U.S. History

Volume 1: Beginnings to 1840

By OpenStax College
at Rice University

Arranged by Traci Hodgson
Chemeketa Community College

A Chemeketa Press Reprint

***U.S. History*, Volume 1: Beginnings to 1840**

ISBN: 978-1-943536-07-8

The contents of this book are reprinted directly from U.S. History by OpenStax College. © May 15, 2015 by OpenStax College. Textbook content produced by OpenStax College is licensed under a Creative Commons Attribution 4.0 license.

Chemeketa Press
Managing Editor: Steve Richardson
Production Editor: Brian Mosher
Production Designer: Kristen MacDonald
Cover Layout: Cierra Maher

Printed in the United States of America.

Volume 1: Beginnings to 1840

1. **The Americas, Europe, and Africa Before 1492** 1
   - 1.1 The Americas 2
   - 1.2 Europe on the Brink of Change 12
   - 1.3 West Africa and the Role of Slavery 18

2. **Early Globalization: The Atlantic World, 1492–1650** 25
   - 2.1 Portuguese Exploration and Spanish Conquest 26
   - 2.2 Religious Upheavals in the Developing Atlantic World 34
   - 2.3 Challenges to Spain's Supremacy 38
   - 2.4 New Worlds in the Americas:
     Labor, Commerce, and the Columbian Exchange 44

3. **Creating New Social Orders: Colonial Societies, 1500–1700** 51
   - 3.1 Spanish Exploration and Colonial Society 52
   - 3.2 Colonial Rivalries: Dutch and French Colonial Ambitions 55
   - 3.3 English Settlements in America 60
   - 3.4 The Impact of Colonization 74

4. **Rule Britannia! The English Empire, 1660–1763** 79
   - 4.1 Charles II and the Restoration Colonies 80
   - 4.2 The Glorious Revolution and the English Empire 86
   - 4.3 An Empire of Slavery and the Consumer Revolution 89
   - 4.4 Great Awakening and Enlightenment 93
   - 4.5 Wars for Empire 98

5. **Imperial Reforms and Colonial Protests, 1763–1774** 103
   - 5.1 Confronting the National Debt:
     The Aftermath of the French and Indian War 104
   - 5.2 The Stamp Act and the Sons and Daughters of Liberty 108
   - 5.3 The Townshend Acts and Colonial Protest 114
   - 5.4 The Destruction of the Tea and the Coercive Acts 121
   - 5.5 Disaffection: The First Continental Congress and American Identity 125

6. **America's War for Independence, 1775–1783** 129
   - 6.1 Britain's Law-and-Order Strategy and Its Consequences 130
   - 6.2 The Early Years of the Revolution 137
   - 6.3 War in the South 143
   - 6.4 Identity during the American Revolution 147

7. Creating Republican Governments, 1776–1790 ... 155
- 7.1 Common Sense: From Monarchy to an American Republic ... 156
- 7.2 How Much Revolutionary Change? ... 159
- 7.3 Debating Democracy ... 167
- 7.4 The Constitutional Convention and Federal Constitution ... 174

8. Growing Pains: The New Republic, 1790–1820 ... 181
- 8.1 Competing Visions: Federalists and Democratic-Republicans ... 182
- 8.2 The New American Republic ... 188
- 8.3 Partisan Politics ... 194
- 8.4 The United States Goes Back to War ... 202

9. Jacksonian Democracy, 1820–1840 ... 207
- 9.1 A New Political Style: From John Quincy Adams to Andrew Jackson ... 208
- 9.2 The Rise of American Democracy ... 214
- 9.3 The Nullification Crisis and the Bank War ... 217
- 9.4 Indian Removal ... 221
- 9.5 The Tyranny and Triumph of the Majority ... 227

Appendix
- A. The Declaration of Independence ... 231
- B. The Constitution of the United States ... 235

CHAPTER 1
The Americas, Europe, and Africa Before 1492

Figure 1.1 In *Europe supported by Africa and America* (1796), artist William Blake, who was an abolitionist, depicts the interdependence of the three continents in the Atlantic World; however, he places gold armbands on the Indian and African women, symbolizing their subjugation. The strand binding the three women may represent tobacco.

Chapter Outline
1.1 The Americas
1.2 Europe on the Brink of Change
1.3 West Africa and the Role of Slavery

Introduction

Globalization, the ever-increasing interconnectedness of the world, is not a new phenomenon, but it accelerated when western Europeans discovered the riches of the East. During the Crusades (1095–1291), Europeans developed an appetite for spices, silk, porcelain, sugar, and other luxury items from the East, for which they traded fur, timber, and Slavic people they captured and sold (hence the word *slave*). But when the Silk Road, the long overland trading route from China to the Mediterranean, became costlier and more dangerous to travel, Europeans searched for a more efficient and inexpensive trade route over water, initiating the development of what we now call the Atlantic World.

In pursuit of commerce in Asia, fifteenth-century traders unexpectedly encountered a "New World" populated by millions and home to sophisticated and numerous peoples. Mistakenly believing they had reached the East Indies, these early explorers called its inhabitants Indians. West Africa, a diverse and culturally rich area, soon entered the stage as other nations exploited its slave trade and brought its peoples to the New World in chains. Although Europeans would come to dominate the New World, they could not have done so without Africans and native peoples (**Figure 1.1**).

CHAPTER 1

1.1 The Americas

By the end of this section, you will be able to:
- Locate on a map the major American civilizations before the arrival of the Spanish
- Discuss the cultural achievements of these civilizations
- Discuss the differences and similarities between lifestyles, religious practices, and customs among the native peoples

Between nine and fifteen thousand years ago, some scholars believe that a land bridge existed between Asia and North America that we now call **Beringia**. The first inhabitants of what would be named the Americas migrated across this bridge in search of food. When the glaciers melted, water engulfed Beringia, and the Bering Strait was formed. Later settlers came by boat across the narrow strait. (The fact that Asians and American Indians share genetic markers on a Y chromosome lends credibility to this migration theory.) Continually moving southward, the settlers eventually populated both North and South America, creating unique cultures that ranged from the highly complex and urban Aztec civilization in what is now Mexico City to the woodland tribes of eastern North America. Recent research along the west coast of South America suggests that migrant populations may have traveled down this coast by water as well as by land.

Researchers believe that about ten thousand years ago, humans also began the domestication of plants and animals, adding agriculture as a means of sustenance to hunting and gathering techniques. With this agricultural revolution, and the more abundant and reliable food supplies it brought, populations grew and people were able to develop a more settled way of life, building permanent settlements. Nowhere in the Americas was this more obvious than in Mesoamerica (**Figure 1.3**).

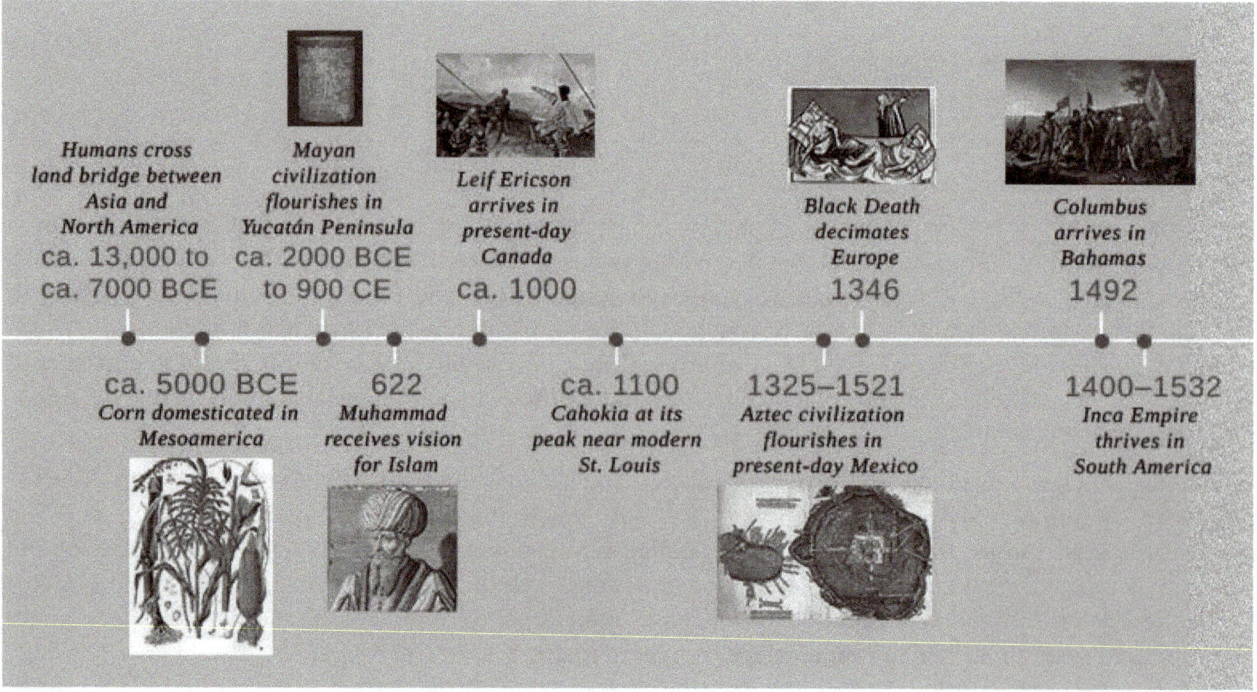

Figure 1.2 (credit: modification of work by Architect of the Capitol)

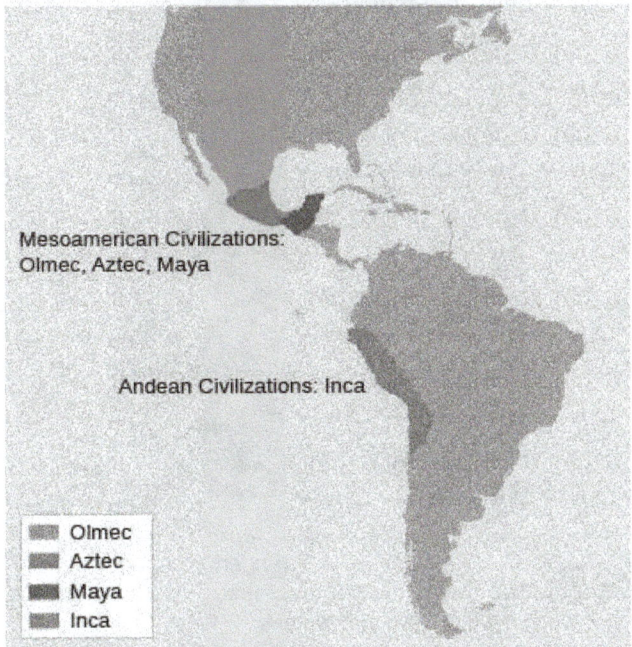

Figure 1.3 This map shows the extent of the major civilizations of the Western Hemisphere. In South America, early civilizations developed along the coast because the high Andes and the inhospitable Amazon Basin made the interior of the continent less favorable for settlement.

THE FIRST AMERICANS: THE OLMEC

Mesoamerica is the geographic area stretching from north of Panama up to the desert of central Mexico. Although marked by great topographic, linguistic, and cultural diversity, this region cradled a number of civilizations with similar characteristics. Mesoamericans were polytheistic; their gods possessed both male and female traits and demanded blood sacrifices of enemies taken in battle or ritual bloodletting. Corn, or maize, domesticated by 5000 BCE, formed the basis of their diet. They developed a mathematical system, built huge edifices, and devised a calendar that accurately predicted eclipses and solstices and that priest-astronomers used to direct the planting and harvesting of crops. Most important for our knowledge of these peoples, they created the only known written language in the Western Hemisphere; researchers have made much progress in interpreting the inscriptions on their temples and pyramids. Though the area had no overarching political structure, trade over long distances helped diffuse culture. Weapons made of obsidian, jewelry crafted from jade, feathers woven into clothing and ornaments, and cacao beans that were whipped into a chocolate drink formed the basis of commerce. The mother of Mesoamerican cultures was the Olmec civilization.

Flourishing along the hot Gulf Coast of Mexico from about 1200 to about 400 BCE, the Olmec produced a number of major works of art, architecture, pottery, and sculpture. Most recognizable are their giant head sculptures (**Figure 1.4**) and the pyramid in La Venta. The Olmec built aqueducts to transport water into their cities and irrigate their fields. They grew maize, squash, beans, and tomatoes. They also bred small domesticated dogs which, along with fish, provided their protein. Although no one knows what happened to the Olmec after about 400 BCE, in part because the jungle reclaimed many of their cities, their culture was the base upon which the Maya and the Aztec built. It was the Olmec who worshipped a rain god, a maize god, and the feathered serpent so important in the future pantheons of the Aztecs (who called him Quetzalcoatl) and the Maya (to whom he was Kukulkan). The Olmec also developed a system of trade throughout Mesoamerica, giving rise to an elite class.

Figure 1.4 The Olmec carved heads from giant boulders that ranged from four to eleven feet in height and could weigh up to fifty tons. All these figures have flat noses, slightly crossed eyes, and large lips. These physical features can be seen today in some of the peoples indigenous to the area.

THE MAYA

After the decline of the Olmec, a city rose in the fertile central highlands of Mesoamerica. One of the largest population centers in pre-Columbian America and home to more than 100,000 people at its height in about 500 CE, Teotihuacan was located about thirty miles northeast of modern Mexico City. The ethnicity of this settlement's inhabitants is debated; some scholars believe it was a multiethnic city. Large-scale agriculture and the resultant abundance of food allowed time for people to develop special trades and skills other than farming. Builders constructed over twenty-two hundred apartment compounds for multiple families, as well as more than a hundred temples. Among these were the Pyramid of the Sun (which is two hundred feet high) and the Pyramid of the Moon (one hundred and fifty feet high). Near the Temple of the Feathered Serpent, graves have been uncovered that suggest humans were sacrificed for religious purposes. The city was also the center for trade, which extended to settlements on Mesoamerica's Gulf Coast.

The Maya were one Mesoamerican culture that had strong ties to Teotihuacan. The Maya's architectural and mathematical contributions were significant. Flourishing from roughly 2000 BCE to 900 CE in what is now Mexico, Belize, Honduras, and Guatemala, the Maya perfected the calendar and written language the Olmec had begun. They devised a written mathematical system to record crop yields and the size of the population, and to assist in trade. Surrounded by farms relying on primitive agriculture, they built the city-states of Copan, Tikal, and Chichen Itza along their major trade routes, as well as temples, statues of gods, pyramids, and astronomical observatories (**Figure 1.5**). However, because of poor soil and a drought that lasted nearly two centuries, their civilization declined by about 900 CE and they abandoned their large population centers.

Figure 1.5 El Castillo, located at Chichen Itza in the eastern Yucatán peninsula, served as a temple for the god Kukulkan. Each side contains ninety-one steps to the top. When counting the top platform, the total number of stairs is three hundred and sixty-five, the number of days in a year. (credit: Ken Thomas)

The Spanish found little organized resistance among the weakened Maya upon their arrival in the 1520s. However, they did find Mayan history, in the form of glyphs, or pictures representing words, recorded in folding books called codices (the singular is *codex*). In 1562, Bishop Diego de Landa, who feared the converted natives had reverted to their traditional religious practices, collected and burned every codex he could find. Today only a few survive.

Visit the **University of Arizona Library Special Collections** (http://openstaxcollege.org/l/mayancodex) to view facsimiles and descriptions of two of the four surviving Mayan codices.

THE AZTEC

When the Spaniard Hernán Cortés arrived on the coast of Mexico in the sixteenth century, at the site of present-day Veracruz, he soon heard of a great city ruled by an emperor named Moctezuma. This city was tremendously wealthy—filled with gold—and took in tribute from surrounding tribes. The riches and complexity Cortés found when he arrived at that city, known as Tenochtitlán, were far beyond anything he or his men had ever seen.

According to legend, a warlike people called the Aztec (also known as the Mexica) had left a city called Aztlán and traveled south to the site of present-day Mexico City. In 1325, they began construction of Tenochtitlán on an island in Lake Texcoco. By 1519, when Cortés arrived, this settlement contained upwards of 200,000 inhabitants and was certainly the largest city in the Western Hemisphere at that time and probably larger than any European city (**Figure 1.6**). One of Cortés's soldiers, Bernal Díaz del Castillo, recorded his impressions upon first seeing it: "When we saw so many cities and villages built in the water and other great towns on dry land we were amazed and said it was like the enchantments . . . on account of the great towers and cues and buildings rising from the water, and all built of masonry. And some of our soldiers even asked whether the things that we saw were not a dream? . . . I do not know how to describe it, seeing things as we did that had never been heard of or seen before, not even dreamed about."

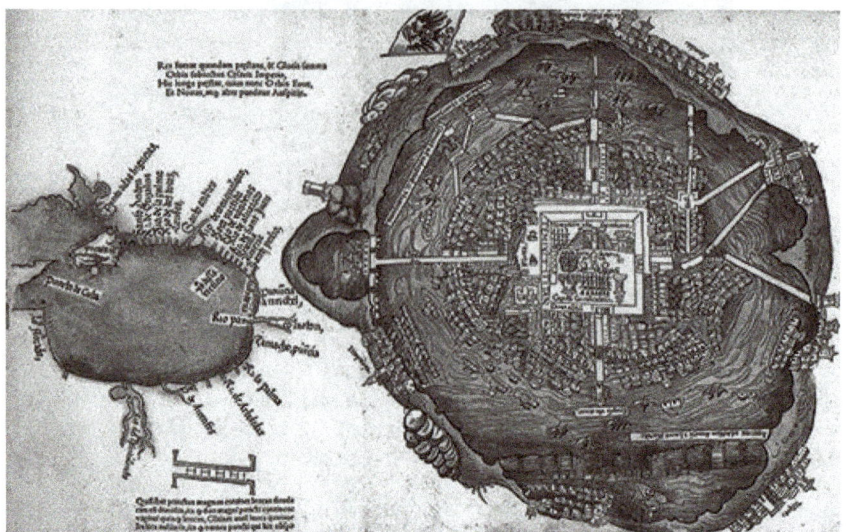

Figure 1.6 This rendering of the Aztec island city of Tenochtitlán depicts the causeways that connected the central city to the surrounding land. Envoys from surrounding tribes brought tribute to the Emperor.

Unlike the dirty, fetid cities of Europe at the time, Tenochtitlán was well planned, clean, and orderly. The city had neighborhoods for specific occupations, a trash collection system, markets, two aqueducts bringing in fresh water, and public buildings and temples. Unlike the Spanish, Aztecs bathed daily, and wealthy homes might even contain a steam bath. A labor force of slaves from subjugated neighboring tribes had built the fabulous city and the three causeways that connected it to the mainland. To farm, the Aztec constructed barges made of reeds and filled them with fertile soil. Lake water constantly irrigated these *chinampas*, or "floating gardens," which are still in use and can be seen today in Xochimilco, a district of Mexico City.

Each god in the Aztec pantheon represented and ruled an aspect of the natural world, such as the heavens, farming, rain, fertility, sacrifice, and combat. A ruling class of warrior nobles and priests performed ritual human sacrifice daily to sustain the sun on its long journey across the sky, to appease or feed the gods, and to stimulate agricultural production. The sacrificial ceremony included cutting open the chest of a criminal or captured warrior with an obsidian knife and removing the still-beating heart (**Figure 1.7**).

Figure 1.7 In this illustration, an Aztec priest cuts out the beating heart of a sacrificial victim before throwing the body down from the temple. Aztec belief centered on supplying the gods with human blood—the ultimate sacrifice—to keep them strong and well.

Click and Explore

Explore Aztec-History.com (http://openstaxcollege.org/l/azteccreation) to learn more about the Aztec creation story.

MY STORY

✺ *The Aztec Predict the Coming of the Spanish*

The following is an excerpt from the sixteenth-century Florentine Codex of the writings of Fray Bernardino de Sahagun, a priest and early chronicler of Aztec history. When an old man from Xochimilco first saw the Spanish in Veracruz, he recounted an earlier dream to Moctezuma, the ruler of the Aztecs.

> Said Quzatli to the sovereign, "Oh mighty lord, if because I tell you the truth I am to die, nevertheless I am here in your presence and you may do what you wish to me!" He narrated that mounted men would come to this land in a great wooden house [ships] this structure was to lodge many men, serving them as a home; within they would eat and sleep. On the surface of this house they would cook their food, walk and play as if they were on firm land. They were to be white, bearded men, dressed in different colors and on their heads they would wear round coverings.

Ten years before the arrival of the Spanish, Moctezuma received several omens which at the time he could not interpret. A fiery object appeared in the night sky, a spontaneous fire broke out in a religious temple and could not be extinguished with water, a water spout appeared in Lake Texcoco, and a woman could be heard wailing, "O my children we are about to go forever." Moctezuma also had dreams and premonitions of impending disaster. These foretellings were recorded after the Aztecs' destruction. They do, however, give us insight into the importance placed upon signs and omens in the pre-Columbian world.

THE INCA

In South America, the most highly developed and complex society was that of the Inca, whose name means "lord" or "ruler" in the Andean language called Quechua. At its height in the fifteenth and sixteenth centuries, the Inca Empire, located on the Pacific coast and straddling the Andes Mountains, extended some twenty-five hundred miles. It stretched from modern-day Colombia in the north to Chile in the south and included cities built at an altitude of 14,000 feet above sea level. Its road system, kept free of debris and repaired by workers stationed at varying intervals, rivaled that of the Romans and efficiently connected the sprawling empire. The Inca, like all other pre-Columbian societies, did not use axle-mounted wheels for transportation. They built stepped roads to ascend and descend the steep slopes of the Andes; these would have been impractical for wheeled vehicles but worked well for pedestrians. These roads enabled the rapid movement of the highly trained Incan army. Also like the Romans, the Inca were effective administrators. Runners called *chasquis* traversed the roads in a continuous relay system, ensuring quick communication over long distances. The Inca had no system of writing, however. They communicated and kept records using a system of colored strings and knots called the *quipu* (Figure 1.8).

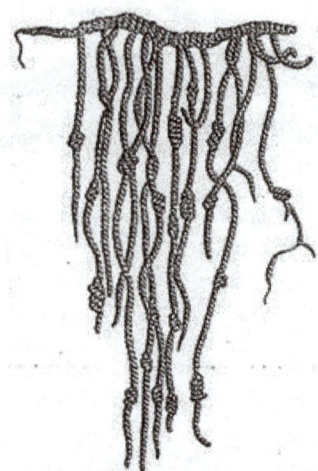

Figure 1.8 The Inca had no written language. Instead, they communicated and kept records by means of a system of knots and colored strings called the *quipu*. Each of these knots and strings possessed a distinct meaning intelligible to those educated in their significance.

The Inca people worshipped their lord who, as a member of an elite ruling class, had absolute authority over every aspect of life. Much like feudal lords in Europe at the time, the ruling class lived off the labor of the peasants, collecting vast wealth that accompanied them as they went, mummified, into the next life. The Inca farmed corn, beans, squash, quinoa (a grain cultivated for its seeds), and the indigenous potato on terraced land they hacked from the steep mountains. Peasants received only one-third of their crops for themselves. The Inca ruler required a third, and a third was set aside in a kind of welfare system for those unable to work. Huge storehouses were filled with food for times of need. Each peasant also worked for the Inca ruler a number of days per month on public works projects, a requirement known as the ***mita***. For example, peasants constructed rope bridges made of grass to span the mountains above fast-flowing icy rivers. In return, the lord provided laws, protection, and relief in times of famine.

The Inca worshipped the sun god Inti and called gold the "sweat" of the sun. Unlike the Maya and the Aztecs, they rarely practiced human sacrifice and usually offered the gods food, clothing, and coca leaves. In times of dire emergency, however, such as in the aftermath of earthquakes, volcanoes, or crop failure, they resorted to sacrificing prisoners. The ultimate sacrifice was children, who were specially selected and well fed. The Inca believed these children would immediately go to a much better afterlife.

In 1911, the American historian Hiram Bingham uncovered the lost Incan city of Machu Picchu (**Figure 1.9**). Located about fifty miles northwest of Cusco, Peru, at an altitude of about 8,000 feet, the city had been built in 1450 and inexplicably abandoned roughly a hundred years later. Scholars believe the city was used for religious ceremonial purposes and housed the priesthood. The architectural beauty of this city is unrivaled. Using only the strength of human labor and no machines, the Inca constructed walls and buildings of polished stones, some weighing over fifty tons, that were fitted together perfectly without the use of mortar. In 1983, UNESCO designated the ruined city a World Heritage Site.

Figure 1.9 Located in today's Peru at an altitude of nearly 8,000 feet, Machu Picchu was a ceremonial Incan city built about 1450 CE.

Browse the British Museum's World Cultures collection (http://openstaxcollege.org/l/inca) to see more examples and descriptions of Incan (as well as Aztec, Mayan, and North American Indian) art.

NORTH AMERICAN INDIANS

With few exceptions, the North American native cultures were much more widely dispersed than the Mayan, Aztec, and Incan societies, and did not have their population size or organized social structures. Although the cultivation of corn had made its way north, many Indians still practiced hunting and gathering. Horses, first introduced by the Spanish, allowed the Plains Indians to more easily follow and hunt the huge herds of bison. A few societies had evolved into relatively complex forms, but they were already in decline at the time of Christopher Columbus's arrival.

In the southwestern part of today's United States dwelled several groups we collectively call the Pueblo. The Spanish first gave them this name, which means "town" or "village," because they lived in towns or villages of permanent stone-and-mud buildings with thatched roofs. Like present-day apartment houses, these buildings had multiple stories, each with multiple rooms. The three main groups of the Pueblo people were the Mogollon, Hohokam, and Anasazi.

The Mogollon thrived in the Mimbres Valley (New Mexico) from about 150 BCE to 1450 CE. They developed a distinctive artistic style for painting bowls with finely drawn geometric figures and wildlife, especially birds, in black on a white background. Beginning about 600 CE, the Hohokam built an extensive irrigation system of canals to irrigate the desert and grow fields of corn, beans, and squash. By 1300, their crop yields were supporting the most highly populated settlements in the southwest. The Hohokam decorated pottery with a red-on-buff design and made jewelry of turquoise. In the high desert of New Mexico, the Anasazi, whose name means "ancient enemy" or "ancient ones," carved homes from steep cliffs accessed by ladders or ropes that could be pulled in at night or in case of enemy attack (**Figure 1.10**).

Figure 1.10 To access their homes, the cliff-dwelling Anasazi used ropes or ladders that could be pulled in at night for safety. These pueblos may be viewed today in Canyon de Chelly National Monument (above) in Arizona and Mesa Verde National Park in Colorado.

Roads extending some 180 miles connected the Pueblos' smaller urban centers to each other and to Chaco Canyon, which by 1050 CE had become the administrative, religious, and cultural center of their civilization. A century later, however, probably because of drought, the Pueblo peoples abandoned their cities. Their present-day descendants include the Hopi and Zuni tribes.

The Indian groups who lived in the present-day Ohio River Valley and achieved their cultural apex from the first century CE to 400 CE are collectively known as the Hopewell culture. Their settlements, unlike those of the southwest, were small hamlets. They lived in wattle-and-daub houses (made from woven lattice branches "daubed" with wet mud, clay, or sand and straw) and practiced agriculture, which they supplemented by hunting and fishing. Utilizing waterways, they developed trade routes stretching from Canada to Louisiana, where they exchanged goods with other tribes and negotiated in many different languages. From the coast they received shells; from Canada, copper; and from the Rocky Mountains, obsidian. With these materials they created necklaces, woven mats, and exquisite carvings. What remains of their culture today are huge burial mounds and earthworks. Many of the mounds that were opened by archaeologists contained artworks and other goods that indicate their society was socially stratified.

Perhaps the largest indigenous cultural and population center in North America was located along the Mississippi River near present-day St. Louis. At its height in about 1100 CE, this five-square-mile city, now called Cahokia, was home to more than ten thousand residents; tens of thousands more lived on farms surrounding the urban center. The city also contained one hundred and twenty earthen mounds or pyramids, each dominating a particular neighborhood and on each of which lived a leader who exercised authority over the surrounding area. The largest mound covered fifteen acres. Cahokia was the hub of political and trading activities along the Mississippi River. After 1300 CE, however, this civilization declined—possibly because the area became unable to support the large population.

INDIANS OF THE EASTERN WOODLAND

Encouraged by the wealth found by the Spanish in the settled civilizations to the south, fifteenth- and sixteenth-century English, Dutch, and French explorers expected to discover the same in North America. What they found instead were small, disparate communities, many already ravaged by European diseases brought by the Spanish and transmitted among the natives. Rather than gold and silver, there was an abundance of land, and the timber and fur that land could produce.

The Indians living east of the Mississippi did not construct the large and complex societies of those to the west. Because they lived in small autonomous clans or tribal units, each group adapted to the specific environment in which it lived (**Figure 1.11**). These groups were by no means unified, and warfare among tribes was common as they sought to increase their hunting and fishing areas. Still, these tribes shared some common traits. A chief or group of tribal elders made decisions, and although the chief was male, usually the women selected and counseled him. Gender roles were not as fixed as they were in the patriarchal societies of Europe, Mesoamerica, and South America.

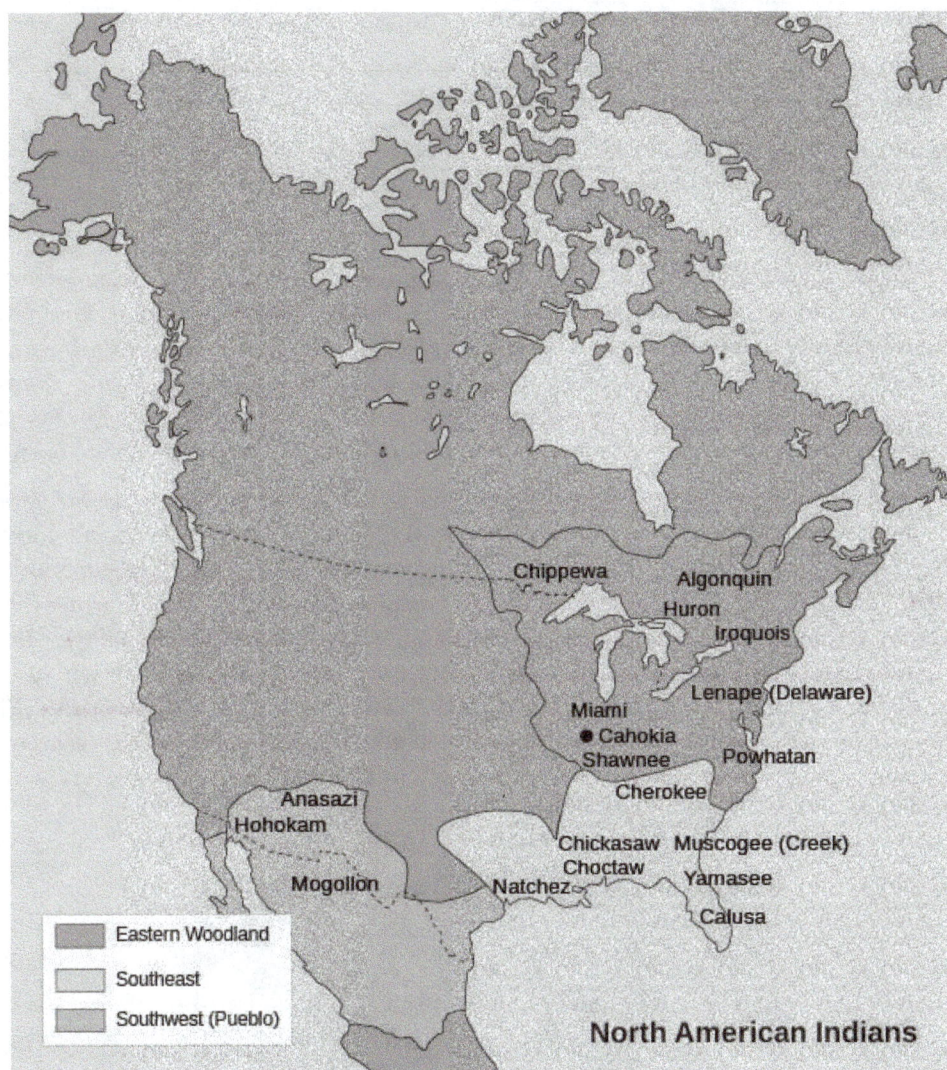

Figure 1.11 This map indicates the locations of the three Pueblo cultures the major Eastern Woodland Indian tribes, and the tribes of the Southeast, as well as the location of the ancient city of Cahokia.

Women typically cultivated corn, beans, and squash and harvested nuts and berries, while men hunted, fished, and provided protection. But both took responsibility for raising children, and most major Indian societies in the east were matriarchal. In tribes such as the Iroquois, Lenape, Muscogee, and Cherokee, women had both power and influence. They counseled the chief and passed on the traditions of the tribe. This **matriarchy** changed dramatically with the coming of the Europeans, who introduced, sometimes forcibly, their own customs and traditions to the natives.

Clashing beliefs about land ownership and use of the environment would be the greatest area of conflict with Europeans. Although tribes often claimed the right to certain hunting grounds—usually identified by some geographical landmark—Indians did not practice, or in general even have the concept of, private ownership of land. There were tribal hunting grounds, usually identified by some geographical landmark, but there was no private ownership of land. A person's possessions included only what he or she had made, such as tools or weapons. The European Christian worldview, on the other hand, viewed land as the source of wealth. According to the Christian Bible, God created humanity in his own image with the command to use and subdue the rest of creation, which included not only land, but also all animal life.

Upon their arrival in North America, Europeans found no fences, no signs designating ownership. Land, and the game that populated it, they believed, were there for the taking.

1.2 Europe on the Brink of Change

By the end of this section, you will be able to:
- Describe the European societies that engaged in conversion, conquest, and commerce
- Discuss the motives for and mechanisms of early European exploration

The fall of the Roman Empire (476 CE) and the beginning of the European Renaissance in the late fourteenth century roughly bookend the period we call the Middle Ages. Without a dominant centralized power or overarching cultural hub, Europe experienced political and military discord during this time. Its inhabitants retreated into walled cities, fearing marauding pillagers including Vikings, Mongols, Arabs, and Magyars. In return for protection, they submitted to powerful lords and their armies of knights. In their brief, hard lives, few people traveled more than ten miles from the place they were born.

The Christian Church remained intact, however, and emerged from the period as a unified and powerful institution. Priests, tucked away in monasteries, kept knowledge alive by collecting and copying religious and secular manuscripts, often adding beautiful drawings or artwork. Social and economic devastation arrived in 1340s, however, when Genoese merchants returning from the Black Sea unwittingly brought with them a rat-borne and highly contagious disease, known as the bubonic plague. In a few short years, it had killed many millions, about one-third of Europe's population. A different strain, spread by airborne germs, also killed many. Together these two are collectively called the **Black Death** (**Figure 1.12**). Entire villages disappeared. A high birth rate, however, coupled with bountiful harvests, meant that the population grew during the next century. By 1450, a newly rejuvenated European society was on the brink of tremendous change.

Figure 1.12 This image depicts the bodily swellings, or buboes, characteristic of the Black Death.

Click and Explore

Visit EyeWitness to History (http://openstaxcollege.org/l/plague) to learn more about the Black Death.

LIFE IN FEUDAL EUROPE

During the Middle Ages, most Europeans lived in small villages that consisted of a manorial house or castle for the lord, a church, and simple homes for the peasants or **serfs**, who made up about 60 percent of western Europe's population. Hundreds of these castles and walled cities remain all over Europe (**Figure 1.13**).

Figure 1.13 One of the most beautifully preserved medieval walled cities is Carcassonne, France. Notice the use of a double wall.

Europe's **feudal society** was a mutually supportive system. The lords owned the land; knights gave military service to a lord and carried out his justice; serfs worked the land in return for the protection offered by the lord's castle or the walls of his city, into which they fled in times of danger from invaders. Much land was communally farmed at first, but as lords became more powerful they extended their ownership and rented land to their subjects. Thus, although they were technically free, serfs were effectively bound to the land they worked, which supported them and their families as well as the lord and all who depended on him. The Catholic Church, the only church in Europe at the time, also owned vast tracts of land and became very wealthy by collecting not only tithes (taxes consisting of 10 percent of annual earnings) but also rents on its lands.

A serf's life was difficult. Women often died in childbirth, and perhaps one-third of children died before the age of five. Without sanitation or medicine, many people perished from diseases we consider inconsequential today; few lived to be older than forty-five. Entire families, usually including grandparents, lived in one- or two-room hovels that were cold, dark, and dirty. A fire was kept lit and was always a danger to the thatched roofs, while its constant smoke affected the inhabitants' health and eyesight. Most individuals owned no more than two sets of clothing, consisting of a woolen jacket or tunic and linen undergarments, and bathed only when the waters melted in spring.

In an agrarian society, the seasons dictate the rhythm of life. Everyone in Europe's feudal society had a job to do and worked hard. The father was the unquestioned head of the family. Idleness meant hunger. When the land began to thaw in early spring, peasants started tilling the soil with primitive wooden plows and crude rakes and hoes. Then they planted crops of wheat, rye, barley, and oats, reaping small yields that barely sustained the population. Bad weather, crop disease, or insect infestation could cause an entire village to starve or force the survivors to move to another location.

Early summer saw the first harvesting of hay, which was stored until needed to feed the animals in winter. Men and boys sheared the sheep, now heavy with wool from the cold weather, while women and children washed the wool and spun it into yarn. The coming of fall meant crops needed to be harvested and prepared for winter. Livestock was butchered and the meat smoked or salted to preserve it. With the harvest in and the provisions stored, fall was also the time for celebrating and giving thanks to God. Winter brought the people indoors to weave yarn into fabric, sew clothing, thresh grain, and keep the fires going. Everyone celebrated the birth of Christ in conjunction with the winter solstice.

THE CHURCH AND SOCIETY

After the fall of Rome, the Christian Church—united in dogma but unofficially divided into western and eastern branches—was the only organized institution in medieval Europe. In 1054, the eastern branch of Christianity, led by the Patriarch of Constantinople (a title that because roughly equivalent to the western Church's pope), established its center in Constantinople and adopted the Greek language for its services. The western branch, under the pope, remained in Rome, becoming known as the Roman Catholic Church and continuing to use Latin. Following this split, known as the Great Schism, each branch of Christianity maintained a strict organizational hierarchy. The pope in Rome, for example, oversaw a huge bureaucracy led by cardinals, known as "princes of the church," who were followed by archbishops, bishops, and then priests. During this period, the Roman Church became the most powerful international organization in western Europe.

Just as agrarian life depended on the seasons, village and family life revolved around the Church. The sacraments, or special ceremonies of the Church, marked every stage of life, from birth to maturation, marriage, and burial, and brought people into the church on a regular basis. As Christianity spread throughout Europe, it replaced pagan and animistic views, explaining supernatural events and forces of nature in its own terms. A benevolent God in heaven, creator of the universe and beyond the realm of nature and the known, controlled all events, warring against the force of darkness, known as the Devil or Satan, here on earth. Although ultimately defeated, Satan still had the power to trick humans and cause them to commit evil or sin.

All events had a spiritual connotation. Sickness, for example, might be a sign that a person had sinned, while crop failure could result from the villagers' not saying their prayers. Penitents confessed their sins to the priest, who absolved them and assigned them penance to atone for their acts and save themselves from eternal damnation. Thus the parish priest held enormous power over the lives of his parishioners.

Ultimately, the pope decided all matters of theology, interpreting the will of God to the people, but he also had authority over temporal matters. Because the Church had the ability to excommunicate people, or send a soul to hell forever, even monarchs feared to challenge its power. It was also the seat of all knowledge. Latin, the language of the Church, served as a unifying factor for a continent of isolated regions, each with its own dialect; in the early Middle Ages, nations as we know them today did not yet exist. The mostly illiterate serfs were thus dependent on those literate priests to read and interpret the Bible, the word of God, for them.

CHRISTIANITY ENCOUNTERS ISLAM

The year 622 brought a new challenge to Christendom. Near Mecca, Saudi Arabia, a prophet named Muhammad received a revelation that became a cornerstone of the Islamic faith. The **Koran**, which Muhammad wrote in Arabic, contained his message, affirming monotheism but identifying Christ not as

God but as a prophet like Moses, Abraham, David, and Muhammad. Following Muhammad's death in 632, Islam spread by both conversion and military conquest across the Middle East and Asia Minor to India and northern Africa, crossing the Straits of Gibraltar into Spain in the year 711 (**Figure 1.14**).

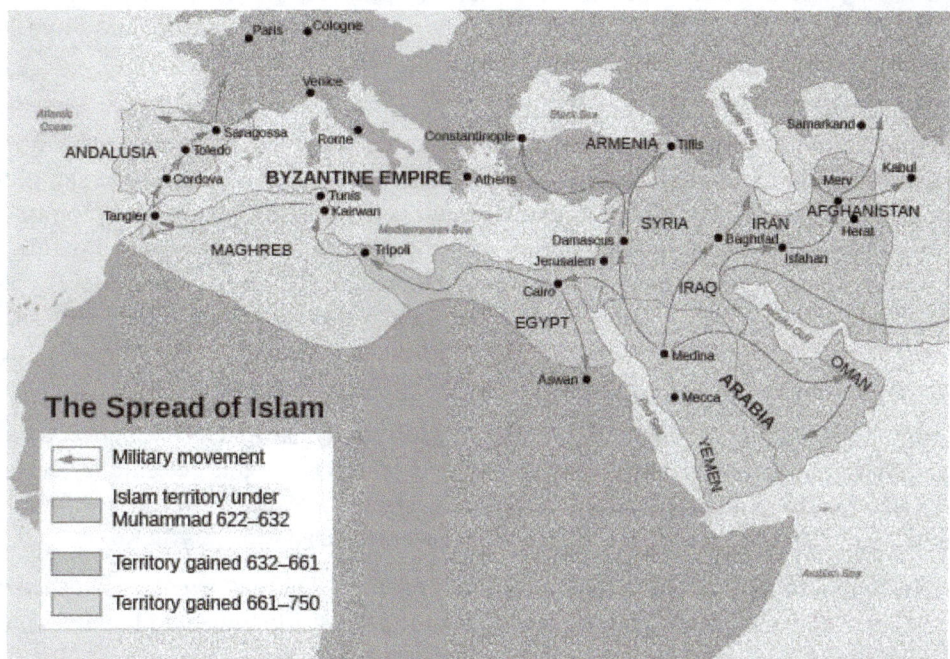

Figure 1.14 In the seventh and eighth centuries, Islam spread quickly across North Africa and into the Middle East. The religion arrived in Europe via Spain in 711 and remained there until 1492, when Catholic monarchs reconquered the last of Muslim-held territory after a long war.

The Islamic conquest of Europe continued until 732. Then, at the Battle of Tours (in modern France), Charles Martel, nicknamed the Hammer, led a Christian force in defeating the army of Abdul Rahman al-Ghafiqi. Muslims, however, retained control of much of Spain, where Córdoba, known for leather and wool production, became a major center of learning and trade. By the eleventh century, a major Christian holy war called the **Reconquista**, or reconquest, had begun to slowly push the Muslims from Spain. This drive was actually an extension of the earlier military conflict between Christians and Muslims for domination of the Holy Land (the Biblical region of Palestine), known as the **Crusades**.

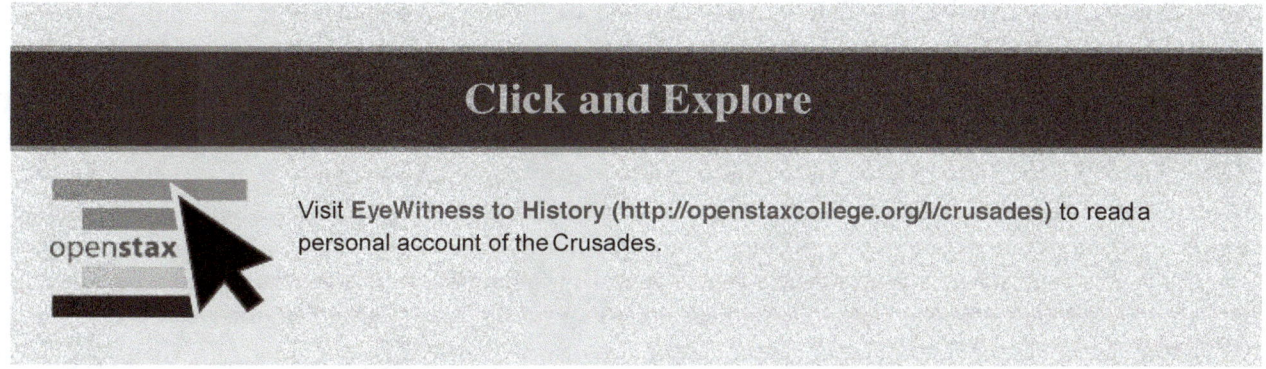

Visit EyeWitness to History (http://openstaxcollege.org/l/crusades) to read a personal account of the Crusades.

JERUSALEM AND THE CRUSADES

The city of Jerusalem is a holy site for Jews, Christians, and Muslims. It was here King Solomon built the Temple in the tenth century BCE. It was here the Romans crucified Jesus in 33 CE, and from here, Christians maintain, he ascended into heaven, promising to return. From here, Muslims believe,

Muhammad traveled to heaven in 621 to receive instructions about prayer. Thus claims on the area go deep, and emotions about it run high, among followers of all three faiths. Evidence exists that the three religions lived in harmony for centuries. In 1095, however, European Christians decided not only to retake the holy city from the Muslim rulers but also to conquer what they called the Holy Lands, an area that extended from modern-day Turkey in the north along the Mediterranean coast to the Sinai Peninsula and that was also held by Muslims. The Crusades had begun.

Religious zeal motivated the knights who participated in the four Crusades. Adventure, the chance to win land and a title, and the Church's promise of wholesale forgiveness of sins also motivated many. The Crusaders, mostly French knights, retook Jerusalem in June 1099 amid horrific slaughter. A French writer who accompanied them recorded this eyewitness account: "On the top of Solomon's Temple, to which they had climbed in fleeing, many were shot to death with arrows and cast down headlong from the roof. Within this Temple, about ten thousand were beheaded. If you had been there, your feet would have been stained up to the ankles with the blood of the slain. What more shall I tell? Not one of them was allowed to live. They did not spare the women and children." A Muslim eyewitness also described how the conquerors stripped the temple of its wealth and looted private homes.

In 1187, under the legendary leader Saladin, Muslim forces took back the city. Reaction from Europe was swift as King Richard I of England, the Lionheart, joined others to mount yet another action. The battle for the Holy Lands did not conclude until the Crusaders lost their Mediterranean stronghold at Acre (in present-day Israel) in 1291 and the last of the Christians left the area a few years later.

The Crusades had lasting effects, both positive and negative. On the negative side, the wide-scale persecution of Jews began. Christians classed them with the infidel Muslims and labeled them "the killers of Christ." In the coming centuries, kings either expelled Jews from their kingdoms or forced them to pay heavy tributes for the privilege of remaining. Muslim-Christian hatred also festered, and intolerance grew.

On the positive side, maritime trade between East and West expanded. As Crusaders experienced the feel of silk, the taste of spices, and the utility of porcelain, desire for these products created new markets for merchants. In particular, the Adriatic port city of Venice prospered enormously from trade with Islamic merchants. Merchants' ships brought Europeans valuable goods, traveling between the port cities of western Europe and the East from the tenth century on, along routes collectively labeled the Silk Road. From the days of the early adventurer Marco Polo, Venetian sailors had traveled to ports on the Black Sea and established their own colonies along the Mediterranean Coast. However, transporting goods along the old Silk Road was costly, slow, and unprofitable. Muslim middlemen collected taxes as the goods changed hands. Robbers waited to ambush the treasure-laden caravans. A direct water route to the East, cutting out the land portion of the trip, had to be found. As well as seeking a water passage to the wealthy cities in the East, sailors wanted to find a route to the exotic and wealthy Spice Islands in modern-day Indonesia, whose location was kept secret by Muslim rulers. Longtime rivals of Venice, the merchants of Genoa and Florence also looked west.

THE IBERIAN PENINSULA

Although Norse explorers such as Leif Ericson, the son of Eric the Red who first settled Greenland, had reached and established a colony in northern Canada roughly five hundred years prior to Christopher Columbus's voyage, it was explorers sailing for Portugal and Spain who traversed the Atlantic throughout the fifteenth century and ushered in an unprecedented age of exploration and permanent contact with North America.

Located on the extreme western edge of Europe, Portugal, with its port city of Lisbon, soon became the center for merchants desiring to undercut the Venetians' hold on trade. With a population of about one million and supported by its ruler Prince Henry, whom historians call "the Navigator," this independent kingdom fostered exploration of and trade with western Africa. Skilled shipbuilders and navigators who took advantage of maps from all over Europe, Portuguese sailors used triangular sails and built lighter vessels called caravels that could sail down the African coast.

Just to the east of Portugal, King Ferdinand of Aragon married Queen Isabella of Castile in 1469, uniting two of the most powerful independent kingdoms on the Iberian peninsula and laying the foundation for the modern nation of Spain. Isabella, motivated by strong religious zeal, was instrumental in beginning the **Inquisition** in 1480, a brutal campaign to root out Jews and Muslims who had seemingly converted to Christianity but secretly continued to practice their faith, as well as other heretics. This powerful couple ruled for the next twenty-five years, centralizing authority and funding exploration and trade with the East. One of their daughters, Catherine of Aragon, became the first wife of King Henry VIII of England.

AMERICANA

✱ Motives for European Exploration

Historians generally recognize three motives for European exploration—God, glory, and gold. Particularly in the strongly Catholic nations of Spain and Portugal, religious zeal motivated the rulers to make converts and retake land from the Muslims. Prince Henry the Navigator of Portugal described his "great desire to make increase in the faith of our Lord Jesus Christ and to bring him all the souls that should be saved."

Sailors' tales about fabulous monsters and fantasy literature about exotic worlds filled with gold, silver, and jewels captured the minds of men who desired to explore these lands and return with untold wealth and the glory of adventure and discovery. They sparked the imagination of merchants like Marco Polo, who made the long and dangerous trip to the realm of the great Mongol ruler Kublai Khan in 1271. The story of his trip, printed in a book entitled *Travels*, inspired Columbus, who had a copy in his possession during his voyage more than two hundred years later. Passages such as the following, which describes China's imperial palace, are typical of the *Travels*:

> You must know that it is the greatest Palace that ever was. . . . The roof is very lofty, and the walls of the Palace are all covered with gold and silver. They are also adorned with representations of dragons [sculptured and gilt], beasts and birds, knights and idols, and sundry other subjects. And on the ceiling too you see nothing but gold and silver and painting. [On each of the four sides there is a great marble staircase leading to the top of the marble wall, and forming the approach to the Palace.]

> The hall of the Palace is so large that it could easily dine 6,000 people; and it is quite a marvel to see how many rooms there are besides. The building is altogether so vast, so rich, and so beautiful, that no man on earth could design anything superior to it. The outside of the roof also is all colored with vermilion and yellow and green and blue and other hues, which are fixed with a varnish so fine and exquisite that they shine like crystal, and lend a resplendent lustre to the Palace as seen for a great way round. This roof is made too with such strength and solidity that it is fit to last forever.

Why might a travel account like this one have influenced an explorer like Columbus? What does this tell us about European explorers' motivations and goals?

The year 1492 witnessed some of the most significant events of Ferdinand and Isabella's reign. The couple oversaw the final expulsion of North African Muslims (Moors) from the Kingdom of Granada, bringing the nearly eight-hundred-year Reconquista to an end. In this same year, they also ordered all unconverted Jews to leave Spain.

Also in 1492, after six years of lobbying, a Genoese sailor named Christopher Columbus persuaded the monarchs to fund his expedition to the Far East. Columbus had already pitched his plan to the rulers of Genoa and Venice without success, so the Spanish monarchy was his last hope. Christian zeal was the prime motivating factor for Isabella, as she imagined her faith spreading to the East. Ferdinand, the more practical of the two, hoped to acquire wealth from trade.

Most educated individuals at the time knew the earth was round, so Columbus's plan to reach the East by sailing west was plausible. Though the calculations of Earth's circumference made by the Greek geographer Eratosthenes in the second century BCE were known (and, as we now know, nearly accurate), most scholars did not believe they were dependable. Thus Columbus would have no way of knowing when he had traveled far enough around the Earth to reach his goal—and in fact, Columbus greatly underestimated the Earth's circumference.

In August 1492, Columbus set sail with his three small caravels (**Figure 1.15**). After a voyage of about three thousand miles lasting six weeks, he landed on an island in the Bahamas named Guanahani by the native Lucayans. He promptly christened it San Salvador, the name it bears today.

Figure 1.15 Columbus sailed in three caravels such as these. The *Santa Maria*, his largest, was only 58 feet long.

1.3 West Africa and the Role of Slavery

At the end of this section, you will be able to:
- Locate the major West African empires on a map
- Discuss the roles of Islam and Europe in the slave trade

It is difficult to generalize about West Africa, which was linked to the rise and diffusion of Islam. This geographical unit, central to the rise of the Atlantic World, stretches from modern-day Mauritania to the Democratic Republic of the Congo and encompasses lush rainforests along the equator, savannas on either side of the forest, and much drier land to the north. Until about 600 CE, most Africans were hunter-gatherers. Where water was too scarce for farming, herders maintained sheep, goats, cattle, or camels. In the more heavily wooded area near the equator, farmers raised yams, palm products, or plantains. The savanna areas yielded rice, millet, and sorghum. Sub-Saharan Africans had little experience in maritime matters. Most of the population lived away from the coast, which is connected to the interior by five main rivers—the Senegal, Gambia, Niger, Volta, and Congo.

Although there were large trading centers along these rivers, most West Africans lived in small villages and identified with their extended family or their clan. Wives, children, and dependents (including slaves) were a sign of wealth among men, and **polygyny**, the practice of having more than one wife at a time, was widespread. In time of need, relatives, however far away, were counted upon to assist in supplying food or security. Because of the clannish nature of African society, "we" was associated with the village and family members, while "they" included everyone else. Hundreds of separate dialects emerged; in modern Nigeria, nearly five hundred are still spoken.

Read The Role of Islam in African Slavery (http://openstaxcollege.org/l/islamslavery) to learn more about the African slave trade.

THE MAJOR AFRICAN EMPIRES

Following the death of the prophet Muhammad in 632 CE, Islam continued to spread quickly across North Africa, bringing not only a unifying faith but a political and legal structure as well. As lands fell under the control of Muslim armies, they instituted Islamic rule and legal structures as local chieftains converted, usually under penalty of death. Only those who had converted to Islam could rule or be engaged in trade. The first major empire to emerge in West Africa was the Ghana Empire (**Figure 1.16**). By 750, the Soninke farmers of the sub-Sahara had become wealthy by taxing the trade that passed through their area. For instance, the Niger River basin supplied gold to the Berber and Arab traders from west of the Nile Valley, who brought cloth, weapons, and manufactured goods into the interior. Huge Saharan salt mines supplied the life-sustaining mineral to the Mediterranean coast of Africa and inland areas. By 900, the monotheistic Muslims controlled most of this trade and had converted many of the African ruling elite. The majority of the population, however, maintained their tribal animistic practices, which gave living attributes to nonliving objects such as mountains, rivers, and wind. Because Ghana's king controlled the gold supply, he was able to maintain price controls and afford a strong military. Soon, however, a new kingdom emerged.

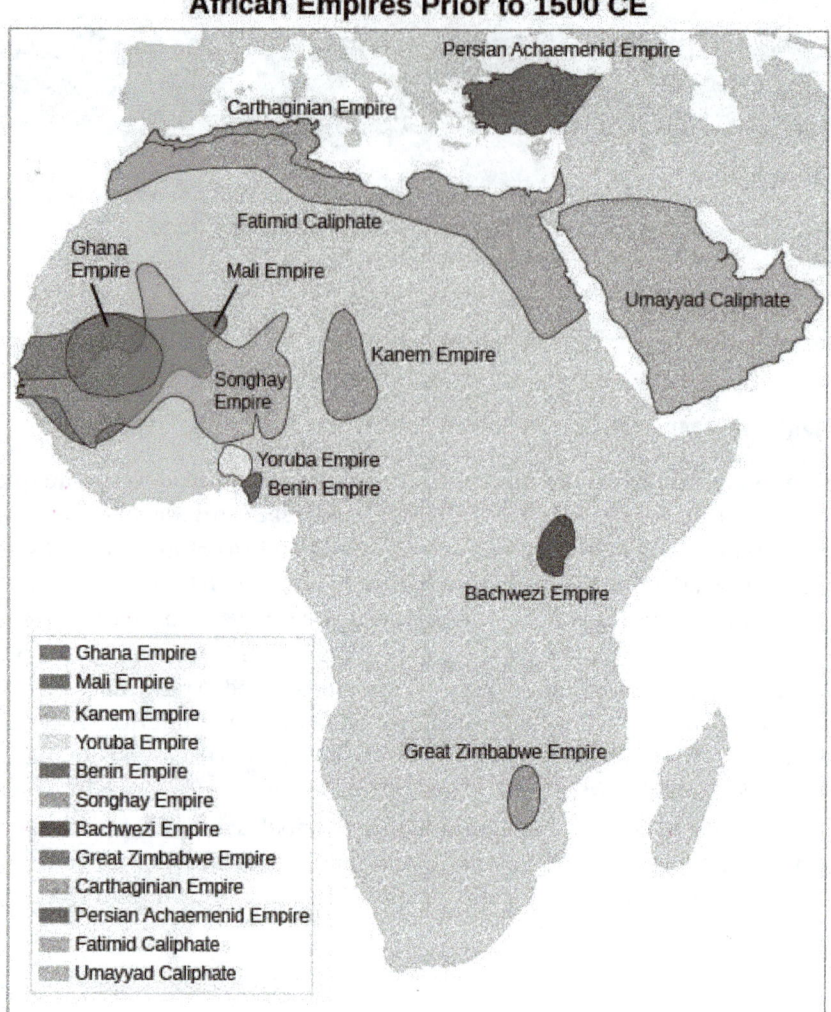

Figure 1.16 This map shows the locations of the major West African empires before 1492. Along the Mediterranean coast, Muslim states prevailed.

By 1200 CE, under the leadership of Sundiata Keita, Mali had replaced Ghana as the leading state in West Africa. After Sundiata's rule, the court converted to Islam, and Muslim scribes played a large part in administration and government. Miners then discovered huge new deposits of gold east of the Niger River. By the fourteenth century, the empire was so wealthy that while on a *hajj*, or pilgrimage to the holy city of Mecca, Mali's ruler Mansu Musa gave away enough gold to create serious price inflation in the cities along his route. Timbuktu, the capital city, became a leading Islamic center for education, commerce and the slave trade. Meanwhile, in the east, the city of Gao became increasingly strong under the leadership of Sonni Ali and soon eclipsed Mali's power. Timbuktu sought Ali's assistance in repelling the Tuaregs from the north. By 1500, however, the Tuareg empire of Songhay had eclipsed Mali, where weak and ineffective leadership prevailed.

THE ROLE OF SLAVERY

The institution of slavery is not a recent phenomenon. Most civilizations have practiced some form of human bondage and servitude, and African empires were no different (**Figure 1.17**). Famine or fear of stronger enemies might force one tribe to ask another for help and give themselves in a type of bondage in exchange. Similar to the European serf system, those seeking protection, or relief from starvation, would become the servants of those who provided relief. Debt might also be worked off through a form of servitude. Typically, these servants became a part of the extended tribal family. There is some evidence of **chattel slavery**, in which people are treated as personal property to be bought and sold, in the Nile Valley. It appears there was a slave-trade route through the Sahara that brought sub-Saharan Africans to Rome, which had slaves from all over the world.

Figure 1.17 Traders with a group of slaves. Note how the slaves are connected at the neck. Muslim traders brought slaves to the North African coast, where they might be sent to Europe or other parts of Africa.

Arab slave trading, which exchanged slaves for goods from the Mediterranean, existed long before Islam's spread across North Africa. Muslims later expanded this trade and enslaved not only Africans but also Europeans, especially from Spain, Sicily, and Italy. Male captives were forced to build coastal fortifications and serve as galley slaves. Women were added to the harem.

The major European slave trade began with Portugal's exploration of the west coast of Africa in search of a trade route to the East. By 1444, slaves were being brought from Africa to work on the sugar plantations of the Madeira Islands, off the coast of modern Morocco. The slave trade then expanded greatly as European colonies in the New World demanded an ever-increasing number of workers for the extensive plantations growing tobacco, sugar, and eventually rice and cotton (**Figure 1.18**).

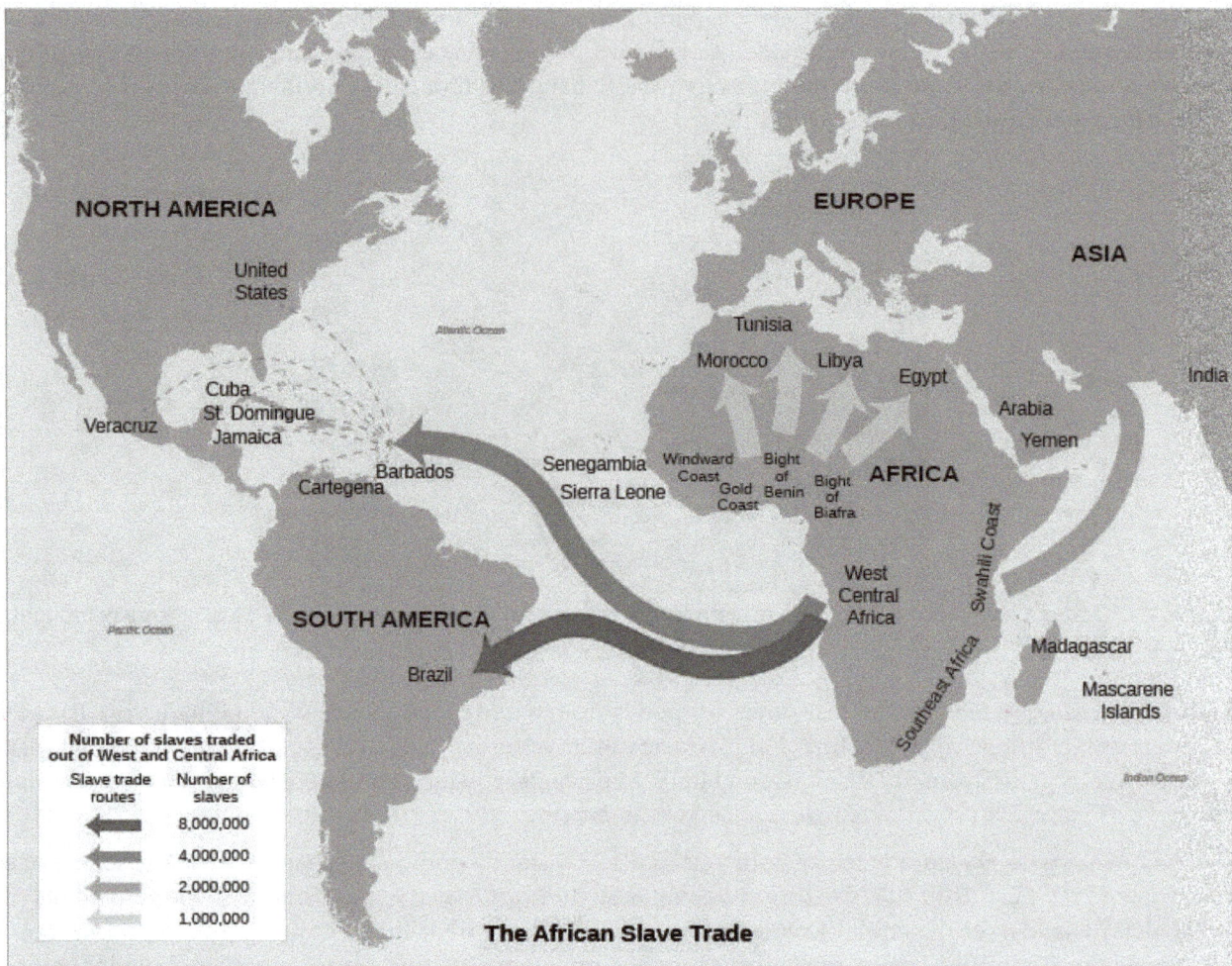

Figure 1.18 This map shows the routes that were used in the course of the slave trade and the number of enslaved people who traveled each route. As the figures indicate, most African slaves were bound for Brazil and the Caribbean. While West Africans made up the vast majority of the enslaved, the east coast of Africa, too, supplied slaves for the trade.

In the New World, the institution of slavery assumed a new aspect when the mercantilist system demanded a permanent, identifiable, and plentiful labor supply. African slaves were both easily identified (by their skin color) and plentiful, because of the thriving slave trade. This led to a race-based slavery system in the New World unlike any bondage system that had come before. Initially, the Spanish tried to force Indians to farm their crops. Most Spanish and Portuguese settlers coming to the New World were gentlemen and did not perform physical labor. They came to "serve God, but also to get rich," as noted by Bernal Díaz del Castillo. However, enslaved natives tended to sicken or die from disease or from the overwork and cruel treatment they were subjected to, and so the indigenous peoples proved not to be a dependable source of labor. Although he later repented of his ideas, the great defender of the Indians, Bartolomé de Las Casas, seeing the near extinction of the native population, suggested the Spanish send black (and white) laborers to the Indies. These workers proved hardier, and within fifty years, a change took place: The profitability of the African slave trade, coupled with the seemingly limitless number of potential slaves and the Catholic Church's denunciation of the enslavement of Christians, led race to become a dominant factor in the institution of slavery.

In the English colonies along the Atlantic coast, indentured servants initially filled the need for labor in the North, where family farms were the norm. In the South, however, labor-intensive crops such as tobacco, rice, and indigo prevailed, and eventually the supply of indentured servants was insufficient to meet the demand. These workers served only for periods of three to seven years before being freed; a more permanent labor supply was needed. Thus, whereas in Africa permanent, inherited slavery was unknown, and children of those bound in slavery to the tribe usually were free and intermarried with their captors, this changed in the Americas; slavery became permanent, and children born to slaves became slaves. This development, along with slavery's identification with race, forever changed the institution and shaped its unique character in the New World.

AMERICANA

The Beginnings of Racial Slavery

Slavery has a long history. The ancient Greek philosopher Aristotle posited that some peoples were *homunculi*, or humanlike but not really people—for instance, if they did not speak Greek. Both the Bible and the Koran sanction slavery. Vikings who raided from Ireland to Russia brought back slaves of all nationalities. During the Middle Ages, traders from the interior of Africa brought slaves along well-established routes to sell them along the Mediterranean coast. Initially, slavers also brought European slaves to the Caribbean. Many of these were orphaned or homeless children captured in the cities of Ireland. The question is, when did slavery become based on race? This appears to have developed in the New World, with the introduction of gruelingly labor-intensive crops such as sugar and coffee. Unable to fill their growing need from the ranks of prisoners or indentured servants, the European colonists turned to African laborers. The Portuguese, although seeking a trade route to India, also set up forts along the West African coast for the purpose of exporting slaves to Europe. Historians believe that by the year 1500, 10 percent of the population of Lisbon and Seville consisted of black slaves. Because of the influence of the Catholic Church, which frowned on the enslavement of Christians, European slave traders expanded their reach down the coast of Africa.

When Europeans settled Brazil, the Caribbean, and North America, they thus established a system of racially based slavery. Here, the need for a massive labor force was greater than in western Europe. The land was ripe for growing sugar, coffee, rice, and ultimately cotton. To fulfill the ever-growing demand for these crops, large plantations were created. The success of these plantations depended upon the availability of a permanent, plentiful, identifiable, and skilled labor supply. As Africans were already familiar with animal husbandry as well as farming, had an identifying skin color, and could be readily supplied by the existing African slave trade, they proved the answer to this need. This process set the stage for the expansion of New World slavery into North America.

CHAPTER 2
Early Globalization: The Atlantic World, 1492–1650

Figure 2.1 After Christopher Columbus "discovered" the New World, he sent letters home to Spain describing the wonders he beheld. These letters were quickly circulated throughout Europe and translated into Italian, German, and Latin. This woodcut is from the first Italian verse translation of the letter Columbus sent to the Spanish court after his first voyage, *Lettera delle isole novamente trovata* by Giuliano Dati.

Chapter Outline
2.1 Portuguese Exploration and Spanish Conquest
2.2 Religious Upheavals in the Developing Atlantic World
2.3 Challenges to Spain's Supremacy
2.4 New Worlds in the Americas: Labor, Commerce, and the Columbian Exchange

Introduction

The story of the Atlantic World is the story of global migration, a migration driven in large part by the actions and aspirations of the ruling heads of Europe. Columbus is hardly visible in this illustration of his ships making landfall on the Caribbean island of Hispaniola (**Figure 2.1**). Instead, Ferdinand II of Spain (in the foreground) sits on his throne and points toward Columbus's landing. As the ships arrive, the Arawak people tower over the Spanish, suggesting the native population density of the islands.

This historic moment in 1492 sparked new rivalries among European powers as they scrambled to create New World colonies, fueled by the quest for wealth and power as well as by religious passions. Almost continuous war resulted. Spain achieved early preeminence, creating a far-flung empire and growing rich with treasures from the Americas. Native Americans who confronted the newcomers from Europe suffered unprecedented losses of life, however, as previously unknown diseases sliced through their populations. They also were victims of the arrogance of the Europeans, who viewed themselves as uncontested masters of the New World, sent by God to bring Christianity to the "Indians." The Spanish enslaved Native Americans, forcing them to bring whatever gold could be found to fill Spanish coffers.

2.1 Portuguese Exploration and Spanish Conquest

By the end of this section, you will be able to:
- Describe Portuguese exploration of the Atlantic and Spanish exploration of the Americas, and the importance of these voyages to the developing Atlantic World
- Explain the importance of Spanish exploration of the Americas in the expansion of Spain's empire and the development of Spanish Renaissance culture

Portuguese colonization of Atlantic islands in the 1400s inaugurated an era of aggressive European expansion across the Atlantic. In the 1500s, Spain surpassed Portugal as the dominant European power. This age of exploration and the subsequent creation of an Atlantic World marked the earliest phase of globalization, in which previously isolated groups—Africans, Native Americans, and Europeans—first came into contact with each other, sometimes with disastrous results.

PORTUGUESE EXPLORATION

Portugal's Prince Henry the Navigator spearheaded his country's exploration of Africa and the Atlantic in the 1400s. With his support, Portuguese mariners successfully navigated an eastward route to Africa, establishing a foothold there that became a foundation of their nation's trade empire in the fifteenth and sixteenth centuries.

Portuguese mariners built an Atlantic empire by colonizing the Canary, Cape Verde, and Azores Islands, as well as the island of Madeira. Merchants then used these Atlantic outposts as debarkation points for subsequent journeys. From these strategic points, Portugal spread its empire down the western coast of Africa to the Congo, along the western coast of India, and eventually to Brazil on the eastern coast of South America. It also established trading posts in China and Japan. While the Portuguese didn't rule over

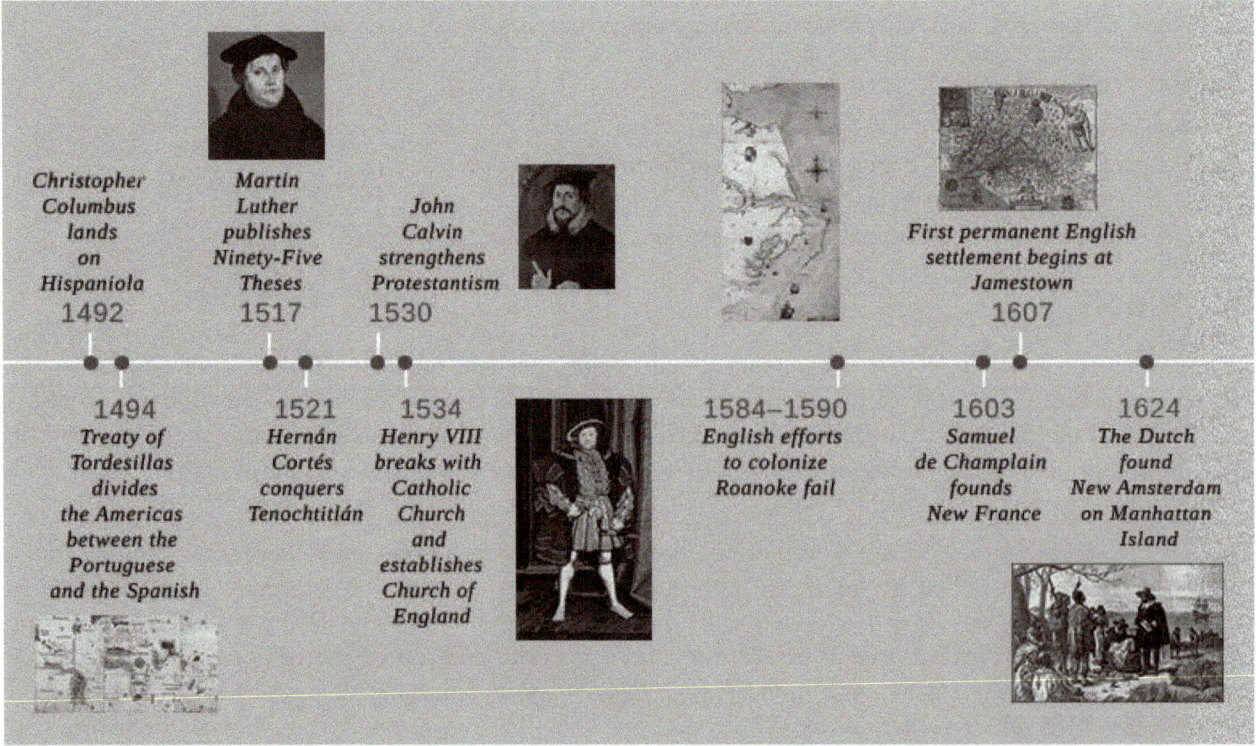

Figure 2.2

an immense landmass, their strategic holdings of islands and coastal ports gave them almost unrivaled control of nautical trade routes and a global empire of trading posts during the 1400s.

The travels of Portuguese traders to western Africa introduced them to the African slave trade, already brisk among African states. Seeing the value of this source of labor in growing the profitable crop of sugar on their Atlantic islands, the Portuguese soon began exporting African slaves along with African ivory and gold. Sugar fueled the Atlantic slave trade, and the Portuguese islands quickly became home to sugar plantations. The Portuguese also traded these slaves, introducing much-needed human capital to other European nations. In the following years, as European exploration spread, slavery spread as well. In time, much of the Atlantic World would become a gargantuan sugar-plantation complex in which Africans labored to produce the highly profitable commodity for European consumers.

AMERICANA

✪ Elmina Castle

In 1482, Portuguese traders built Elmina Castle (also called São Jorge da Mina, or Saint George's of the Mine) in present-day Ghana, on the west coast of Africa (**Figure 2.3**). A fortified trading post, it had mounted cannons facing out to sea, not inland toward continental Africa; the Portuguese had greater fear of a naval attack from other Europeans than of a land attack from Africans. Portuguese traders soon began to settle around the fort and established the town of Elmina.

Figure 2.3 Elmina Castle on the west coast of Ghana was used as a holding pen for slaves before they were brought across the Atlantic and sold. Originally built by the Portuguese in the fifteenth century, it appears in this image as it was in the 1660s, after being seized by Dutch slave traders in 1637.

Although the Portuguese originally used the fort primarily for trading gold, by the sixteenth century they had shifted their focus. The dungeon of the fort now served as a holding pen for African slaves from the interior of the continent, while on the upper floors Portuguese traders ate, slept, and prayed in a chapel. Slaves lived in the dungeon for weeks or months until ships arrived to transport them to Europe or the Americas. For them, the dungeon of Elmina was their last sight of their home country.

SPANISH EXPLORATION AND CONQUEST

The Spanish established the first European settlements in the Americas, beginning in the Caribbean and, by 1600, extending throughout Central and South America. Thousands of Spaniards flocked to the

Americas seeking wealth and status. The most famous of these Spanish adventurers are Christopher Columbus (who, though Italian himself, explored on behalf of the Spanish monarchs), Hernán Cortés, and Francisco Pizarro.

The history of Spanish exploration begins with the history of Spain itself. During the fifteenth century, Spain hoped to gain advantage over its rival, Portugal. The marriage of Ferdinand of Aragon and Isabella of Castile in 1469 unified Catholic Spain and began the process of building a nation that could compete for worldwide power. Since the 700s, much of Spain had been under Islamic rule, and King Ferdinand II and Queen Isabella I, arch-defenders of the Catholic Church against Islam, were determined to defeat the Muslims in Granada, the last Islamic stronghold in Spain. In 1492, they completed the Reconquista: the centuries-long Christian conquest of the Iberian Peninsula. The Reconquista marked another step forward in the process of making Spain an imperial power, and Ferdinand and Isabella were now ready to look further afield.

Their goals were to expand Catholicism and to gain a commercial advantage over Portugal. To those ends, Ferdinand and Isabella sponsored extensive Atlantic exploration. Spain's most famous explorer, Christopher Columbus, was actually from Genoa, Italy. He believed that, using calculations based on other mariners' journeys, he could chart a westward route to India, which could be used to expand European trade and spread Christianity. Starting in 1485, he approached Genoese, Venetian, Portuguese, English, and Spanish monarchs, asking for ships and funding to explore this westward route. All those he petitioned—including Ferdinand and Isabella at first—rebuffed him; their nautical experts all concurred that Columbus's estimates of the width of the Atlantic Ocean were far too low. However, after three years of entreaties, and, more important, the completion of the Reconquista, Ferdinand and Isabella agreed to finance Columbus's expedition in 1492, supplying him with three ships: the *Nina*, the *Pinta*, and the *Santa Maria*. The Spanish monarchs knew that Portuguese mariners had reached the southern tip of Africa and sailed the Indian Ocean. They understood that the Portuguese would soon reach Asia and, in this competitive race to reach the Far East, the Spanish rulers decided to act.

Columbus held erroneous views that shaped his thinking about what he would encounter as he sailed west. He believed the earth to be much smaller than its actual size and, since he did not know of the existence of the Americas, he fully expected to land in Asia. On October 12, 1492, however, he made landfall on an island in the Bahamas. He then sailed to an island he named **Hispaniola** (present-day Dominican Republic and Haiti) (**Figure 2.4**). Believing he had landed in the East Indies, Columbus called the native Taínos he found there "Indios," giving rise to the term "Indian" for any native people of the New World. Upon Columbus's return to Spain, the Spanish crown bestowed on him the title of Admiral of the Ocean Sea and named him governor and viceroy of the lands he had discovered. As a devoted Catholic, Columbus had agreed with Ferdinand and Isabella prior to sailing west that part of the expected wealth from his voyage would be used to continue the fight against Islam.

Figure 2.4 This sixteenth-century map shows the island of Hispaniola (present-day Haiti and Dominican Republic). Note the various fanciful elements, such as the large-scale ships and sea creatures, and consider what the creator of this map hoped to convey. In addition to navigation, what purpose would such a map have served?

Columbus's 1493 letter—or *probanza de mérito* (proof of merit)—describing his "discovery" of a New World did much to inspire excitement in Europe. *Probanzas de méritos* were reports and letters written by Spaniards in the New World to the Spanish crown, designed to win royal patronage. Today they highlight the difficult task of historical work; while the letters are primary sources, historians need to understand the context and the culture in which the conquistadors, as the Spanish adventurers came to be called, wrote them and distinguish their bias and subjective nature. While they are filled with distortions and fabrications, *probanzas de méritos* are still useful in illustrating the expectation of wealth among the explorers as well as their view that native peoples would not pose a serious obstacle to colonization.

In 1493, Columbus sent two copies of a *probanza de mérito* to the Spanish king and queen and their minister of finance, Luis de Santángel. Santángel had supported Columbus's voyage, helping him to obtain funding from Ferdinand and Isabella. Copies of the letter were soon circulating all over Europe, spreading news of the wondrous new land that Columbus had "discovered." Columbus would make three more voyages over the next decade, establishing Spain's first settlement in the New World on the island of Hispaniola. Many other Europeans followed in Columbus's footsteps, drawn by dreams of winning wealth by sailing west. Another Italian, Amerigo Vespucci, sailing for the Portuguese crown, explored the South American coastline between 1499 and 1502. Unlike Columbus, he realized that the Americas were not part of Asia but lands unknown to Europeans. Vespucci's widely published accounts of his voyages fueled speculation and intense interest in the New World among Europeans. Among those who read Vespucci's reports was the German mapmaker Martin Waldseemuller. Using the explorer's first name as a label for the new landmass, Waldseemuller attached "America" to his map of the New World in 1507, and the name stuck.

DEFINING "AMERICAN"

✪ Columbus's Probanza de mérito of 1493

The exploits of the most famous Spanish explorers have provided Western civilization with a narrative of European supremacy and Indian savagery. However, these stories are based on the self-aggrandizing efforts of conquistadors to secure royal favor through the writing of *probanzas de méritos* (proofs of merit). Below are excerpts from Columbus's 1493 letter to Luis de Santángel, which illustrates how fantastic reports from European explorers gave rise to many myths surrounding the Spanish conquest and the New World.

> This island, like all the others, is most extensive. It has many ports along the sea-coast excelling any in Christendom—and many fine, large, flowing rivers. The land there is elevated, with many mountains and peaks incomparably higher than in the centre isle. They are most beautiful, of a thousand varied forms, accessible, and full of trees of endless varieties, so high that they seem to touch the sky, and I have been told that they never lose their foliage. . . . There is honey, and there are many kinds of birds, and a great variety of fruits. Inland there are numerous mines of metals and innumerable people. Hispaniola is a marvel. Its hills and mountains, fine plains and open country, are rich and fertile for planting and for pasturage, and for building towns and villages. The seaports there are incredibly fine, as also the magnificent rivers, most of which bear gold. The trees, fruits and grasses differ widely from those in Juana. There are many spices and vast mines of gold and other metals in this island. They have no iron, nor steel, nor weapons, nor are they fit for them, because although they are well-made men of commanding stature, they appear extraordinarily timid. The only arms they have are sticks of cane, cut when in seed, with a sharpened stick at the end, and they are afraid to use these. Often I have sent two or three men ashore to some town to converse with them, and the natives came out in great numbers, and as soon as they saw our men arrive, fled without a moment's delay although I protected them from all injury.

What does this letter show us about Spanish objectives in the New World? How do you think it might have influenced Europeans reading about the New World for the first time?

The 1492 Columbus landfall accelerated the rivalry between Spain and Portugal, and the two powers vied for domination through the acquisition of new lands. In the 1480s, Pope Sixtus IV had granted Portugal the right to all land south of the Cape Verde islands, leading the Portuguese king to claim that the lands discovered by Columbus belonged to Portugal, not Spain. Seeking to ensure that Columbus's finds would remain Spanish, Spain's monarchs turned to the Spanish-born Pope Alexander VI, who issued two papal decrees in 1493 that gave legitimacy to Spain's Atlantic claims at the expense of Portugal. Hoping to salvage Portugal's Atlantic holdings, King João II began negotiations with Spain. The resulting Treaty of Tordesillas in 1494 drew a north-to-south line through South America (**Figure 2.5**); Spain gained territory west of the line, while Portugal retained the lands east of the line, including the east coast of Brazil.

Figure 2.5 This 1502 map, known as the Cantino World Map, depicts the cartographer's interpretation of the world in light of recent discoveries. The map shows areas of Portuguese and Spanish exploration, the two nations' claims under the Treaty of Tordesillas, and a variety of flora, fauna, figures, and structures. What does it reveal about the state of geographical knowledge, as well as European perceptions of the New World, at the beginning of the sixteenth century?

Columbus's discovery opened a floodgate of Spanish exploration. Inspired by tales of rivers of gold and timid, malleable natives, later Spanish explorers were relentless in their quest for land and gold. Hernán Cortés hoped to gain hereditary privilege for his family, tribute payments and labor from natives, and an annual pension for his service to the crown. Cortés arrived on Hispaniola in 1504 and took part in the conquest of that island. In anticipation of winning his own honor and riches, Cortés later explored the Yucatán Peninsula. In 1519, he entered Tenochtitlán, the capital of the Aztec (Mexica) Empire. He and his men were astonished by the incredibly sophisticated causeways, gardens, and temples in the city, but they were horrified by the practice of human sacrifice that was part of the Aztec religion. Above all else, the Aztec wealth in gold fascinated the Spanish adventurers.

Hoping to gain power over the city, Cortés took Moctezuma, the Aztec ruler, hostage. The Spanish then murdered hundreds of high-ranking Mexica during a festival to celebrate Huitzilopochtli, the god of war. This angered the people of Tenochtitlán, who rose up against the interlopers in their city. Cortés and his people fled for their lives, running down one of Tenochtitlán's causeways to safety on the shore. Smarting from their defeat at the hands of the Aztec, Cortés slowly created alliances with native peoples who resented Aztec rule. It took nearly a year for the Spanish and the tens of thousands of native allies who joined them to defeat the Mexica in Tenochtitlán, which they did by laying siege to the city. Only by playing upon the disunity among the diverse groups in the Aztec Empire were the Spanish able to capture the grand city of Tenochtitlán. In August 1521, having successfully fomented civil war as well as fended off rival Spanish explorers, Cortés claimed Tenochtitlán for Spain and renamed it Mexico City.

The traditional European narrative of exploration presents the victory of the Spanish over the Aztec as an example of the superiority of the Europeans over the savage Indians. However, the reality is far more complex. When Cortés explored central Mexico, he encountered a region simmering with native conflict. Far from being unified and content under Aztec rule, many peoples in Mexico resented it and were ready to rebel. One group in particular, the Tlaxcalan, threw their lot in with the Spanish, providing as many as 200,000 fighters in the siege of Tenochtitlán. The Spanish also brought smallpox into the valley of Mexico. The disease took a heavy toll on the people in Tenochtitlán, playing a much greater role in the city's demise than did Spanish force of arms.

Cortés was also aided by a Nahua woman called Malintzin (also known as La Malinche or Doña Marina, her Spanish name), whom the natives of Tabasco gave him as tribute. Malintzin translated for Cortés in his dealings with Moctezuma and, whether willingly or under pressure, entered into a physical relationship with him. Their son, Martín, may have been the first mestizo (person of mixed indigenous American and European descent). Malintzin remains a controversial figure in the history of the Atlantic World; some people view her as a traitor because she helped Cortés conquer the Aztecs, while others see her as a victim of European expansion. In either case, she demonstrates one way in which native peoples responded to the arrival of the Spanish. Without her, Cortés would not have been able to communicate, and without the language bridge, he surely would have been less successful in destabilizing the Aztec Empire. By this and other means, native people helped shape the conquest of the Americas.

Spain's acquisitiveness seemingly knew no bounds as groups of its explorers searched for the next trove of instant riches. One such explorer, Francisco Pizarro, made his way to the Spanish Caribbean in 1509, drawn by the promise of wealth and titles. He participated in successful expeditions in Panama before following rumors of Inca wealth to the south. Although his first efforts against the Inca Empire in the 1520s failed, Pizarro captured the Inca emperor Atahualpa in 1532 and executed him one year later. In 1533, Pizarro founded Lima, Peru. Like Cortés, Pizarro had to combat not only the natives of the new worlds he was conquering, but also competitors from his own country; a Spanish rival assassinated him in 1541.

Spain's drive to enlarge its empire led other hopeful conquistadors to push further into the Americas, hoping to replicate the success of Cortés and Pizarro. Hernando de Soto had participated in Pizarro's conquest of the Inca, and from 1539 to 1542 he led expeditions to what is today the southeastern United States, looking for gold. He and his followers explored what is now Florida, Georgia, the Carolinas, Tennessee, Alabama, Mississippi, Arkansas, Oklahoma, Louisiana, and Texas. Everywhere they traveled, they brought European diseases, which claimed thousands of native lives as well as the lives of the explorers. In 1542, de Soto himself died during the expedition. The surviving Spaniards, numbering a little over three hundred, returned to Mexico City without finding the much-anticipated mountains of gold and silver.

Francisco Vásquez de Coronado was born into a noble family and went to Mexico, then called New Spain, in 1535. He presided as governor over the province of Nueva Galicia, where he heard rumors of wealth to the north: a golden city called Quivira. Between 1540 and 1542, Coronado led a large expedition of Spaniards and native allies to the lands north of Mexico City, and for the next several years, they explored the area that is now the southwestern United States (**Figure 2.6**). During the winter of 1540–41, the explorers waged war against the Tiwa in present-day New Mexico. Rather than leading to the discovery of gold and silver, however, the expedition simply left Coronado bankrupt.

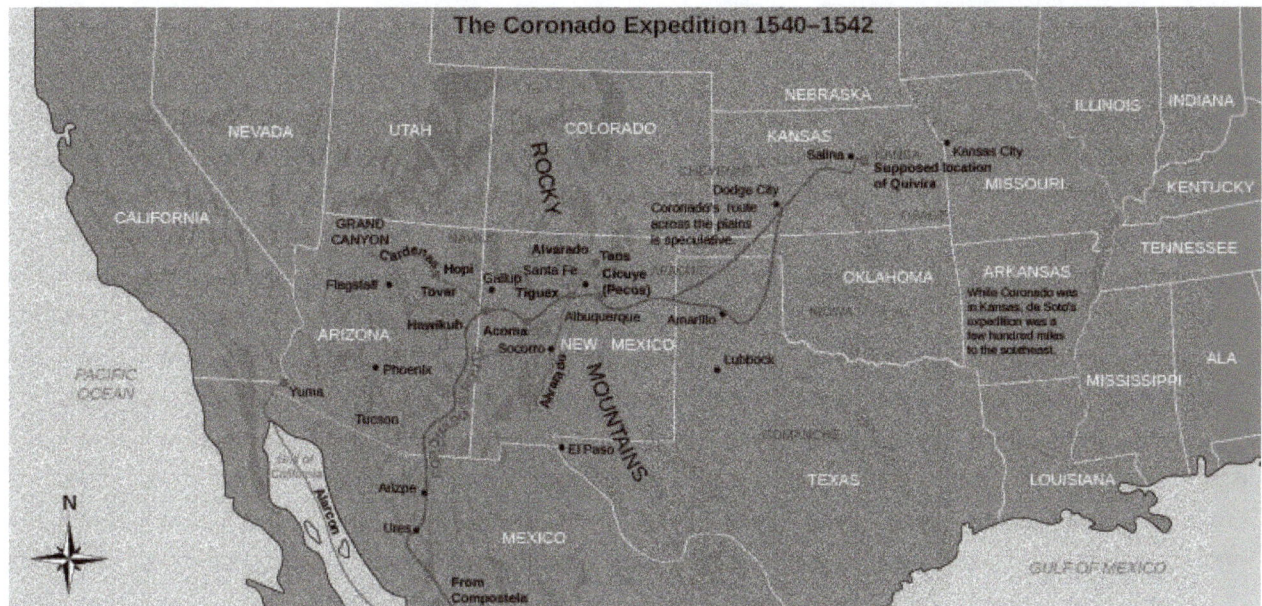

Figure 2.6 This map traces Coronado's path through the American Southwest and the Great Plains. The regions through which he traveled were not empty areas waiting to be "discovered": rather, they were populated and controlled by the groups of native peoples indicated. (credit: modification of work by National Park Service)

THE SPANISH GOLDEN AGE

The exploits of European explorers had a profound impact both in the Americas and back in Europe. An exchange of ideas, fueled and financed in part by New World commodities, began to connect European nations and, in turn, to touch the parts of the world that Europeans conquered. In Spain, gold and silver from the Americas helped to fuel a golden age, the Siglo de Oro, when Spanish art and literature flourished. Riches poured in from the colonies, and new ideas poured in from other countries and new lands. The Hapsburg dynasty, which ruled a collection of territories including Austria, the Netherlands, Naples, Sicily, and Spain, encouraged and financed the work of painters, sculptors, musicians, architects, and writers, resulting in a blooming of Spanish Renaissance culture. One of this period's most famous works is the novel *The Ingenious Gentleman Don Quixote of La Mancha*, by Miguel de Cervantes. This two-volume book (1605 and 1618) told a colorful tale of an *hidalgo* (gentleman) who reads so many tales of chivalry and knighthood that he becomes unable to tell reality from fiction. With his faithful sidekick Sancho Panza, Don Quixote leaves reality behind and sets out to revive chivalry by doing battle with what he perceives as the enemies of Spain.

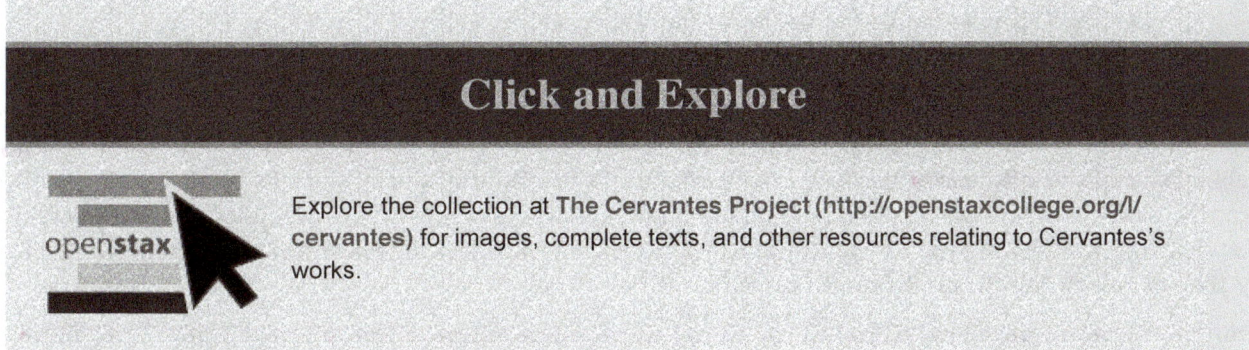

Explore the collection at **The Cervantes Project** (http://openstaxcollege.org/l/cervantes) for images, complete texts, and other resources relating to Cervantes's works.

Spain attracted innovative foreign painters such as El Greco, a Greek who had studied with Italian Renaissance masters like Titian and Michelangelo before moving to Toledo. Native Spaniards created equally enduring works. *Las Meninas (The Maids of Honor)*, painted by Diego Velázquez in 1656, is one of the best-known paintings in history. Velázquez painted himself into this imposingly large royal portrait (he's shown holding his brush and easel on the left) and boldly placed the viewer where the king and queen would stand in the scene (**Figure 2.7**).

Figure 2.7 *Las Meninas (The Maids of Honor)*, painted by Diego Velázquez in 1656, is unique for its time because it places the viewer in the place of King Philip IV and his wife, Queen Mariana.

2.2 Religious Upheavals in the Developing Atlantic World

By the end of this section, you will be able to:
- Explain the changes brought by the Protestant Reformation and how it influenced the development of the Atlantic World
- Describe Spain's response to the Protestant Reformation

Until the 1500s, the Catholic Church provided a unifying religious structure for Christian Europe. The Vatican in Rome exercised great power over the lives of Europeans; it controlled not only learning and scholarship but also finances, because it levied taxes on the faithful. Spain, with its New World wealth, was the bastion of the Catholic faith. Beginning with the reform efforts of Martin Luther in 1517 and John Calvin in the 1530s, however, Catholic dominance came under attack as the **Protestant Reformation**, a split or schism among European Christians, began.

During the sixteenth century, Protestantism spread through northern Europe, and Catholic countries responded by attempting to extinguish what was seen as the Protestant menace. Religious turmoil between Catholics and Protestants influenced the history of the Atlantic World as well, since different nation-states competed not only for control of new territories but also for the preeminence of their religious beliefs there. Just as the history of Spain's rise to power is linked to the Reconquista, so too is the history of early globalization connected to the history of competing Christian groups in the Atlantic World.

MARTIN LUTHER

Martin Luther (Figure 2.8) was a German Catholic monk who took issue with the Catholic Church's practice of selling **indulgences**, documents that absolved sinners of their errant behavior. He also objected to the Catholic Church's taxation of ordinary Germans and the delivery of Mass in Latin, arguing that it failed to instruct German Catholics, who did not understand the language.

Figure 2.8 Martin Luther, a German Catholic monk and leader of the Protestant Reformation, was a close friend of the German painter Lucas Cranach the Elder. Cranach painted this and several other portraits of Luther.

Many Europeans had called for reforms of the Catholic Church before Martin Luther did, but his protest had the unintended consequence of splitting European Christianity. Luther compiled a list of what he viewed as needed Church reforms, a document that came to be known as *The Ninety-Five Theses*, and nailed it to the door of a church in Wittenberg, Germany, in 1517. He called for the publication of the Bible in everyday language, took issue with the Church's policy of imposing tithes (a required payment to the Church that appeared to enrich the clergy), and denounced the buying and selling of indulgences. Although he had hoped to reform the Catholic Church while remaining a part of it, Luther's action instead triggered a movement called the Protestant Reformation that divided the Church in two. The Catholic Church condemned him as a heretic, but a doctrine based on his reforms, called Lutheranism, spread through northern Germany and Scandinavia.

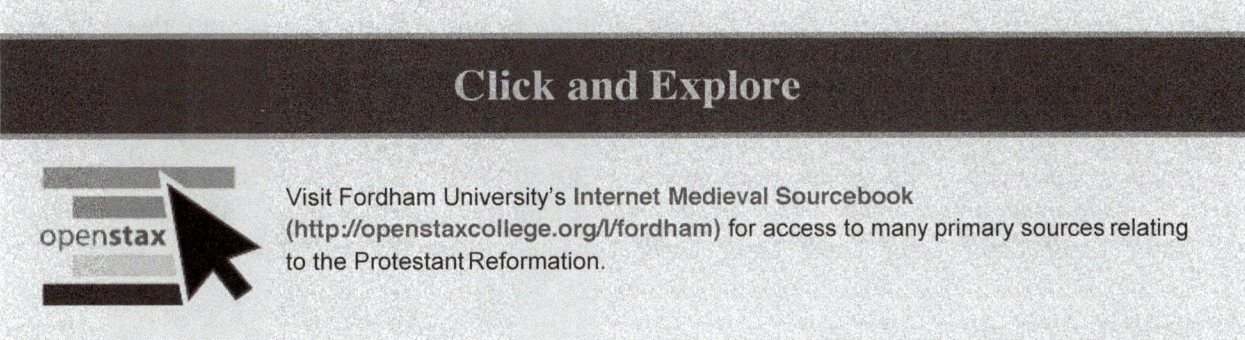

Visit Fordham University's Internet Medieval Sourcebook (http://openstaxcollege.org/l/fordham) for access to many primary sources relating to the Protestant Reformation.

JOHN CALVIN

Like Luther, the French lawyer John Calvin advocated making the Bible accessible to ordinary people; only by reading scripture and reflecting daily about their spiritual condition, he argued, could believers begin to understand the power of God. In 1535, Calvin fled Catholic France and led the Reformation movement from Geneva, Switzerland.

Calvinism emphasized human powerlessness before an omniscient God and stressed the idea of predestination, the belief that God selected a few chosen people for salvation while everyone else was predestined to damnation. Calvinists believed that reading scripture prepared sinners, if they were among the elect, to receive God's grace. In Geneva, Calvin established a Bible commonwealth, a community of believers whose sole source of authority was their interpretation of the Bible, not the authority of any prince or monarch. Soon Calvin's ideas spread to the Netherlands and Scotland.

PROTESTANTISM IN ENGLAND

Protestantism spread beyond the German states and Geneva to England, which had been a Catholic nation for centuries. Luther's idea that scripture should be available in the everyday language of worshippers inspired English scholar William Tyndale to translate the Bible into English in 1526. The seismic break with the Catholic Church in England occurred in the 1530s, when Henry VIII established a new, Protestant state religion.

A devout Catholic, Henry had initially stood in opposition to the Reformation. Pope Leo X even awarded him the title "Defender of the Faith." The tides turned, however, when Henry desired a male heir to the Tudor monarchy. When his Spanish Catholic wife, Catherine (the daughter of Ferdinand and Isabella), did not give birth to a boy, the king sought an annulment to their marriage. When the Pope refused his request, Henry created a new national Protestant church, the Church of England, with himself at its head. This left him free to annul his own marriage and marry Anne Boleyn.

Anne Boleyn also failed to produce a male heir, and when she was accused of adultery, Henry had her executed. His third wife, Jane Seymour, at long last delivered a son, Edward, who ruled for only a short time before dying in 1553 at the age of fifteen. Mary, the daughter of Henry VIII and his discarded first wife Catherine, then came to the throne, committed to restoring Catholicism. She earned the nickname "Bloody Mary" for the many executions of Protestants, often by burning alive, that she ordered during her reign.

Religious turbulence in England was finally quieted when Elizabeth, the Protestant daughter of Henry VIII and Anne Boleyn, ascended the throne in 1558. Under Elizabeth, the Church of England again became the state church, retaining the hierarchical structure and many of the rituals of the Catholic Church. However, by the late 1500s, some English members of the Church began to agitate for more reform. Known as **Puritans**, they worked to erase all vestiges of Catholicism from the Church of England. At the time, the term "puritan" was a pejorative one; many people saw Puritans as holier-than-thou frauds who used religion to swindle their neighbors. Worse still, many in power saw Puritans as a security threat because of their opposition to the national church.

Under Elizabeth, whose long reign lasted from 1558 to 1603, Puritans grew steadily in number. After James I died in 1625 and his son Charles I ascended the throne, Puritans became the target of increasing state pressure to conform. Many crossed the Atlantic in the 1620s and 1630s instead to create a New England, a haven for reformed Protestantism where Puritan was no longer a term of abuse. Thus, the religious upheavals that affected England so much had equally momentous consequences for the Americas.

RELIGIOUS WAR

By the early 1500s, the Protestant Reformation threatened the massive Spanish Catholic empire. As the preeminent Catholic power, Spain would not tolerate any challenge to the Holy Catholic Church. Over the course of the 1500s, it devoted vast amounts of treasure and labor to leading an unsuccessful effort to eradicate Protestantism in Europe.

This content is available for free at http://cnx.org/content/col11740/latest/

Spain's main enemies at this time were the runaway Spanish provinces of the North Netherlands. By 1581, these seven northern provinces had declared their independence from Spain and created the Dutch Republic, also called Holland, where Protestantism was tolerated. Determined to deal a death blow to Protestantism in England and Holland, King Philip of Spain assembled a massive force of over thirty thousand men and 130 ships, and in 1588 he sent this navy, the Spanish Armada, north. But English sea power combined with a maritime storm destroyed the fleet.

The defeat of the Spanish Armada in 1588 was but one part of a larger but undeclared war between Protestant England and Catholic Spain. Between 1585 and 1604, the two rivals sparred repeatedly. England launched its own armada in 1589 in an effort to cripple the Spanish fleet and capture Spanish treasure. However, the foray ended in disaster for the English, with storms, disease, and the strength of the Spanish Armada combining to bring about defeat.

The conflict between Spain and England dragged on into the early seventeenth century, and the newly Protestant nations, especially England and the Dutch Republic, posed a significant challenge to Spain (and also to Catholic France) as imperial rivalries played out in the Atlantic World. Spain retained its mighty American empire, but by the early 1600s, the nation could no longer keep England and other European rivals—the French and Dutch—from colonizing smaller islands in the Caribbean (**Figure 2.9**).

Figure 2.9 This portrait of Elizabeth I of England, painted by George Gower in about 1588, shows Elizabeth with her hand on a globe, signifying her power over the world. The pictures in the background show the English defeat of the Spanish Armada.

Religious intolerance characterized the sixteenth and seventeenth centuries, an age of powerful state religions with the authority to impose and enforce belief systems on the population. In this climate, religious violence was common. One of the most striking examples is the St. Bartholomew's Day Massacre of 1572, in which French Catholic troops began to kill unarmed French Protestants (**Figure 2.10**). The murders touched off mob violence that ultimately claimed nine thousand lives, a bloody episode that highlights the degree of religious turmoil that gripped Europe in the aftermath of the Protestant Reformation.

Figure 2.10 *Saint Bartholomew's Day Massacre* (1772-84), by François Dubois, shows the horrific violence of the St. Bartholomew's Day Massacre. In this scene, French Catholic troops slaughter French Protestant Calvinists.

2.3 Challenges to Spain's Supremacy

By the end of this section, you will be able to:
- Identify regions where the English, French, and Dutch explored and established settlements
- Describe the differences among the early colonies
- Explain the role of the American colonies in European nations' struggles for domination

For Europeans, the discovery of an Atlantic World meant newfound wealth in the form of gold and silver as well as valuable furs. The Americas also provided a new arena for intense imperial rivalry as different European nations jockeyed for preeminence in the New World. The religious motives for colonization spurred European expansion as well, and as the Protestant Reformation gained ground beginning in the 1520s, rivalries between Catholic and Protestant Christians spilled over into the Americas.

ENGLISH EXPLORATION

Disruptions during the Tudor monarchy—especially the creation of the Protestant Church of England by Henry VIII in the 1530s, the return of the nation to Catholicism under Queen Mary in the 1550s, and the restoration of Protestantism under Queen Elizabeth—left England with little energy for overseas projects. More important, England lacked the financial resources for such endeavors. Nonetheless, English monarchs carefully monitored developments in the new Atlantic World and took steps to assert England's claim to the Americas. As early as 1497, Henry VII of England had commissioned John Cabot, an Italian mariner, to explore new lands. Cabot sailed from England that year and made landfall somewhere along the North American coastline. For the next century, English fishermen routinely crossed the Atlantic to fish the rich waters off the North American coast. However, English colonization efforts in the 1500s were closer to home, as England devoted its energy to the colonization of Ireland.

Queen Elizabeth favored England's advance into the Atlantic World, though her main concern was blocking Spain's effort to eliminate Protestantism. Indeed, England could not commit to large-scale colonization in the Americas as long as Spain appeared ready to invade Ireland or Scotland. Nonetheless,

Elizabeth approved of English **privateers**, sea captains to whom the home government had given permission to raid the enemy at will. These skilled mariners cruised the Caribbean, plundering Spanish ships whenever they could. Each year the English took more than £100,000 from Spain in this way; English privateer Francis Drake first made a name for himself when, in 1573, he looted silver, gold, and pearls worth £40,000.

Elizabeth did sanction an early attempt at colonization in 1584, when Sir Walter Raleigh, a favorite of the queen's, attempted to establish a colony at **Roanoke**, an island off the coast of present-day North Carolina. The colony was small, consisting of only 117 people, who suffered a poor relationship with the local Indians, the Croatans, and struggled to survive in their new land (**Figure 2.11**). Their governor, John White, returned to England in late 1587 to secure more people and supplies, but events conspired to keep him away from Roanoke for three years. By the time he returned in 1590, the entire colony had vanished. The only trace the colonists left behind was the word *Croatoan* carved into a fence surrounding the village. Governor White never knew whether the colonists had decamped for nearby Croatoan Island (now Hatteras) or whether some disaster had befallen them all. Roanoke is still called "the lost colony."

Figure 2.11 In 1588, a promoter of English colonization named Thomas Hariot published *A Briefe and True Report of the New Found Land of Virginia*, which contained many engravings of the native peoples who lived on the Carolina coast in the 1580s. This print, "The brovvyllinge of their fishe ouer the flame" (1590) by Theodor de Bry, shows the ingenuity and wisdom of the "savages" of the New World. (credit: UNC Chapel Hill)

English promoters of colonization pushed its commercial advantages and the religious justification that English colonies would allow the establishment of Protestantism in the Americas. Both arguments struck a chord. In the early 1600s, wealthy English merchants and the landed elite began to pool their resources to form **joint stock companies**. In this novel business arrangement, which was in many ways the precursor to the modern corporation, investors provided the capital for and assumed the risk of a venture in order to reap significant returns. The companies gained the approval of the English crown to establish colonies, and their investors dreamed of reaping great profits from the money they put into overseas colonization.

The first permanent English settlement was established by a joint stock company, the Virginia Company. Named for Elizabeth, the "virgin queen," the company gained royal approval to establish a colony on the east coast of North America, and in 1606, it sent 144 men and boys to the New World. In early 1607, this group sailed up Chesapeake Bay. Finding a river they called the James in honor of their new king, James I, they established a ramshackle settlement and named it Jamestown. Despite serious struggles, the colony survived.

Many of Jamestown's settlers were desperate men; although they came from elite families, they were younger sons who would not inherit their father's estates. The Jamestown adventurers believed they would find instant wealth in the New World and did not actually expect to have to perform work. Henry Percy, the eighth son of the Earl of Northumberland, was among them. His account, excerpted below, illustrates the hardships the English confronted in Virginia in 1607.

MY STORY

George Percy and the First Months at Jamestown

The 144 men and boys who started the Jamestown colony faced many hardships; by the end of the first winter, only 38 had survived. Disease, hunger, and poor relationships with local natives all contributed to the colony's high death toll. George Percy, who served twice as governor of Jamestown, kept records of the colonists' first months in the colony. These records were later published in London in 1608. This excerpt is from his account of August and September of 1607.

> The fourth day of September died Thomas Jacob Sergeant. The fifth day, there died Benjamin Beast. Our men were destroyed with cruel diseases, as Swellings, Fluxes, Burning Fevers, and by wars, and some departed suddenly, but for the most part they died of mere famine. There were never Englishmen left in a foreign Country in such misery as we were in this new discovered Virginia. . . . Our food was but a small Can of Barley sod* in water, to five men a day, our drink cold water taken out of the River, which was at a flood very salty, at a low tide full of slime and filth, which was the destruction of many of our men. Thus we lived for the space of five months in this miserable distress, not having five able men to man our Bulwarks upon any occasion. If it had not pleased God to have put a terror in the Savages' hearts, we had all perished by those wild and cruel Pagans, being in that weak estate as we were; our men night and day groaning in every corner of the Fort most pitiful to hear. If there were any conscience in men, it would make their hearts to bleed to hear the pitiful murmurings and outcries of our sick men without relief, every night and day, for the space of six weeks, some departing out of the World, many times three or four in a night; in the morning, their bodies trailed out of their Cabins like Dogs to be buried. In this sort did I see the mortality of diverse of our people.
>
> *soaked

According to George Percy's account, what were the major problems the Jamestown settlers encountered? What kept the colony from complete destruction?

By any measure, England came late to the race to colonize. As Jamestown limped along in the 1610s, the Spanish Empire extended around the globe and grew rich from its global colonial project. Yet the English persisted, and for this reason the Jamestown settlement has a special place in history as the first permanent colony in what later became the United States.

After Jamestown's founding, English colonization of the New World accelerated. In 1609, a ship bound for Jamestown foundered in a storm and landed on Bermuda. (Some believe this incident helped inspire Shakespeare's 1611 play *The Tempest*.) The admiral of the ship, George Somers, claimed the island for the English crown. The English also began to colonize small islands in the Caribbean, an incursion into the Spanish American empire. They established themselves on small islands such as St. Christopher (1624), Barbados (1627), Nevis (1628), Montserrat (1632), and Antigua (1632).

From the start, the English West Indies had a commercial orientation, for these islands produced cash crops: first tobacco and then sugar. Very quickly, by the mid-1600s, Barbados had become one of the most important English colonies because of the sugar produced there. Barbados was the first English colony dependent on slaves, and it became a model for other English slave societies on the American mainland. These differed radically from England itself, where slavery was not practiced.

English Puritans also began to colonize the Americas in the 1620s and 1630s. These intensely religious migrants dreamed of creating communities of reformed Protestantism where the corruption of England would be eliminated. One of the first groups of Puritans to remove to North America, known as **Pilgrims** and led by William Bradford, had originally left England to live in the Netherlands. Fearing their children were losing their English identity among the Dutch, however, they sailed for North America in 1620 to settle at Plymouth, the first English settlement in New England. The Pilgrims differed from other Puritans in their insistence on separating from what they saw as the corrupt Church of England. For this reason, Pilgrims are known as **Separatists**.

Like Jamestown, Plymouth occupies an iconic place in American national memory. The tale of the 102 migrants who crossed the Atlantic aboard the *Mayflower* and their struggle for survival is a well-known narrative of the founding of the country. Their story includes the signing of the Mayflower Compact, a written agreement whereby the English voluntarily agreed to help each other. Some interpret this 1620 document as an expression of democratic spirit because of the cooperative and inclusive nature of the agreement to live and work together. In 1630, a much larger contingent of Puritans left England to escape conformity to the Church of England and founded the Massachusetts Bay Colony. In the following years, thousands more arrived to create a new life in the rocky soils and cold climates of New England.

In comparison to Catholic Spain, however, Protestant England remained a very weak imperial player in the early seventeenth century, with only a few infant colonies in the Americas in the early 1600s. The English never found treasure equal to that of the Aztec city of Tenochtitlán, and England did not quickly grow rich from its small American outposts. The English colonies also differed from each other; Barbados and Virginia had a decidedly commercial orientation from the start, while the Puritan colonies of New England were intensely religious at their inception. All English settlements in America, however, marked the increasingly important role of England in the Atlantic World.

FRENCH EXPLORATION

Spanish exploits in the New World whetted the appetite of other would-be imperial powers, including France. Like Spain, France was a Catholic nation and committed to expanding Catholicism around the globe. In the early sixteenth century, it joined the race to explore the New World and exploit the resources of the Western Hemisphere. Navigator Jacques Cartier claimed northern North America for France, naming the area New France. From 1534 to 1541, he made three voyages of discovery on the Gulf of St. Lawrence and the St. Lawrence River. Like other explorers, Cartier made exaggerated claims of mineral wealth in America, but he was unable to send great riches back to France. Due to resistance from the native peoples as well as his own lack of planning, he could not establish a permanent settlement in North America.

Explorer Samuel de Champlain occupies a special place in the history of the Atlantic World for his role in establishing the French presence in the New World. Champlain explored the Caribbean in 1601 and then the coast of New England in 1603 before traveling farther north. In 1608 he founded Quebec, and he made numerous Atlantic crossings as he worked tirelessly to promote New France. Unlike other imperial powers, France—through Champlain's efforts—fostered especially good relationships with native peoples, paving the way for French exploration further into the continent: around the Great Lakes, around Hudson Bay, and eventually to the Mississippi. Champlain made an alliance with the Huron confederacy and the Algonquins and agreed to fight with them against their enemy, the Iroquois (**Figure 2.12**).

Figure 2.12 In this engraving, titled *Defeat of the Iroquois* and based on a drawing by explorer Samuel de Champlain, Champlain is shown fighting on the side of the Huron and Algonquins against the Iroquois. He portrays himself in the middle of the battle, firing a gun, while the native people around him shoot arrows at each other. What does this engraving suggest about the impact of European exploration and settlement on the Americas?

The French were primarily interested in establishing commercially viable colonial outposts, and to that end, they created extensive trading networks in New France. These networks relied on native hunters to harvest furs, especially beaver pelts, and to exchange these items for French glass beads and other trade goods. (French fashion at the time favored broad-brimmed hats trimmed in beaver fur, so French traders had a ready market for their North American goods.) The French also dreamed of replicating the wealth of Spain by colonizing the tropical zones. After Spanish control of the Caribbean began to weaken, the French turned their attention to small islands in the West Indies, and by 1635 they had colonized two, Guadeloupe and Martinique. Though it lagged far behind Spain, France now boasted its own West Indian colonies. Both islands became lucrative sugar plantation sites that turned a profit for French planters by relying on African slave labor.

DUTCH COLONIZATION

Dutch entrance into the Atlantic World is part of the larger story of religious and imperial conflict in the early modern era. In the 1500s, Calvinism, one of the major Protestant reform movements, had found adherents in the northern provinces of the Spanish Netherlands. During the sixteenth century, these provinces began a long struggle to achieve independence from Catholic Spain. Established in 1581 but not recognized as independent by Spain until 1648, the Dutch Republic, or Holland, quickly made itself a powerful force in the race for Atlantic colonies and wealth. The Dutch distinguished themselves as commercial leaders in the seventeenth century (**Figure 2.13**), and their mode of colonization relied on powerful corporations: the Dutch East India Company, chartered in 1602 to trade in Asia, and the Dutch West India Company, established in 1621 to colonize and trade in the Americas.

Figure 2.13 Amsterdam was the richest city in the world in the 1600s. In *Courtyard of the Exchange in Amsterdam*, a 1653 painting by Emanuel de Witt, merchants involved in the global trade eagerly attend to news of shipping and the prices of commodities.

While employed by the Dutch East India Company in 1609, the English sea captain Henry Hudson explored New York Harbor and the river that now bears his name. Like many explorers of the time, Hudson was actually seeking a northwest passage to Asia and its wealth, but the ample furs harvested from the region he explored, especially the coveted beaver pelts, provided a reason to claim it for the Netherlands. The Dutch named their colony New Netherlands, and it served as a fur-trading outpost for the expanding and powerful Dutch West India Company. With headquarters in New Amsterdam on the island of Manhattan, the Dutch set up several regional trading posts, including one at Fort Orange—named for the royal Dutch House of Orange-Nassau—in present-day Albany. (The color orange remains significant to the Dutch, having become particularly associated with William of Orange, Protestantism, and the Glorious Revolution of 1688.) A brisk trade in furs with local Algonquian and Iroquois peoples brought the Dutch and native peoples together in a commercial network that extended throughout the Hudson River Valley and beyond.

The Dutch West India Company in turn established colonies on Aruba, Bonaire, and Curaçao, St. Martin, St. Eustatius, and Saba. With their outposts in New Netherlands and the Caribbean, the Dutch had established themselves in the seventeenth century as a commercially powerful rival to Spain. Amsterdam became a trade hub for all the Atlantic World.

2.4 New Worlds in the Americas: Labor, Commerce, and the Columbian Exchange

By the end of this section, you will be able to:
- Describe how Europeans solved their labor problems
- Describe the theory of mercantilism and the process of commodification
- Analyze the effects of the Columbian Exchange

European promoters of colonization claimed the Americas overflowed with a wealth of treasures. Burnishing national glory and honor became entwined with carving out colonies, and no nation wanted to be left behind. However, the realities of life in the Americas—violence, exploitation, and particularly the need for workers—were soon driving the practice of slavery and forced labor. Everywhere in America a stark contrast existed between freedom and slavery. The Columbian Exchange, in which Europeans transported plants, animals, and diseases across the Atlantic in both directions, also left a lasting impression on the Americas.

LABOR SYSTEMS

Physical power—to work the fields, build villages, process raw materials—is a necessity for maintaining a society. During the sixteenth and seventeenth centuries, humans could derive power only from the wind, water, animals, or other humans. Everywhere in the Americas, a crushing demand for labor bedeviled Europeans because there were not enough colonists to perform the work necessary to keep the colonies going. Spain granted *encomiendas*—legal rights to native labor—to conquistadors who could prove their service to the crown. This system reflected the Spanish view of colonization: the king rewarded successful conquistadors who expanded the empire. Some native peoples who had sided with the conquistadors, like the Tlaxcalan, also gained *encomiendas*; Malintzin, the Nahua woman who helped Cortés defeat the Mexica, was granted one.

The Spanish believed native peoples would work for them by right of conquest, and, in return, the Spanish would bring them Catholicism. In theory the relationship consisted of reciprocal obligations, but in practice the Spaniards ruthlessly exploited it, seeing native people as little more than beasts of burden. Convinced of their right to the land and its peoples, they sought both to control native labor and to impose what they viewed as correct religious beliefs upon the land's inhabitants. Native peoples everywhere resisted both the labor obligations and the effort to change their ancient belief systems. Indeed, many retained their religion or incorporated only the parts of Catholicism that made sense to them.

The system of *encomiendas* was accompanied by a great deal of violence (**Figure 2.14**). One Spaniard, Bartolomé de Las Casas, denounced the brutality of Spanish rule. A Dominican friar, Las Casas had been one of the earliest Spanish settlers in the Spanish West Indies. In his early life in the Americas, he owned Indian slaves and was the recipient of an *encomienda*. However, after witnessing the savagery with which *encomenderos* (recipients of *encomiendas*) treated the native people, he reversed his views. In 1515, Las Casas released his native slaves, gave up his *encomienda*, and began to advocate for humane treatment of native peoples. He lobbied for new legislation, eventually known as the New Laws, which would eliminate slavery and the *encomienda* system.

Figure 2.14 In this startling image from the Kingsborough Codex (a book written and drawn by native Mesoamericans), a well-dressed Spaniard is shown pulling the hair of a bleeding, severely injured native. The drawing was part of a complaint about Spanish abuses of their *encomiendas*.

Las Casas's writing about the Spaniards' horrific treatment of Indians helped inspire the so-called **Black Legend**, the idea that the Spanish were bloodthirsty conquerors with no regard for human life. Perhaps not surprisingly, those who held this view of the Spanish were Spain's imperial rivals. English writers and others seized on the idea of Spain's ruthlessness to support their own colonization projects. By demonizing the Spanish, they justified their own efforts as more humane. All European colonizers, however, shared a disregard for Indians.

> # MY STORY
>
> ## ✪ *Bartolomé de Las Casas on the Mistreatment of Indians*
>
> Bartolomé de Las Casas's *A Short Account of the Destruction of the Indies*, written in 1542 and published ten years later, detailed for Prince Philip II of Spain how Spanish colonists had been mistreating natives.
>
>> Into and among these gentle sheep, endowed by their Maker and Creator with all the qualities aforesaid, did creep the Spaniards, who no sooner had knowledge of these people than they became like fierce wolves and tigers and lions who have gone many days without food or nourishment. And no other thing have they done for forty years until this day, and still today see fit to do, but dismember, slay, perturb, afflict, torment, and destroy the Indians by all manner of cruelty—new and divers and most singular manners such as never before seen or read or heard of—some few of which shall be recounted below, and they do this to such a degree that on the Island of Hispaniola, of the above three millions souls that we once saw, today there be no more than two hundred of those native people remaining. . . .
>>
>> Two principal and general customs have been employed by those, calling themselves Christians, who have passed this way, in extirpating and striking from the face of the earth those suffering nations. The first being unjust, cruel, bloody, and tyrannical warfare. The other—after having slain all those who might yearn toward or suspire after or think of freedom, or consider escaping from the torments that they are made to suffer, by which I mean all the native-born lords and adult males, for it is the Spaniards' custom in their wars to allow only young boys and females to live—being to oppress them with the hardest, harshest, and most heinous bondage to which men or beasts might ever be bound into.
>
> How might these writings have been used to promote the "black legend" against Spain as well as subsequent English exploration and colonization?

Indians were not the only source of cheap labor in the Americas; by the middle of the sixteenth century, Africans formed an important element of the labor landscape, producing the cash crops of sugar and tobacco for European markets. Europeans viewed Africans as non-Christians, which they used as a justification for enslavement. Denied control over their lives, slaves endured horrendous conditions. At every opportunity, they resisted enslavement, and their resistance was met with violence. Indeed, physical, mental, and sexual violence formed a key strategy among European slaveholders in their effort to assert mastery and impose their will. The Portuguese led the way in the evolving transport of slaves across the Atlantic; slave "factories" on the west coast of Africa, like Elmina Castle in Ghana, served as holding pens for slaves brought from Africa's interior. In time, other European imperial powers would follow in the footsteps of the Portuguese by constructing similar outposts on the coast of West Africa.

The Portuguese traded or sold slaves to Spanish, Dutch, and English colonists in the Americas, particularly in South America and the Caribbean, where sugar was a primary export. Thousands of African slaves found themselves growing, harvesting, and processing **sugarcane** in an arduous routine of physical labor. Slaves had to cut the long cane stalks by hand and then bring them to a mill, where the cane juice was extracted. They boiled the extracted cane juice down to a brown, crystalline sugar, which then had to be cured in special curing houses to have the molasses drained from it. The result was refined sugar, while the leftover molasses could be distilled into rum. Every step was labor-intensive and often dangerous.

Las Casas estimated that by 1550, there were fifty thousand slaves on Hispaniola. However, it is a mistake to assume that during the very early years of European exploration all Africans came to America as slaves; some were free men who took part in expeditions, for example, serving as conquistadors alongside Cortés in his assault on Tenochtitlán. Nonetheless, African slavery was one of the most tragic outcomes in the emerging Atlantic World.

Click and Explore

Browse the PBS collection **Africans in America: Part 1** (http://openstaxcollege.org/l/afinam) to see information and primary sources for the period 1450 through 1750.

COMMERCE IN THE NEW WORLD

The economic philosophy of **mercantilism** shaped European perceptions of wealth from the 1500s to the late 1700s. Mercantilism held that only a limited amount of wealth, as measured in gold and silver bullion, existed in the world. In order to gain power, nations had to amass wealth by mining these precious raw materials from their colonial possessions. During the age of European exploration, nations employed conquest, colonization, and trade as ways to increase their share of the bounty of the New World. Mercantilists did not believe in free trade, arguing instead that the nation should control trade to create wealth. In this view, colonies existed to strengthen the colonizing nation. Mercantilists argued against allowing their nations to trade freely with other nations.

Spain's mercantilist ideas guided its economic policy. Every year, slaves or native workers loaded shipments of gold and silver aboard Spanish treasure fleets that sailed from Cuba for Spain. These ships groaned under the sheer weight of bullion, for the Spanish had found huge caches of silver and gold in the New World. In South America, for example, Spaniards discovered rich veins of silver ore in the mountain called Potosí and founded a settlement of the same name there. Throughout the sixteenth century, Potosí was a boom town, attracting settlers from many nations as well as native people from many different cultures.

Colonial mercantilism, which was basically a set of protectionist policies designed to benefit the nation, relied on several factors: colonies rich in raw materials, cheap labor, colonial loyalty to the home government, and control of the shipping trade. Under this system, the colonies sent their raw materials, harvested by slaves or native workers, back to their mother country. The mother country sent back finished materials of all sorts: textiles, tools, clothing. The colonists could purchase these goods *only* from their mother country; trade with other countries was forbidden.

The 1500s and early 1600s also introduced the process of **commodification** to the New World. American silver, tobacco, and other items, which were used by native peoples for ritual purposes, became European commodities with a monetary value that could be bought and sold. Before the arrival of the Spanish, for example, the Inca people of the Andes consumed *chicha*, a corn beer, for ritual purposes only. When the Spanish discovered chicha, they bought and traded for it, turning it into a commodity instead of a ritual substance. Commodification thus recast native economies and spurred the process of early commercial capitalism. New World resources, from plants to animal pelts, held the promise of wealth for European imperial powers.

THE COLUMBIAN EXCHANGE

As Europeans traversed the Atlantic, they brought with them plants, animals, and diseases that changed lives and landscapes on both sides of the ocean. These two-way exchanges between the Americas and Europe/Africa are known collectively as the **Columbian Exchange** (Figure 2.15).

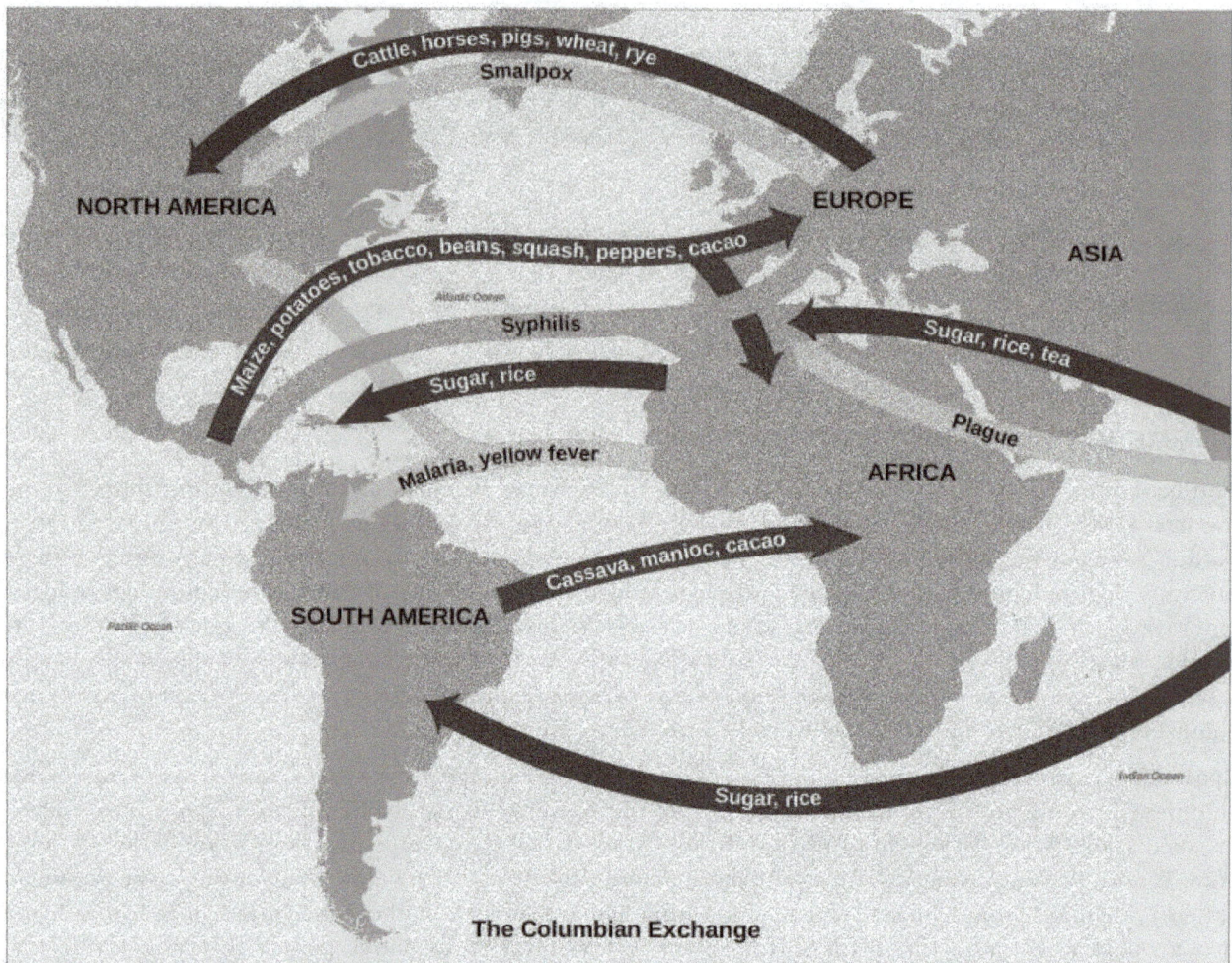

Figure 2.15 With European exploration and settlement of the New World, goods and diseases began crossing the Atlantic Ocean in both directions. This "Columbian Exchange" soon had global implications.

Of all the commodities in the Atlantic World, sugar proved to be the most important. Indeed, sugar carried the same economic importance as oil does today. European rivals raced to create sugar plantations in the Americas and fought wars for control of some of the best sugar production areas. Although refined sugar was available in the Old World, Europe's harsher climate made sugarcane difficult to grow, and it was not plentiful. Columbus brought sugar to Hispaniola in 1493, and the new crop was growing there by the end of the 1490s. By the first decades of the 1500s, the Spanish were building sugar mills on the island. Over the next century of colonization, Caribbean islands and most other tropical areas became centers of sugar production.

Though of secondary importance to sugar, tobacco achieved great value for Europeans as a cash crop as well. Native peoples had been growing it for medicinal and ritual purposes for centuries before European contact, smoking it in pipes or powdering it to use as snuff. They believed tobacco could improve concentration and enhance wisdom. To some, its use meant achieving an entranced, altered, or divine state; entering a spiritual place.

Tobacco was unknown in Europe before 1492, and it carried a negative stigma at first. The early Spanish explorers considered natives' use of tobacco to be proof of their savagery and, because of the fire and smoke produced in the consumption of tobacco, evidence of the Devil's sway in the New World. Gradually, however, European colonists became accustomed to and even took up the habit of smoking, and they brought it across the Atlantic. As did the Indians, Europeans ascribed medicinal properties to tobacco, claiming that it could cure headaches and skin irritations. Even so, Europeans did not import

This content is available for free at http://cnx.org/content/col11740/latest/

tobacco in great quantities until the 1590s. At that time, it became the first truly global commodity; English, French, Dutch, Spanish, and Portuguese colonists all grew it for the world market.

Native peoples also introduced Europeans to chocolate, made from cacao seeds and used by the Aztec in Mesoamerica as currency. Mesoamerican Indians consumed unsweetened chocolate in a drink with chili peppers, vanilla, and a spice called achiote. This chocolate drink—*xocolatl*—was part of ritual ceremonies like marriage and an everyday item for those who could afford it. Chocolate contains theobromine, a stimulant, which may be why native people believed it brought them closer to the sacred world.

Spaniards in the New World considered drinking chocolate a vile practice; one called chocolate "the Devil's vomit." In time, however, they introduced the beverage to Spain. At first, chocolate was available only in the Spanish court, where the elite mixed it with sugar and other spices. Later, as its availability spread, chocolate gained a reputation as a love potion.

Click and Explore

Visit **Nature Transformed** (http://openstaxcollege.org/l/naturetrans) for a collection of scholarly essays on the environment in American history.

The crossing of the Atlantic by plants like cacao and tobacco illustrates the ways in which the discovery of the New World changed the habits and behaviors of Europeans. Europeans changed the New World in turn, not least by bringing Old World animals to the Americas. On his second voyage, Christopher Columbus brought pigs, horses, cows, and chickens to the islands of the Caribbean. Later explorers followed suit, introducing new animals or reintroducing ones that had died out (like horses). With less vulnerability to disease, these animals often fared better than humans in their new home, thriving both in the wild and in domestication.

Europeans encountered New World animals as well. Because European Christians understood the world as a place of warfare between God and Satan, many believed the Americas, which lacked Christianity, were home to the Devil and his minions. The exotic, sometimes bizarre, appearances and habits of animals in the Americas that were previously unknown to Europeans, such as manatees, sloths, and poisonous snakes, confirmed this association. Over time, however, they began to rely more on observation of the natural world than solely on scripture. This shift—from seeing the Bible as the source of all received wisdom to trusting observation or empiricism—is one of the major outcomes of the era of early globalization.

Travelers between the Americas, Africa, and Europe also included microbes: silent, invisible life forms that had profound and devastating consequences. Native peoples had no immunity to diseases from across the Atlantic, to which they had never been exposed. European explorers unwittingly brought with them chickenpox, measles, mumps, and **smallpox**, which ravaged native peoples despite their attempts to treat the diseases, decimating some populations and wholly destroying others (**Figure 2.16**).

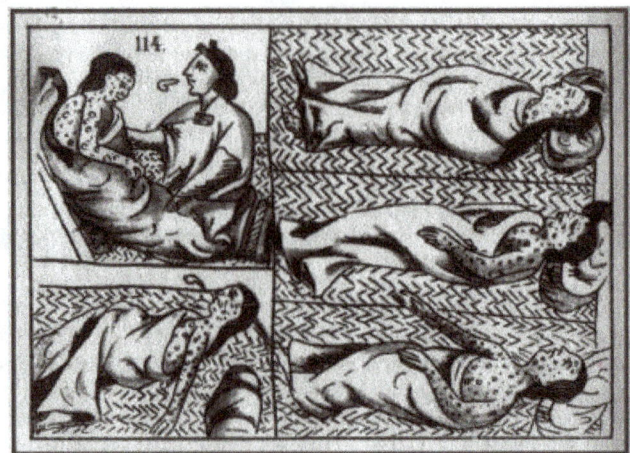

Figure 2.16 This sixteenth-century Aztec drawing shows the suffering of a typical victim of smallpox. Smallpox and other contagious diseases brought by European explorers decimated Indian populations in the Americas.

In eastern North America, some native peoples interpreted death from disease as a hostile act. Some groups, including the Iroquois, engaged in raids or "**mourning wars**," taking enemy prisoners in order to assuage their grief and replace the departed. In a special ritual, the prisoners were "requickened"—assigned the identity of a dead person—and adopted by the bereaved family to take the place of their dead. As the toll from disease rose, mourning wars intensified and expanded.

CHAPTER 3

Creating New Social Orders: Colonial Societies, 1500–1700

Figure 3.1 John Smith's famous map of Virginia (1622) illustrates many geopolitical features of early colonization. In the upper left, Powhatan, who governed a powerful local confederation of Algonquian communities, sits above other local chiefs, denoting his authority. Another native figure, Susquehannock, who appears in the upper right, visually reinforces the message that the English did not control the land beyond a few outposts along the Chesapeake.

Chapter Outline

3.1 Spanish Exploration and Colonial Society
3.2 Colonial Rivalries: Dutch and French Colonial Ambitions
3.3 English Settlements in America
3.4 The Impact of Colonization

Introduction

By the mid-seventeenth century, the geopolitical map of North America had become a patchwork of imperial designs and ambitions as the Spanish, Dutch, French, and English reinforced their claims to parts of the land. Uneasiness, punctuated by violent clashes, prevailed in the border zones between the Europeans' territorial claims. Meanwhile, still-powerful native peoples waged war to drive the invaders from the continent. In the Chesapeake Bay and New England colonies, conflicts erupted as the English pushed against their native neighbors (**Figure 3.1**).

The rise of colonial societies in the Americas brought Native Americans, Africans, and Europeans together for the first time, highlighting the radical social, cultural, and religious differences that hampered their ability to understand each other. European settlement affected every aspect of the land and its people, bringing goods, ideas, and diseases that transformed the Americas. Reciprocally, Native American practices, such as the use of tobacco, profoundly altered European habits and tastes.

3.1 Spanish Exploration and Colonial Society

By the end of this section, you will be able to:
- Identify the main Spanish American colonial settlements of the 1500s and 1600s
- Discuss economic, political, and demographic similarities and differences between the Spanish colonies

During the 1500s, Spain expanded its colonial empire to the Philippines in the Far East and to areas in the Americas that later became the United States. The Spanish dreamed of mountains of gold and silver and imagined converting thousands of eager Indians to Catholicism. In their vision of colonial society, everyone would know his or her place. Patriarchy (the rule of men over family, society, and government) shaped the Spanish colonial world. Women occupied a lower status. In all matters, the Spanish held themselves to be atop the social pyramid, with native peoples and Africans beneath them. Both Africans and native peoples, however, contested Spanish claims to dominance. Everywhere the Spanish settled, they brought devastating diseases, such as smallpox, that led to a horrific loss of life among native peoples. European diseases killed far more native inhabitants than did Spanish swords.

The world native peoples had known before the coming of the Spanish was further upset by Spanish colonial practices. The Spanish imposed the *encomienda* system in the areas they controlled. Under this system, authorities assigned Indian workers to mine and plantation owners with the understanding that the recipients would defend the colony and teach the workers the tenets of Christianity. In reality, the *encomienda* system exploited native workers. It was eventually replaced by another colonial labor system, the *repartimiento*, which required Indian towns to supply a pool of labor for Spanish overlords.

ST. AUGUSTINE, FLORIDA

Spain gained a foothold in present-day Florida, viewing that area and the lands to the north as a logical extension of their Caribbean empire. In 1513, Juan Ponce de León had claimed the area around today's St. Augustine for the Spanish crown, naming the land Pascua Florida (Feast of Flowers, or Easter) for the nearest feast day. Ponce de León was unable to establish a permanent settlement there, but by 1565, Spain was in need of an outpost to confront the French and English privateers using Florida as a base from which

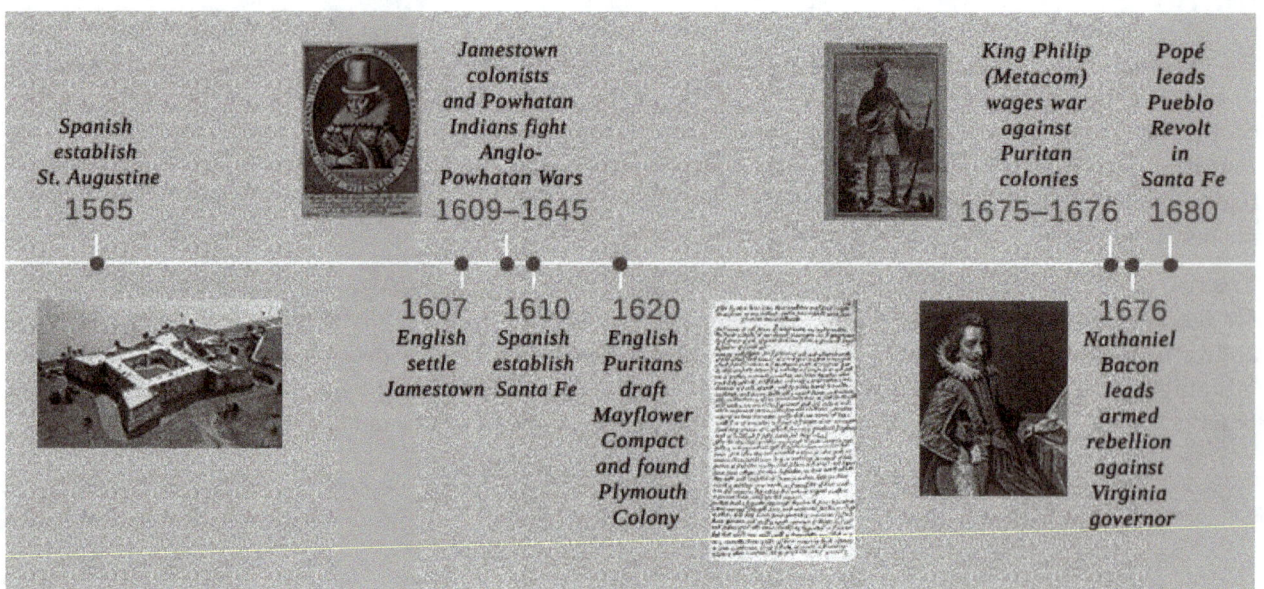

Figure 3.2

to attack treasure-laden Spanish ships heading from Cuba to Spain. The threat to Spanish interests took a new turn in 1562 when a group of French Protestants (Huguenots) established a small settlement they called Fort Caroline, north of St. Augustine. With the authorization of King Philip II, Spanish nobleman Pedro Menéndez led an attack on Fort Caroline, killing most of the colonists and destroying the fort. Eliminating Fort Caroline served dual purposes for the Spanish—it helped reduce the danger from French privateers and eradicated the French threat to Spain's claim to the area. The contest over Florida illustrates how European rivalries spilled over into the Americas, especially religious conflict between Catholics and Protestants.

In 1565, the victorious Menéndez founded St. Augustine, now the oldest European settlement in the Americas. In the process, the Spanish displaced the local **Timucua** Indians from their ancient town of Seloy, which had stood for thousands of years (**Figure 3.3**). The Timucua suffered greatly from diseases introduced by the Spanish, shrinking from a population of around 200,000 pre-contact to fifty thousand in 1590. By 1700, only one thousand Timucua remained. As in other areas of Spanish conquest, Catholic priests worked to bring about a spiritual conquest by forcing the surviving Timucua, demoralized and reeling from catastrophic losses of family and community, to convert to Catholicism.

Figure 3.3 In this drawing by French artist Jacques le Moyne de Morgues, Timucua flee the Spanish settlers, who arrive by ship. Le Moyne lived at Fort Caroline, the French outpost, before the Spanish destroyed the colony in 1562.

Spanish Florida made an inviting target for Spain's imperial rivals, especially the English, who wanted to gain access to the Caribbean. In 1586, Spanish settlers in St. Augustine discovered their vulnerability to attack when the English pirate Sir Francis Drake destroyed the town with a fleet of twenty ships and one hundred men. Over the next several decades, the Spanish built more wooden forts, all of which were burnt by raiding European rivals. Between 1672 and 1695, the Spanish constructed a stone fort, Castillo de San Marcos (**Figure 3.4**), to better defend St. Augustine against challengers.

Figure 3.4 The Spanish fort of Castillo de San Marcos helped Spanish colonists in St. Augustine fend off marauding privateers from rival European countries.

Browse the National Park Service's multimedia resources on Castillo de San Marcos (http://openstaxcollege.org/l/castillo) to see how the fort and gates have looked throughout history.

SANTA FE, NEW MEXICO

Further west, the Spanish in Mexico, intent on expanding their empire, looked north to the land of the Pueblo Indians. Under orders from King Philip II, Juan de Oñate explored the American southwest for Spain in the late 1590s. The Spanish hoped that what we know as New Mexico would yield gold and silver, but the land produced little of value to them. In 1610, Spanish settlers established themselves at Santa Fe—originally named La Villa Real de la Santa Fe de San Francisco de Asís, or "Royal City of the Holy Faith of St. Francis of Assisi"—where many Pueblo villages were located. Santa Fe became the capital of the Kingdom of New Mexico, an outpost of the larger Spanish Viceroyalty of New Spain, which had its headquarters in Mexico City.

As they had in other Spanish colonies, Franciscan missionaries labored to bring about a spiritual conquest by converting the Pueblo to Catholicism. At first, the Pueblo adopted the parts of Catholicism that dovetailed with their own long-standing view of the world. However, Spanish priests insisted that natives discard their old ways entirely and angered the Pueblo by focusing on the young, drawing them away from their parents. This deep insult, combined with an extended period of drought and increased attacks by local Apache and Navajo in the 1670s—troubles that the Pueblo came to believe were linked to the Spanish presence—moved the Pueblo to push the Spanish and their religion from the area. Pueblo leader Popé demanded a return to native ways so the hardships his people faced would end. To him and to thousands of others, it seemed obvious that "when Jesus came, the Corn Mothers went away." The expulsion of the Spanish would bring a return to prosperity and a pure, native way of life.

In 1680, the Pueblo launched a coordinated rebellion against the Spanish. The Pueblo Revolt killed over four hundred Spaniards and drove the rest of the settlers, perhaps as many as two thousand, south toward Mexico. However, as droughts and attacks by rival tribes continued, the Spanish sensed an opportunity to regain their foothold. In 1692, they returned and reasserted their control of the area. Some of the Spanish explained the Pueblo success in 1680 as the work of the Devil. Satan, they believed, had stirred up the Pueblo to take arms against God's chosen people—the Spanish—but the Spanish, and their God, had prevailed in the end.

3.2 Colonial Rivalries: Dutch and French Colonial Ambitions

By the end of this section, you will be able to:
- Compare and contrast the development and character of the French and Dutch colonies in North America
- Discuss the economies of the French and Dutch colonies in North America

Seventeenth-century French and Dutch colonies in North America were modest in comparison to Spain's colossal global empire. New France and New Netherland remained small commercial operations focused on the fur trade and did not attract an influx of migrants. The Dutch in New Netherland confined their operations to Manhattan Island, Long Island, the Hudson River Valley, and what later became New Jersey. Dutch trade goods circulated widely among the native peoples in these areas and also traveled well into the interior of the continent along preexisting native trade routes. French *habitants*, or farmer-settlers, eked out an existence along the St. Lawrence River. French fur traders and missionaries, however, ranged far into the interior of North America, exploring the Great Lakes region and the Mississippi River. These pioneers gave France somewhat inflated imperial claims to lands that nonetheless remained firmly under the dominion of native peoples.

FUR TRADING IN NEW NETHERLAND

The Dutch Republic emerged as a major commercial center in the 1600s. Its fleets plied the waters of the Atlantic, while other Dutch ships sailed to the Far East, returning with prized spices like pepper to be sold in the bustling ports at home, especially Amsterdam. In North America, Dutch traders established themselves first on Manhattan Island.

One of the Dutch directors-general of the North American settlement, Peter Stuyvesant, served from 1647 to 1664 and expanded the fledgling outpost of New Netherland east to present-day Long Island and for many miles north along the Hudson River. The resulting elongated colony served primarily as a fur-trading post, with the powerful Dutch West India Company controlling all commerce. Fort Amsterdam, on the southern tip of Manhattan Island, defended the growing city of New Amsterdam. In 1655, Stuyvesant took over the small outpost of New Sweden along the banks of the Delaware River in present-day New Jersey, Pennsylvania, and Delaware. He also defended New Amsterdam from Indian attacks by ordering African slaves to build a protective wall on the city's northeastern border, giving present-day Wall Street its name (**Figure 3.5**).

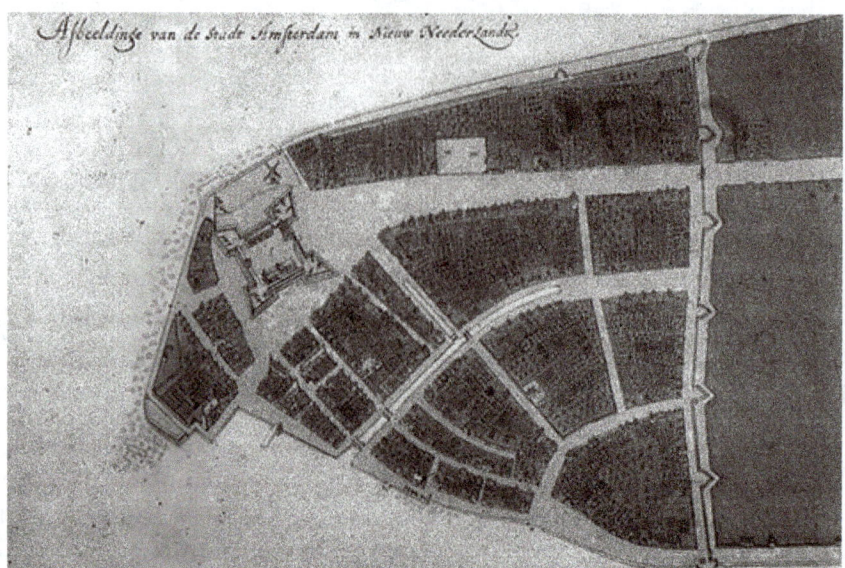

Figure 3.5 The Castello Plan is the only extant map of 1660 New Amsterdam (present-day New York City). The line with spikes on the right side of the colony is the northeastern wall for which Wall Street was named.

New Netherland failed to attract many Dutch colonists; by 1664, only nine thousand people were living there. Conflict with native peoples, as well as dissatisfaction with the Dutch West India Company's trading practices, made the Dutch outpost an undesirable place for many migrants. The small size of the population meant a severe labor shortage, and to complete the arduous tasks of early settlement, the Dutch West India Company imported some 450 African slaves between 1626 and 1664. (The company had involved itself heavily in the slave trade and in 1637 captured Elmina, the slave-trading post on the west coast of Africa, from the Portuguese.) The shortage of labor also meant that New Netherland welcomed non-Dutch immigrants, including Protestants from Germany, Sweden, Denmark, and England, and embraced a degree of religious tolerance, allowing Jewish immigrants to become residents beginning in the 1650s. Thus, a wide variety of people lived in New Netherland from the start. Indeed, one observer claimed eighteen different languages could be heard on the streets of New Amsterdam. As new settlers arrived, the colony of New Netherland stretched farther to the north and the west (**Figure 3.6**).

Figure 3.6 This 1684 map of New Netherland shows the extent of Dutch settlement.

The Dutch West India Company found the business of colonization in New Netherland to be expensive. To share some of the costs, it granted Dutch merchants who invested heavily in it **patroonships**, or large tracts of land and the right to govern the tenants there. In return, the shareholder who gained the patroonship promised to pay for the passage of at least thirty Dutch farmers to populate the colony. One of the largest patroonships was granted to Kiliaen van Rensselaer, one of the directors of the Dutch West India Company; it covered most of present-day Albany and Rensselaer Counties. This pattern of settlement created a yawning gap in wealth and status between the tenants, who paid rent, and the wealthy patroons.

During the summer trading season, Indians gathered at trading posts such as the Dutch site at Beverwijck (present-day Albany), where they exchanged furs for guns, blankets, and alcohol. The furs, especially beaver pelts destined for the lucrative European millinery market, would be sent down the Hudson River to New Amsterdam. There, slaves or workers would load them aboard ships bound for Amsterdam.

Click and Explore

Explore an **interactive map of New Amsterdam in 1660** (http://openstaxcollege.org/l/WNET) that shows the city plan and the locations of various structures, including houses, businesses, and public buildings. Rolling over the map reveals relevant historical details, such as street names, the identities of certain buildings and businesses, and the names of residents of the houses (when known).

COMMERCE AND CONVERSION IN NEW FRANCE

After Jacques Cartier's voyages of discovery in the 1530s, France showed little interest in creating permanent colonies in North America until the early 1600s, when Samuel de Champlain established Quebec as a French fur-trading outpost. Although the fur trade was lucrative, the French saw Canada as an inhospitable frozen wasteland, and by 1640, fewer than four hundred settlers had made their home there. The sparse French presence meant that colonists depended on the local native Algonquian people; without them, the French would have perished. French fishermen, explorers, and fur traders made extensive contact with the Algonquian. The Algonquian, in turn, tolerated the French because the colonists supplied them with firearms for their ongoing war with the Iroquois. Thus, the French found themselves escalating native wars and supporting the Algonquian against the Iroquois, who received weapons from their Dutch trading partners. These seventeenth-century conflicts centered on the lucrative trade in beaver pelts, earning them the name of the Beaver Wars. In these wars, fighting between rival native peoples spread throughout the Great Lakes region.

A handful of French Jesuit priests also made their way to Canada, intent on converting the native inhabitants to Catholicism. The **Jesuits** were members of the Society of Jesus, an elite religious order founded in the 1540s to spread Catholicism and combat the spread of Protestantism. The first Jesuits arrived in Quebec in the 1620s, and for the next century, their numbers did not exceed forty priests. Like the Spanish Franciscan missionaries, the Jesuits in the colony called New France labored to convert the native peoples to Catholicism. They wrote detailed annual reports about their progress in bringing the faith to the Algonquian and, beginning in the 1660s, to the Iroquois. These documents are known as the *Jesuit Relations* (**Figure 3.7**), and they provide a rich source for understanding both the Jesuit view of the Indians and the Indian response to the colonizers.

One native convert to Catholicism, a Mohawk woman named Katherine Tekakwitha, so impressed the priests with her piety that a Jesuit named Claude Chauchetière attempted to make her a saint in the Church. However, the effort to canonize Tekakwitha faltered when leaders of the Church balked at elevating a "savage" to such a high status; she was eventually canonized in 2012. French colonizers pressured the native inhabitants of New France to convert, but they virtually never saw native peoples as their equals.

DEFINING "AMERICAN"

✪ *A Jesuit Priest on Indian Healing Traditions*

The *Jesuit Relations* (Figure 3.7) provide incredible detail about Indian life. For example, the 1636 edition, written by the Catholic priest Jean de Brébeuf, addresses the devastating effects of disease on native peoples and the efforts made to combat it.

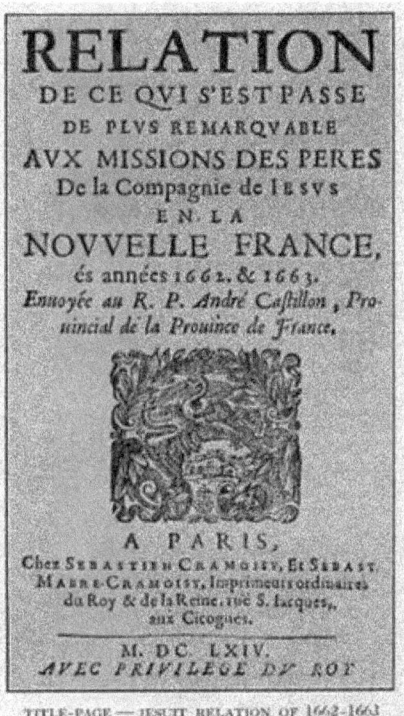

Figure 3.7 French Jesuit missionaries to New France kept detailed records of their interactions with—and observations of—the Algonquian and Iroquois that they converted to Catholicism. (credit: Project Gutenberg).

> Let us return to the feasts. The *Aoutaerohi* is a remedy which is only for one particular kind of disease, which they call also *Aoutaerohi*, from the name of a little Demon as large as the fist, which they say is in the body of the sick man, especially in the part which pains him. They find out that they are sick of this disease, by means of a dream, or by the intervention of some Sorcerer. . . .
>
> Of three kinds of games especially in use among these Peoples,—namely, the games of crosse [lacrosse], dish, and straw,—the first two are, they say, most healing. Is not this worthy of compassion? There is a poor sick man, fevered of body and almost dying, and a miserable Sorcerer will order for him, as a cooling remedy, a game of crosse. Or the sick man himself, sometimes, will have dreamed that he must die unless the whole country shall play crosse for his health; and, no matter how little may be his credit, you will see then in a beautiful field, Village contending against Village, as to who will play crosse the better, and betting against one another Beaver robes and Porcelain collars, so as to excite greater interest.

According to this account, how did Indians attempt to cure disease? Why did they prescribe a game of lacrosse? What benefits might these games have for the sick?

3.3 English Settlements in America

By the end of this section, you will be able to:
- Identify the first English settlements in America
- Describe the differences between the Chesapeake Bay colonies and the New England colonies
- Compare and contrast the wars between native inhabitants and English colonists in both the Chesapeake Bay and New England colonies
- Explain the role of Bacon's Rebellion in the rise of chattel slavery in Virginia

At the start of the seventeenth century, the English had not established a permanent settlement in the Americas. Over the next century, however, they outpaced their rivals. The English encouraged emigration far more than the Spanish, French, or Dutch. They established nearly a dozen colonies, sending swarms of immigrants to populate the land. England had experienced a dramatic rise in population in the sixteenth century, and the colonies appeared a welcoming place for those who faced overcrowding and grinding poverty at home. Thousands of English migrants arrived in the Chesapeake Bay colonies of Virginia and Maryland to work in the tobacco fields. Another stream, this one of pious Puritan families, sought to live as they believed scripture demanded and established the Plymouth, Massachusetts Bay, New Haven, Connecticut, and Rhode Island colonies of New England (**Figure 3.8**).

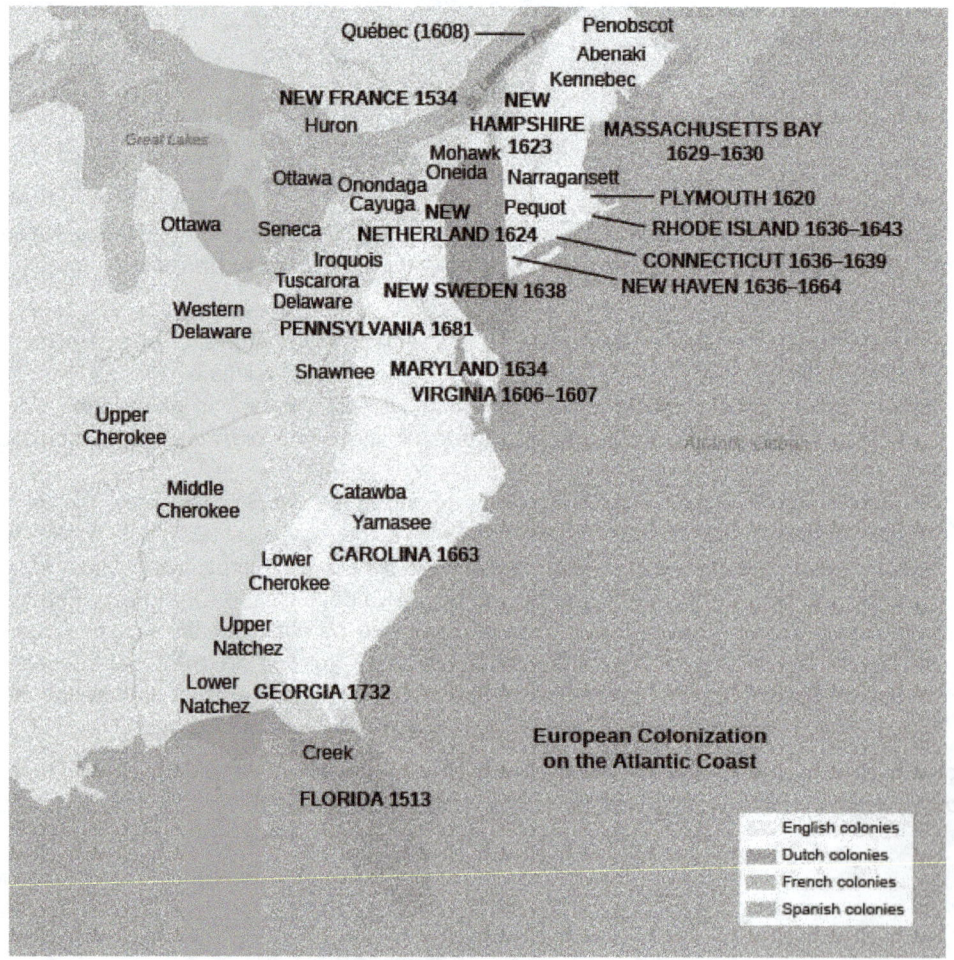

Figure 3.8 In the early seventeenth century, thousands of English settlers came to what are now Virginia, Maryland, and the New England states in search of opportunity and a better life.

THE DIVERGING CULTURES OF THE NEW ENGLAND AND CHESAPEAKE COLONIES

Promoters of English colonization in North America, many of whom never ventured across the Atlantic, wrote about the bounty the English would find there. These boosters of colonization hoped to turn a profit—whether by importing raw resources or providing new markets for English goods—and spread Protestantism. The English migrants who actually made the journey, however, had different goals. In Chesapeake Bay, English migrants established Virginia and Maryland with a decidedly commercial orientation. Though the early Virginians at Jamestown hoped to find gold, they and the settlers in Maryland quickly discovered that growing tobacco was the only sure means of making money. Thousands of unmarried, unemployed, and impatient young Englishmen, along with a few Englishwomen, pinned their hopes for a better life on the tobacco fields of these two colonies.

A very different group of English men and women flocked to the cold climate and rocky soil of New England, spurred by religious motives. Many of the Puritans crossing the Atlantic were people who brought families and children. Often they were following their ministers in a migration "beyond the seas," envisioning a new English Israel where reformed Protestantism would grow and thrive, providing a model for the rest of the Christian world and a counter to what they saw as the Catholic menace. While the English in Virginia and Maryland worked on expanding their profitable tobacco fields, the English in New England built towns focused on the church, where each congregation decided what was best for itself. The Congregational Church is the result of the Puritan enterprise in America. Many historians believe the fault lines separating what later became the North and South in the United States originated in the profound differences between the Chesapeake and New England colonies.

The source of those differences lay in England's domestic problems. Increasingly in the early 1600s, the English state church—the Church of England, established in the 1530s—demanded conformity, or compliance with its practices, but Puritans pushed for greater reforms. By the 1620s, the Church of England began to see leading Puritan ministers and their followers as outlaws, a national security threat because of their opposition to its power. As the noose of conformity tightened around them, many Puritans decided to remove to New England. By 1640, New England had a population of twenty-five thousand. Meanwhile, many loyal members of the Church of England, who ridiculed and mocked Puritans both at home and in New England, flocked to Virginia for economic opportunity.

The troubles in England escalated in the 1640s when civil war broke out, pitting Royalist supporters of King Charles I and the Church of England against Parliamentarians, the Puritan reformers and their supporters in Parliament. In 1649, the Parliamentarians gained the upper hand and, in an unprecedented move, executed Charles I. In the 1650s, therefore, England became a republic, a state without a king. English colonists in America closely followed these events. Indeed, many Puritans left New England and returned home to take part in the struggle against the king and the national church. Other English men and women in the Chesapeake colonies and elsewhere in the English Atlantic World looked on in horror at the mayhem the Parliamentarians, led by the Puritan insurgents, appeared to unleash in England. The turmoil in England made the administration and imperial oversight of the Chesapeake and New England colonies difficult, and the two regions developed divergent cultures.

THE CHESAPEAKE COLONIES: VIRGINIA AND MARYLAND

The Chesapeake colonies of Virginia and Maryland served a vital purpose in the developing seventeenth-century English empire by providing tobacco, a cash crop. However, the early history of Jamestown did not suggest the English outpost would survive. From the outset, its settlers struggled both with each other and with the native inhabitants, the powerful Powhatan, who controlled the area. Jealousies and infighting among the English destabilized the colony. One member, John Smith, whose famous map begins this chapter, took control and exercised near-dictatorial powers, which furthered aggravated the squabbling. The settlers' inability to grow their own food compounded this unstable situation. They were essentially employees of the Virginia Company of London, an English joint-stock company, in which investors provided the capital and assumed the risk in order to reap the profit, and they had to make a profit for their shareholders as well as for themselves. Most initially devoted themselves to finding gold and silver instead of finding ways to grow their own food.

Early Struggles and the Development of the Tobacco Economy

Poor health, lack of food, and fighting with native peoples took the lives of many of the original Jamestown settlers. The winter of 1609–1610, which became known as "the starving time," came close to annihilating the colony. By June 1610, the few remaining settlers had decided to abandon the area; only the last-minute arrival of a supply ship from England prevented another failed colonization effort. The supply ship brought new settlers, but only twelve hundred of the seventy-five hundred who came to Virginia between 1607 and 1624 survived.

MY STORY

◯ *George Percy on "The Starving Time"*

George Percy, the youngest son of an English nobleman, was in the first group of settlers at the Jamestown Colony. He kept a journal describing their experiences; in the excerpt below, he reports on the privations of the colonists' third winter.

> Now all of us at James Town, beginning to feel that sharp prick of hunger which no man truly describe but he which has tasted the bitterness thereof, a world of miseries ensued as the sequel will express unto you, in so much that some to satisfy their hunger have robbed the store for the which I caused them to be executed. Then having fed upon horses and other beasts as long as they lasted, we were glad to make shift with vermin as dogs, cats, rats, and mice. All was fish that came to net to satisfy cruel hunger as to eat boots, shoes, or any other leather some could come by, and, those being spent and devoured, some were enforced to search the woods and to feed upon serpents and snakes and to dig the earth for wild and unknown roots, where many of our men were cut off of and slain by the savages. And now famine beginning to look ghastly and pale in every face that nothing was spared to maintain life and to do those things which seem incredible as to dig up dead corpses out of graves and to eat them, and some have licked up the blood which has fallen from their weak fellows.
> —George Percy, "A True Relation of the Proceedings and Occurances of Moment which have happened in Virginia from the Time Sir Thomas Gates shipwrecked upon the Bermudes anno 1609 until my departure out of the Country which was in anno Domini 1612," London 1624

What is your reaction to George Percy's story? How do you think Jamestown managed to survive after such an experience? What do you think the Jamestown colonists learned?

By the 1620s, Virginia had weathered the worst and gained a degree of permanence. Political stability came slowly, but by 1619, the fledgling colony was operating under the leadership of a governor, a council, and a House of Burgesses. Economic stability came from the lucrative cultivation of tobacco. Smoking tobacco was a long-standing practice among native peoples, and English and other European consumers soon adopted it. In 1614, the Virginia colony began exporting tobacco back to England, which earned it a sizable profit and saved the colony from ruin. A second tobacco colony, Maryland, was formed in 1634, when King Charles I granted its charter to the Calvert family for their loyal service to England. Cecilius Calvert, the second Lord Baltimore, conceived of Maryland as a refuge for English Catholics.

Growing tobacco proved very labor-intensive (**Figure 3.9**), and the Chesapeake colonists needed a steady workforce to do the hard work of clearing the land and caring for the tender young plants. The mature leaf of the plant then had to be cured (dried), which necessitated the construction of drying barns. Once cured, the tobacco had to be packaged in hogsheads (large wooden barrels) and loaded aboard ship, which also required considerable labor.

Figure 3.9 In this 1670 painting by an unknown artist, slaves work in tobacco-drying sheds.

To meet these labor demands, early Virginians relied on indentured servants. An **indenture** is a labor contract that young, impoverished, and often illiterate Englishmen and occasionally Englishwomen signed in England, pledging to work for a number of years (usually between five and seven) growing tobacco in the Chesapeake colonies. In return, indentured servants received paid passage to America and food, clothing, and lodging. At the end of their indenture servants received "freedom dues," usually food and other provisions, including, in some cases, land provided by the colony. The promise of a new life in America was a strong attraction for members of England's underclass, who had few if any options at home. In the 1600s, some 100,000 indentured servants traveled to the Chesapeake Bay. Most were poor young men in their early twenties.

Life in the colonies proved harsh, however. Indentured servants could not marry, and they were subject to the will of the tobacco planters who bought their labor contracts. If they committed a crime or disobeyed their masters, they found their terms of service lengthened, often by several years. Female indentured servants faced special dangers in what was essentially a bachelor colony. Many were exploited by unscrupulous tobacco planters who seduced them with promises of marriage. These planters would then sell their pregnant servants to other tobacco planters to avoid the costs of raising a child.

Nonetheless, those indentured servants who completed their term of service often began new lives as tobacco planters. To entice even more migrants to the New World, the Virginia Company also implemented the **headright system**, in which those who paid their own passage to Virginia received fifty acres plus an additional fifty for each servant or family member they brought with them. The headright system and the promise of a new life for servants acted as powerful incentives for English migrants to hazard the journey to the New World.

Click and Explore

Visit Virtual Jamestown (http://openstaxcollege.org/l/jamestown1) to access a database of contracts of indentured servants. Search it by name to find an ancestor or browse by occupation, destination, or county of origin.

The Anglo-Powhatan Wars

By choosing to settle along the rivers on the banks of the Chesapeake, the English unknowingly placed themselves at the center of the Powhatan Empire, a powerful Algonquian confederacy of thirty native groups with perhaps as many as twenty-two thousand people. The territory of the equally impressive Susquehannock people also bordered English settlements at the north end of the Chesapeake Bay.

Tensions ran high between the English and the Powhatan, and near-constant war prevailed. The First Anglo-Powhatan War (1609–1614) resulted not only from the English colonists' intrusion onto Powhatan land, but also from their refusal to follow native protocol by giving gifts. English actions infuriated and insulted the Powhatan. In 1613, the settlers captured Pocahontas (also called Matoaka), the daughter of a Powhatan headman named Wahunsonacook, and gave her in marriage to Englishman John Rolfe. Their union, and her choice to remain with the English, helped quell the war in 1614. Pocahontas converted to Christianity, changing her name to Rebecca, and sailed with her husband and several other Powhatan to England where she was introduced to King James I (**Figure 3.10**). Promoters of colonization publicized Pocahontas as an example of the good work of converting the Powhatan to Christianity.

Figure 3.10 This 1616 engraving by Simon van de Passe, completed when Pocahontas and John Rolfe were presented at court in England, is the only known contemporary image of Pocahontas. Note her European garb and pose. What message did the painter likely intend to convey with this portrait of Pocahontas, the daughter of a powerful Indian chief?

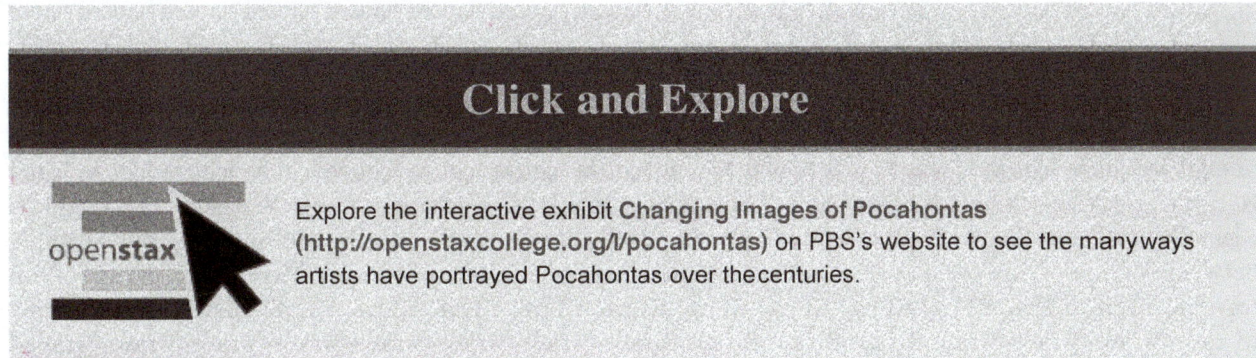

Click and Explore

Explore the interactive exhibit **Changing Images of Pocahontas** (http://openstaxcollege.org/l/pocahontas) on PBS's website to see the many ways artists have portrayed Pocahontas over the centuries.

Peace in Virginia did not last long. The Second Anglo-Powhatan War (1620s) broke out because of the expansion of the English settlement nearly one hundred miles into the interior, and because of the continued insults and friction caused by English activities. The Powhatan attacked in 1622 and succeeded in killing almost 350 English, about a third of the settlers. The English responded by annihilating every Powhatan village around Jamestown and from then on became even more intolerant. The Third Anglo-Powhatan War (1644–1646) began with a surprise attack in which the Powhatan killed around five hundred English colonists. However, their ultimate defeat in this conflict forced the Powhatan to acknowledge King Charles I as their sovereign. The Anglo-Powhatan Wars, spanning nearly forty years, illustrate the degree of native resistance that resulted from English intrusion into the Powhatan confederacy.

The Rise of Slavery in the Chesapeake Bay Colonies

The transition from indentured servitude to slavery as the main labor source for some English colonies happened first in the West Indies. On the small island of Barbados, colonized in the 1620s, English planters first grew tobacco as their main export crop, but in the 1640s, they converted to sugarcane and began increasingly to rely on African slaves. In 1655, England wrestled control of Jamaica from the Spanish and quickly turned it into a lucrative sugar island, run on slave labor, for its expanding empire. While slavery was slower to take hold in the Chesapeake colonies, by the end of the seventeenth century, both Virginia and Maryland had also adopted chattel slavery—which legally defined Africans as property and not people—as the dominant form of labor to grow tobacco. Chesapeake colonists also enslaved native people.

When the first Africans arrived in Virginia in 1619, slavery—which did not exist in England—had not yet become an institution in colonial America. Many Africans worked as servants and, like their white counterparts, could acquire land of their own. Some Africans who converted to Christianity became free landowners with white servants. The change in the status of Africans in the Chesapeake to that of slaves occurred in the last decades of the seventeenth century.

Bacon's Rebellion, an uprising of both whites and blacks who believed that the Virginia government was impeding their access to land and wealth and seemed to do little to clear the land of Indians, hastened the transition to African slavery in the Chesapeake colonies. The rebellion takes its name from Nathaniel Bacon, a wealthy young Englishman who arrived in Virginia in 1674. Despite an early friendship with Virginia's royal governor, William Berkeley, Bacon found himself excluded from the governor's circle of influential friends and councilors. He wanted land on the Virginia frontier, but the governor, fearing war with neighboring Indian tribes, forbade further expansion. Bacon marshaled others, especially former indentured servants who believed the governor was limiting their economic opportunities and denying them the right to own tobacco farms. Bacon's followers believed Berkeley's frontier policy didn't protect English settlers enough. Worse still in their eyes, Governor Berkeley tried to keep peace in Virginia by signing treaties with various local native peoples. Bacon and his followers, who saw all Indians as an obstacle to their access to land, pursued a policy of extermination.

Tensions between the English and the native peoples in the Chesapeake colonies led to open conflict. In 1675, war broke out when Susquehannock warriors attacked settlements on Virginia's frontier, killing English planters and destroying English plantations, including one owned by Bacon. In 1676, Bacon and other Virginians attacked the Susquehannock without the governor's approval. When Berkeley ordered Bacon's arrest, Bacon led his followers to Jamestown, forced the governor to flee to the safety of Virginia's eastern shore, and then burned the city. The civil war known as Bacon's Rebellion, a vicious struggle between supporters of the governor and those who supported Bacon, ensued. Reports of the rebellion traveled back to England, leading Charles II to dispatch both royal troops and English commissioners to restore order in the tobacco colonies. By the end of 1676, Virginians loyal to the governor gained the upper hand, executing several leaders of the rebellion. Bacon escaped the hangman's noose, instead dying of dysentery. The rebellion fizzled in 1676, but Virginians remained divided as supporters of Bacon continued to harbor grievances over access to Indian land.

Bacon's Rebellion helped to catalyze the creation of a system of racial slavery in the Chesapeake colonies. At the time of the rebellion, indentured servants made up the majority of laborers in the region. Wealthy whites worried over the presence of this large class of laborers and the relative freedom they enjoyed, as well as the alliance that black and white servants had forged in the course of the rebellion. Replacing indentured servitude with black slavery diminished these risks, alleviating the reliance on white indentured servants, who were often dissatisfied and troublesome, and creating a caste of racially defined laborers whose movements were strictly controlled. It also lessened the possibility of further alliances between black and white workers. Racial slavery even served to heal some of the divisions between wealthy and poor whites, who could now unite as members of a "superior" racial group.

While colonial laws in the tobacco colonies had made slavery a legal institution before Bacon's Rebellion, new laws passed in the wake of the rebellion severely curtailed black freedom and laid the foundation for racial slavery. Virginia passed a law in 1680 prohibiting free blacks and slaves from bearing arms, banning blacks from congregating in large numbers, and establishing harsh punishments for slaves who assaulted Christians or attempted escape. Two years later, another Virginia law stipulated that all Africans brought to the colony would be slaves for life. Thus, the increasing reliance on slaves in the tobacco colonies—and the draconian laws instituted to control them—not only helped planters meet labor demands, but also served to assuage English fears of further uprisings and alleviate class tensions between rich and poor whites.

DEFINING "AMERICAN"

✪ Robert Beverley on Servants and Slaves

Robert Beverley was a wealthy Jamestown planter and slaveholder. This excerpt from his *History and Present State of Virginia*, published in 1705, clearly illustrates the contrast between white servants and black slaves.

> Their Servants, they distinguish by the Names of Slaves for Life, and Servants for a time. Slaves are the Negroes, and their Posterity, following the condition of the Mother, according to the Maxim, partus sequitur ventrem [status follows the womb]. They are call'd Slaves, in respect of the time of their Servitude, because it is for Life.
>
> Servants, are those which serve only for a few years, according to the time of their Indenture, or the Custom of the Country. The Custom of the Country takes place upon such as have no Indentures. The Law in this case is, that if such Servants be under Nineteen years of Age, they must be brought into Court, to have their Age adjudged; and from the Age they are judg'd to be of, they must serve until they reach four and twenty: But if they be adjudged upwards of Nineteen, they are then only to be Servants for the term of five Years.
>
> The Male-Servants, and Slaves of both Sexes, are employed together in Tilling and Manuring the Ground, in Sowing and Planting Tobacco, Corn, &c. Some Distinction indeed is made between them in their Cloaths, and Food; but the Work of both, is no other than what the Overseers, the Freemen, and the Planters themselves do.
>
> Sufficient Distinction is also made between the Female-Servants, and Slaves; for a White Woman is rarely or never put to work in the Ground, if she be good for any thing else: And to Discourage all Planters from using any Women so, their Law imposes the heaviest Taxes upon Female Servants working in the Ground, while it suffers all other white Women to be absolutely exempted: Whereas on the other hand, it is a common thing to work a Woman Slave out of Doors; nor does the Law make any Distinction in her Taxes, whether her Work be Abroad, or at Home.

According to Robert Beverley, what are the differences between servants and slaves? What protections did servants have that slaves did not?

PURITAN NEW ENGLAND

The second major area to be colonized by the English in the first half of the seventeenth century, New England, differed markedly in its founding principles from the commercially oriented Chesapeake tobacco colonies. Settled largely by waves of Puritan families in the 1630s, New England had a religious orientation from the start. In England, reform-minded men and women had been calling for greater changes to the English national church since the 1580s. These reformers, who followed the teachings of John Calvin and other Protestant reformers, were called Puritans because of their insistence on "purifying" the Church of England of what they believed to be un-scriptural, especially Catholic elements that lingered in its institutions and practices.

Many who provided leadership in early New England were learned ministers who had studied at Cambridge or Oxford but who, because they had questioned the practices of the Church of England, had been deprived of careers by the king and his officials in an effort to silence all dissenting voices. Other Puritan leaders, such as the first governor of the Massachusetts Bay Colony, John Winthrop, came from the privileged class of English gentry. These well-to-do Puritans and many thousands more left their English homes not to establish a land of religious freedom, but to practice their own religion without persecution. Puritan New England offered them the opportunity to live as they believed the Bible demanded. In their "New" England, they set out to create a model of reformed Protestantism, a new English Israel.

The conflict generated by Puritanism had divided English society, because the Puritans demanded reforms that undermined the traditional festive culture. For example, they denounced popular pastimes like bear-baiting—letting dogs attack a chained bear—which were often conducted on Sundays when people had a few leisure hours. In the culture where William Shakespeare had produced his masterpieces, Puritans called for an end to the theater, censuring playhouses as places of decadence. Indeed, the Bible itself became part of the struggle between Puritans and James I, who headed the Church of England. Soon after ascending the throne, James commissioned a new version of the Bible in an effort to stifle Puritan reliance on the Geneva Bible, which followed the teachings of John Calvin and placed God's authority above the monarch's. The King James Version, published in 1611, instead emphasized the majesty of kings.

During the 1620s and 1630s, the conflict escalated to the point where the state church prohibited Puritan ministers from preaching. In the Church's view, Puritans represented a national security threat, because their demands for cultural, social, and religious reforms undermined the king's authority. Unwilling to conform to the Church of England, many Puritans found refuge in the New World. Yet those who emigrated to the Americas were not united. Some called for a complete break with the Church of England, while others remained committed to reforming the national church.

Plymouth: The First Puritan Colony

The first group of Puritans to make their way across the Atlantic was a small contingent known as the Pilgrims. Unlike other Puritans, they insisted on a complete separation from the Church of England and had first migrated to the Dutch Republic seeking religious freedom. Although they found they could worship without hindrance there, they grew concerned that they were losing their Englishness as they saw their children begin to learn the Dutch language and adopt Dutch ways. In addition, the English Pilgrims (and others in Europe) feared another attack on the Dutch Republic by Catholic Spain. Therefore, in 1620, they moved on to found the Plymouth Colony in present-day Massachusetts. The governor of Plymouth, William Bradford, was a Separatist, a proponent of complete separation from the English state church. Bradford and the other Pilgrim Separatists represented a major challenge to the prevailing vision of a unified English national church and empire. On board the *Mayflower*, which was bound for Virginia but landed on the tip of Cape Cod, Bradford and forty other adult men signed the Mayflower Compact (**Figure 3.11**), which presented a religious (rather than an economic) rationale for colonization. The compact expressed a community ideal of working together. When a larger exodus of Puritans established the Massachusetts Bay Colony in the 1630s, the Pilgrims at Plymouth welcomed them and the two colonies cooperated with each other.

AMERICANA

� *The Mayflower Compact and Its Religious Rationale*

The Mayflower Compact, which forty-one Pilgrim men signed on board the *Mayflower* in Plymouth Harbor, has been called the first American governing document, predating the U.S. Constitution by over 150 years. But was the Mayflower Compact a constitution? How much authority did it convey, and to whom?

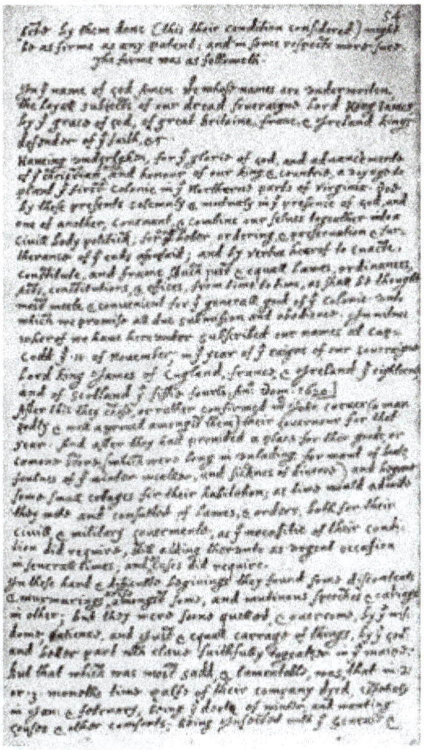

Figure 3.11 The original Mayflower Compact is no longer extant; only copies, such as this ca.1645 transcription by William Bradford, remain.

> In the name of God, Amen. We, whose names are underwritten, the loyal subjects of our dread Sovereign Lord King James, by the Grace of God, of Great Britain, France, and Ireland, King, defender of the Faith, etc.
>
> Having undertaken, for the Glory of God, and advancements of the Christian faith and honor of our King and Country, a voyage to plant the first colony in the Northern parts of Virginia, do by these presents, solemnly and mutually, in the presence of God, and one another, covenant and combine ourselves together into a civil body politic; for our better ordering, and preservation and furtherance of the ends aforesaid; and by virtue hereof to enact, constitute, and frame, such just and equal laws, ordinances, acts, constitutions, and offices, from time to time, as shall be thought most meet and convenient for the general good of the colony; unto which we promise all due submission and obedience.
>
> In witness whereof we have hereunto subscribed our names at Cape Cod the 11th of November, in the year of the reign of our Sovereign Lord King James, of England, France, and Ireland, the eighteenth, and of Scotland the fifty-fourth, 1620

Different labor systems also distinguished early Puritan New England from the Chesapeake colonies. Puritans expected young people to work diligently at their calling, and all members of their large families, including children, did the bulk of the work necessary to run homes, farms, and businesses. Very few migrants came to New England as laborers; in fact, New England towns protected their disciplined homegrown workforce by refusing to allow outsiders in, assuring their sons and daughters of steady employment. New England's labor system produced remarkable results, notably a powerful maritime-based economy with scores of oceangoing ships and the crews necessary to sail them. New England mariners sailing New England–made ships transported Virginian tobacco and West Indian sugar throughout the Atlantic World.

"A City upon a Hill"

A much larger group of English Puritans left England in the 1630s, establishing the Massachusetts Bay Colony, the New Haven Colony, the Connecticut Colony, and Rhode Island. Unlike the exodus of young males to the Chesapeake colonies, these migrants were families with young children and their university-trained ministers. Their aim, according to John Winthrop (**Figure 3.12**), the first governor of Massachusetts Bay, was to create a model of reformed Protestantism—a "city upon a hill," a new English Israel. The idea of a "city upon a hill" made clear the religious orientation of the New England settlement, and the charter of the Massachusetts Bay Colony stated as a goal that the colony's people "may be soe religiously, peaceablie, and civilly governed, as their good Life and orderlie Conversacon, maie wynn and incite the Natives of Country, to the Knowledg and Obedience of the onlie true God and Saulor of Mankinde, and the Christian Fayth." To illustrate this, the seal of the Massachusetts Bay Company (**Figure 3.12**) shows a half-naked Indian who entreats more of the English to "come over and help us."

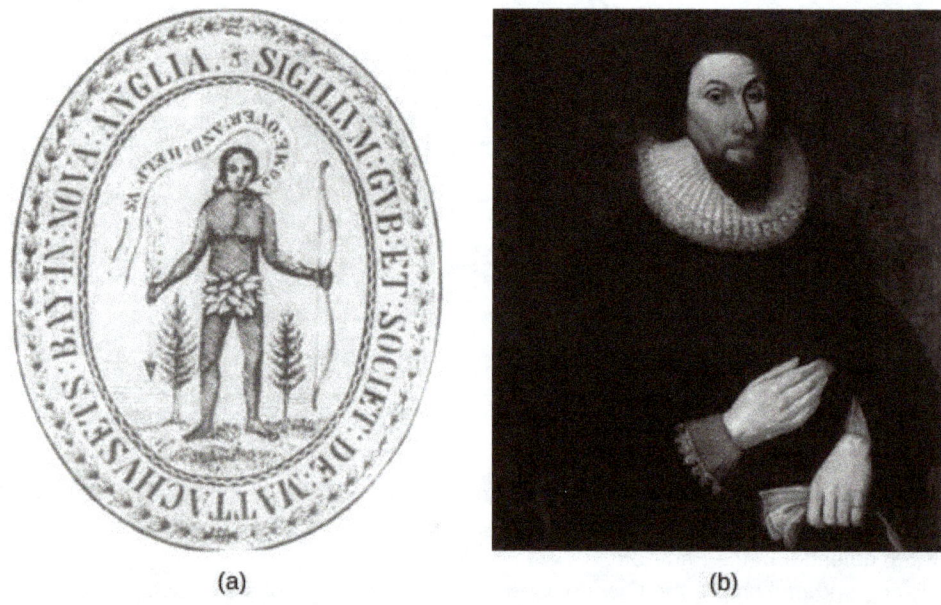

Figure 3.12 In the 1629 seal of the Massachusetts Bay Colony (a), an Indian is shown asking colonists to "Come over and help us." This seal indicates the religious ambitions of John Winthrop (b), the colony's first governor, for his "city upon a hill."

Puritan New England differed in many ways from both England and the rest of Europe. Protestants emphasized literacy so that everyone could read the Bible. This attitude was in stark contrast to that of Catholics, who refused to tolerate private ownership of Bibles in the vernacular. The Puritans, for their part, placed a special emphasis on reading scripture, and their commitment to literacy led to the establishment of the first printing press in English America in 1636. Four years later, in 1640, they published the first book in North America, the Bay Psalm Book. As Calvinists, Puritans adhered to the doctrine of predestination, whereby a few "elect" would be saved and all others damned. No one could be sure whether they were predestined for salvation, but through introspection, guided by scripture, Puritans hoped to find a glimmer of redemptive grace. Church membership was restricted to those Puritans who were willing to provide a conversion narrative telling how they came to understand their spiritual estate by hearing sermons and studying the Bible.

Although many people assume Puritans escaped England to establish religious freedom, they proved to be just as intolerant as the English state church. When dissenters, including Puritan minister Roger Williams and Anne Hutchinson, challenged Governor Winthrop in Massachusetts Bay in the 1630s, they were banished. Roger Williams questioned the Puritans' taking of Indian land. Williams also argued for a complete separation from the Church of England, a position other Puritans in Massachusetts rejected, as well as the idea that the state could not punish individuals for their beliefs. Although he did accept that nonbelievers were destined for eternal damnation, Williams did not think the state could compel true orthodoxy. Puritan authorities found him guilty of spreading dangerous ideas, but he went on to found Rhode Island as a colony that sheltered dissenting Puritans from their brethren in Massachusetts. In Rhode Island, Williams wrote favorably about native peoples, contrasting their virtues with Puritan New England's intolerance.

Anne Hutchinson also ran afoul of Puritan authorities for her criticism of the evolving religious practices in the Massachusetts Bay Colony. In particular, she held that Puritan ministers in New England taught a shallow version of Protestantism emphasizing hierarchy and actions—a "covenant of works" rather than a "covenant of grace." Literate Puritan women like Hutchinson presented a challenge to the male ministers' authority. Indeed, her major offense was her claim of direct religious revelation, a type of spiritual experience that negated the role of ministers. Because of Hutchinson's beliefs and her defiance of authority in the colony, especially that of Governor Winthrop, Puritan authorities tried and convicted her of holding false beliefs. In 1638, she was excommunicated and banished from the colony. She went to Rhode Island and later, in 1642, sought safety among the Dutch in New Netherland. The following year, Algonquian warriors killed Hutchinson and her family. In Massachusetts, Governor Winthrop noted her death as the righteous judgment of God against a heretic.

Like many other Europeans, the Puritans believed in the supernatural. Every event appeared to be a sign of God's mercy or judgment, and people believed that witches allied themselves with the Devil to carry out evil deeds and deliberate harm such as the sickness or death of children, the loss of cattle, and other catastrophes. Hundreds were accused of witchcraft in Puritan New England, including townspeople whose habits or appearance bothered their neighbors or who appeared threatening for any reason. Women, seen as more susceptible to the Devil because of their supposedly weaker constitutions, made up the vast majority of suspects and those who were executed. The most notorious cases occurred in Salem Village in 1692. Many of the accusers who prosecuted the suspected witches had been traumatized by the Indian wars on the frontier and by unprecedented political and cultural changes in New England. Relying on their belief in witchcraft to help make sense of their changing world, Puritan authorities executed nineteen people and caused the deaths of several others.

Explore the Salem Witchcraft Trials (http://openstaxcollege.org/l/salemwitch) to learn more about the prosecution of witchcraft in seventeenth-century New England.

Puritan Relationships with Native Peoples

Like their Spanish and French Catholic rivals, English Puritans in America took steps to convert native peoples to their version of Christianity. John Eliot, the leading Puritan missionary in New England, urged natives in Massachusetts to live in "praying towns" established by English authorities for converted

Indians, and to adopt the Puritan emphasis on the centrality of the Bible. In keeping with the Protestant emphasis on reading scripture, he translated the Bible into the local Algonquian language and published his work in 1663. Eliot hoped that as a result of his efforts, some of New England's native inhabitants would become preachers.

Tensions had existed from the beginning between the Puritans and the native people who controlled southern New England (**Figure 3.13**). Relationships deteriorated as the Puritans continued to expand their settlements aggressively and as European ways increasingly disrupted native life. These strains led to King Philip's War (1675–1676), a massive regional conflict that was nearly successful in pushing the English out of New England.

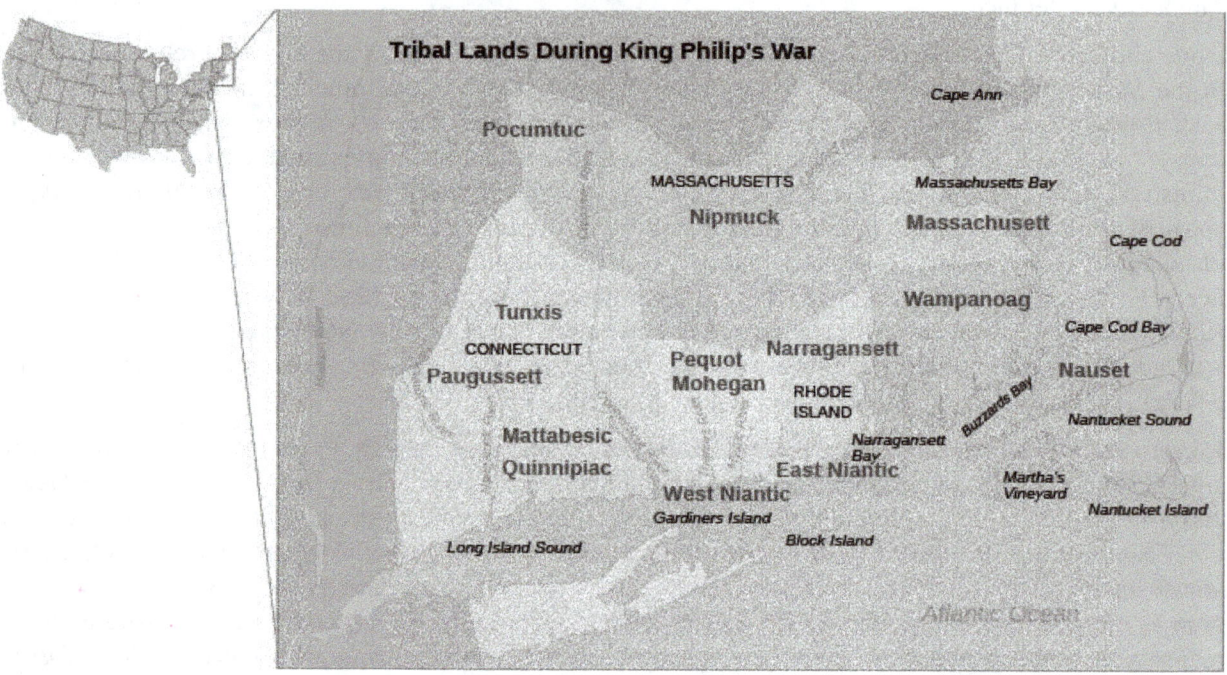

Figure 3.13 This map indicates the domains of New England's native inhabitants in 1670, a few years before King Philip's War.

When the Puritans began to arrive in the 1620s and 1630s, local Algonquian peoples had viewed them as potential allies in the conflicts already simmering between rival native groups. In 1621, the Wampanoag, led by Massasoit, concluded a peace treaty with the Pilgrims at Plymouth. In the 1630s, the Puritans in Massachusetts and Plymouth allied themselves with the Narragansett and Mohegan people against the Pequot, who had recently expanded their claims into southern New England. In May 1637, the Puritans attacked a large group of several hundred Pequot along the Mystic River in Connecticut. To the horror of their native allies, the Puritans massacred all but a handful of the men, women, and children they found.

By the mid-seventeenth century, the Puritans had pushed their way further into the interior of New England, establishing outposts along the Connecticut River Valley. There seemed no end to their expansion. Wampanoag leader Metacom or Metacomet, also known as King Philip among the English, was determined to stop the encroachment. The Wampanoag, along with the Nipmuck, Pocumtuck, and Narragansett, took up the hatchet to drive the English from the land. In the ensuing conflict, called King Philip's War, native forces succeeded in destroying half of the frontier Puritan towns; however, in the end, the English (aided by Mohegans and Christian Indians) prevailed and sold many captives into slavery in the West Indies. (The severed head of King Philip was publicly displayed in Plymouth.) The war also forever changed the English perception of native peoples; from then on, Puritan writers took great pains to vilify the natives as bloodthirsty savages. A new type of racial hatred became a defining feature of Indian-English relationships in the Northeast.

MY STORY

◎ *Mary Rowlandson's Captivity Narrative*

Mary Rowlandson was a Puritan woman whom Indian tribes captured and imprisoned for several weeks during King Philip's War. After her release, she wrote *The Narrative of the Captivity and the Restoration of Mrs. Mary Rowlandson*, which was published in 1682 (**Figure 3.14**). The book was an immediate sensation that was reissued in multiple editions for over a century.

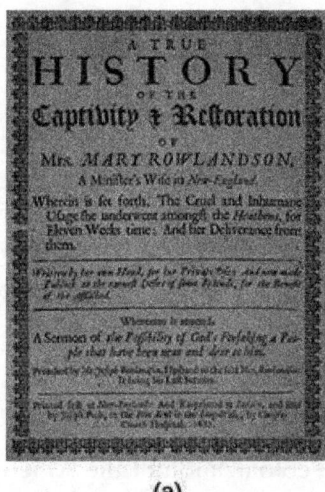

(a)   (b)

Figure 3.14 Puritan woman Mary Rowlandson wrote her captivity narrative, the front cover of which is shown here (a), after her imprisonment during King Philip's War. In her narrative, she tells of her treatment by the Indians holding her as well as of her meetings with the Wampanoag leader Metacom (b), shown in a contemporary portrait.

> But now, the next morning, I must turn my back upon the town, and travel with them into the vast and desolate wilderness, I knew not whither. It is not my tongue, or pen, can express the sorrows of my heart, and bitterness of my spirit that I had at this departure: but God was with me in a wonderful manner, carrying me along, and bearing up my spirit, that it did not quite fail. One of the Indians carried my poor wounded babe upon a horse; it went moaning all along, "I shall die, I shall die." I went on foot after it, with sorrow that cannot be expressed. At length I took it off the horse, and carried it in my arms till my strength failed, and I fell down with it. Then they set me upon a horse with my wounded child in my lap, and there being no furniture upon the horse's back, as we were going down a steep hill we both fell over the horse's head, at which they, like inhumane creatures, laughed, and rejoiced to see it, though I thought we should there have ended our days, as overcome with so many difficulties. But the Lord renewed my strength still, and carried me along, that I might see more of His power; yea, so much that I could never have thought of, had I not experienced it.

What sustains Rowlandson her during her ordeal? How does she characterize her captors? What do you think made her narrative so compelling to readers?

> **Click and Explore**
>
>  Access the entire text of Mary Rowlandson's captivity narrative (http://openstaxcollege.org/l/captivenarr) at the Gutenberg Project.

3.4 The Impact of Colonization

By the end of this section, you will be able to:
- Explain the reasons for the rise of slavery in the American colonies
- Describe changes to Indian life, including warfare and hunting
- Contrast European and Indian views on property
- Assess the impact of European settlement on the environment

As Europeans moved beyond exploration and into colonization of the Americas, they brought changes to virtually every aspect of the land and its people, from trade and hunting to warfare and personal property. European goods, ideas, and diseases shaped the changing continent.

As Europeans established their colonies, their societies also became segmented and divided along religious and racial lines. Most people in these societies were not free; they labored as servants or slaves, doing the work required to produce wealth for others. By 1700, the American continent had become a place of stark contrasts between slavery and freedom, between the haves and the have-nots.

THE INSTITUTION OF SLAVERY

Everywhere in the American colonies, a crushing demand for labor existed to grow New World cash crops, especially sugar and tobacco. This need led Europeans to rely increasingly on Africans, and after 1600, the movement of Africans across the Atlantic accelerated. The English crown chartered the Royal African Company in 1672, giving the company a monopoly over the transport of African slaves to the English colonies. Over the next four decades, the company transported around 350,000 Africans from their homelands. By 1700, the tiny English sugar island of Barbados had a population of fifty thousand slaves, and the English had encoded the institution of chattel slavery into colonial law.

This new system of African slavery came slowly to the English colonists, who did not have slavery at home and preferred to use servant labor. Nevertheless, by the end of the seventeenth century, the English everywhere in America—and particularly in the Chesapeake Bay colonies—had come to rely on African slaves. While Africans had long practiced slavery among their own people, it had not been based on race. Africans enslaved other Africans as war captives, for crimes, and to settle debts; they generally used their slaves for domestic and small-scale agricultural work, not for growing cash crops on large plantations. Additionally, African slavery was often a temporary condition rather than a lifelong sentence, and, unlike New World slavery, it was typically not heritable (passed from a slave mother to her children).

The growing slave trade with Europeans had a profound impact on the people of West Africa, giving prominence to local chieftains and merchants who traded slaves for European textiles, alcohol, guns, tobacco, and food. Africans also charged Europeans for the right to trade in slaves and imposed taxes on slave purchases. Different African groups and kingdoms even staged large-scale raids on each other to meet the demand for slaves.

Once sold to traders, all slaves sent to America endured the hellish **Middle Passage**, the transatlantic crossing, which took one to two months. By 1625, more than 325,800 Africans had been shipped to the New World, though many thousands perished during the voyage. An astonishing number, some four million, were transported to the Caribbean between 1501 and 1830. When they reached their destination in America, Africans found themselves trapped in shockingly brutal slave societies. In the Chesapeake colonies, they faced a lifetime of harvesting and processing tobacco.

Everywhere, Africans resisted slavery, and running away was common. In Jamaica and elsewhere, runaway slaves created **maroon communities**, groups that resisted recapture and eked a living from the land, rebuilding their communities as best they could. When possible, they adhered to traditional ways, following spiritual leaders such as Vodun priests.

CHANGES TO INDIAN LIFE

While the Americas remained firmly under the control of native peoples in the first decades of European settlement, conflict increased as colonization spread and Europeans placed greater demands upon the native populations, including expecting them to convert to Christianity (either Catholicism or Protestantism). Throughout the seventeenth century, the still-powerful native peoples and confederacies that retained control of the land waged war against the invading Europeans, achieving a degree of success in their effort to drive the newcomers from the continent.

At the same time, European goods had begun to change Indian life radically. In the 1500s, some of the earliest objects Europeans introduced to Indians were glass beads, copper kettles, and metal utensils. Native people often adapted these items for their own use. For example, some cut up copper kettles and refashioned the metal for other uses, including jewelry that conferred status on the wearer, who was seen as connected to the new European source of raw materials.

As European settlements grew throughout the 1600s, European goods flooded native communities. Soon native people were using these items for the same purposes as the Europeans. For example, many native inhabitants abandoned their animal-skin clothing in favor of European textiles. Similarly, clay cookware gave way to metal cooking implements, and Indians found that European flint and steel made starting fires much easier (**Figure 3.15**).

Figure 3.15 In this 1681 portrait, the Niantic-Narragansett chief Ninigret wears a combination of European and Indian goods. Which elements of each culture are evident in this portrait?

The abundance of European goods gave rise to new artistic objects. For example, iron awls made the creation of shell beads among the native people of the Eastern Woodlands much easier, and the result was an astonishing increase in the production of **wampum**, shell beads used in ceremonies and as jewelry and currency. Native peoples had always placed goods in the graves of their departed, and this practice escalated with the arrival of European goods. Archaeologists have found enormous caches of European trade goods in the graves of Indians on the East Coast.

Native weapons changed dramatically as well, creating an arms race among the peoples living in European colonization zones. Indians refashioned European brassware into arrow points and turned axes used for chopping wood into weapons. The most prized piece of European weaponry to obtain was a **musket**, or light, long-barreled European gun. In order to trade with Europeans for these, native peoples intensified their harvesting of beaver, commercializing their traditional practice.

The influx of European materials made warfare more lethal and changed traditional patterns of authority among tribes. Formerly weaker groups, if they had access to European metal and weapons, suddenly gained the upper hand against once-dominant groups. The Algonquian, for instance, traded with the French for muskets and gained power against their enemies, the Iroquois. Eventually, native peoples also used their new weapons against the European colonizers who had provided them.

Click and Explore

Explore the complexity of **Indian-European relationships** (http://openstaxcollege.org/l/NHC) in the series of primary source documents on the National Humanities Center site.

ENVIRONMENTAL CHANGES

The European presence in America spurred countless changes in the environment, setting into motion chains of events that affected native animals as well as people. The popularity of beaver-trimmed hats in Europe, coupled with Indians' desire for European weapons, led to the overhunting of beaver in the Northeast. Soon, beavers were extinct in New England, New York, and other areas. With their loss came the loss of beaver ponds, which had served as habitats for fish as well as water sources for deer, moose, and other animals. Furthermore, Europeans introduced pigs, which they allowed to forage in forests and other wildlands. Pigs consumed the foods on which deer and other indigenous species depended, resulting in scarcity of the game native peoples had traditionally hunted.

European ideas about owning land as private property clashed with natives' understanding of land use. Native peoples did not believe in private ownership of land; instead, they viewed land as a resource to be held in common for the benefit of the group. The European idea of usufruct—the right to common land use and enjoyment—comes close to the native understanding, but colonists did not practice usufruct widely in America. Colonizers established fields, fences, and other means of demarcating private property. Native peoples who moved seasonally to take advantage of natural resources now found areas off limits, claimed by colonizers because of their insistence on private-property rights.

The Introduction of Disease

Perhaps European colonization's single greatest impact on the North American environment was the introduction of disease. Microbes to which native inhabitants had no immunity led to death everywhere Europeans settled. Along the New England coast between 1616 and 1618, epidemics claimed the lives of 75 percent of the native people. In the 1630s, half the Huron and Iroquois around the Great Lakes died of smallpox. As is often the case with disease, the very young and the very old were the most vulnerable and had the highest mortality rates. The loss of the older generation meant the loss of knowledge and tradition, while the death of children only compounded the trauma, creating devastating implications for future generations.

Some native peoples perceived disease as a weapon used by hostile spiritual forces, and they went to war to exorcise the disease from their midst. These "mourning wars" in eastern North America were designed to gain captives who would either be adopted ("requickened" as a replacement for a deceased loved one) or ritually tortured and executed to assuage the anger and grief caused by loss.

The Cultivation of Plants

European expansion in the Americas led to an unprecedented movement of plants across the Atlantic. A prime example is tobacco, which became a valuable export as the habit of smoking, previously unknown in Europe, took hold (**Figure 3.16**). Another example is sugar. Columbus brought sugarcane to the Caribbean on his second voyage in 1494, and thereafter a wide variety of other herbs, flowers, seeds, and roots made the transatlantic voyage.

Figure 3.16 Adriaen van Ostade, a Dutch artist, painted *An Apothecary Smoking in an Interior* in 1646. The large European market for American tobacco strongly influenced the development of some of the American colonies.

Just as pharmaceutical companies today scour the natural world for new drugs, Europeans traveled to America to discover new medicines. The task of cataloging the new plants found there helped give birth to the science of botany. Early botanists included the English naturalist Sir Hans Sloane, who traveled to Jamaica in 1687 and there recorded hundreds of new plants (**Figure 3.17**). Sloane also helped popularize the drinking of chocolate, made from the cacao bean, in England.

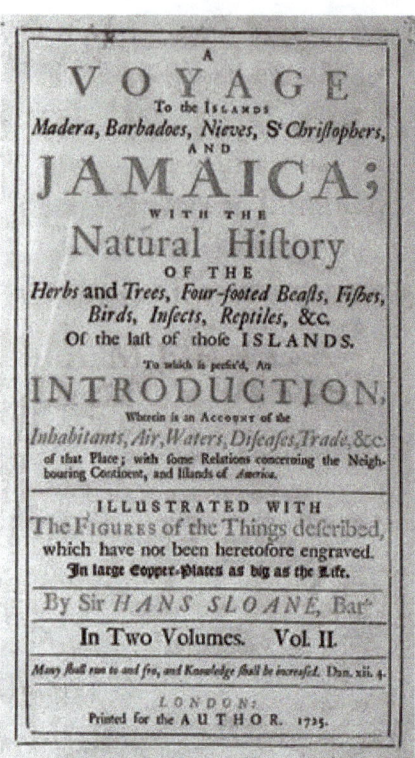

Figure 3.17 English naturalist Sir Hans Sloane traveled to Jamaica and other Caribbean islands to catalog the flora of the new world.

Indians, who possessed a vast understanding of local New World plants and their properties, would have been a rich source of information for those European botanists seeking to find and catalog potentially useful plants. Enslaved Africans, who had a tradition of the use of medicinal plants in their native land, adapted to their new surroundings by learning the use of New World plants through experimentation or from the native inhabitants. Native peoples and Africans employed their knowledge effectively within their own communities. One notable example was the use of the peacock flower to induce abortions: Indian and enslaved African women living in oppressive colonial regimes are said to have used this herb to prevent the birth of children into slavery. Europeans distrusted medical knowledge that came from African or native sources, however, and thus lost the benefit of this source of information.

CHAPTER 4
Rule Britannia! The English Empire, 1660–1763

Figure 4.1 Isaac Royall and his family, seen here in a 1741 portrait by Robert Feke, moved to Medford, Massachusetts, from the West Indian island of Antigua, bringing their slaves with them. They were an affluent British colonial family, proud of their success and the success of the British Empire.

Chapter Outline

- 4.1 Charles II and the Restoration Colonies
- 4.2 The Glorious Revolution and the English Empire
- 4.3 An Empire of Slavery and the Consumer Revolution
- 4.4 Great Awakening and Enlightenment
- 4.5 Wars for Empire

Introduction

The eighteenth century witnessed the birth of Great Britain (after the union of England and Scotland in 1707) and the expansion of the British Empire. By the mid-1700s, Great Britain had developed into a commercial and military powerhouse; its economic sway ranged from India, where the British East India Company had gained control over both trade and territory, to the West African coast, where British slave traders predominated, and to the British West Indies, whose lucrative sugar plantations, especially in Barbados and Jamaica, provided windfall profits for British planters. Meanwhile, the population rose dramatically in Britain's North American colonies. In the early 1700s the population in the colonies had reached 250,000. By 1750, however, over a million British migrants and African slaves had established a near-continuous zone of settlement on the Atlantic coast from Maine to Georgia.

During this period, the ties between Great Britain and the American colonies only grew stronger. Anglo-American colonists considered themselves part of the British Empire in all ways: politically, militarily, religiously (as Protestants), intellectually, and racially. The portrait of the Royall family (**Figure 4.1**) exemplifies the colonial American gentry of the eighteenth century. Successful and well-to-do, they display fashions, hairstyles, and furnishings that all speak to their identity as proud and loyal British subjects.

4.1 Charles II and the Restoration Colonies

By the end of this section, you will be able to:
- Analyze the causes and consequences of the Restoration
- Identify the Restoration colonies and their role in the expansion of the Empire

When Charles II ascended the throne in 1660, English subjects on both sides of the Atlantic celebrated the restoration of the English monarchy after a decade of living without a king as a result of the English Civil Wars. Charles II lost little time in strengthening England's global power. From the 1660s to the 1680s, Charles II added more possessions to England's North American holdings by establishing the Restoration colonies of New York and New Jersey (taking these areas from the Dutch) as well as Pennsylvania and the Carolinas. In order to reap the greatest economic benefit from England's overseas possessions, Charles II enacted the mercantilist Navigation Acts, although many colonial merchants ignored them because enforcement remained lax.

CHARLES II

The chronicle of Charles II begins with his father, Charles I. Charles I ascended the English throne in 1625 and soon married a French Catholic princess, Henrietta Maria, who was not well liked by English Protestants because she openly practiced Catholicism during her husband's reign. The most outspoken Protestants, the Puritans, had a strong voice in Parliament in the 1620s, and they strongly opposed the king's marriage and his ties to Catholicism. When Parliament tried to contest his edicts, including the king's efforts to impose taxes without Parliament's consent, Charles I suspended Parliament in 1629 and ruled without one for the next eleven years.

The ensuing struggle between the king and Parliament led to the outbreak of war. The English Civil War lasted from 1642 to 1649 and pitted the king and his Royalist supporters against Oliver Cromwell and his Parliamentary forces. After years of fighting, the Parliamentary forces gained the upper hand, and in 1649, they charged Charles I with treason and beheaded him. The monarchy was dissolved, and England

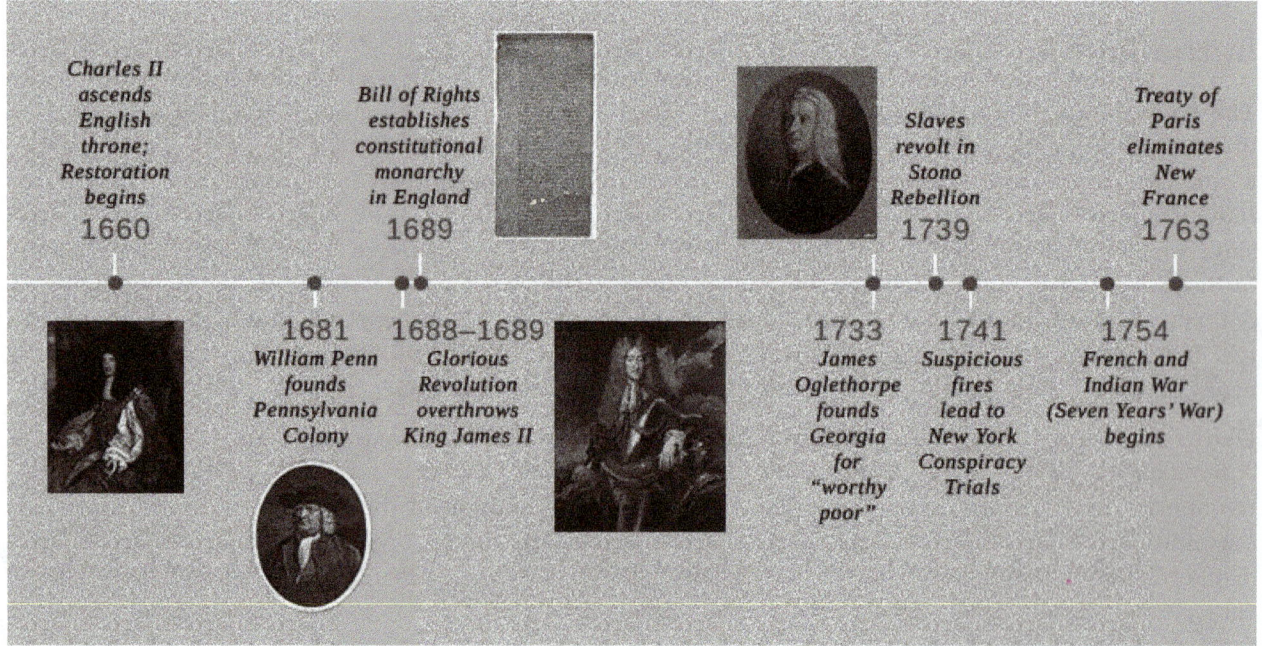

Figure 4.2

became a republic: a state without a king. Oliver Cromwell headed the new English Commonwealth, and the period known as the **English interregnum**, or the time between kings, began.

Though Cromwell enjoyed widespread popularity at first, over time he appeared to many in England to be taking on the powers of a military dictator. Dissatisfaction with Cromwell grew. When he died in 1658 and control passed to his son Richard, who lacked the political skills of his father, a majority of the English people feared an alternate hereditary monarchy in the making. They had had enough and asked Charles II to be king. In 1660, they welcomed the son of the executed king Charles I back to the throne to resume the English monarchy and bring the interregnum to an end (**Figure 4.3**). The return of Charles II is known as the Restoration.

Figure 4.3 The monarchy and Parliament fought for control of England during the seventeenth century. Though Oliver Cromwell (a), shown here in a 1656 portrait by Samuel Cooper, appeared to offer England a better mode of government, he assumed broad powers for himself and disregarded cherished English liberties established under Magna Carta in 1215. As a result, the English people welcomed Charles II (b) back to the throne in 1660. This portrait by John Michael Wright was painted ca. 1660–1665, soon after the new king gained the throne.

Charles II was committed to expanding England's overseas possessions. His policies in the 1660s through the 1680s established and supported the **Restoration colonies**: the Carolinas, New Jersey, New York, and Pennsylvania. All the Restoration colonies started as **proprietary colonies**, that is, the king gave each colony to a trusted individual, family, or group.

THE CAROLINAS

Charles II hoped to establish English control of the area between Virginia and Spanish Florida. To that end, he issued a royal charter in 1663 to eight trusted and loyal supporters, each of whom was to be a feudal-style proprietor of a region of the province of Carolina.

These proprietors did not relocate to the colonies, however. Instead, English plantation owners from the tiny Caribbean island of Barbados, already a well-established English sugar colony fueled by slave labor, migrated to the southern part of Carolina to settle there. In 1670, they established Charles Town (later Charleston), named in honor of Charles II, at the junction of the Ashley and Cooper Rivers (**Figure 4.4**). As the settlement around Charles Town grew, it began to produce livestock for export to the West Indies. In the northern part of Carolina, settlers turned sap from pine trees into turpentine used to waterproof wooden ships. Political disagreements between settlers in the northern and southern parts of Carolina escalated in the 1710s through the 1720s and led to the creation, in 1729, of two colonies, North and South Carolina. The southern part of Carolina had been producing rice and indigo (a plant that yields a dark blue dye used by English royalty) since the 1700s, and South Carolina continued to depend on these main crops.

North Carolina continued to produce items for ships, especially turpentine and tar, and its population increased as Virginians moved there to expand their tobacco holdings. Tobacco was the primary export of both Virginia and North Carolina, which also traded in deerskins and slaves from Africa.

Figure 4.4 The port of colonial Charles Towne, depicted here on a 1733 map of North America, was the largest in the South and played a significant role in the Atlantic slave trade.

Slavery developed quickly in the Carolinas, largely because so many of the early migrants came from Barbados, where slavery was well established. By the end of the 1600s, a very wealthy class of rice planters who relied on slaves had attained dominance in the southern part of the Carolinas, especially around Charles Town. By 1715, South Carolina had a black majority because of the number of slaves in the colony. The legal basis for slavery was established in the early 1700s as the Carolinas began to pass slave laws based on the Barbados slave codes of the late 1600s. These laws reduced Africans to the status of property to be bought and sold as other commodities.

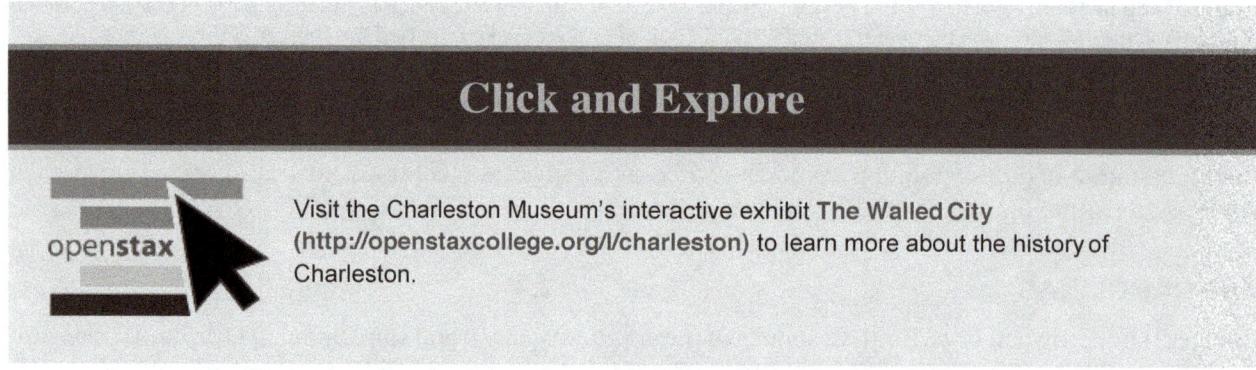

Visit the Charleston Museum's interactive exhibit The Walled City (http://openstaxcollege.org/l/charleston) to learn more about the history of Charleston.

As in other areas of English settlement, native peoples in the Carolinas suffered tremendously from the introduction of European diseases. Despite the effects of disease, Indians in the area endured and, following the pattern elsewhere in the colonies, grew dependent on European goods. Local Yamasee and Creek tribes built up a trade deficit with the English, trading deerskins and captive slaves for European guns. English settlers exacerbated tensions with local Indian tribes, especially the Yamasee, by expanding their rice and tobacco fields into Indian lands. Worse still, English traders took native women captive as payment for debts.

The outrages committed by traders, combined with the seemingly unstoppable expansion of English settlement onto native land, led to the outbreak of the Yamasee War (1715–1718), an effort by a coalition of local tribes to drive away the European invaders. This native effort to force the newcomers back across the

Atlantic nearly succeeded in annihilating the Carolina colonies. Only when the Cherokee allied themselves with the English did the coalition's goal of eliminating the English from the region falter. The Yamasee War demonstrates the key role native peoples played in shaping the outcome of colonial struggles and, perhaps most important, the disunity that existed between different native groups.

NEW YORK AND NEW JERSEY

Charles II also set his sights on the Dutch colony of New Netherland. The English takeover of New Netherland originated in the imperial rivalry between the Dutch and the English. During the Anglo-Dutch wars of the 1650s and 1660s, the two powers attempted to gain commercial advantages in the Atlantic World. During the Second Anglo-Dutch War (1664–1667), English forces gained control of the Dutch fur trading colony of New Netherland, and in 1664, Charles II gave this colony (including present-day New Jersey) to his brother James, Duke of York (later James II). The colony and city were renamed New York in his honor. The Dutch in New York chafed under English rule. In 1673, during the Third Anglo-Dutch War (1672–1674), the Dutch recaptured the colony. However, at the end of the conflict, the English had regained control (**Figure 4.5**).

Figure 4.5 "View of New Amsterdam" (ca. 1665), a watercolor by Johannes Vingboons, was painted during the Anglo-Dutch wars of the 1660s and 1670s. New Amsterdam was officially reincorporated as New York City in 1664, but alternated under Dutch and English rule until 1674.

The Duke of York had no desire to govern locally or listen to the wishes of local colonists. It wasn't until 1683, therefore, almost 20 years after the English took control of the colony, that colonists were able to convene a local representative legislature. The assembly's 1683 Charter of Liberties and Privileges set out the traditional rights of Englishmen, like the right to trial by jury and the right to representative government.

The English continued the Dutch patroonship system, granting large estates to a favored few families. The largest of these estates, at 160,000 acres, was given to Robert Livingston in 1686. The Livingstons and the other manorial families who controlled the Hudson River Valley formed a formidable political and economic force. Eighteenth-century New York City, meanwhile, contained a variety of people and religions—as well as Dutch and English people, it held French Protestants (Huguenots), Jews, Puritans, Quakers, Anglicans, and a large population of slaves. As they did in other zones of colonization, native peoples played a key role in shaping the history of colonial New York. After decades of war in the 1600s, the powerful Five Nations of the Iroquois, composed of the Mohawk, Oneida, Onondaga, Cayuga, and Seneca, successfully pursued a policy of neutrality with both the English and, to the north, the French in Canada during the first half of the 1700s. This native policy meant that the Iroquois continued to live in their own villages under their own government while enjoying the benefits of trade with both the French and the English.

PENNSYLVANIA

The Restoration colonies also included Pennsylvania, which became the geographic center of British colonial America. Pennsylvania (which means "Penn's Woods" in Latin) was created in 1681, when Charles II bestowed the largest proprietary colony in the Americas on William Penn (**Figure 4.6**) to settle the large debt he owed the Penn family. William Penn's father, Admiral William Penn, had served the English crown by helping take Jamaica from the Spanish in 1655. The king personally owed the Admiral money as well.

Figure 4.6 Charles II granted William Penn the land that eventually became the Commonwealth of Pennsylvania in order to settle a debt the English crown owed to Penn's father.

Like early settlers of the New England colonies, Pennsylvania's first colonists migrated mostly for religious reasons. William Penn himself was a Quaker, a member of a new Protestant denomination called the Society of Friends. George Fox had founded the Society of Friends in England in the late 1640s, having grown dissatisfied with Puritanism and the idea of predestination. Rather, Fox and his followers stressed that everyone had an "inner light" inside him or her, a spark of divinity. They gained the name Quakers because they were said to quake when the inner light moved them. Quakers rejected the idea of worldly rank, believing instead in a new and radical form of social equality. Their speech reflected this belief in that they addressed all others as equals, using "thee" and "thou" rather than terms like "your lordship" or "my lady" that were customary for privileged individuals of the hereditary elite.

The English crown persecuted Quakers in England, and colonial governments were equally harsh; Massachusetts even executed several early Quakers who had gone to proselytize there. To avoid such persecution, Quakers and their families at first created a community on the sugar island of Barbados. Soon after its founding, however, Pennsylvania became the destination of choice. Quakers flocked to Pennsylvania as well as New Jersey, where they could preach and practice their religion in peace. Unlike New England, whose official religion was Puritanism, Pennsylvania did not establish an official church. Indeed, the colony allowed a degree of religious tolerance found nowhere else in English America. To help encourage immigration to his colony, Penn promised fifty acres of land to people who agreed to come to Pennsylvania and completed their term of service. Not surprisingly, those seeking a better life came in large numbers, so much so that Pennsylvania relied on indentured servants more than any other colony.

One of the primary tenets of Quakerism is pacifism, leading William Penn to establish friendly relationships with local native peoples. He formed a covenant of friendship with the Lenni Lenape (Delaware) tribe, buying their land for a fair price instead of taking it by force. In 1701, he also signed a treaty with the Susquehannocks to avoid war. Unlike other colonies, Pennsylvania did not experience war on the frontier with native peoples during its early history.

This content is available for free at http://cnx.org/content/col11740/latest/

As an important port city, Philadelphia grew rapidly. Quaker merchants there established contacts throughout the Atlantic world and participated in the thriving African slave trade. Some Quakers, who were deeply troubled by the contradiction between their belief in the "inner light" and the practice of slavery, rejected the practice and engaged in efforts to abolish it altogether. Philadelphia also acted as a magnet for immigrants, who came not only from England, but from all over Europe by the hundreds of thousands. The city, and indeed all of Pennsylvania, appeared to be the best country for poor men and women, many of whom arrived as servants and dreamed of owning land. A very few, like the fortunate Benjamin Franklin, a runaway from Puritan Boston, did extraordinarily well. Other immigrant groups in the colony, most notably Germans and Scotch-Irish (families from Scotland and England who had first lived in Ireland before moving to British America), greatly improved their lot in Pennsylvania. Of course, Africans imported into the colony to labor for white masters fared far worse.

AMERICANA

✪ *John Wilson Offers Reward for Escaped Prisoners*

The *American Weekly Mercury*, published by William Bradford, was Philadelphia's first newspaper. This advertisement from "John Wilson, *Goaler*" (jailer) offers a reward for anyone capturing several men who escaped from the jail.

> BROKE out of the Common Goal of Philadelphia, the 15th of this Instant February, 1721, the following Persons:
>
> John Palmer, also Plumly, *alias* Paine, *Servant to Joseph Jones, run away and was lately taken up at New-York. He is fully described in the* American Mercury, Novem. 23, 1721. *He has a Cinnamon coloured Coat on, a middle sized fresh coloured Man. His Master will give a Pistole Reward to any who Shall Secure him, besides what is here offered.*
>
> Daniel Oughtopay, *A Dutchman, aged about 24 Years, Servant to Dr. Johnston in Amboy. He is a thin Spare man, grey Drugget Waistcoat and Breeches and a light-coloured Coat on.*
>
> Ebenezor Mallary, *a New-England, aged about 24 Years, is a middle-sized thin Man, having on a Snuff colour'd Coat, and ordinary Ticking Waistcoat and Breeches. He has dark brown strait Hair.*
>
> Matthew Dulany, *an Irish Man, down-look'd Swarthy Complexion, and has on an Olive-coloured Cloth Coat and Waistcoat with Cloth Buttons.*
>
> John Flemming, *an Irish Lad, aged about 18, belonging to Mr. Miranda, Merchant in this City. He has no Coat, a grey Drugget Waistcoat, and a narrow brim'd Hat on.*
>
> John Corbet, *a Shropshire Man, a Runaway Servant from Alexander Faulkner of Maryland, broke out on the 12th Instant. He has got a double-breasted Sailor's Jacket on lined with red Bays, pretends to be a Sailor, and once taught School at Josephs Collings's in the Jerseys. Whoever takes up and secures all, or any One of these Felons, shall have a Pistole Reward for each of them and reasonable Charges, paid them by* John Wilson, *Goaler*
>
> —Advertisement from the *American Weekly Mercury*, 1722

What do the descriptions of the men tell you about life in colonial Philadelphia?

Click and Explore

Browse a number of issues of the American Weekly Mercury (http://openstaxcollege.org/l/philly1) that were digitized by New Jersey's Stockton University. Read through several to get a remarkable flavor of life in early eighteenth-century Philadelphia.

THE NAVIGATION ACTS

Creating wealth for the Empire remained a primary goal, and in the second half of the seventeenth century, especially during the Restoration, England attempted to gain better control of trade with the American colonies. The mercantilist policies by which it tried to achieve this control are known as the **Navigation Acts**.

The 1651 Navigation Ordnance, a product of Cromwell's England, required that only English ships carry goods between England and the colonies, and that the captain and three-fourths of the crew had to be English. The ordnance further listed "enumerated articles" that could be transported only to England or to English colonies, including the most lucrative commodities like sugar and tobacco as well as indigo, rice, molasses, and naval stores such as turpentine. All were valuable goods not produced in England or in demand by the British navy. After ascending the throne, Charles II approved the 1660 Navigation Act, which restated the 1651 act to ensure a monopoly on imports from the colonies.

Other Navigation Acts included the 1663 Staple Act and the 1673 Plantation Duties Act. The Staple Act barred colonists from importing goods that had not been made in England, creating a profitable monopoly for English exporters and manufacturers. The Plantation Duties Act taxed enumerated articles exported from one colony to another, a measure aimed principally at New Englanders, who transported great quantities of molasses from the West Indies, including smuggled molasses from French-held islands, to make into rum.

In 1675, Charles II organized the Lords of Trade and Plantation, commonly known as the Lords of Trade, an administrative body intended to create stronger ties between the colonial governments and the crown. However, the 1696 Navigation Act created the Board of Trade, replacing the Lords of Trade. This act, meant to strengthen enforcement of customs laws, also established vice-admiralty courts where the crown could prosecute customs violators without a jury. Under this act, customs officials were empowered with warrants known as "writs of assistance" to board and search vessels suspected of containing smuggled goods.

Despite the Navigation Acts, however, Great Britain exercised lax control over the English colonies during most of the eighteenth century because of the policies of Prime Minister Robert Walpole. During his long term (1721–1742), Walpole governed according to his belief that commerce flourished best when it was not encumbered with restrictions. Historians have described this lack of strict enforcement of the Navigation Acts as **salutary neglect**. In addition, nothing prevented colonists from building their own fleet of ships to engage in trade. New England especially benefited from both salutary neglect and a vibrant maritime culture made possible by the scores of trading vessels built in the northern colonies. The case of the 1733 Molasses Act illustrates the weaknesses of British mercantilist policy. The 1733 act placed a sixpence-per-gallon duty on raw sugar, rum, and molasses from Britain's competitors, the French and the Dutch, in order to give an advantage to British West Indian producers. Because the British did not enforce the 1733 law, however, New England mariners routinely smuggled these items from the French and Dutch West Indies more cheaply than they could buy them on English islands.

4.2 The Glorious Revolution and the English Empire

By the end of this section, you will be able to:
- Identify the causes of the Glorious Revolution
- Explain the outcomes of the Glorious Revolution

During the brief rule of King James II, many in England feared the imposition of a Catholic absolute monarchy by the man who modeled his rule on that of his French Catholic cousin, Louis XIV. Opposition to James II, spearheaded by the English Whig party, overthrew the king in the Glorious Revolution of

1688–1689. This paved the way for the Protestant reign of William of Orange and his wife Mary (James's Protestant daughter).

JAMES II AND THE GLORIOUS REVOLUTION

King James II (**Figure 4.7**), the second son of Charles I, ascended the English throne in 1685 on the death of his brother, Charles II. James then worked to model his rule on the reign of the French Catholic King Louis XIV, his cousin. This meant centralizing English political strength around the throne, giving the monarchy absolute power. Also like Louis XIV, James II practiced a strict and intolerant form of Roman Catholicism after he converted from Protestantism in the late 1660s. He had a Catholic wife, and when they had a son, the potential for a Catholic heir to the English throne became a threat to English Protestants. James also worked to modernize the English army and navy. The fact that the king kept a standing army in times of peace greatly alarmed the English, who believed that such a force would be used to crush their liberty. As James's strength grew, his opponents feared their king would turn England into a Catholic monarchy with absolute power over her people.

Figure 4.7 James II (shown here in a painting ca. 1690) worked to centralize the English government. The Catholic king of France, Louis XIV, provided a template for James's policies.

In 1686, James II applied his concept of a centralized state to the colonies by creating an enormous colony called the **Dominion of New England**. The Dominion included all the New England colonies (Massachusetts, New Hampshire, Plymouth, Connecticut, New Haven, and Rhode Island) and in 1688 was enlarged by the addition of New York and New Jersey. James placed in charge Sir Edmund Andros, a former colonial governor of New York. Loyal to James II and his family, Andros had little sympathy for New Englanders. His regime caused great uneasiness among New England Puritans when it called into question the many land titles that did not acknowledge the king and imposed fees for their reconfirmation. Andros also committed himself to enforcing the Navigation Acts, a move that threatened to disrupt the region's trade, which was based largely on smuggling.

In England, opponents of James II's efforts to create a centralized Catholic state were known as Whigs. The Whigs worked to depose James, and in late 1688 they succeeded, an event they celebrated as the **Glorious Revolution** while James fled to the court of Louis XIV in France. William III (William of Orange) and his wife Mary II ascended the throne in 1689.

The Glorious Revolution spilled over into the colonies. In 1689, Bostonians overthrew the government of the Dominion of New England and jailed Sir Edmund Andros as well as other leaders of the regime (**Figure 4.8**). The removal of Andros from power illustrates New England's animosity toward the English overlord who had, during his tenure, established Church of England worship in Puritan Boston and vigorously enforced the Navigation Acts, to the chagrin of those in port towns. In New York, the same year that Andros fell from power, Jacob Leisler led a group of Protestant New Yorkers against the dominion government. Acting on his own authority, Leisler assumed the role of King William's governor and organized intercolonial military action independent of British authority. Leisler's actions usurped the crown's prerogative and, as a result, he was tried for treason and executed. In 1691, England restored control over the Province of New York.

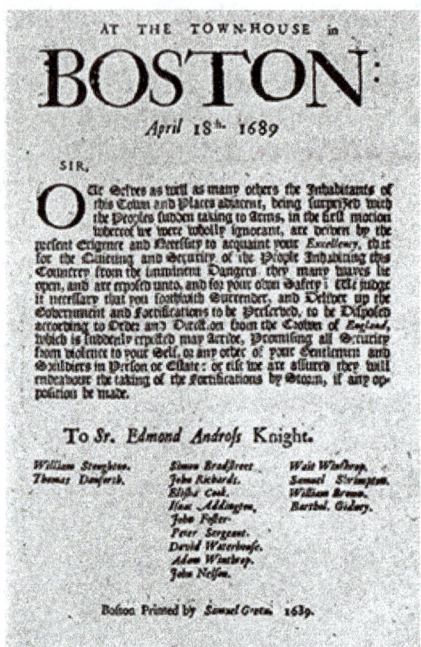

Figure 4.8 This broadside, signed by several citizens, demands the surrender of Sir Edmund (spelled here "Edmond") Andros, James II's hand-picked leader of the Dominion of New England.

The Glorious Revolution provided a shared experience for those who lived through the tumult of 1688 and 1689. Subsequent generations kept the memory of the Glorious Revolution alive as a heroic defense of English liberty against a would-be tyrant.

ENGLISH LIBERTY

The Glorious Revolution led to the establishment of an English nation that limited the power of the king and provided protections for English subjects. In October 1689, the same year that William and Mary took the throne, the 1689 Bill of Rights established a constitutional monarchy. It stipulated Parliament's independence from the monarchy and protected certain of Parliament's rights, such as the right to freedom of speech, the right to regular elections, and the right to petition the king. The 1689 Bill of Rights also guaranteed certain rights to all English subjects, including trial by jury and habeas corpus (the requirement that authorities bring an imprisoned person before a court to demonstrate the cause of the imprisonment).

John Locke (1632–1704), a doctor and educator who had lived in exile in Holland during the reign of James II and returned to England after the Glorious Revolution, published his *Two Treatises of Government* in 1690. In it, he argued that government was a form of contract between the leaders and the people, and that representative government existed to protect "life, liberty and property." Locke rejected the divine right of kings and instead advocated for the central role of Parliament with a limited monarchy. Locke's political philosophy had an enormous impact on future generations of colonists and established the paramount importance of representation in government.

> ### Click and Explore
>
>
> Visit the **Digital Locke Project** (http://openstaxcollege.org/l/jlocke) to read more of John Locke's writings. This digital collection contains over thirty of his philosophical texts.

The Glorious Revolution also led to the English Toleration Act of 1689, a law passed by Parliament that allowed for greater religious diversity in the Empire. This act granted religious tolerance to **nonconformist** Trinitarian Protestants (those who believed in the Holy Trinity of God the Father, Son, and Holy Ghost), such as Baptists (those who advocated adult baptism) and Congregationalists (those who followed the Puritans' lead in creating independent churches). While the Church of England remained the official state religious establishment, the Toleration Act gave much greater religious freedom to nonconformists. However, this tolerance did not extend to Catholics, who were routinely excluded from political power. The 1689 Toleration Act extended to the British colonies, where several colonies—Pennsylvania, Rhode Island, Delaware, and New Jersey—refused to allow the creation of an established colonial church, a major step toward greater religious diversity.

4.3 An Empire of Slavery and the Consumer Revolution

> By the end of this section, you will be able to:
> - Analyze the role slavery played in the history and economy of the British Empire
> - Explain the effects of the 1739 Stono Rebellion and the 1741 New York Conspiracy Trials
> - Describe the consumer revolution and its effect on the life of the colonial gentry and other settlers

Slavery formed a cornerstone of the British Empire in the eighteenth century. Every colony had slaves, from the southern rice plantations in Charles Town, South Carolina, to the northern wharves of Boston. Slavery was more than a labor system; it also influenced every aspect of colonial thought and culture. The uneven relationship it engendered gave white colonists an exaggerated sense of their own status. English liberty gained greater meaning and coherence for whites when they contrasted their status to that of the unfree class of black slaves in British America. African slavery provided whites in the colonies with a shared racial bond and identity.

SLAVERY AND THE STONO REBELLION

The transport of slaves to the American colonies accelerated in the second half of the seventeenth century. In 1660, Charles II created the Royal African Company (**Figure 4.9**) to trade in slaves and African goods. His brother, James II, led the company before ascending the throne. Under both these kings, the Royal African Company enjoyed a monopoly to transport slaves to the English colonies. Between 1672 and 1713, the company bought 125,000 captives on the African coast, losing 20 percent of them to death on the Middle Passage, the journey from the African coast to the Americas.

Figure 4.9 The 1686 English guinea shows the logo of the Royal African Company, an elephant and castle, beneath a bust of King James II. The coins were commonly called guineas because most British gold came from Guinea in West Africa.

The Royal African Company's monopoly ended in 1689 as a result of the Glorious Revolution. After that date, many more English merchants engaged in the slave trade, greatly increasing the number of slaves being transported. Africans who survived the brutal Middle Passage usually arrived in the West Indies, often in Barbados. From there, they were transported to the mainland English colonies on company ships. While merchants in London, Bristol, and Liverpool lined their pockets, Africans trafficked by the company endured a nightmare of misery, privation, and dislocation.

Slaves strove to adapt to their new lives by forming new communities among themselves, often adhering to traditional African customs and healing techniques. Indeed, the development of families and communities formed the most important response to the trauma of being enslaved. Other slaves dealt with the trauma of their situation by actively resisting their condition, whether by defying their masters or running away. Runaway slaves formed what were called "maroon" communities, groups that successfully resisted recapture and formed their own autonomous groups. The most prominent of these communities lived in the interior of Jamaica, controlling the area and keeping the British away.

Slaves everywhere resisted their exploitation and attempted to gain freedom. They fully understood that rebellions would bring about massive retaliation from whites and therefore had little chance of success. Even so, rebellions occurred frequently. One notable uprising that became known as the Stono Rebellion took place in South Carolina in September 1739. A literate slave named Jemmy led a large group of slaves in an armed insurrection against white colonists, killing several before militia stopped them. The militia suppressed the rebellion after a battle in which both slaves and militiamen were killed, and the remaining slaves were executed or sold to the West Indies.

Jemmy is believed to have been taken from the Kingdom of Kongo, an area where the Portuguese had introduced Catholicism. Other slaves in South Carolina may have had a similar background: Africa-born and familiar with whites. If so, this common background may have made it easier for Jemmy to communicate with the other slaves, enabling them to work together to resist their enslavement even though slaveholders labored to keep slaves from forging such communities.

In the wake of the Stono Rebellion, South Carolina passed a new slave code in 1740 called An Act for the Better Ordering and Governing of Negroes and Other Slaves in the Province, also known as the Negro Act of 1740. This law imposed new limits on slaves' behavior, prohibiting slaves from assembling, growing their own food, learning to write, and traveling freely.

THE NEW YORK CONSPIRACY TRIALS OF 1741

Eighteenth-century New York City contained many different ethnic groups, and conflicts among them created strain. In addition, one in five New Yorkers was a slave, and tensions ran high between slaves and the free population, especially in the aftermath of the Stono Rebellion. These tensions burst forth in 1741.

That year, thirteen fires broke out in the city, one of which reduced the colony's Fort George to ashes. Ever fearful of an uprising among enslaved New Yorkers, the city's whites spread rumors that the fires were part of a massive slave revolt in which slaves would murder whites, burn the city, and take over the colony. The Stono Rebellion was only a few years in the past, and throughout British America, fears of similar incidents were still fresh. Searching for solutions, and convinced slaves were the principal danger, nervous British authorities interrogated almost two hundred slaves and accused them of conspiracy. Rumors that Roman Catholics had joined the suspected conspiracy and planned to murder Protestant inhabitants of the city only added to the general hysteria. Very quickly, two hundred people were arrested, including a large number of the city's slave population.

After a quick series of trials at City Hall, known as the New York Conspiracy Trials of 1741, the government executed seventeen New Yorkers. Thirteen black men were publicly burned at the stake, while the others (including four whites) were hanged (**Figure 4.10**). Seventy slaves were sold to the West Indies. Little evidence exists to prove that an elaborate conspiracy, like the one white New Yorkers imagined, actually existed.

Figure 4.10 In the wake of a series of fires throughout New York City, rumors of a slave revolt led authorities to convict and execute thirty people, including thirteen black men who were publicly burned at the stake.

The events of 1741 in New York City illustrate the racial divide in British America, where panic among whites spurred great violence against and repression of the feared slave population. In the end, the Conspiracy Trials furthered white dominance and power over enslaved New Yorkers.

COLONIAL GENTRY AND THE CONSUMER REVOLUTION

British Americans' reliance on indentured servitude and slavery to meet the demand for colonial labor helped give rise to a wealthy colonial class—the gentry—in the Chesapeake tobacco colonies and elsewhere. To be "genteel," that is, a member of the gentry, meant to be refined, free of all rudeness. The British American gentry modeled themselves on the English aristocracy, who embodied the ideal of refinement and gentility. They built elaborate mansions to advertise their status and power. William Byrd II of Westover, Virginia, exemplifies the colonial gentry; a wealthy planter and slaveholder, he is known for founding Richmond and for his diaries documenting the life of a gentleman planter (**Figure 4.11**).

Figure 4.11 This painting by Hans Hysing, ca. 1724, depicts William Byrd II. Byrd was a wealthy gentleman planter in Virginia and a member of the colonial gentry.

MY STORY

William Byrd's Secret Diary

The diary of William Byrd, a Virginia planter, provides a unique way to better understand colonial life on a plantation (**Figure 4.12**). What does it show about daily life for a gentleman planter? What does it show about slavery?

> August 27, 1709
> I rose at 5 o'clock and read two chapters in Hebrew and some Greek in Josephus. I said my prayers and ate milk for breakfast. I danced my dance. I had like to have whipped my maid Anaka for her laziness but I forgave her. I read a little geometry. I denied my man G-r-l to go to a horse race because there was nothing but swearing and drinking there. I ate roast mutton for dinner. In the afternoon I played at piquet with my own wife and made her out of humor by cheating her. I read some Greek in Homer. Then I walked about the plantation. I lent John H-ch £7 [7 English pounds] in his distress. I said my prayers and had good health, good thoughts, and good humor, thanks be to God Almighty.
>
> September 6, 1709
> About one o'clock this morning my wife was happily delivered of a son, thanks be to God Almighty. I was awake in a blink and rose and my cousin Harrison met me on the stairs and told me it was a boy. We drank some French wine and went to bed again and rose at 7 o'clock. I read a chapter in Hebrew and then drank chocolate with the women for breakfast. I returned God humble thanks for so great a blessing and recommended my young son to His divine protection. . . .
>
> September 15, 1710
> I rose at 5 o'clock and read two chapters in Hebrew and some Greek in Thucydides. I said my prayers and ate milk and pears for breakfast. About 7 o'clock the negro boy [*or* Betty] that ran away was brought home. My wife against my will caused little Jenny to be burned with a hot iron, for which I quarreled with her. . . .

This content is available for free at http://cnx.org/content/col11740/latest/

Figure 4.12 This photograph shows the view down the stairway from the third floor of Westover Plantation, home of William Byrd II. What does this image suggest about the lifestyle of the inhabitants—masters and servants—of this house?

One of the ways in which the gentry set themselves apart from others was through their purchase, consumption, and display of goods. An increased supply of consumer goods from England that became available in the eighteenth century led to a phenomenon called the consumer revolution. These products linked the colonies to Great Britain in real and tangible ways. Indeed, along with the colonial gentry, ordinary settlers in the colonies also participated in the frenzy of consumer spending on goods from Great Britain. Tea, for example, came to be regarded as the drink of the Empire, with or without fashionable tea sets.

The consumer revolution also made printed materials more widely available. Before 1680, for instance, no newspapers had been printed in colonial America. In the eighteenth century, however, a flood of journals, books, pamphlets, and other publications became available to readers on both sides of the Atlantic. This shared trove of printed matter linked members of the Empire by creating a community of shared tastes and ideas.

Cato's Letters, by Englishmen John Trenchard and Thomas Gordon, was one popular series of 144 pamphlets. These Whig circulars were published between 1720 and 1723 and emphasized the glory of England, especially its commitment to liberty. However, the pamphlets cautioned readers to be ever vigilant and on the lookout for attacks upon that liberty. Indeed, *Cato's Letters* suggested that there were constant efforts to undermine and destroy it.

Another very popular publication was the English gentlemen's magazine the *Spectator*, published between 1711 and 1714. In each issue, "Mr. Spectator" observed and commented on the world around him. What made the *Spectator* so wildly popular was its style; the essays were meant to persuade, and to cultivate among readers a refined set of behaviors, rejecting deceit and intolerance and focusing instead on the polishing of genteel taste and manners.

Novels, a new type of literature, made their first appearance in the eighteenth century and proved very popular in the British Atlantic. Daniel Defoe's *Robinson Crusoe* and Samuel Richardson's *Pamela: Or, Virtue Rewarded* found large and receptive audiences. Reading also allowed female readers the opportunity to interpret what they read without depending on a male authority to tell them what to think. Few women beyond the colonial gentry, however, had access to novels.

4.4 Great Awakening and Enlightenment

By the end of this section, you will be able to:
- Explain the significance of the Great Awakening
- Describe the genesis, central ideas, and effects of the Enlightenment in British North America

Two major cultural movements further strengthened Anglo-American colonists' connection to Great Britain: the Great Awakening and the Enlightenment. Both movements began in Europe, but they advocated very different ideas: the Great Awakening promoted a fervent, emotional religiosity, while the Enlightenment encouraged the pursuit of reason in all things. On both sides of the Atlantic, British subjects grappled with these new ideas.

THE FIRST GREAT AWAKENING

During the eighteenth century, the British Atlantic experienced an outburst of Protestant revivalism known as the **First Great Awakening**. (A Second Great Awakening would take place in the 1800s.) During the First Great Awakening, evangelists came from the ranks of several Protestant denominations: Congregationalists, Anglicans (members of the Church of England), and Presbyterians. They rejected what appeared to be sterile, formal modes of worship in favor of a vigorous emotional religiosity. Whereas Martin Luther and John Calvin had preached a doctrine of predestination and close reading of scripture, new evangelical ministers spread a message of personal and experiential faith that rose above mere book learning. Individuals could bring about their own salvation by accepting Christ, an especially welcome message for those who had felt excluded by traditional Protestantism: women, the young, and people at the lower end of the social spectrum.

The Great Awakening caused a split between those who followed the evangelical message (the "New Lights") and those who rejected it (the "Old Lights"). The elite ministers in British America were firmly Old Lights, and they censured the new revivalism as chaos. Indeed, the revivals did sometimes lead to excess. In one notorious incident in 1743, an influential New Light minister named James Davenport urged his listeners to burn books. The next day, he told them to burn their clothes as a sign of their casting off the sinful trappings of the world. He then took off his own pants and threw them into the fire, but a woman saved them and tossed them back to Davenport, telling him he had gone too far.

Another outburst of Protestant revivalism began in New Jersey, led by a minister of the Dutch Reformed Church named Theodorus Frelinghuysen. Frelinghuysen's example inspired other ministers, including Gilbert Tennent, a Presbyterian. Tennant helped to spark a Presbyterian revival in the Middle Colonies (Pennsylvania, New York, and New Jersey), in part by founding a seminary to train other evangelical clergyman. New Lights also founded colleges in Rhode Island and New Hampshire that would later become Brown University and Dartmouth College.

In Northampton, Massachusetts, Jonathan Edwards led still another explosion of evangelical fervor. Edwards's best-known sermon, "Sinners in the Hands of an Angry God," used powerful word imagery to describe the terrors of hell and the possibilities of avoiding damnation by personal conversion (**Figure 4.13**). One passage reads: "The wrath of God burns against them [sinners], their damnation don't slumber, the pit is prepared, the fire is made ready, the furnace is now hot, ready to receive them, the flames do now rage and glow. The glittering sword is whet, and held over them, and the pit hath opened her mouth under them." Edwards's revival spread along the Connecticut River Valley, and news of the event spread rapidly through the frequent reprinting of his famous sermon.

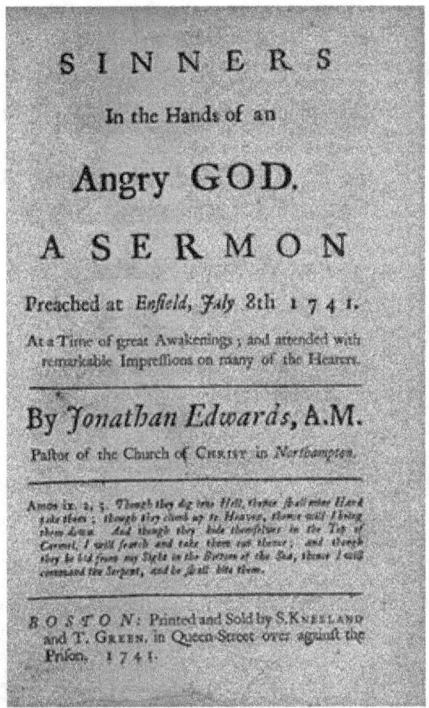

Figure 4.13 This image shows the frontispiece of *Sinners in the Hands of an Angry God, A Sermon Preached at Enfield, July 8, 1741* by Jonathan Edwards. Edwards was an evangelical preacher who led a Protestant revival in New England. This was his most famous sermon, the text of which was reprinted often and distributed widely.

The foremost evangelical of the Great Awakening was an Anglican minister named George Whitefield. Like many evangelical ministers, Whitefield was itinerant, traveling the countryside instead of having his own church and congregation. Between 1739 and 1740, he electrified colonial listeners with his brilliant oratory.

AMERICANA

✪ Two Opposing Views of George Whitefield

Not everyone embraced George Whitefield and other New Lights. Many established Old Lights decried the way the new evangelical religions appealed to people's passions, rather than to traditional religious values. The two illustrations below present two very different visions of George Whitefield (**Figure 4.14**).

(a)

(b)

Figure 4.14 In the 1774 portrait of George Whitefield by engraver Elisha Gallaudet (a), Whitefield appears with a gentle expression on his face. Although his hands are raised in exultation or entreaty, he does not look particularly roused or rousing. In the 1763 British political cartoon to the right, "Dr. Squintum's Exaltation or the Reformation" (b), Whitefield's hands are raised in a similar position, but there the similarities end.

Compare the two images above. On the left is an illustration for Whitefield's memoirs, while on the right is a cartoon satirizing the circus-like atmosphere that his preaching seemed to attract (Dr. Squintum was a nickname for Whitefield, who was cross-eyed). How do these two artists portray the same man? What emotions are the illustration for his memoirs intended to evoke? What details can you find in the cartoon that indicate the artist's distaste for the preacher?

The Great Awakening saw the rise of several Protestant denominations, including Methodists, Presbyterians, and Baptists (who emphasized adult baptism of converted Christians rather than infant baptism). These new churches gained converts and competed with older Protestant groups like Anglicans (members of the Church of England), Congregationalists (the heirs of Puritanism in America), and Quakers. The influence of these older Protestant groups, such as the New England Congregationalists, declined because of the Great Awakening. Nonetheless, the Great Awakening touched the lives of thousands on both sides of the Atlantic and provided a shared experience in the eighteenth-century British Empire.

THE ENLIGHTENMENT

The **Enlightenment**, or the Age of Reason, was an intellectual and cultural movement in the eighteenth century that emphasized reason over superstition and science over blind faith. Using the power of the press, Enlightenment thinkers like John Locke, Isaac Newton, and Voltaire questioned accepted knowledge and spread new ideas about openness, investigation, and religious tolerance throughout

Europe and the Americas. Many consider the Enlightenment a major turning point in Western civilization, an age of light replacing an age of darkness.

Several ideas dominated Enlightenment thought, including rationalism, empiricism, progressivism, and cosmopolitanism. Rationalism is the idea that humans are capable of using their faculty of reason to gain knowledge. This was a sharp turn away from the prevailing idea that people needed to rely on scripture or church authorities for knowledge. Empiricism promotes the idea that knowledge comes from experience and observation of the world. Progressivism is the belief that through their powers of reason and observation, humans could make unlimited, linear progress over time; this belief was especially important as a response to the carnage and upheaval of the English Civil Wars in the seventeenth century. Finally, cosmopolitanism reflected Enlightenment thinkers' view of themselves as citizens of the world and actively engaged in it, as opposed to being provincial and close-minded. In all, Enlightenment thinkers endeavored to be ruled by reason, not prejudice.

The **Freemasons** were a fraternal society that advocated Enlightenment principles of inquiry and tolerance. Freemasonry originated in London coffeehouses in the early eighteenth century, and Masonic lodges (local units) soon spread throughout Europe and the British colonies. One prominent Freemason, Benjamin Franklin, stands as the embodiment of the Enlightenment in British America (**Figure 4.15**). Born in Boston in 1706 to a large Puritan family, Franklin loved to read, although he found little beyond religious publications in his father's house. In 1718 he was apprenticed to his brother to work in a print shop, where he learned how to be a good writer by copying the style he found in the *Spectator*, which his brother printed. At the age of seventeen, the independent-minded Franklin ran away, eventually ending up in Quaker Philadelphia. There he began publishing the *Pennsylvania Gazette* in the late 1720s, and in 1732 he started his annual publication *Poor Richard: An Almanack*, in which he gave readers much practical advice, such as "Early to bed, early to rise, makes a man healthy, wealthy, and wise."

Figure 4.15 In this 1748 portrait by Robert Feke, a forty-year-old Franklin wears a stylish British wig, as befitted a proud and loyal member of the British Empire.

Franklin subscribed to **deism**, an Enlightenment-era belief in a God who created, but has no continuing involvement in, the world and the events within it. Deists also advanced the belief that personal morality—an individual's moral compass, leading to good works and actions—is more important than strict church doctrines. Franklin's deism guided his many philanthropic projects. In 1731, he established a reading library that became the Library Company of Philadelphia. In 1743, he founded the American Philosophical Society to encourage the spirit of inquiry. In 1749, he provided the foundation for the University of Pennsylvania, and in 1751, he helped found Pennsylvania Hospital.

His career as a printer made Franklin wealthy and well-respected. When he retired in 1748, he devoted himself to politics and scientific experiments. His most famous work, on electricity, exemplified Enlightenment principles. Franklin observed that lightning strikes tended to hit metal objects and reasoned that he could therefore direct lightning through the placement of metal objects during an electrical storm. He used this knowledge to advocate the use of lightning rods: metal poles connected to wires directing lightning's electrical charge into the ground and saving wooden homes in cities like Philadelphia from catastrophic fires. He published his findings in 1751, in *Experiments and Observations on Electricity*.

Franklin also wrote of his "rags to riches" tale, his *Memoir*, in the 1770s and 1780s. This story laid the foundation for the American Dream of upward social mobility.

Click and Explore

Visit the Worldly Ways section (http://openstaxcollege.org/l/bfranklin1) of PBS's Benjamin Franklin site to see an interactive map showing Franklin's overseas travels and his influence around the world. His diplomatic, political, scientific, and business achievements had great effects in many countries.

THE FOUNDING OF GEORGIA

The reach of Enlightenment thought was both broad and deep. In the 1730s, it even prompted the founding of a new colony. Having witnessed the terrible conditions of debtors' prison, as well as the results of releasing penniless debtors onto the streets of London, James Oglethorpe, a member of Parliament and advocate of social reform, petitioned King George II for a charter to start a new colony. George II, understanding the strategic advantage of a British colony standing as a buffer between South Carolina and Spanish Florida, granted the charter to Oglethorpe and twenty like-minded proprietors in 1732. Oglethorpe led the settlement of the colony, which was called Georgia in honor of the king. In 1733, he and 113 immigrants arrived on the ship *Anne*. Over the next decade, Parliament funded the migration of twenty-five hundred settlers, making Georgia the only government-funded colonial project.

Oglethorpe's vision for Georgia followed the ideals of the Age of Reason, seeing it as a place for England's "worthy poor" to start anew. To encourage industry, he gave each male immigrant fifty acres of land, tools, and a year's worth of supplies. In Savannah, the Oglethorpe Plan provided for a utopia: "an agrarian model of sustenance while sustaining egalitarian values holding all men as equal."

Oglethorpe's vision called for alcohol and slavery to be banned. However, colonists who relocated from other colonies, especially South Carolina, disregarded these prohibitions. Despite its proprietors' early vision of a colony guided by Enlightenment ideals and free of slavery, by the 1750s, Georgia was producing quantities of rice grown and harvested by slaves.

4.5 Wars for Empire

By the end of this section, you will be able to:
- Describe the wars for empire
- Analyze the significance of these conflicts

Wars for empire composed a final link connecting the Atlantic sides of the British Empire. Great Britain fought four separate wars against Catholic France from the late 1600s to the mid-1700s. Another war, the War of Jenkins' Ear, pitted Britain against Spain. These conflicts for control of North America also helped colonists forge important alliances with native peoples, as different tribes aligned themselves with different European powers.

GENERATIONS OF WARFARE

Generations of British colonists grew up during a time when much of North America, especially the Northeast, engaged in war. Colonists knew war firsthand. In the eighteenth century, fighting was seasonal. Armies mobilized in the spring, fought in the summer, and retired to winter quarters in the fall. The British army imposed harsh discipline on its soldiers, who were drawn from the poorer classes, to ensure they did not step out of line during engagements. If they did, their officers would kill them. On the battlefield, armies dressed in bright uniforms to advertise their bravery and lack of fear. They stood in tight formation and exchanged volleys with the enemy. They often feared their officers more than the enemy.

Click and Explore

Read the diary of a provincial soldier who fought in the French and Indian War on the Captain David Perry Web Site (http://openstaxcollege.org/l/DPerry) hosted by Rootsweb. David Perry's journal, which includes a description of the 1758 campaign, provides a glimpse of warfare in the eighteenth century.

Most imperial conflicts had both American and European fronts, leaving us with two names for each war. For instance, King William's War (1688–1697) is also known as the War of the League of Augsburg. In America, the bulk of the fighting in this conflict took place between New England and New France. The war proved inconclusive, with no clear victor (**Figure 4.16**).

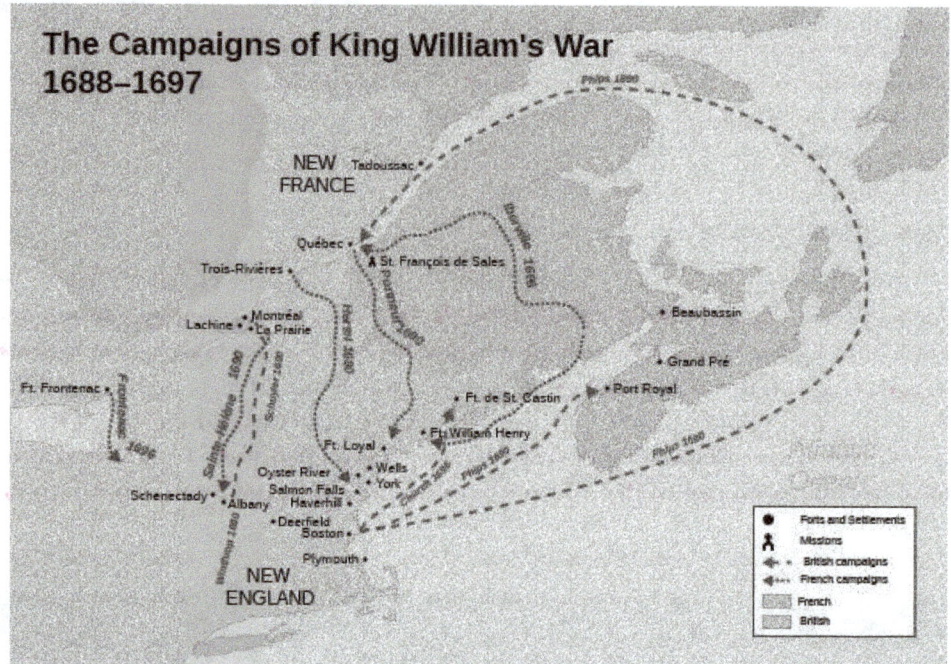

Figure 4.16 This map shows the French and British armies' movements during King William's War, in which there was no clear victor.

Queen Anne's War (1702–1713) is also known as the War of Spanish Succession. England fought against both Spain and France over who would ascend the Spanish throne after the last of the Hapsburg rulers died. In North America, fighting took place in Florida, New England, and New France. In Canada, the French prevailed but lost Acadia and Newfoundland; however, the victory was again not decisive because the English failed to take Quebec, which would have given them control of Canada.

This conflict is best remembered in the United States for the French and Indian raid against Deerfield, Massachusetts, in 1704. A small French force, combined with a native group made up of Catholic Mohawks and Abenaki (Pocumtucs), attacked the frontier outpost of Deerfield, killing scores and taking 112 prisoners. Among the captives was the seven-year-old daughter of Deerfield's minister John Williams, named Eunice. She was held by the Mohawks for years as her family tried to get her back, and became assimilated into the tribe. To the horror of the Puritan leaders, when she grew up Eunice married a Mohawk and refused to return to New England.

In North America, possession of Georgia and trade with the interior was the focus of the War of Jenkins' Ear (1739–1742), a conflict between Britain and Spain over contested claims to the land occupied by the fledgling colony between South Carolina and Florida. The war got its name from an incident in 1731 in which a Spanish Coast Guard captain severed the ear of British captain Robert Jenkins as punishment for raiding Spanish ships in Panama. Jenkins fueled the growing animosity between England and Spain by presenting his ear to Parliament and stirring up British public outrage. More than anything else, the War of Jenkins' Ear disrupted the Atlantic trade, a situation that hurt both Spain and Britain and was a major reason the war came to a close in 1742. Georgia, founded six years earlier, remained British and a buffer against Spanish Florida.

King George's War (1744–1748), known in Europe as the War of Austrian Succession (1740–1748), was fought in the northern colonies and New France. In 1745, the British took the massive French fortress at Louisbourg on Cape Breton Island, Nova Scotia (**Figure 4.17**). However, three years later, under the terms of the Treaty of Aix-la-Chapelle, Britain relinquished control of the fortress to the French. Once again, war resulted in an incomplete victory for both Britain and France.

Figure 4.17 In this 1747 painting by J. Stevens, *View of the landing of the New England forces in ye expedition against Cape Breton*, British forces land on the island of Cape Breton to capture Fort Louisbourg.

THE FRENCH AND INDIAN WAR

The final imperial war, the **French and Indian War** (1754–1763), known as the Seven Years' War in Europe, proved to be the decisive contest between Britain and France in America. It began over rival claims along the frontier in present-day western Pennsylvania. Well-connected planters from Virginia faced stagnant tobacco prices and hoped expanding into these western lands would stabilize their wealth and status. Some of them established the Ohio Company of Virginia in 1748, and the British crown granted the company half a million acres in 1749. However, the French also claimed the lands of the Ohio Company, and to protect the region they established Fort Duquesne in 1754, where the Ohio, Monongahela, and Allegheny Rivers met.

The war began in May 1754 because of these competing claims between Britain and France. Twenty-two-year-old Virginian George Washington, a surveyor whose family helped to found the Ohio Company, gave the command to fire on French soldiers near present-day Uniontown, Pennsylvania. This incident on the Pennsylvania frontier proved to be a decisive event that led to imperial war. For the next decade, fighting took place along the frontier of New France and British America from Virginia to Maine. The war also spread to Europe as France and Britain looked to gain supremacy in the Atlantic World.

The British fared poorly in the first years of the war. In 1754, the French and their native allies forced Washington to surrender at Fort Necessity, a hastily built fort constructed after his attack on the French. In 1755, Britain dispatched General Edward Braddock to the colonies to take Fort Duquesne. The French, aided by the Potawotomis, Ottawas, Shawnees, and Delawares, ambushed the fifteen hundred British soldiers and Virginia militia who marched to the fort. The attack sent panic through the British force, and hundreds of British soldiers and militiamen died, including General Braddock. The campaign of 1755 proved to be a disaster for the British. In fact, the only British victory that year was the capture of Nova Scotia. In 1756 and 1757, Britain suffered further defeats with the fall of Fort Oswego and Fort William Henry (**Figure 4.18**).

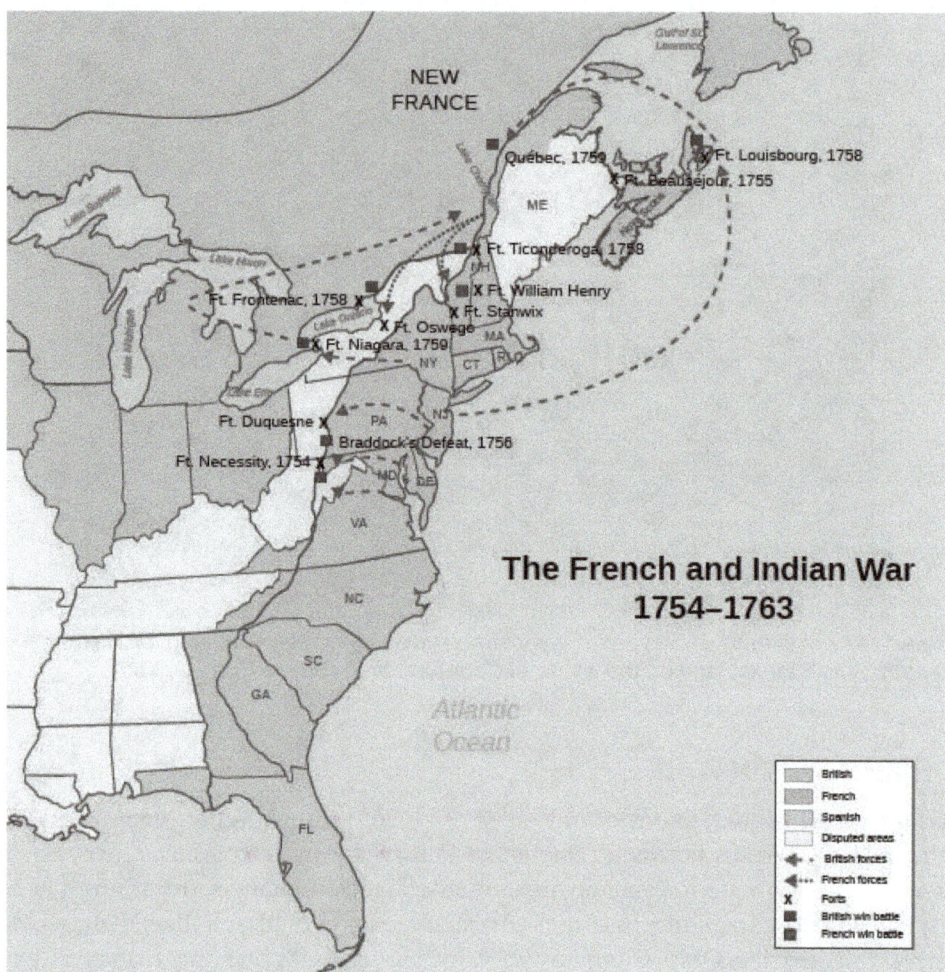

Figure 4.18 This schematic map depicts the events of the French and Indian War. Note the scarcity of British victories.

The war began to turn in favor of the British in 1758, due in large part to the efforts of William Pitt, a very popular member of Parliament. Pitt pledged huge sums of money and resources to defeating the hated Catholic French, and Great Britain spent part of the money on bounties paid to new young recruits in the colonies, helping invigorate the British forces. In 1758, the Iroquois, Delaware, and Shawnee signed the Treaty of Easton, aligning themselves with the British in return for some contested land around Pennsylvania and Virginia. In 1759, the British took Quebec, and in 1760, Montreal. The French empire in North America had crumbled.

The war continued until 1763, when the French signed the Treaty of Paris. This treaty signaled a dramatic reversal of fortune for France. Indeed, New France, which had been founded in the early 1600s, ceased to exist. The British Empire had now gained mastery over North America. The Empire not only gained New France under the treaty; it also acquired French sugar islands in the West Indies, French trading posts in India, and French-held posts on the west coast of Africa. Great Britain's victory in the French and Indian War meant that it had become a truly global empire. British colonists joyously celebrated, singing the refrain of "Rule, Britannia! / Britannia, rule the waves! / Britons never, never, never shall be slaves!"

In the American colonies, ties with Great Britain were closer than ever. Professional British soldiers had fought alongside Anglo-American militiamen, forging a greater sense of shared identity. With Great Britain's victory, colonial pride ran high as colonists celebrated their identity as British subjects. This last of the wars for empire, however, also sowed the seeds of trouble. The war led Great Britain deeply into debt, and in the 1760s and 1770s, efforts to deal with the debt through imperial reforms would have the unintended consequence of causing stress and strain that threatened to tear the Empire apart.

This content is available for free at http://cnx.org/content/col11740/latest/

CHAPTER 5
Imperial Reforms and Colonial Protests, 1763-1774

Figure 5.1 *The Bostonians Paying the Excise-man, or Tarring and Feathering* (1774), attributed to Philip Dawe, depicts the most publicized tarring and feathering incident of the American Revolution. The victim is John Malcolm, a customs official loyal to the British crown.

Chapter Outline
5.1 Confronting the National Debt: The Aftermath of the French and Indian War
5.2 The Stamp Act and the Sons and Daughters of Liberty
5.3 The Townshend Acts and Colonial Protest
5.4 The Destruction of the Tea and the Coercive Acts
5.5 Disaffection: The First Continental Congress and American Identity

Introduction

The Bostonians Paying the Excise-man, or Tarring and Feathering (**Figure 5.1**), shows five Patriots tarring and feathering the Commissioner of Customs, John Malcolm, a sea captain, army officer, and staunch **Loyalist**. The print shows the Boston Tea Party, a protest against the Tea Act of 1773, and the Liberty Tree, an elm tree near Boston Common that became a rallying point against the Stamp Act of 1765. When the crowd threatened to hang Malcolm if he did not renounce his position as a royal customs officer, he reluctantly agreed and the protestors allowed him to go home. The scene represents the animosity toward those who supported royal authority and illustrates the high tide of unrest in the colonies after the British government imposed a series of imperial reform measures during the years 1763–1774.

The government's formerly lax oversight of the colonies ended as the architects of the British Empire put these new reforms in place. The British hoped to gain greater control over colonial trade and frontier settlement as well as to reduce the administrative cost of the colonies and the enormous debt left by the French and Indian War. Each step the British took, however, generated a backlash. Over time, imperial reforms pushed many colonists toward separation from the British Empire.

5.1 Confronting the National Debt: The Aftermath of the French and Indian War

> By the end of this section, you will be able to:
> - Discuss the status of Great Britain's North American colonies in the years directly following the French and Indian War
> - Describe the size and scope of the British debt at the end of the French and Indian War
> - Explain how the British Parliament responded to the debt crisis
> - Outline the purpose of the Proclamation Line, the Sugar Act, and the Currency Act

Great Britain had much to celebrate in 1763. The long and costly war with France had finally ended, and Great Britain had emerged victorious. British subjects on both sides of the Atlantic celebrated the strength of the British Empire. Colonial pride ran high; to live under the British Constitution and to have defeated the hated French Catholic menace brought great joy to British Protestants everywhere in the Empire. From Maine to Georgia, British colonists joyously celebrated the victory and sang the refrain of "Rule, Britannia! Britannia, rule the waves! Britons never, never, never shall be slaves!"

Despite the celebratory mood, the victory over France also produced major problems within the British Empire, problems that would have serious consequences for British colonists in the Americas. During the war, many Indian tribes had sided with the French, who supplied them with guns. After the 1763 Treaty of Paris that ended the French and Indian War (or the Seven Years' War), British colonists had to defend the frontier, where French colonists and their tribal allies remained a powerful force. The most organized resistance, Pontiac's Rebellion, highlighted tensions the settlers increasingly interpreted in racial terms.

The massive debt the war generated at home, however, proved to be the most serious issue facing Great Britain. The frontier had to be secure in order to prevent another costly war. Greater enforcement of imperial trade laws had to be put into place. Parliament had to find ways to raise revenue to pay off the crippling debt from the war. Everyone would have to contribute their expected share, including the British subjects across the Atlantic.

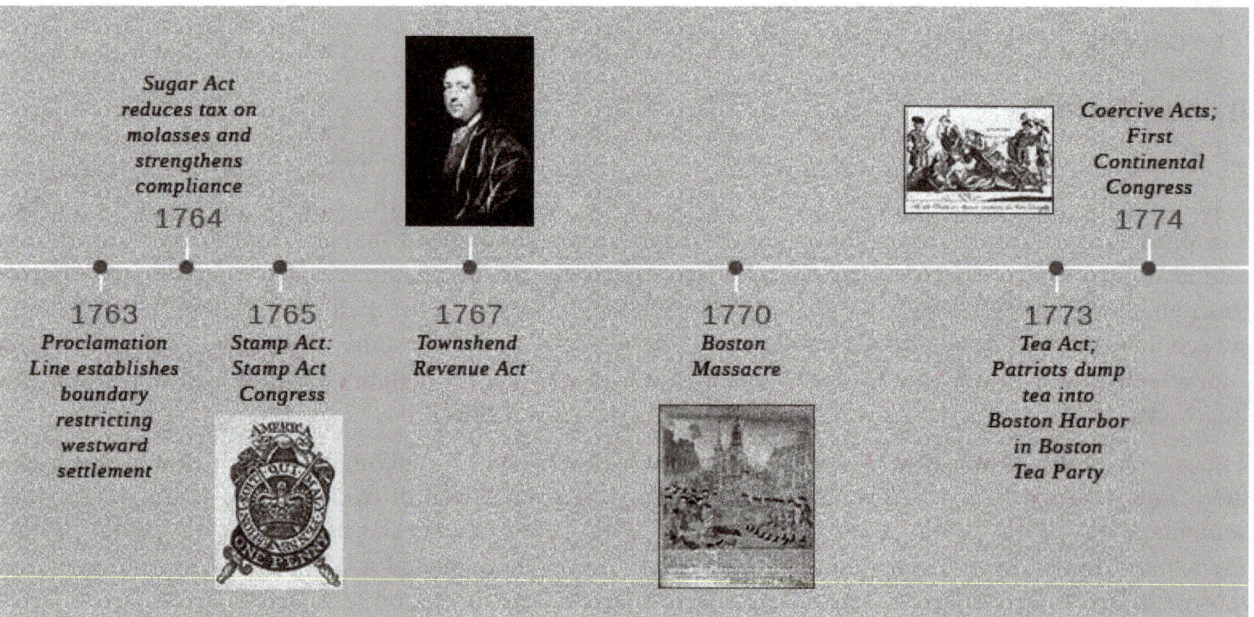

Figure 5.2 (credit "1765": modification of work by the United Kingdom Government)

PROBLEMS ON THE AMERICAN FRONTIER

With the end of the French and Indian War, Great Britain claimed a vast new expanse of territory, at least on paper. Under the terms of the Treaty of Paris, the French territory known as New France had ceased to exist. British territorial holdings now extended from Canada to Florida, and British military focus shifted to maintaining peace in the king's newly enlarged lands. However, much of the land in the American British Empire remained under the control of powerful native confederacies, which made any claims of British mastery beyond the Atlantic coastal settlements hollow. Great Britain maintained ten thousand troops in North America after the war ended in 1763 to defend the borders and repel any attack by their imperial rivals.

British colonists, eager for fresh land, poured over the Appalachian Mountains to stake claims. The western frontier had long been a "middle ground" where different imperial powers (British, French, Spanish) had interacted and compromised with native peoples. That era of accommodation in the "middle ground" came to an end after the French and Indian War. Virginians (including George Washington) and other land-hungry colonists had already raised tensions in the 1740s with their quest for land. Virginia landowners in particular eagerly looked to diversify their holdings beyond tobacco, which had stagnated in price and exhausted the fertility of the lands along the Chesapeake Bay. They invested heavily in the newly available land. This westward movement brought the settlers into conflict as never before with Indian tribes, such as the Shawnee, Seneca-Cayuga, Wyandot, and Delaware, who increasingly held their ground against any further intrusion by white settlers.

The treaty that ended the war between France and Great Britain proved to be a significant blow to native peoples, who had viewed the conflict as an opportunity to gain additional trade goods from both sides. With the French defeat, many Indians who had sided with France lost a valued trading partner as well as bargaining power over the British. Settlers' encroachment on their land, as well as the increased British military presence, changed the situation on the frontier dramatically. After the war, British troops took over the former French forts but failed to court favor with the local tribes by distributing ample gifts, as the French had done. They also significantly reduced the amount of gunpowder and ammunition they sold to the Indians, worsening relationships further.

Indians' resistance to colonists drew upon the teachings of Delaware (Lenni Lenape) prophet Neolin and the leadership of Ottawa war chief Pontiac. Neolin was a spiritual leader who preached a doctrine of shunning European culture and expelling Europeans from native lands. Neolin's beliefs united Indians from many villages. In a broad-based alliance that came to be known as Pontiac's Rebellion, Pontiac led a loose coalition of these native tribes against the colonists and the British army.

Pontiac started bringing his coalition together as early as 1761, urging Indians to "drive [the Europeans] out and make war upon them." The conflict began in earnest in 1763, when Pontiac and several hundred Ojibwas, Potawatomis, and Hurons laid siege to Fort Detroit. At the same time, Senecas, Shawnees, and Delawares laid siege to Fort Pitt. Over the next year, the war spread along the backcountry from Virginia to Pennsylvania. Pontiac's Rebellion (also known as Pontiac's War) triggered horrific violence on both sides. Firsthand reports of Indian attacks tell of murder, scalping, dismemberment, and burning at the stake. These stories incited a deep racial hatred among colonists against all Indians.

The actions of a group of Scots-Irish settlers from Paxton (or Paxtang), Pennsylvania, in December 1763, illustrates the deadly situation on the frontier. Forming a mob known as the Paxton Boys, these frontiersmen attacked a nearby group of Conestoga of the Susquehannock tribe. The Conestoga had lived peacefully with local settlers, but the Paxton Boys viewed all Indians as savages and they brutally murdered the six Conestoga they found at home and burned their houses. When Governor John Penn put the remaining fourteen Conestoga in protective custody in Lancaster, Pennsylvania, the Paxton Boys broke into the building and killed and scalped the Conestoga they found there (**Figure 5.3**). Although Governor Penn offered a reward for the capture of any Paxton Boys involved in the murders, no one ever identified the attackers. Some colonists reacted to the incident with outrage. Benjamin Franklin described the Paxton Boys as "the barbarous Men who committed the atrocious act, in Defiance of Government, of all Laws human and divine, and to the eternal Disgrace of their Country and Colour," stating that "the Wickedness cannot be covered, the Guilt will lie on the whole Land, till Justice is done on the Murderers. The blood of the innocent will cry to heaven for vengeance." Yet, as the inability to bring the perpetrators to justice clearly indicates, the Paxton Boys had many more supporters than critics.

Figure 5.3 This nineteenth-century lithograph depicts the massacre of Conestoga in 1763 at Lancaster, Pennsylvania, where they had been placed in protective custody. None of the attackers, members of the Paxton Boys, were ever identified.

Click and Explore

Visit **Explore PAhistory.com** (http://openstaxcollege.org/l/paxton) to read the full text of Benjamin Franklin's "Benjamin Franklin, An Account of the Paxton Boys' Murder of the Conestoga Indians, 1764."

Pontiac's Rebellion and the Paxton Boys' actions were examples of early American race wars, in which both sides saw themselves as inherently different from the other and believed the other needed to be eradicated. The prophet Neolin's message, which he said he received in a vision from the Master of Life, was: "Wherefore do you suffer the whites to dwell upon your lands? Drive them away; wage war against them." Pontiac echoed this idea in a meeting, exhorting tribes to join together against the British: "It is important for us, my brothers, that we exterminate from our lands this nation which seeks only to destroy us." In his letter suggesting "gifts" to the natives of smallpox-infected blankets, Field Marshal Jeffrey Amherst said, "You will do well to inoculate the Indians by means of blankets, as well as every other method that can serve to extirpate this execrable race." Pontiac's Rebellion came to an end in 1766, when it became clear that the French, whom Pontiac had hoped would side with his forces, would not be returning. The repercussions, however, would last much longer. Race relations between Indians and whites remained poisoned on the frontier.

Well aware of the problems on the frontier, the British government took steps to try to prevent bloodshed and another costly war. At the beginning of Pontiac's uprising, the British issued the Proclamation of 1763, which forbade white settlement west of the **Proclamation Line**, a borderline running along the spine of the Appalachian Mountains (**Figure 5.4**). The Proclamation Line aimed to forestall further conflict on the frontier, the clear flashpoint of tension in British North America. British colonists who had hoped to move west after the war chafed at this restriction, believing the war had been fought and won to ensure the right to settle west. The Proclamation Line therefore came as a setback to their vision of westward expansion.

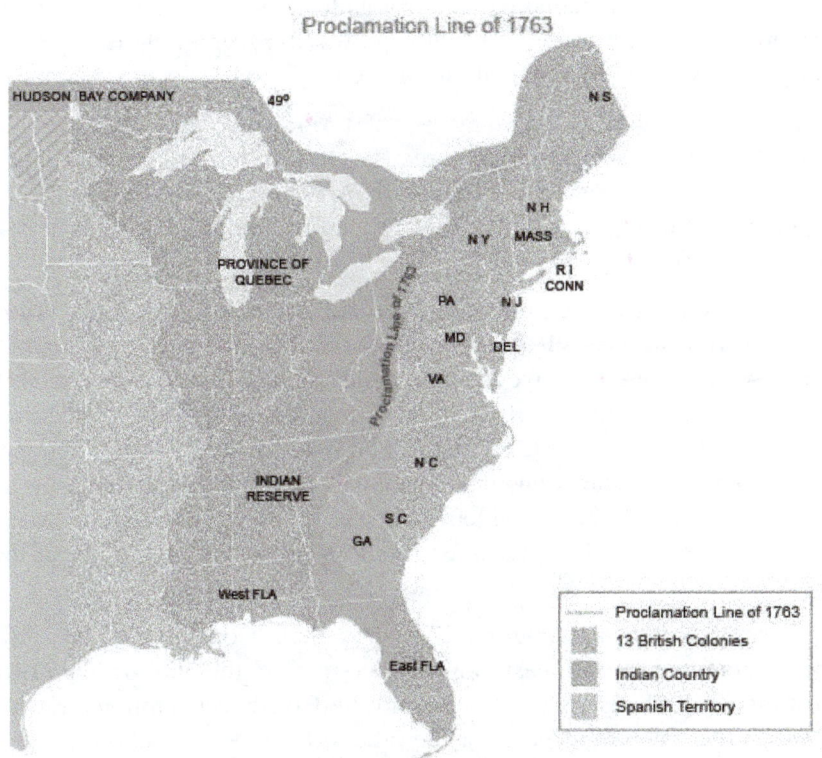

Figure 5.4 This map shows the status of the American colonies in 1763, after the end of the French and Indian War. Although Great Britain won control of the territory east of the Mississippi, the Proclamation Line of 1763 prohibited British colonists from settling west of the Appalachian Mountains. (credit: modification of work by the National Atlas of the United States)

THE BRITISH NATIONAL DEBT

Great Britain's newly enlarged empire meant a greater financial burden, and the mushrooming debt from the war was a major cause of concern. The war nearly doubled the British national debt, from £75 million in 1756 to £133 million in 1763. Interest payments alone consumed over half the national budget, and the continuing military presence in North America was a constant drain. The Empire needed more revenue to replenish its dwindling coffers. Those in Great Britain believed that British subjects in North America, as the major beneficiaries of Great Britain's war for global supremacy, should certainly shoulder their share of the financial burden.

The British government began increasing revenues by raising taxes at home, even as various interest groups lobbied to keep their taxes low. Powerful members of the aristocracy, well represented in Parliament, successfully convinced Prime Minister John Stuart, third earl of Bute, to refrain from raising taxes on land. The greater tax burden, therefore, fell on the lower classes in the form of increased import duties, which raised the prices of imported goods such as sugar and tobacco. George Grenville succeeded Bute as prime minister in 1763. Grenville determined to curtail government spending and make sure that, as subjects of the British Empire, the American colonists did their part to pay down the massive debt.

IMPERIAL REFORMS

The new era of greater British interest in the American colonies through imperial reforms picked up in pace in the mid-1760s. In 1764, Prime Minister Grenville introduced the Currency Act of 1764, prohibiting the colonies from printing additional paper money and requiring colonists to pay British merchants in gold and silver instead of the colonial paper money already in circulation. The Currency Act aimed to standardize the currency used in Atlantic trade, a logical reform designed to help stabilize the Empire's economy. This rule brought American economic activity under greater British control. Colonists relied on their own paper currency to conduct trade and, with gold and silver in short supply, they found their finances tight. Not surprisingly, they grumbled about the new imperial currency regulations.

Grenville also pushed Parliament to pass the Sugar Act of 1764, which actually lowered duties on British molasses by half, from six pence per gallon to three. Grenville designed this measure to address the problem of rampant colonial smuggling with the French sugar islands in the West Indies. The act attempted to make it easier for colonial traders, especially New England mariners who routinely engaged in illegal trade, to comply with the imperial law.

To give teeth to the 1764 Sugar Act, the law intensified enforcement provisions. Prior to the 1764 act, colonial violations of the Navigation Acts had been tried in local courts, where sympathetic colonial juries refused to convict merchants on trial. However, the Sugar Act required violators to be tried in **vice-admiralty courts**. These crown-sanctioned tribunals, which settled disputes that occurred at sea, operated without juries. Some colonists saw this feature of the 1764 act as dangerous. They argued that trial by jury had long been honored as a basic right of Englishmen under the British Constitution. To deprive defendants of a jury, they contended, meant reducing liberty-loving British subjects to political slavery. In the British Atlantic world, some colonists perceived this loss of liberty as parallel to the enslavement of Africans.

As loyal British subjects, colonists in America cherished their Constitution, an unwritten system of government that they celebrated as the best political system in the world. The British Constitution prescribed the roles of the King, the House of Lords, and the House of Commons. Each entity provided a check and balance against the worst tendencies of the others. If the King had too much power, the result would be tyranny. If the Lords had too much power, the result would be oligarchy. If the Commons had the balance of power, democracy or mob rule would prevail. The British Constitution promised representation of the will of British subjects, and without such representation, even the **indirect tax** of the Sugar Act was considered a threat to the settlers' rights as British subjects. Furthermore, some American colonists felt the colonies were on equal political footing with Great Britain. The Sugar Act meant they were secondary, mere adjuncts to the Empire. All subjects of the British crown knew they had liberties under the constitution. The Sugar Act suggested that some in Parliament labored to deprive them of what made them uniquely British.

5.2 The Stamp Act and the Sons and Daughters of Liberty

By the end of this section, you will be able to:
- Explain the purpose of the 1765 Stamp Act
- Describe the colonial responses to the Stamp Act

In 1765, the British Parliament moved beyond the efforts during the previous two years to better regulate westward expansion and trade by putting in place the Stamp Act. As a **direct tax** on the colonists, the Stamp Act imposed an internal tax on almost every type of printed paper colonists used, including newspapers, legal documents, and playing cards. While the architects of the Stamp Act saw the measure as a way to defray the costs of the British Empire, it nonetheless gave rise to the first major colonial protest against British imperial control as expressed in the famous slogan "no taxation without representation." The Stamp Act reinforced the sense among some colonists that Parliament was not treating them as equals of their peers across the Atlantic.

THE STAMP ACT AND THE QUARTERING ACT

Prime Minister Grenville, author of the Sugar Act of 1764, introduced the Stamp Act in the early spring of 1765. Under this act, anyone who used or purchased anything printed on paper had to buy a revenue stamp (**Figure 5.5**) for it. In the same year, 1765, Parliament also passed the Quartering Act, a law that attempted to solve the problems of stationing troops in North America. The Parliament understood the Stamp Act and the Quartering Act as an assertion of their power to control colonial policy.

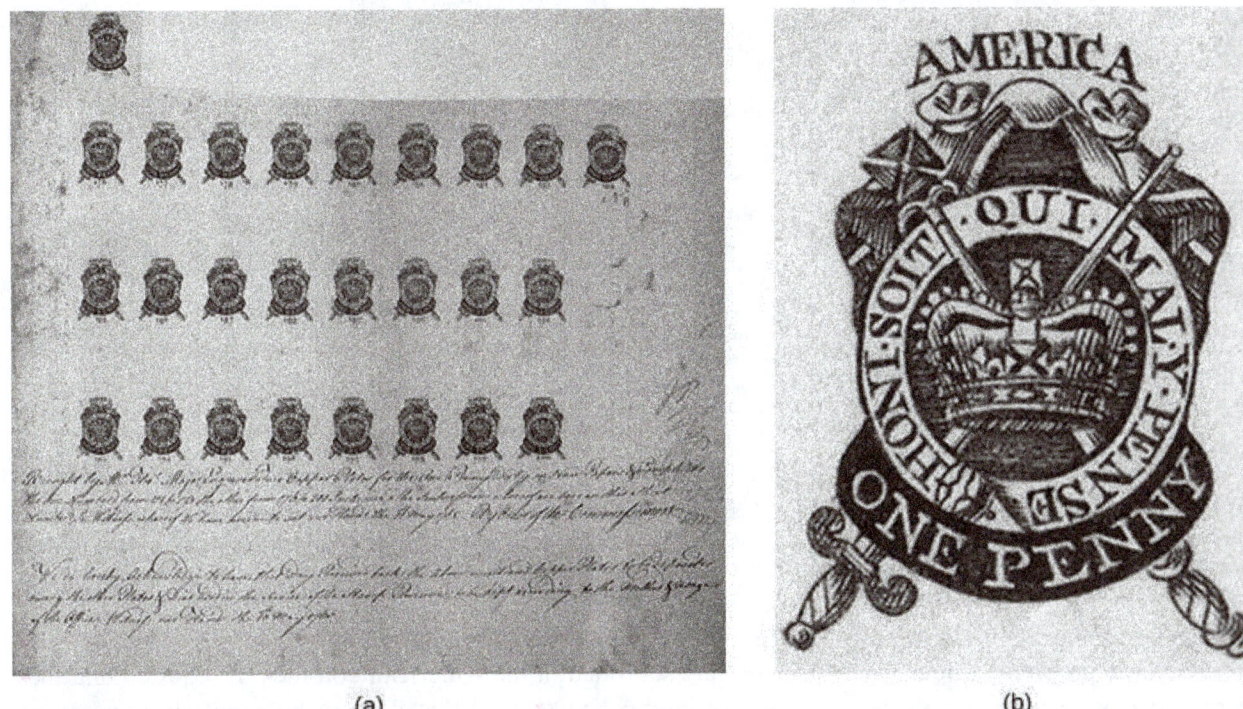

Figure 5.5 Under the Stamp Act, anyone who used or purchased anything printed on paper had to buy a revenue stamp for it. Image (a) shows a partial proof sheet of one-penny stamps. Image (b) provides a close-up of a one-penny stamp. (credit a: modification of work by the United Kingdom Government; credit b: modification of work by the United Kingdom Government)

The Stamp Act signaled a shift in British policy after the French and Indian War. Before the Stamp Act, the colonists had paid taxes to their colonial governments or indirectly through higher prices, not directly to the Crown's appointed governors. This was a time-honored liberty of representative legislatures of the colonial governments. The passage of the Stamp Act meant that starting on November 1, 1765, the colonists would contribute £60,000 per year—17 percent of the total cost—to the upkeep of the ten thousand British soldiers in North America (**Figure 5.6**). Because the Stamp Act raised constitutional issues, it triggered the first serious protest against British imperial policy.

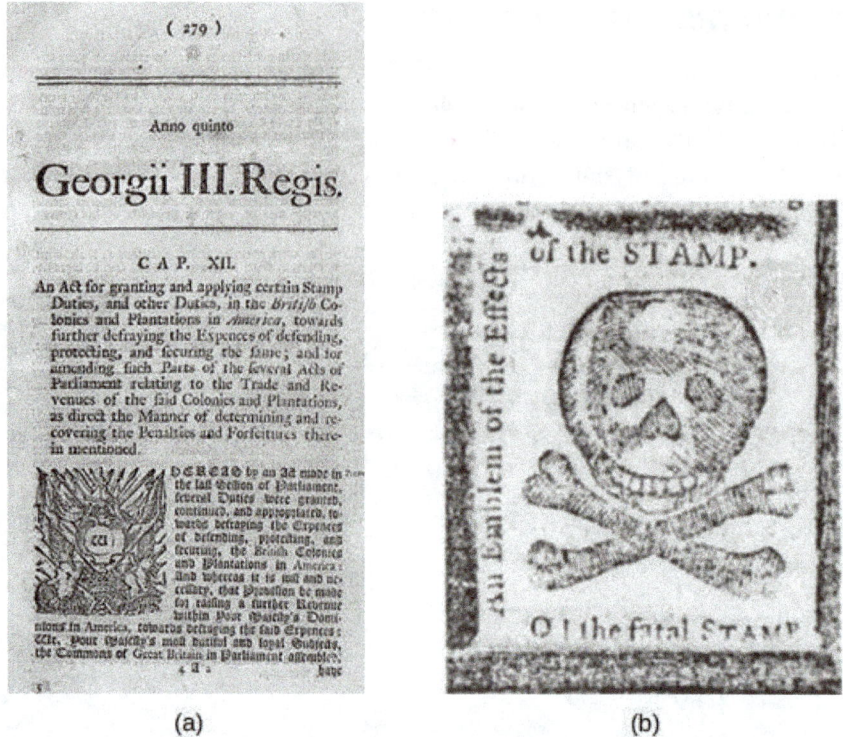

Figure 5.6 The announcement of the Stamp Act, seen in this newspaper publication (a), raised numerous concerns among colonists in America. Protests against British imperial policy took many forms, such as this mock stamp (b) whose text reads "An Emblem of the Effects of the STAMP. O! the Fatal STAMP."

Parliament also asserted its prerogative in 1765 with the Quartering Act. The Quartering Act of 1765 addressed the problem of housing British soldiers stationed in the American colonies. It required that they be provided with barracks or places to stay in public houses, and that if extra housing were necessary, then troops could be stationed in barns and other uninhabited private buildings. In addition, the costs of the troops' food and lodging fell to the colonists. Since the time of James II, who ruled from 1685 to 1688, many British subjects had mistrusted the presence of a standing army during peacetime, and having to pay for the soldiers' lodging and food was especially burdensome. Widespread evasion and disregard for the law occurred in almost all the colonies, but the issue was especially contentious in New York, the headquarters of British forces. When fifteen hundred troops arrived in New York in 1766, the New York Assembly refused to follow the Quartering Act.

COLONIAL PROTEST: GENTRY, MERCHANTS, AND THE STAMP ACT CONGRESS

For many British colonists living in America, the Stamp Act raised many concerns. As a direct tax, it appeared to be an unconstitutional measure, one that deprived freeborn British subjects of their liberty, a concept they defined broadly to include various rights and privileges they enjoyed as British subjects, including the right to representation. According to the unwritten British Constitution, only representatives for whom British subjects voted could tax them. Parliament was in charge of taxation, and although it was a representative body, the colonies did not have "actual" (or direct) representation in it. Parliamentary members who supported the Stamp Act argued that the colonists had virtual representation, because the architects of the British Empire knew best how to maximize returns from its possessions overseas. However, this argument did not satisfy the protesters, who viewed themselves as having the same right as all British subjects to avoid taxation without their consent. With no representation in the House of Commons, where bills of taxation originated, they felt themselves deprived of this inherent right.

The British government knew the colonists might object to the Stamp Act's expansion of parliamentary power, but Parliament believed the relationship of the colonies to the Empire was one of dependence, not equality. However, the Stamp Act had the unintended and ironic consequence of drawing colonists from very different areas and viewpoints together in protest. In Massachusetts, for instance, James Otis, a lawyer and defender of British liberty, became the leading voice for the idea that "Taxation without representation is tyranny." In the Virginia House of Burgesses, firebrand and slaveholder Patrick Henry introduced the Virginia Stamp Act Resolutions, which denounced the Stamp Act and the British crown in language so strong that some conservative Virginians accused him of treason (**Figure 5.7**). Henry replied that Virginians were subject only to taxes that they themselves—or their representatives—imposed. In short, there could be **no taxation without representation**.

Figure 5.7 *Patrick Henry Before the Virginia House of Burgesses* (1851), painted by Peter F. Rothermel, offers a romanticized depiction of Henry's speech denouncing the Stamp Act of 1765. Supporters and opponents alike debated the stark language of the speech, which quickly became legendary.

The colonists had never before formed a unified political front, so Grenville and Parliament did not fear true revolt. However, this was to change in 1765. In response to the Stamp Act, the Massachusetts Assembly sent letters to the other colonies, asking them to attend a meeting, or congress, to discuss how to respond to the act. Many American colonists from very different colonies found common cause in their opposition to the Stamp Act. Representatives from nine colonial legislatures met in New York in the fall of 1765 to reach a consensus. Could Parliament impose taxation without representation? The members of this first congress, known as the Stamp Act Congress, said no. These nine representatives had a vested interest in repealing the tax. Not only did it weaken their businesses and the colonial economy, but it also threatened their liberty under the British Constitution. They drafted a rebuttal to the Stamp Act, making clear that they desired only to protect their liberty as loyal subjects of the Crown. The document, called the Declaration of Rights and Grievances, outlined the unconstitutionality of taxation without representation and trials without juries. Meanwhile, popular protest was also gaining force.

Click and Explore

Browse the collection of the **Massachusetts Historical Society** (http://openstaxcollege.org/l/masshist1) to examine digitized primary sources of the documents that paved the way to the fight for liberty.

MOBILIZATION: POPULAR PROTEST AGAINST THE STAMP ACT

The Stamp Act Congress was a gathering of landowning, educated white men who represented the political elite of the colonies and was the colonial equivalent of the British landed aristocracy. While these gentry were drafting their grievances during the Stamp Act Congress, other colonists showed their distaste for the new act by boycotting British goods and protesting in the streets. Two groups, the **Sons of Liberty** and the **Daughters of Liberty**, led the popular resistance to the Stamp Act. Both groups considered themselves British patriots defending their liberty, just as their forebears had done in the time of James II.

Forming in Boston in the summer of 1765, the Sons of Liberty were artisans, shopkeepers, and small-time merchants willing to adopt extralegal means of protest. Before the act had even gone into effect, the Sons of Liberty began protesting. On August 14, they took aim at Andrew Oliver, who had been named the Massachusetts Distributor of Stamps. After hanging Oliver in effigy—that is, using a crudely made figure as a representation of Oliver—the unruly crowd stoned and ransacked his house, finally beheading the effigy and burning the remains. Such a brutal response shocked the royal governmental officials, who hid until the violence had spent itself. Andrew Oliver resigned the next day. By that time, the mob had moved on to the home of Lieutenant Governor Thomas Hutchinson who, because of his support of Parliament's actions, was considered an enemy of English liberty. The Sons of Liberty barricaded Hutchinson in his home and demanded that he renounce the Stamp Act; he refused, and the protesters looted and burned his house. Furthermore, the Sons (also called "True Sons" or "True-born Sons" to make clear their commitment to liberty and distinguish them from the likes of Hutchinson) continued to lead violent protests with the goal of securing the resignation of all appointed stamp collectors (**Figure 5.8**).

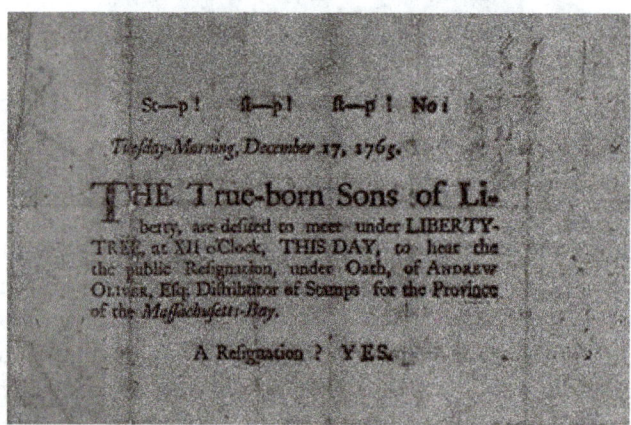

Figure 5.8 With this broadside of December 17, 1765, the Sons of Liberty call for the resignation of Andrew Oliver, the Massachusetts Distributor of Stamps.

Starting in early 1766, the Daughters of Liberty protested the Stamp Act by refusing to buy British goods and encouraging others to do the same. They avoided British tea, opting to make their own teas with local herbs and berries. They built a community—and a movement—around creating homespun cloth instead of buying British linen. Well-born women held "spinning bees," at which they competed to see who could spin the most and the finest linen. An entry in *The Boston Chronicle* of April 7, 1766, states that on March 12, in Providence, Rhode Island, "18 Daughters of Liberty, young ladies of good reputation, assembled at the house of Doctor Ephraim Bowen, in this town. . . . There they exhibited a fine example of industry, by spinning from sunrise until dark, and displayed a spirit for saving their sinking country rarely to be found among persons of more age and experience." At dinner, they "cheerfully agreed to omit tea, to render their conduct consistent. Besides this instance of their patriotism, before they separated, they unanimously resolved that the Stamp Act was unconstitutional, that they would purchase no more British manufactures unless it be repealed, and that they would not even admit the addresses of any gentlemen should they have the opportunity, without they determined to oppose its execution to the last extremity, if the occasion required."

The Daughters' **non-importation movement** broadened the protest against the Stamp Act, giving women a new and active role in the political dissent of the time. Women were responsible for purchasing goods for the home, so by exercising the power of the purse, they could wield more power than they had in the past. Although they could not vote, they could mobilize others and make a difference in the political landscape.

From a local movement, the protests of the Sons and Daughters of Liberty soon spread until there was a chapter in every colony. The Daughters of Liberty promoted the boycott on British goods while the Sons enforced it, threatening retaliation against anyone who bought imported goods or used stamped paper. In the protest against the Stamp Act, wealthy, lettered political figures like John Adams supported the goals of the Sons and Daughters of Liberty, even if they did not engage in the Sons' violent actions. These men, who were lawyers, printers, and merchants, ran a propaganda campaign parallel to the Sons' campaign of violence. In newspapers and pamphlets throughout the colonies, they published article after article outlining the reasons the Stamp Act was unconstitutional and urging peaceful protest. They officially condemned violent actions but did not have the protesters arrested; a degree of cooperation prevailed, despite the groups' different economic backgrounds. Certainly, all the protesters saw themselves as acting in the best British tradition, standing up against the corruption (especially the extinguishing of their right to representation) that threatened their liberty (**Figure 5.9**).

Figure 5.9 This 1766 illustration shows a funeral procession for the Stamp Act. Reverend William Scott leads the procession of politicians who had supported the act, while a dog urinates on his leg. George Grenville, pictured fourth in line, carries a small coffin. What point do you think this cartoon is trying to make?

THE DECLARATORY ACT

Back in Great Britain, news of the colonists' reactions worsened an already volatile political situation. Grenville's imperial reforms had brought about increased domestic taxes and his unpopularity led to his dismissal by King George III. While many in Parliament still wanted such reforms, British merchants argued strongly for their repeal. These merchants had no interest in the philosophy behind the colonists' desire for liberty; rather, their motive was that the non-importation of British goods by North American colonists was hurting their business. Many of the British at home were also appalled by the colonists' violent reaction to the Stamp Act. Other Britons cheered what they saw as the manly defense of liberty by their counterparts in the colonies.

In March 1766, the new prime minister, Lord Rockingham, compelled Parliament to repeal the Stamp Act. Colonists celebrated what they saw as a victory for their British liberty; in Boston, merchant John Hancock treated the entire town to drinks. However, to appease opponents of the repeal, who feared that it would weaken parliamentary power over the American colonists, Rockingham also proposed the Declaratory Act. This stated in no uncertain terms that Parliament's power was supreme and that any laws the colonies may have passed to govern and tax themselves were null and void if they ran counter to parliamentary law.

Click and Explore

Visit **USHistory.org** (http://openstaxcollege.org/l/decact) to read the full text of the Declaratory Act, in which Parliament asserted the supremacy of parliamentary power.

5.3 The Townshend Acts and Colonial Protest

By the end of this section, you will be able to:
- Describe the purpose of the 1767 Townshend Acts
- Explain why many colonists protested the 1767 Townshend Acts and the consequences of their actions

Colonists' joy over the repeal of the Stamp Act and what they saw as their defense of liberty did not last long. The Declaratory Act of 1766 had articulated Great Britain's supreme authority over the colonies, and Parliament soon began exercising that authority. In 1767, with the passage of the Townshend Acts, a tax on consumer goods in British North America, colonists believed their liberty as loyal British subjects had come under assault for a second time.

THE TOWNSHEND ACTS

Lord Rockingham's tenure as prime minister was not long (1765–1766). Rich landowners feared that if he were not taxing the colonies, Parliament would raise their taxes instead, sacrificing them to the interests of merchants and colonists. George III duly dismissed Rockingham. William Pitt, also sympathetic to the colonists, succeeded him. However, Pitt was old and ill with gout. His chancellor of the exchequer, Charles Townshend (**Figure 5.10**), whose job was to manage the Empire's finances, took on many of his duties. Primary among these was raising the needed revenue from the colonies.

Figure 5.10 Charles Townshend, chancellor of the exchequer, shown here in a 1765 painting by Joshua Reynolds, instituted the Townshend Revenue Act of 1767 in order to raise money to support the British military presence in the colonies.

Townshend's first act was to deal with the unruly New York Assembly, which had voted not to pay for supplies for the garrison of British soldiers that the Quartering Act required. In response, Townshend proposed the Restraining Act of 1767, which disbanded the New York Assembly until it agreed to pay for the garrison's supplies, which it eventually agreed to do.

The Townshend Revenue Act of 1767 placed duties on various consumer items like paper, paint, lead, tea, and glass. These British goods had to be imported, since the colonies did not have the manufacturing base to produce them. Townshend hoped the new duties would not anger the colonists because they were external taxes, not internal ones like the Stamp Act. In 1766, in arguing before Parliament for the repeal of the Stamp Act, Benjamin Franklin had stated, "I never heard any objection to the right of laying duties to regulate commerce; but a right to lay internal taxes was never supposed to be in parliament, as we are not represented there."

The Indemnity Act of 1767 exempted tea produced by the British East India Company from taxation when it was imported into Great Britain. When the tea was re-exported to the colonies, however, the colonists had to pay taxes on it because of the Revenue Act. Some critics of Parliament on both sides of the Atlantic saw this tax policy as an example of corrupt politicians giving preferable treatment to specific corporate interests, creating a monopoly. The sense that corruption had become entrenched in Parliament only increased colonists' alarm.

In fact, the revenue collected from these duties was only nominally intended to support the British army in America. It actually paid the salaries of some royally appointed judges, governors, and other officials whom the colonial assemblies had traditionally paid. Thanks to the Townshend Revenue Act of 1767, however, these officials no longer relied on colonial leadership for payment. This change gave them a measure of independence from the assemblies, so they could implement parliamentary acts without fear that their pay would be withheld in retaliation. The Revenue Act thus appeared to sever the relationship between governors and assemblies, drawing royal officials closer to the British government and further away from the colonial legislatures.

The Revenue Act also gave the customs board greater powers to counteract smuggling. It granted "writs of assistance"—basically, search warrants—to customs commissioners who suspected the presence of contraband goods, which also opened the door to a new level of bribery and trickery on the waterfronts of colonial America. Furthermore, to ensure compliance, Townshend introduced the Commissioners of Customs Act of 1767, which created an American Board of Customs to enforce trade laws. Customs enforcement had been based in Great Britain, but rules were difficult to implement at such a distance, and smuggling was rampant. The new customs board was based in Boston and would severely curtail smuggling in this large colonial seaport.

Townshend also orchestrated the Vice-Admiralty Court Act, which established three more vice-admiralty courts, in Boston, Philadelphia, and Charleston, to try violators of customs regulations without a jury. Before this, the only colonial vice-admiralty court had been in far-off Halifax, Nova Scotia, but with three local courts, smugglers could be tried more efficiently. Since the judges of these courts were paid a percentage of the worth of the goods they recovered, leniency was rare. All told, the Townshend Acts resulted in higher taxes and stronger British power to enforce them. Four years after the end of the French and Indian War, the Empire continued to search for solutions to its debt problem and the growing sense that the colonies needed to be brought under control.

REACTIONS: THE NON-IMPORTATION MOVEMENT

Like the Stamp Act, the Townshend Acts produced controversy and protest in the American colonies. For a second time, many colonists resented what they perceived as an effort to tax them without representation and thus to deprive them of their liberty. The fact that the revenue the Townshend Acts raised would pay royal governors only made the situation worse, because it took control away from colonial legislatures that otherwise had the power to set and withhold a royal governor's salary. The Restraining Act, which had been intended to isolate New York without angering the other colonies, had the opposite effect, showing the rest of the colonies how far beyond the British Constitution some members of Parliament were willing to go.

The Townshend Acts generated a number of protest writings, including "Letters from a Pennsylvania Farmer" by John Dickinson. In this influential pamphlet, which circulated widely in the colonies, Dickinson conceded that the Empire could regulate trade but argued that Parliament could not impose either internal taxes, like stamps, on goods or external taxes, like customs duties, on imports.

AMERICANA

"Address to the Ladies" Verse from The Boston Post-Boy and Advertiser

This verse, which ran in a Boston newspaper in November 1767, highlights how women were encouraged to take political action by boycotting British goods. Notice that the writer especially encourages women to avoid British tea (Bohea and Green Hyson) and linen, and to manufacture their own homespun cloth. Building on the protest of the 1765 Stamp Act by the Daughters of Liberty, the non-importation movement of 1767–1768 mobilized women as political actors.

> Young ladies in town, and those that live round,
> Let a friend at this season advise you:
> Since money's so scarce, and times growing worse
> Strange things may soon hap and surprize you:
> First then, throw aside your high top knots of pride
> Wear none but your own country linnen;
> of economy boast, let your pride be the most
> What, if homespun they say is not quite so gay
> As brocades, yet be not in a passion,
> For when once it is known this is much wore in town,
> One and all will cry out, 'tis the fashion!
> And as one, all agree that you'll not married be
> To such as will wear London Fact'ry:
> But at first sight refuse, tell 'em such you do chuse
> As encourage our own Manufact'ry.
> No more Ribbons wear, nor in rich dress appear,
> Love your country much better than fine things,
> Begin without passion, 'twill soon be the fashion
> To grace your smooth locks with a twine string.
> Throw aside your Bohea, and your Green Hyson Tea,
> And all things with a new fashion duty;
> Procure a good store of the choice Labradore,
> For there'll soon be enough here to suit ye;
> These do without fear and to all you'll appear
> Fair, charming, true, lovely, and cleaver;
> Tho' the times remain darkish, young men may be sparkish.
> And love you much stronger than ever. !O!

In Massachusetts in 1768, Samuel Adams wrote a letter that became known as the **Massachusetts Circular**. Sent by the Massachusetts House of Representatives to the other colonial legislatures, the letter laid out the unconstitutionality of taxation without representation and encouraged the other colonies to again protest the taxes by boycotting British goods. Adams wrote, "It is, moreover, [the Massachusetts House of Representatives] humble opinion, which they express with the greatest deference to the wisdom of the Parliament, that the acts made there, imposing duties on the people of this province, with the sole and express purpose of raising a revenue, are infringements of their natural and constitutional rights; because, as they are not represented in the Parliament, his Majesty's Commons in Britain, by those acts, grant their property without their consent." Note that even in this letter of protest, the humble and submissive tone shows the Massachusetts Assembly's continued deference to parliamentary authority. Even in that hotbed of political protest, it is a clear expression of allegiance and the hope for a restoration of "natural and constitutional rights."

Great Britain's response to this threat of disobedience served only to unite the colonies further. The colonies' initial response to the Massachusetts Circular was lukewarm at best. However, back in Great

Britain, the secretary of state for the colonies—Lord Hillsborough—demanded that Massachusetts retract the letter, promising that any colonial assemblies that endorsed it would be dissolved. This threat had the effect of pushing the other colonies to Massachusetts's side. Even the city of Philadelphia, which had originally opposed the Circular, came around.

The Daughters of Liberty once again supported and promoted the boycott of British goods. Women resumed spinning bees and again found substitutes for British tea and other goods. Many colonial merchants signed non-importation agreements, and the Daughters of Liberty urged colonial women to shop only with those merchants. The Sons of Liberty used newspapers and circulars to call out by name those merchants who refused to sign such agreements; sometimes they were threatened by violence. For instance, a broadside from 1769–1770 reads:

> WILLIAM JACKSON,
> an IMPORTER;
> at the BRAZEN HEAD,
> North Side of the TOWN-HOUSE,
> and Opposite the Town-Pump, [in]
> Corn-hill, BOSTON
> It is desired that the SONS
> and DAUGHTERS of LIBERTY,
> would not buy any one thing of
> him, for in so doing they will bring
> disgrace upon themselves, and their
> Posterity, for ever and ever, AMEN.

The boycott in 1768–1769 turned the purchase of consumer goods into a political gesture. It mattered what you consumed. Indeed, the very clothes you wore indicated whether you were a defender of liberty in homespun or a protector of parliamentary rights in superfine British attire.

Click and Explore

For examples of the types of luxury items that many American colonists favored, visit the National Humanities Center (http://openstaxcollege.org/l/britlux) to see pictures and documents relating to home interiors of the wealthy.

TROUBLE IN BOSTON

The Massachusetts Circular got Parliament's attention, and in 1768, Lord Hillsborough sent four thousand British troops to Boston to deal with the unrest and put down any potential rebellion there. The troops were a constant reminder of the assertion of British power over the colonies, an illustration of an unequal relationship between members of the same empire. As an added aggravation, British soldiers moonlighted as dockworkers, creating competition for employment. Boston's labor system had traditionally been closed, privileging native-born laborers over outsiders, and jobs were scarce. Many Bostonians, led by the Sons of Liberty, mounted a campaign of harassment against British troops. The Sons of Liberty also helped protect the smuggling actions of the merchants; smuggling was crucial for the colonists' ability to maintain their boycott of British goods.

John Hancock was one of Boston's most successful merchants and prominent citizens. While he maintained too high a profile to work actively with the Sons of Liberty, he was known to support their aims, if not their means of achieving them. He was also one of the many prominent merchants who had made their fortunes by smuggling, which was rampant in the colonial seaports. In 1768, customs officials seized the *Liberty*, one of his ships, and violence erupted. Led by the Sons of Liberty, Bostonians rioted against customs officials, attacking the customs house and chasing out the officers, who ran to safety at Castle William, a British fort on a Boston harbor island. British soldiers crushed the riots, but over the next few years, clashes between British officials and Bostonians became common.

Conflict turned deadly on March 5, 1770, in a confrontation that came to be known as the **Boston Massacre**. On that night, a crowd of Bostonians from many walks of life started throwing snowballs, rocks, and sticks at the British soldiers guarding the customs house. In the resulting scuffle, some soldiers, goaded by the mob who hectored the soldiers as "lobster backs" (the reference to lobster equated the soldiers with bottom feeders, i.e., aquatic animals that feed on the lowest organisms in the food chain), fired into the crowd, killing five people. Crispus Attucks, the first man killed—and, though no one could have known it then, the first official casualty in the war for independence—was of Wampanoag and African descent. The bloodshed illustrated the level of hostility that had developed as a result of Boston's occupation by British troops, the competition for scarce jobs between Bostonians and the British soldiers stationed in the city, and the larger question of Parliament's efforts to tax the colonies.

The Sons of Liberty immediately seized on the event, characterizing the British soldiers as murderers and their victims as martyrs. Paul Revere, a silversmith and member of the Sons of Liberty, circulated an engraving that showed a line of grim redcoats firing ruthlessly into a crowd of unarmed, fleeing civilians. Among colonists who resisted British power, this view of the "massacre" confirmed their fears of a tyrannous government using its armies to curb the freedom of British subjects. But to others, the attacking mob was equally to blame for pelting the British with rocks and insulting them.

It was not only British Loyalists who condemned the unruly mob. John Adams, one of the city's strongest supporters of peaceful protest against Parliament, represented the British soldiers at their murder trial. Adams argued that the mob's lawlessness required the soldiers' response, and that without law and order, a society was nothing. He argued further that the soldiers were the tools of a much broader program, which transformed a street brawl into the injustice of imperial policy. Of the eight soldiers on trial, the jury acquitted six, convicting the other two of the reduced charge of manslaughter.

Adams argued: "Facts are stubborn things; and whatever may be our wishes, our inclinations, or the dictates of our passions, they cannot alter the state of facts and evidence: nor is the law less stable than the fact; if an assault was made to endanger their lives, the law is clear, they had a right to kill in their own defense; if it was not so severe as to endanger their lives, yet if they were assaulted at all, struck and abused by blows of any sort, by snow-balls, oyster-shells, cinders, clubs, or sticks of any kind; this was a provocation, for which the law reduces the offence of killing, down to manslaughter, in consideration of those passions in our nature, which cannot be eradicated. To your candour and justice I submit the prisoners and their cause."

AMERICANA

✪ *Propaganda and the Sons of Liberty*

Long after the British soldiers had been tried and punished, the Sons of Liberty maintained a relentless propaganda campaign against British oppression. Many of them were printers or engravers, and they were able to use public media to sway others to their cause. Shortly after the incident outside the customs house, Paul Revere created "The bloody massacre perpetrated in King Street Boston on March 5th 1770 by a party of the 29th Regt." (**Figure 5.11**), based on an image by engraver Henry Pelham. The picture—which represents only the protesters' point of view—shows the ruthlessness of the British soldiers and the helplessness of the crowd of civilians. Notice the subtle details Revere uses to help convince the viewer of the civilians' innocence and the soldiers' cruelty. Although eyewitnesses said the crowd started the fight by throwing snowballs and rocks, in the engraving they are innocently standing by. Revere also depicts the crowd as well dressed and well-to-do, when in fact they were laborers and probably looked quite a bit rougher.

Figure 5.11 The Sons of Liberty circulated this sensationalized version of the events of March 5, 1770, in order to promote the rightness of their cause. The verses below the image begin as follows: "Unhappy Boston! see thy Sons deplore, Thy hallowed Walks besmeared with guiltless Gore."

Newspaper articles and pamphlets that the Sons of Liberty circulated implied that the "massacre" was a planned murder. In the *Boston Gazette* on March 12, 1770, an article describes the soldiers as striking first. It goes on to discuss this version of the events: "On hearing the noise, one Samuel Atwood came up to see what was the matter; and entering the alley from dock square, heard the latter part of the combat; and when the boys had dispersed he met the ten or twelve soldiers aforesaid rushing down the alley towards the square and asked them if they intended to murder people? They answered Yes, by God, root and branch! With that one of them struck Mr. Atwood with a club which was repeated by another; and being unarmed, he turned to go off and received a wound on the left shoulder which reached the bone and gave him much pain."

What do you think most people in the United States think of when they consider the Boston Massacre? How does the propaganda of the Sons of Liberty still affect the way we think of this event?

PARTIAL REPEAL

As it turned out, the Boston Massacre occurred after Parliament had partially repealed the Townshend Acts. By the late 1760s, the American boycott of British goods had drastically reduced British trade. Once again, merchants who lost money because of the boycott strongly pressured Parliament to loosen its restrictions on the colonies and break the non-importation movement. Charles Townshend died suddenly in 1767 and was replaced by Lord North, who was inclined to look for a more workable solution with the colonists. North convinced Parliament to drop all the Townshend duties except the tax on tea. The administrative and enforcement provisions under the Townshend Acts—the American Board of Customs Commissioners and the vice-admiralty courts—remained in place.

To those who had protested the Townshend Acts for several years, the partial repeal appeared to be a major victory. For a second time, colonists had rescued liberty from an unconstitutional parliamentary measure. The hated British troops in Boston departed. The consumption of British goods skyrocketed after the partial repeal, an indication of the American colonists' desire for the items linking them to the Empire.

5.4 The Destruction of the Tea and the Coercive Acts

By the end of this section, you will be able to:
- Describe the socio-political environment in the colonies in the early 1770s
- Explain the purpose of the Tea Act of 1773 and discuss colonial reactions to it
- Identify and describe the Coercive Acts

The Tea Act of 1773 triggered a reaction with far more significant consequences than either the 1765 Stamp Act or the 1767 Townshend Acts. Colonists who had joined in protest against those earlier acts renewed their efforts in 1773. They understood that Parliament had again asserted its right to impose taxes without representation, and they feared the Tea Act was designed to seduce them into conceding this important principle by lowering the price of tea to the point that colonists might abandon their scruples. They also deeply resented the East India Company's monopoly on the sale of tea in the American colonies; this resentment sprang from the knowledge that some members of Parliament had invested heavily in the company.

SMOLDERING RESENTMENT

Even after the partial repeal of the Townshend duties, however, suspicion of Parliament's intentions remained high. This was especially true in port cities like Boston and New York, where British customs agents were a daily irritant and reminder of British power. In public houses and squares, people met and discussed politics. Philosopher John Locke's *Two Treatises of Government*, published almost a century earlier, influenced political thought about the role of government to protect life, liberty, and property. The Sons of Liberty issued propaganda ensuring that colonists remained aware when Parliament overreached itself.

Violence continued to break out on occasion, as in 1772, when Rhode Island colonists boarded and burned the British revenue ship *Gaspée* in Narragansett Bay (**Figure 5.12**). Colonists had attacked or burned British customs ships in the past, but after the Gaspée Affair, the British government convened a Royal Commission of Inquiry. This Commission had the authority to remove the colonists, who were charged with treason, to Great Britain for trial. Some colonial protestors saw this new ability as another example of the overreach of British power.

Figure 5.12 This 1883 engraving, which appeared in *Harper's New Monthly Magazine*, depicts the burning of the *Gaspée*. This attack provoked the British government to convene a Royal Commission of Inquiry; some regarded the Commission as an example of excessive British power and control over the colonies.

Samuel Adams, along with Joseph Warren and James Otis, re-formed the Boston **Committee of Correspondence**, which functioned as a form of shadow government, to address the fear of British overreach. Soon towns all over Massachusetts had formed their own committees, and many other colonies followed suit. These committees, which had between seven and eight thousand members in all, identified enemies of the movement and communicated the news of the day. Sometimes they provided a version of events that differed from royal interpretations, and slowly, the committees began to supplant royal governments as sources of information. They later formed the backbone of communication among the colonies in the rebellion against the Tea Act, and eventually in the revolt against the British crown.

THE TEA ACT OF 1773

Parliament did not enact the Tea Act of 1773 in order to punish the colonists, assert parliamentary power, or even raise revenues. Rather, the act was a straightforward order of economic protectionism for a British tea firm, the East India Company, that was on the verge of bankruptcy. In the colonies, tea was the one remaining consumer good subject to the hated Townshend duties. Protest leaders and their followers still avoided British tea, drinking smuggled Dutch tea as a sign of patriotism.

The Tea Act of 1773 gave the British East India Company the ability to export its tea directly to the colonies without paying import or export duties and without using middlemen in either Great Britain or the colonies. Even with the Townshend tax, the act would allow the East India Company to sell its tea at lower prices than the smuggled Dutch tea, thus undercutting the smuggling trade.

This act was unwelcome to those in British North America who had grown displeased with the pattern of imperial measures. By granting a monopoly to the East India Company, the act not only cut out colonial merchants who would otherwise sell the tea themselves; it also reduced their profits from smuggled foreign tea. These merchants were among the most powerful and influential people in the colonies, so their dissatisfaction carried some weight. Moreover, because the tea tax that the Townshend Acts imposed remained in place, tea had intense power to symbolize the idea of "no taxation without representation."

COLONIAL PROTEST: THE DESTRUCTION OF THE TEA

The 1773 act reignited the worst fears among the colonists. To the Sons and Daughters of Liberty and those who followed them, the act appeared to be proof positive that a handful of corrupt members of Parliament were violating the British Constitution. Veterans of the protest movement had grown accustomed to interpreting British actions in the worst possible light, so the 1773 act appeared to be part of a large conspiracy against liberty.

As they had done to protest earlier acts and taxes, colonists responded to the Tea Act with a boycott. The Committees of Correspondence helped to coordinate resistance in all of the colonial port cities, so up and down the East Coast, British tea-carrying ships were unable to come to shore and unload their wares. In Charlestown, Boston, Philadelphia, and New York, the equivalent of millions of dollars' worth of tea was held hostage, either locked in storage warehouses or rotting in the holds of ships as they were forced to sail back to Great Britain.

In Boston, Thomas Hutchinson, now the royal governor of Massachusetts, vowed that radicals like Samuel Adams would not keep the ships from unloading their cargo. He urged the merchants who would have accepted the tea from the ships to stand their ground and receive the tea once it had been unloaded. When the *Dartmouth* sailed into Boston Harbor in November 1773, it had twenty days to unload its cargo of tea and pay the duty before it had to return to Great Britain. Two more ships, the *Eleanor* and the *Beaver*, followed soon after. Samuel Adams and the Sons of Liberty tried to keep the captains of the ships from paying the duties and posted groups around the ships to make sure the tea would not be unloaded.

On December 16, just as the *Dartmouth*'s deadline approached, townspeople gathered at the Old South Meeting House determined to take action. From this gathering, a group of Sons of Liberty and their followers approached the three ships. Some were disguised as Mohawks. Protected by a crowd of spectators, they systematically dumped all the tea into the harbor, destroying goods worth almost $1 million in today's dollars, a very significant loss. This act soon inspired further acts of resistance up and down the East Coast. However, not all colonists, and not even all Patriots, supported the dumping of the tea. The wholesale destruction of property shocked people on both sides of the Atlantic.

Click and Explore

To learn more about the Boston Tea Party, explore the extensive resources in the Boston Tea Party Ships and Museum collection (http://openstaxcollege.org/l/teapartyship) of articles, photos, and video. At the museum itself, you can board replicas of the *Eleanor* and the *Beaver* and experience a recreation of the dumping of the tea.

PARLIAMENT RESPONDS: THE COERCIVE ACTS

In London, response to the destruction of the tea was swift and strong. The violent destruction of property infuriated King George III and the prime minister, Lord North (**Figure 5.13**), who insisted the loss be repaid. Though some American merchants put forward a proposal for restitution, the Massachusetts Assembly refused to make payments. Massachusetts's resistance to British authority united different factions in Great Britain against the colonies. North had lost patience with the unruly British subjects in Boston. He declared: "The Americans have tarred and feathered your subjects, plundered your merchants, burnt your ships, denied all obedience to your laws and authority; yet so clement and so long forbearing has our conduct been that it is incumbent on us now to take a different course. Whatever may be the consequences, we must risk something; if we do not, all is over." Both Parliament and the king agreed that Massachusetts should be forced to both pay for the tea and yield to British authority.

Figure 5.13 Lord North, seen here in *Portrait of Frederick North, Lord North* (1773–1774), painted by Nathaniel Dance, was prime minister at the time of the destruction of the tea and insisted that Massachusetts make good on the loss.

In early 1774, leaders in Parliament responded with a set of four measures designed to punish Massachusetts, commonly known at the **Coercive Acts**. The Boston Port Bill shut down Boston Harbor until the East India Company was repaid. The Massachusetts Government Act placed the colonial government under the direct control of crown officials and made traditional town meetings subject to the governor's approval. The Administration of Justice Act allowed the royal governor to unilaterally move any trial of a crown officer out of Massachusetts, a change designed to prevent hostile Massachusetts juries from deciding these cases. This act was especially infuriating to John Adams and others who emphasized the time-honored rule of law. They saw this part of the Coercive Acts as striking at the heart of fair and equitable justice. Finally, the Quartering Act encompassed all the colonies and allowed British troops to be housed in occupied buildings.

At the same time, Parliament also passed the Quebec Act, which expanded the boundaries of Quebec westward and extended religious tolerance to Roman Catholics in the province. For many Protestant colonists, especially Congregationalists in New England, this forced tolerance of Catholicism was the most objectionable provision of the act. Additionally, expanding the boundaries of Quebec raised troubling questions for many colonists who eyed the West, hoping to expand the boundaries of their provinces. The Quebec Act appeared gratuitous, a slap in the face to colonists already angered by the Coercive Acts.

American Patriots renamed the Coercive and Quebec measures the **Intolerable Acts**. Some in London also thought the acts went too far; see the cartoon "The Able Doctor, or America Swallowing the Bitter Draught" (**Figure 5.14**) for one British view of what Parliament was doing to the colonies. Meanwhile, punishments designed to hurt only one colony (Massachusetts, in this case) had the effect of mobilizing all the colonies to its side. The Committees of Correspondence had already been active in coordinating an approach to the Tea Act. Now the talk would turn to these new, intolerable assaults on the colonists' rights as British subjects.

Figure 5.14 The artist of "The Able Doctor, or America Swallowing the Bitter Draught" (*London Magazine*, May 1, 1774) targets select members of Parliament as the perpetrators of a devilish scheme to overturn the constitution; this is why Mother Britannia weeps. Note that this cartoon came from a British publication; Great Britain was not united in support of Parliament's policies toward the American colonies.

5.5 Disaffection: The First Continental Congress and American Identity

By the end of this section, you will be able to:
- Describe the state of affairs between the colonies and the home government in 1774
- Explain the purpose and results of the First Continental Congress

Disaffection—the loss of affection toward the home government—had reached new levels by 1774. Many colonists viewed the Intolerable Acts as a turning point; they now felt they had to take action. The result was the First Continental Congress, a direct challenge to Lord North and British authority in the colonies. Still, it would be a mistake to assume there was a groundswell of support for separating from the British Empire and creating a new, independent nation. Strong ties still bound the Empire together, and colonists did not agree about the proper response. Loyalists tended to be property holders, established residents who feared the loss of their property. To them the protests seemed to promise nothing but mob rule, and the violence and disorder they provoked were shocking. On both sides of the Atlantic, opinions varied.

After the passage of the Intolerable Acts in 1774, the Committees of Correspondence and the Sons of Liberty went straight to work, spreading warnings about how the acts would affect the liberty of all colonists, not just urban merchants and laborers. The Massachusetts Government Act had shut down the colonial government there, but resistance-minded colonists began meeting in extralegal assemblies. One of these assemblies, the Massachusetts Provincial Congress, passed the **Suffolk Resolves** in September 1774, which laid out a plan of resistance to the Intolerable Acts. Meanwhile, the First Continental Congress was convening to discuss how to respond to the acts themselves.

The First Continental Congress was made up of elected representatives of twelve of the thirteen American colonies. (Georgia's royal governor blocked the move to send representatives from that colony, an indication of the continued strength of the royal government despite the crisis.) The representatives met in Philadelphia from September 5 through October 26, 1774, and at first they did not agree at all about the appropriate response to the Intolerable Acts. Joseph Galloway of Pennsylvania argued for a conciliatory approach; he proposed that an elected Grand Council in America, like the Parliament in Great Britain, should be paired with a royally appointed President General, who would represent the authority of the Crown. More radical factions argued for a move toward separation from the Crown.

In the end, Paul Revere rode from Massachusetts to Philadelphia with the Suffolk Resolves, which became the basis of the Declaration and Resolves of the First Continental Congress. In the Declaration and Resolves, adopted on October 14, the colonists demanded the repeal of all repressive acts passed since 1773 and agreed to a non-importation, non-exportation, and non-consumption pact against all British goods until the acts were repealed. In the "Petition of Congress to the King" on October 24, the delegates adopted a further recommendation of the Suffolk Resolves and proposed that the colonies raise and regulate their own militias.

The representatives at the First Continental Congress created a Continental Association to ensure that the full boycott was enforced across all the colonies. The Continental Association served as an umbrella group for colonial and local committees of observation and inspection. By taking these steps, the First Continental Congress established a governing network in opposition to royal authority.

Click and Explore

Visit the Massachusetts Historical Society (http://openstaxcollege.org/l/firstcongress) to see a digitized copy and read the transcript of the First Continental Congress's petition to King George.

DEFINING "AMERICAN"

⚙ *The First List of Un-American Activities*

In her book *Toward A More Perfect Union: Virtue and the Formation of American Republics*, historian Ann Fairfax Withington explores actions the delegates to the First Continental Congress took during the weeks they were together. Along with their efforts to bring about the repeal of the Intolerable Acts, the delegates also banned certain activities they believed would undermine their fight against what they saw as British corruption.

In particular, the delegates prohibited horse races, cockfights, the theater, and elaborate funerals. The reasons for these prohibitions provide insight into the state of affairs in 1774. Both horse races and cockfights encouraged gambling and, for the delegates, gambling threatened to prevent the unity of action and purpose they desired. In addition, cockfighting appeared immoral and corrupt because the roosters were fitted with razors and fought to the death (**Figure 5.15**).

Figure 5.15 Cockfights, as depicted in *The Cockpit* (1759) by British artist and engraver William Hogarth, were among the entertainments the First Continental Congress sought to outlaw, considering them un-American.

The ban on the theater aimed to do away with another corrupt British practice. Critics had long believed that theatrical performances drained money from working people. Moreover, they argued, theatergoers learned to lie and deceive from what they saw on stage. The delegates felt banning the theater would demonstrate their resolve to act honestly and without pretence in their fight against corruption.

Finally, eighteenth-century mourning practices often required lavish spending on luxury items and even the employment of professional mourners who, for a price, would shed tears at the grave. Prohibiting these practices reflected the idea that luxury bred corruption, and the First Continental Congress wanted to demonstrate that the colonists would do without British vices. Congress emphasized the need to be frugal and self-sufficient when confronted with corruption.

The First Continental Congress banned all four activities—horse races, cockfights, the theater, and elaborate funerals—and entrusted the Continental Association with enforcement. Rejecting what they saw as corruption coming from Great Britain, the delegates were also identifying themselves as standing apart from their British relatives. They cast themselves as virtuous defenders of liberty against a corrupt Parliament.

In the Declaration and Resolves and the Petition of Congress to the King, the delegates to the First Continental Congress refer to George III as "Most Gracious Sovereign" and to themselves as "inhabitants of the English colonies in North America" or "inhabitants of British America," indicating that they still considered themselves British subjects of the king, not American citizens. At the same time, however, they were slowly moving away from British authority, creating their own de facto government in the First Continental Congress. One of the provisions of the Congress was that it meet again in one year to mark its progress; the Congress was becoming an elected government.

CHAPTER 6
America's War for Independence, 1775-1783

Figure 6.1 This famous 1819 painting by John Trumbull shows members of the committee entrusted with drafting the Declaration of Independence presenting their work to the Continental Congress in 1776. Note the British flags on the wall. Separating from the British Empire proved to be very difficult as the colonies and the Empire were linked with strong cultural, historical, and economic bonds forged over several generations.

Chapter Outline

6.1 Britain's Law-and-Order Strategy and Its Consequences
6.2 The Early Years of the Revolution
6.3 War in the South
6.4 Identity during the American Revolution

Introduction

By the 1770s, Great Britain ruled a vast empire, with its American colonies producing useful raw materials and profitably consuming British goods. From Britain's perspective, it was inconceivable that the colonies would wage a successful war for independence; in 1776, they appeared weak and disorganized, no match for the Empire. Yet, although the Revolutionary War did indeed drag on for eight years, in 1783, the thirteen colonies, now the United States, ultimately prevailed against the British.

The Revolution succeeded because colonists from diverse economic and social backgrounds united in their opposition to Great Britain. Although thousands of colonists remained loyal to the crown and many others preferred to remain neutral, a sense of community against a common enemy prevailed among Patriots. The signing of the Declaration of Independence (**Figure 6.1**) exemplifies the spirit of that common cause. Representatives asserted: "That these United Colonies are, and of Right ought to be Free and Independent States; that they are Absolved from all Allegiance to the British Crown, . . . And for the support of this Declaration, . . . we mutually pledge to each other our Lives, our Fortunes and our sacred Honor."

6.1 Britain's Law-and-Order Strategy and Its Consequences

By the end of this section, you will be able to:
- Explain how Great Britain's response to the destruction of a British shipment of tea in Boston Harbor in 1773 set the stage for the Revolution
- Describe the beginnings of the American Revolution

Great Britain pursued a policy of law and order when dealing with the crises in the colonies in the late 1760s and 1770s. Relations between the British and many American Patriots worsened over the decade, culminating in an unruly mob destroying a fortune in tea by dumping it into Boston Harbor in December 1773 as a protest against British tax laws. The harsh British response to this act in 1774, which included sending British troops to Boston and closing Boston Harbor, caused tensions and resentments to escalate further. The British tried to disarm the insurgents in Massachusetts by confiscating their weapons and ammunition and arresting the leaders of the patriotic movement. However, this effort faltered on April 19, when Massachusetts militias and British troops fired on each other as British troops marched to Lexington and Concord, an event immortalized by poet Ralph Waldo Emerson as the "shot heard round the world." The American Revolution had begun.

ON THE EVE OF REVOLUTION

The decade from 1763 to 1774 was a difficult one for the British Empire. Although Great Britain had defeated the French in the French and Indian War, the debt from that conflict remained a stubborn and seemingly unsolvable problem for both Great Britain and the colonies. Great Britain tried various methods of raising revenue on both sides of the Atlantic to manage the enormous debt, including instituting a tax on tea and other goods sold to the colonies by British companies, but many subjects resisted these taxes. In the colonies, Patriot groups like the Sons of Liberty led boycotts of British goods and took violent measures that stymied British officials.

Boston proved to be the epicenter of protest. In December 1773, a group of Patriots protested the Tea Act passed that year—which, among other provisions, gave the East India Company a monopoly on tea—by boarding British tea ships docked in Boston Harbor and dumping tea worth over $1 million (in current

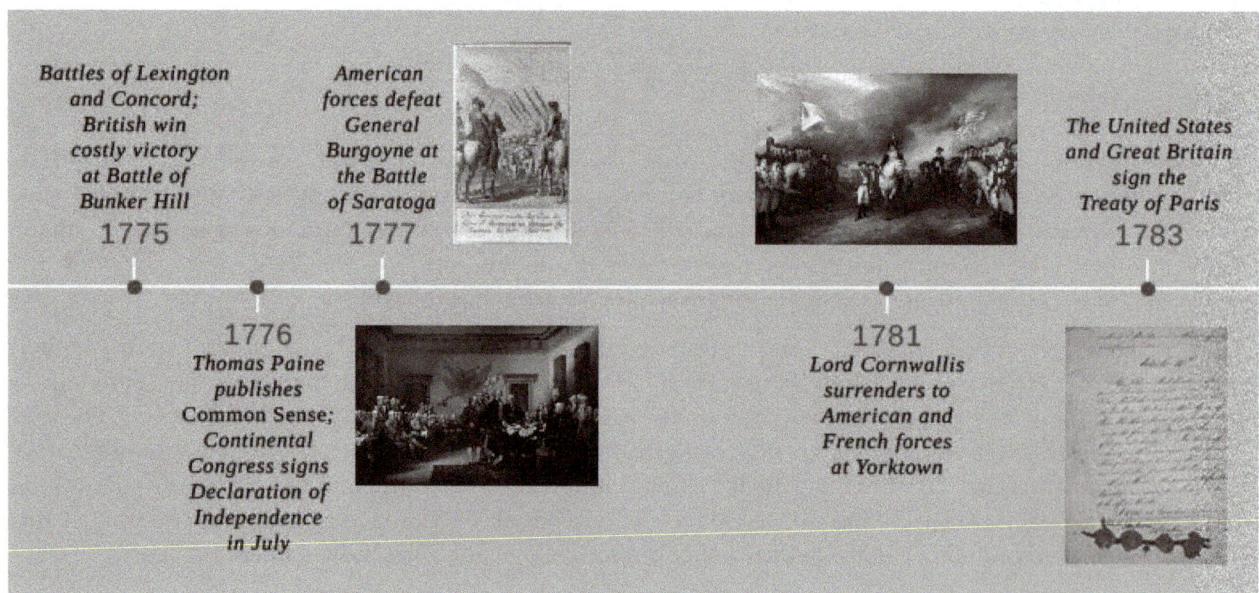

Figure 6.2

prices) into the water. The destruction of the tea radically escalated the crisis between Great Britain and the American colonies. When the Massachusetts Assembly refused to pay for the tea, Parliament enacted a series of laws called the Coercive Acts, which some colonists called the Intolerable Acts. Parliament designed these laws, which closed the port of Boston, limited the meetings of the colonial assembly, and disbanded all town meetings, to punish Massachusetts and bring the colony into line. However, many British Americans in other colonies were troubled and angered by Parliament's response to Massachusetts. In September and October 1774, all the colonies except Georgia participated in the First Continental Congress in Philadelphia. The Congress advocated a boycott of all British goods and established the Continental Association to enforce local adherence to the boycott. The Association supplanted royal control and shaped resistance to Great Britain.

AMERICANA

Joining the Boycott

Many British colonists in Virginia, as in the other colonies, disapproved of the destruction of the tea in Boston Harbor. However, after the passage of the Coercive Acts, the Virginia House of Burgesses declared its solidarity with Massachusetts by encouraging Virginians to observe a day of fasting and prayer on May 24 in sympathy with the people of Boston. Almost immediately thereafter, Virginia's colonial governor dissolved the House of Burgesses, but many of its members met again in secret on May 30 and adopted a resolution stating that "the Colony of Virginia will concur with the other Colonies in such Measures as shall be judged most effectual for the preservation of the Common Rights and Liberty of British America."

After the First Continental Congress in Philadelphia, Virginia's Committee of Safety ensured that all merchants signed the non-importation agreements that the Congress had proposed. This British cartoon (**Figure 6.3**) shows a Virginian signing the Continental Association boycott agreement.

Figure 6.3 In "The Alternative of Williams-Burg" (1775), a merchant has to sign a non-importation agreement or risk being covered with the tar and feathers suspended behind him.

Note the tar and feathers hanging from the gallows in the background of this image and the demeanor of the people surrounding the signer. What is the message of this engraving? Where are the sympathies of the artist? What is the meaning of the title "The Alternative of Williams-Burg?"

In an effort to restore law and order in Boston, the British dispatched General Thomas Gage to the New England seaport. He arrived in Boston in May 1774 as the new royal governor of the Province of Massachusetts, accompanied by several regiments of British troops. As in 1768, the British again occupied the town. Massachusetts delegates met in a Provincial Congress and published the Suffolk Resolves, which officially rejected the Coercive Acts and called for the raising of colonial militias to take military action if needed. The Suffolk Resolves signaled the overthrow of the royal government in Massachusetts.

Both the British and the rebels in New England began to prepare for conflict by turning their attention to supplies of weapons and gunpowder. General Gage stationed thirty-five hundred troops in Boston, and from there he ordered periodic raids on towns where guns and gunpowder were stockpiled, hoping to impose law and order by seizing them. As Boston became the headquarters of British military operations, many residents fled the city.

Gage's actions led to the formation of local rebel militias that were able to mobilize in a minute's time. These **minutemen**, many of whom were veterans of the French and Indian War, played an important role in the war for independence. In one instance, General Gage seized munitions in Cambridge and Charlestown, but when he arrived to do the same in Salem, his troops were met by a large crowd of minutemen and had to leave empty-handed. In New Hampshire, minutemen took over Fort William and Mary and confiscated weapons and cannons there. New England readied for war.

THE OUTBREAK OF FIGHTING

Throughout late 1774 and into 1775, tensions in New England continued to mount. General Gage knew that a powder magazine was stored in Concord, Massachusetts, and on April 19, 1775, he ordered troops to seize these munitions. Instructions from London called for the arrest of rebel leaders Samuel Adams and John Hancock. Hoping for secrecy, his troops left Boston under cover of darkness, but riders from Boston let the militias know of the British plans. (Paul Revere was one of these riders, but the British captured him and he never finished his ride. Henry Wadsworth Longfellow memorialized Revere in his 1860 poem, "Paul Revere's Ride," incorrectly implying that he made it all the way to Concord.) Minutemen met the British troops and skirmished with them, first at Lexington and then at Concord (**Figure 6.4**). The British retreated to Boston, enduring ambushes from several other militias along the way. Over four thousand militiamen took part in these skirmishes with British soldiers. Seventy-three British soldiers and forty-nine Patriots died during the British retreat to Boston. The famous confrontation is the basis for Emerson's "Concord Hymn" (1836), which begins with the description of the "shot heard round the world." Although propagandists on both sides pointed fingers, it remains unclear who fired that shot.

Figure 6.4 Amos Doolittle was an American printmaker who volunteered to fight against the British. His engravings of the battles of Lexington and Concord—such as this detail from *The Battle of Lexington, April 19th 1775*—are the only contemporary American visual records of the events there.

After the battles of Lexington and Concord, New England fully mobilized for war. Thousands of militias from towns throughout New England marched to Boston, and soon the city was besieged by a sea of rebel forces (**Figure 6.5**). In May 1775, Ethan Allen and Colonel Benedict Arnold led a group of rebels against

Fort Ticonderoga in New York. They succeeded in capturing the fort, and cannons from Ticonderoga were brought to Massachusetts and used to bolster the Siege of Boston.

Figure 6.5 This 1779 map shows details of the British and Patriot troops in and around Boston, Massachusetts, at the beginning of the war.

In June, General Gage resolved to take Breed's Hill and Bunker Hill, the high ground across the Charles River from Boston, a strategic site that gave the rebel militias an advantage since they could train their cannons on the British. In the Battle of Bunker Hill (**Figure 6.6**), on June 17, the British launched three assaults on the hills, gaining control only after the rebels ran out of ammunition. British losses were very high—over two hundred were killed and eight hundred wounded—and, despite his victory, General Gage was unable to break the colonial forces' siege of the city. In August, King George III declared the colonies to be in a state of rebellion. Parliament and many in Great Britain agreed with their king. Meanwhile, the British forces in Boston found themselves in a terrible predicament, isolated in the city and with no control over the countryside.

(a) (b)

Figure 6.6 The British cartoon "Bunkers Hill or America's Head Dress" (a) depicts the initial rebellion as an elaborate colonial coiffure. The illustration pokes fun at both the colonial rebellion and the overdone hairstyles for women that had made their way from France and Britain to the American colonies. Despite gaining control of the high ground after the colonial militias ran out of ammunition, General Thomas Gage (b), shown here in a painting made in 1768–1769 by John Singleton Copley, was unable to break the siege of the city.

In the end, General George Washington, commander in chief of the Continental Army since June 15, 1775, used the Fort Ticonderoga cannons to force the evacuation of the British from Boston. Washington had positioned these cannons on the hills overlooking both the fortified positions of the British and Boston Harbor, where the British supply ships were anchored. The British could not return fire on the colonial positions because they could not elevate their cannons. They soon realized that they were in an untenable position and had to withdraw from Boston. On March 17, 1776, the British evacuated their troops to Halifax, Nova Scotia, ending the nearly year-long siege.

By the time the British withdrew from Boston, fighting had broken out in other colonies as well. In May 1775, Mecklenburg County in North Carolina issued the **Mecklenburg Resolves**, stating that a rebellion against Great Britain had begun, that colonists did not owe any further allegiance to Great Britain, and that governing authority had now passed to the Continental Congress. The resolves also called upon the formation of militias to be under the control of the Continental Congress. Loyalists and Patriots clashed in North Carolina in February 1776 at the Battle of Moore's Creek Bridge.

In Virginia, the royal governor, Lord Dunmore, raised Loyalist forces to combat the rebel colonists and also tried to use the large slave population to put down the rebellion. In November 1775, he issued a decree, known as **Dunmore's Proclamation,** promising freedom to slaves and indentured servants of rebels who remained loyal to the king and who pledged to fight with the Loyalists against the insurgents. Dunmore's Proclamation exposed serious problems for both the Patriot cause and for the British. In order for the British to put down the rebellion, they needed the support of Virginia's landowners, many of whom owned slaves. (While Patriot slaveholders in Virginia and elsewhere proclaimed they acted in defense of liberty, they kept thousands in bondage, a fact the British decided to exploit.) Although a number of slaves did join Dunmore's side, the proclamation had the unintended effect of galvanizing Patriot resistance to Britain. From the rebels' point of view, the British looked to deprive them of their slave property and incite a race war. Slaveholders feared a slave uprising and increased their commitment to the cause against Great Britain, calling for independence. Dunmore fled Virginia in 1776.

COMMON SENSE

With the events of 1775 fresh in their minds, many colonists reached the conclusion in 1776 that the time had come to secede from the Empire and declare independence. Over the past ten years, these colonists had argued that they deserved the same rights as Englishmen enjoyed in Great Britain, only to find themselves relegated to an intolerable subservient status in the Empire. The groundswell of support for their cause of independence in 1776 also owed much to the appearance of an anonymous pamphlet, first published in January 1776, entitled *Common Sense*. Thomas Paine, who had emigrated from England to Philadelphia in 1774, was the author. Arguably the most radical pamphlet of the revolutionary era, *Common Sense* made a powerful argument for independence.

Paine's pamphlet rejected the monarchy, calling King George III a "royal brute" and questioning the right of an island (England) to rule over America. In this way, Paine helped to channel colonial discontent toward the king himself and not, as had been the case, toward the British Parliament—a bold move that signaled the desire to create a new political order disavowing monarchy entirely. He argued for the creation of an American republic, a state without a king, and extolled the blessings of **republicanism**, a political philosophy that held that elected representatives, not a hereditary monarch, should govern states. The vision of an American republic put forward by Paine included the idea of **popular sovereignty**: citizens in the republic would determine who would represent them, and decide other issues, on the basis of majority rule. Republicanism also served as a social philosophy guiding the conduct of the Patriots in their struggle against the British Empire. It demanded adherence to a code of virtue, placing the public good and community above narrow self-interest.

Paine wrote *Common Sense* (**Figure 6.7**) in simple, direct language aimed at ordinary people, not just the learned elite. The pamphlet proved immensely popular and was soon available in all **thirteen colonies**, where it helped convince many to reject monarchy and the British Empire in favor of independence and a republican form of government.

Figure 6.7 Thomas Paine's *Common Sense* (a) helped convince many colonists of the need for independence from Great Britain. Paine, shown here in a portrait by Laurent Dabos (b), was a political activist and revolutionary best known for his writings on both the American and French Revolutions.

THE DECLARATION OF INDEPENDENCE

In the summer of 1776, the Continental Congress met in Philadelphia and agreed to sever ties with Great Britain. Virginian Thomas Jefferson and John Adams of Massachusetts, with the support of the Congress, articulated the justification for liberty in the Declaration of Independence (**Figure 6.8**). The Declaration, written primarily by Jefferson, included a long list of grievances against King George III and laid out the foundation of American government as a republic in which the consent of the governed would be of paramount importance.

Figure 6.8 The Dunlap Broadsides, one of which is shown here, are considered the first published copies of the Declaration of Independence. This one was printed on July 4, 1776.

The preamble to the Declaration began with a statement of Enlightenment principles about universal human rights and values: "We hold these Truths to be self-evident, that all Men are created equal, that they are endowed by their Creator with certain unalienable Rights, that among these are Life, Liberty, and the pursuit of Happiness—That to secure these Rights, Governments are instituted among Men, deriving their just Powers from the Consent of the Governed, that whenever any Form of Government becomes destructive of these Ends, it is the Right of the People to alter or abolish it." In addition to this statement of principles, the document served another purpose: Patriot leaders sent copies to France and Spain in hopes of winning their support and aid in the contest against Great Britain. They understood how important foreign recognition and aid would be to the creation of a new and independent nation.

The Declaration of Independence has since had a global impact, serving as the basis for many subsequent movements to gain independence from other colonial powers. It is part of America's civil religion, and thousands of people each year make pilgrimages to see the original document in Washington, DC.

The Declaration also reveals a fundamental contradiction of the American Revolution: the conflict between the existence of slavery and the idea that "all men are created equal." One-fifth of the population in 1776 was enslaved, and at the time he drafted the Declaration, Jefferson himself owned more than one hundred slaves. Further, the Declaration framed equality as existing only among white men; women and nonwhites were entirely left out of a document that referred to native peoples as "merciless Indian savages" who indiscriminately killed men, women, and children. Nonetheless, the promise of equality for all planted the seeds for future struggles waged by slaves, women, and many others to bring about its full realization. Much of American history is the story of the slow realization of the promise of equality expressed in the Declaration of Independence.

This content is available for free at http://cnx.org/content/col11740/latest/

> ### Click and Explore
>
>
> Visit Digital History (http://openstaxcollege.org/l/fcombatants) to view "The Female Combatants." In this 1776 engraving by an anonymous artist, Great Britain is depicted on the left as a staid, stern matron, while America, on the right, is shown as a half-dressed American Indian. Why do you think the artist depicted the two opposing sides this way?

6.2 The Early Years of the Revolution

By the end of this section, you will be able to:
- Explain the British and American strategies of 1776 through 1778
- Identify the key battles of the early years of the Revolution

After the British quit Boston, they slowly adopted a strategy to isolate New England from the rest of the colonies and force the insurgents in that region into submission, believing that doing so would end the conflict. At first, British forces focused on taking the principal colonial centers. They began by easily capturing New York City in 1776. The following year, they took over the American capital of Philadelphia. The larger British effort to isolate New England was implemented in 1777. That effort ultimately failed when the British surrendered a force of over five thousand to the Americans in the fall of 1777 at the Battle of Saratoga.

The major campaigns over the next several years took place in the middle colonies of New York, New Jersey, and Pennsylvania, whose populations were sharply divided between Loyalists and Patriots. Revolutionaries faced many hardships as British superiority on the battlefield became evident and the difficulty of funding the war caused strains.

THE BRITISH STRATEGY IN THE MIDDLE COLONIES

After evacuating Boston in March 1776, British forces sailed to Nova Scotia to regroup. They devised a strategy, successfully implemented in 1776, to take New York City. The following year, they planned to end the rebellion by cutting New England off from the rest of the colonies and starving it into submission. Three British armies were to move simultaneously from New York City, Montreal, and Fort Oswego to converge along the Hudson River; British control of that natural boundary would isolate New England.

General William Howe (Figure 6.9), commander in chief of the British forces in America, amassed thirty-two thousand troops on Staten Island in June and July 1776. His brother, Admiral Richard Howe, controlled New York Harbor. Command of New York City and the Hudson River was their goal. In August 1776, General Howe landed his forces on Long Island and easily routed the American Continental Army there in the Battle of Long Island (August 27). The Americans were outnumbered and lacked both military experience and discipline. Sensing victory, General and Admiral Howe arranged a peace conference in September 1776, where Benjamin Franklin, John Adams, and South Carolinian John Rutledge represented the Continental Congress. Despite the Howes' hopes, however, the Americans demanded recognition of their independence, which the Howes were not authorized to grant, and the conference disbanded.

Figure 6.9 General William Howe, shown here in a 1777 portrait by Richard Purcell, led British forces in America in the first years of the war.

On September 16, 1776, George Washington's forces held up against the British at the Battle of Harlem Heights. This important American military achievement, a key reversal after the disaster on Long Island, occurred as most of Washington's forces retreated to New Jersey. A few weeks later, on October 28, General Howe's forces defeated Washington's at the Battle of White Plains and New York City fell to the British. For the next seven years, the British made the city the headquarters for their military efforts to defeat the rebellion, which included raids on surrounding areas. In 1777, the British burned Danbury, Connecticut, and in July 1779, they set fire to homes in Fairfield and Norwalk. They held American prisoners aboard ships in the waters around New York City; the death toll was shocking, with thousands perishing in the holds. Meanwhile, New York City served as a haven for Loyalists who disagreed with the effort to break away from the Empire and establish an American republic.

GEORGE WASHINGTON AND THE CONTINENTAL ARMY

When the Second Continental Congress met in Philadelphia in May 1775, members approved the creation of a professional Continental Army with Washington as commander in chief (**Figure 6.10**). Although sixteen thousand volunteers enlisted, it took several years for the Continental Army to become a truly professional force. In 1775 and 1776, militias still composed the bulk of the Patriots' armed forces, and these soldiers returned home after the summer fighting season, drastically reducing the army's strength.

Figure 6.10 This 1775 etching shows George Washington taking command of the Continental Army at Cambridge, Massachusetts, just two weeks after his appointment by the Continental Congress.

That changed in late 1776 and early 1777, when Washington broke with conventional eighteenth-century military tactics that called for fighting in the summer months only. Intent on raising revolutionary morale after the British captured New York City, he launched surprise strikes against British forces in their winter quarters. In Trenton, New Jersey, he led his soldiers across the Delaware River and surprised an encampment of **Hessians**, German mercenaries hired by Great Britain to put down the American rebellion. Beginning the night of December 25, 1776, and continuing into the early hours of December 26, Washington moved on Trenton where the Hessians were encamped. Maintaining the element of surprise by attacking at Christmastime, he defeated them, taking over nine hundred captive. On January 3, 1777, Washington achieved another much-needed victory at the Battle of Princeton. He again broke with eighteenth-century military protocol by attacking unexpectedly after the fighting season had ended.

DEFINING "AMERICAN"

Thomas Paine on "The American Crisis"

During the American Revolution, following the publication of *Common Sense* in January 1776, Thomas Paine began a series of sixteen pamphlets known collectively as *The American Crisis* (**Figure 6.11**). He wrote the first volume in 1776, describing the dire situation facing the revolutionaries at the end of that hard year.

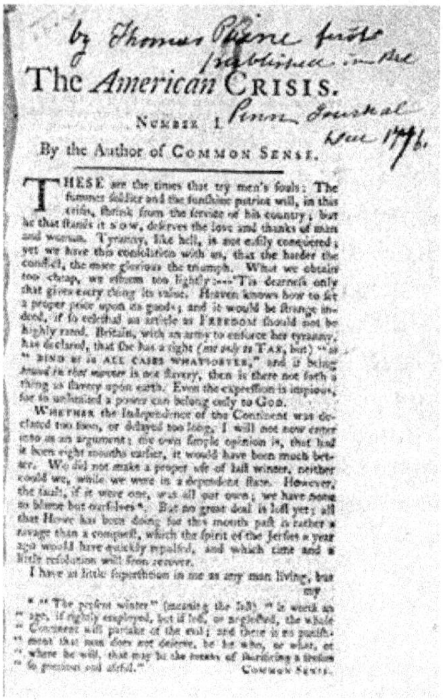

by Thomas Paine first published in the Penn Journal Dec 1776.

The *American* CRISIS.

NUMBER I.

By the Author of COMMON SENSE.

THESE are the times that try men's souls: The summer soldier and the sunshine patriot will, in this crisis, shrink from the service of his country; but he that stands it NOW, deserves the love and thanks of man and woman. Tyranny, like hell, is not easily conquered; yet we have this consolation with us, that the harder the conflict, the more glorious the triumph. What we obtain too cheap, we esteem too lightly:—'Tis dearness only that gives every thing its value. Heaven knows how to set a proper price upon its goods; and it would be strange indeed, if so celestial an article as FREEDOM should not be highly rated. Britain, with an army to enforce her tyranny, has declared, that she has a right (*not only to* TAX, but) "to "BIND US IN ALL CASES WHATSOEVER," and if being *bound in that manner* is not slavery, then is there not such a thing as slavery upon earth. Even the expression is impious, for so unlimited a power can belong only to GOD.

WHETHER the Independence of the Continent was declared too soon, or delayed too long, I will not now enter into as an argument; my own simple opinion is, that had it been eight months earlier, it would have been much better. We did not make a proper use of last winter, neither could we, while we were in a dependent state. However, the fault, if it were one, was all our own; we have none to blame but ourselves*. But no great deal is lost yet; all that Howe has been doing for this month past is rather a ravage than a conquest, which the spirit of the Jersies a year ago would have quickly repulsed, and which time and a little resolution will soon recover.

I have as little superstition in me as any man living, but my

* "The present winter" (meaning the last) "is worth an "age, if rightly employed, but if lost, or neglected, the whole "Continent will partake of the evil; and there is no punish-"ment that man does not deserve, be he who, or what, or "where he will, that may be the means of sacrificing a season "so precious and useful." COMMON SENSE.

Figure 6.11 Thomas Paine wrote the pamphlet *The American Crisis*, the first page of which is shown here, in 1776.

> These are the times that try men's souls. The summer soldier and the sunshine patriot will, in this crisis, shrink from the service of their country; but he that stands it now, deserves the love and thanks of man and woman. . . . Britain, with an army to enforce her tyranny, has declared that she has a right (not only to tax) but "to bind us in all cases whatsoever," and if being bound in that manner, is not slavery, then is there not such a thing as slavery upon earth. Even the expression is impious; for so unlimited a power can belong only to God. . . .
>
> I shall conclude this paper with some miscellaneous remarks on the state of our affairs; and shall begin with asking the following question, Why is it that the enemy have left the New England provinces, and made these middle ones the seat of war? The answer is easy: New England is not infested with Tories, and we are. I have been tender in raising the cry against these men, and used numberless arguments to show them their danger, but it will not do to sacrifice a world either to their folly or their baseness. The period is now arrived, in which either they or we must change our sentiments, or one or both must fall. . . .
>
> By perseverance and fortitude we have the prospect of a glorious issue; by cowardice and submission, the sad choice of a variety of evils—a ravaged country—a depopulated city—habitations without safety, and slavery without hope—our homes turned into barracks and bawdy-houses for Hessians, and a future race to provide for, whose fathers we shall doubt of. Look on this picture and weep over it! and if there yet remains one thoughtless wretch who believes it not, let him suffer it unlamented.
>
> —Thomas Paine, "The American Crisis," December 23, 1776

What topics does Paine address in this pamphlet? What was his purpose in writing? What does he write about Tories (Loyalists), and why does he consider them a problem?

> **Click and Explore**
>
>  Visit Wikisource (http://openstaxcollege.org/l/amcrisis) to read the rest of Thomas Paine's first *American Crisis* pamphlet, as well as the other fifteen in the series.

PHILADELPHIA AND SARATOGA: BRITISH AND AMERICAN VICTORIES

In August 1777, General Howe brought fifteen thousand British troops to Chesapeake Bay as part of his plan to take Philadelphia, where the Continental Congress met. That fall, the British defeated Washington's soldiers in the Battle of Brandywine Creek and took control of Philadelphia, forcing the Continental Congress to flee. During the winter of 1777–1778, the British occupied the city, and Washington's army camped at Valley Forge, Pennsylvania.

Washington's winter at Valley Forge was a low point for the American forces. A lack of supplies weakened the men, and disease took a heavy toll. Amid the cold, hunger, and sickness, soldiers deserted in droves. On February 16, Washington wrote to George Clinton, governor of New York: "For some days past, there has been little less than a famine in camp. A part of the army has been a week without any kind of flesh & the rest three or four days. Naked and starving as they are, we cannot enough admire the incomparable patience and fidelity of the soldiery, that they have not been ere [before] this excited by their sufferings to a general mutiny and dispersion." Of eleven thousand soldiers encamped at Valley Forge, twenty-five hundred died of starvation, malnutrition, and disease. As Washington feared, nearly one hundred soldiers deserted every week. (Desertions continued, and by 1780, Washington was executing recaptured deserters every Saturday.) The low morale extended all the way to Congress, where some wanted to replace Washington with a more seasoned leader.

Assistance came to Washington and his soldiers in February 1778 in the form of the Prussian soldier Friedrich Wilhelm von Steuben (**Figure 6.12**). Baron von Steuben was an experienced military man, and he implemented a thorough training course for Washington's ragtag troops. By drilling a small corps of soldiers and then having them train others, he finally transformed the Continental Army into a force capable of standing up to the professional British and Hessian soldiers. His drill manual—*Regulations for the Order and Discipline of the Troops of the United States*—informed military practices in the United States for the next several decades.

Figure 6.12 Prussian soldier Friedrich Wilhelm von Steuben, shown here in a 1786 portrait by Ralph Earl, was instrumental in transforming Washington's Continental Army into a professional armed force.

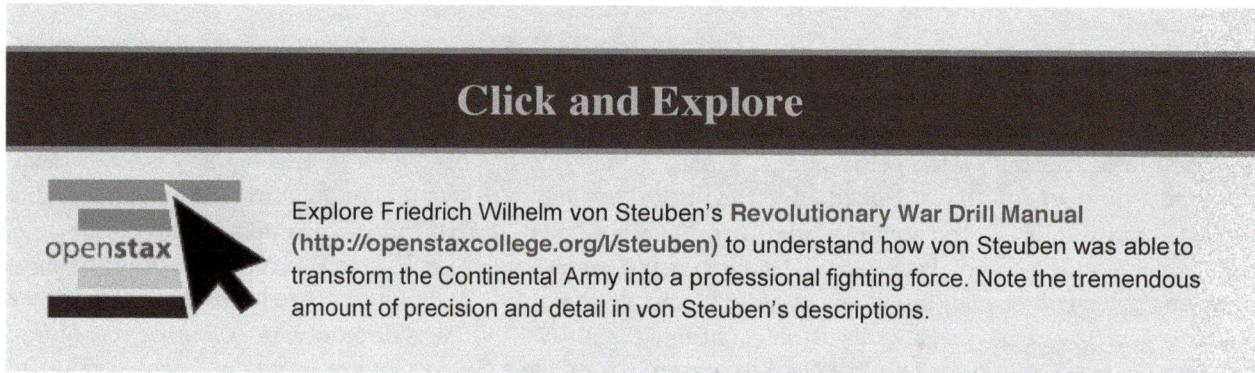

Explore Friedrich Wilhelm von Steuben's **Revolutionary War Drill Manual** (http://openstaxcollege.org/l/steuben) to understand how von Steuben was able to transform the Continental Army into a professional fighting force. Note the tremendous amount of precision and detail in von Steuben's descriptions.

Meanwhile, the campaign to sever New England from the rest of the colonies had taken an unexpected turn during the fall of 1777. The British had attempted to implement the plan, drawn up by Lord George Germain and Prime Minister Lord North, to isolate New England with the combined forces of three armies. One army, led by General John Burgoyne, would march south from Montreal. A second force, led by Colonel Barry St. Leger and made up of British troops and Iroquois, would march east from Fort Oswego on the banks of Lake Ontario. A third force, led by General Sir Henry Clinton, would march north from New York City. The armies would converge at Albany and effectively cut the rebellion in two by isolating New England. This northern campaign fell victim to competing strategies, however, as General Howe had meanwhile decided to take Philadelphia. His decision to capture that city siphoned off troops that would have been vital to the overall success of the campaign in 1777.

The British plan to isolate New England ended in disaster. St. Leger's efforts to bring his force of British regulars, Loyalist fighters, and Iroquois allies east to link up with General Burgoyne failed, and he retreated to Quebec. Burgoyne's forces encountered ever-stiffer resistance as he made his way south from Montreal, down Lake Champlain and the upper Hudson River corridor. Although they did capture Fort Ticonderoga when American forces retreated, Burgoyne's army found themselves surrounded by a sea of colonial militias in Saratoga, New York. In the meantime, the small British force under Clinton that left New York City to aid Burgoyne advanced slowly up the Hudson River, failing to provide the much-needed support for the troops at Saratoga. On October 17, 1777, Burgoyne surrendered his five thousand soldiers to the Continental Army (**Figure 6.13**).

Figure 6.13 This German engraving, created by Daniel Chodowiecki in 1784, shows British soldiers laying down their arms before the American forces.

The American victory at the Battle of Saratoga was the major turning point in the war. This victory convinced the French to recognize American independence and form a military alliance with the new nation, which changed the course of the war by opening the door to badly needed military support from France. Still smarting from their defeat by Britain in the Seven Years' War, the French supplied the United States with gunpowder and money, as well as soldiers and naval forces that proved decisive in the defeat of Great Britain. The French also contributed military leaders, including the Marquis de Lafayette, who arrived in America in 1777 as a volunteer and served as Washington's aide-de-camp.

The war quickly became more difficult for the British, who had to fight the rebels in North America as well as the French in the Caribbean. Following France's lead, Spain joined the war against Great Britain in 1779, though it did not recognize American independence until 1783. The Dutch Republic also began to support the American revolutionaries and signed a treaty of commerce with the United States in 1782.

Great Britain's effort to isolate New England in 1777 failed. In June 1778, the occupying British force in Philadelphia evacuated and returned to New York City in order to better defend that city, and the British then turned their attention to the southern colonies.

6.3 War in the South

By the end of this section, you will be able to:
- Outline the British southern strategy and its results
- Describe key American victories and the end of the war
- Identify the main terms of the Treaty of Paris (1783)

By 1778, the war had turned into a stalemate. Although some in Britain, including Prime Minister Lord North, wanted peace, King George III demanded that the colonies be brought to obedience. To break the deadlock, the British revised their strategy and turned their attention to the southern colonies, where they could expect more support from Loyalists. The southern colonies soon became the center of the fighting. The southern strategy brought the British success at first, but thanks to the leadership of George Washington and General Nathanael Greene and the crucial assistance of French forces, the Continental Army defeated the British at Yorktown, effectively ending further large-scale operations during the war.

GEORGIA AND SOUTH CAROLINA

The British architect of the war strategy, Lord George Germain, believed Britain would gain the upper hand with the support of Loyalists, slaves, and Indian allies in the South, and indeed, this southern strategy initially achieved great success. The British began their southern campaign by capturing Savannah, the capital of Georgia, in December 1778. In Georgia, they found support from thousands of slaves who ran to the British side to escape their bondage. As the British regained political control in Georgia, they forced the inhabitants to swear allegiance to the king and formed twenty Loyalist regiments. The Continental Congress had suggested that slaves be given freedom if they joined the Patriot army against the British, but revolutionaries in Georgia and South Carolina refused to consider this proposal. Once again, the Revolution served to further divisions over race and slavery.

After taking Georgia, the British turned their attention to South Carolina. Before the Revolution, South Carolina had been starkly divided between the backcountry, which harbored revolutionary partisans, and the coastal regions, where Loyalists remained a powerful force. Waves of violence rocked the backcountry from the late 1770s into the early 1780s. The Revolution provided an opportunity for residents to fight over their local resentments and antagonisms with murderous consequences. Revenge killings and the destruction of property became mainstays in the savage civil war that gripped the South.

In April 1780, a British force of eight thousand soldiers besieged American forces in Charleston (**Figure 6.14**). After six weeks of the Siege of Charleston, the British triumphed. General Benjamin Lincoln, who led the effort for the revolutionaries, had to surrender his entire force, the largest American loss during the entire war. Many of the defeated Americans were placed in jails or in British prison ships anchored in Charleston Harbor. The British established a military government in Charleston under the command of General Sir Henry Clinton. From this base, Clinton ordered General Charles Cornwallis to subdue the rest of South Carolina.

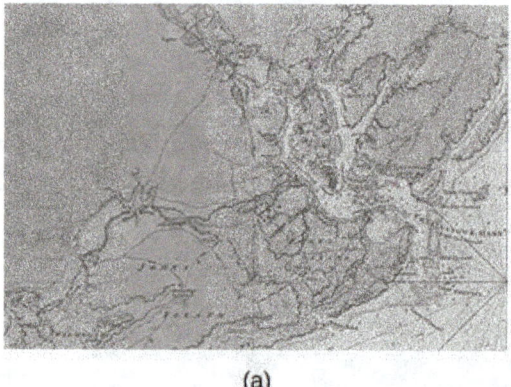 

(a) (b)

Figure 6.14 This 1780 map of Charleston (a), which shows details of the Continental defenses, was probably drawn by British engineers in anticipation of the attack on the city. The Siege of Charleston was one of a series of defeats for the Continental forces in the South, which led the Continental Congress to place General Nathanael Greene (b), shown here in a 1783 portrait by Charles Wilson Peale, in command in late 1780. Greene led his troops to two crucial victories.

The disaster at Charleston led the Continental Congress to change leadership by placing General Horatio Gates in charge of American forces in the South. However, General Gates fared no better than General Lincoln; at the Battle of Camden, South Carolina, in August 1780, Cornwallis forced General Gates to retreat into North Carolina. Camden was one of the worst disasters suffered by American armies during the entire Revolutionary War. Congress again changed military leadership, this time by placing General Nathanael Greene (**Figure 6.14**) in command in December 1780.

As the British had hoped, large numbers of Loyalists helped ensure the success of the southern strategy, and thousands of slaves seeking freedom arrived to aid Cornwallis's army. However, the war turned in the Americans' favor in 1781. General Greene realized that to defeat Cornwallis, he did not have to win a single battle. So long as he remained in the field, he could continue to destroy isolated British forces. Greene therefore made a strategic decision to divide his own troops to wage war—and the strategy worked. American forces under General Daniel Morgan decisively beat the British at the Battle of Cowpens in South Carolina. General Cornwallis now abandoned his strategy of defeating the backcountry rebels in South Carolina. Determined to destroy Greene's army, he gave chase as Greene strategically retreated north into North Carolina. At the Battle of Guilford Courthouse in March 1781, the British prevailed on the battlefield but suffered extensive losses, an outcome that paralleled the Battle of Bunker Hill nearly six years earlier in June 1775.

YORKTOWN

In the summer of 1781, Cornwallis moved his army to **Yorktown**, Virginia. He expected the Royal Navy to transport his army to New York, where he thought he would join General Sir Henry Clinton. Yorktown was a tobacco port on a peninsula, and Cornwallis believed the British navy would be able to keep the coast clear of rebel ships. Sensing an opportunity, a combined French and American force of sixteen thousand men swarmed the peninsula in September 1781. Washington raced south with his forces, now a disciplined army, as did the Marquis de Lafayette and the Comte de Rochambeau with their French troops. The French Admiral de Grasse sailed his naval force into Chesapeake Bay, preventing Lord Cornwallis from taking a seaward escape route.

In October 1781, the American forces began the battle for Yorktown, and after a siege that lasted eight days, Lord Cornwallis capitulated on October 19 (**Figure 6.15**). Tradition says that during the surrender of his troops, the British band played "The World Turned Upside Down," a song that befitted the Empire's unexpected reversal of fortune.

Figure 6.15 The 1820 painting above, by John Trumbull, is titled *Surrender of Lord Cornwallis*, but Cornwallis actually sent his general, Charles O'Hara, to perform the ceremonial surrendering of the sword. The painting depicts General Benjamin Lincoln holding out his hand to receive the sword. General George Washington is in the background on the brown horse, since he refused to accept the sword from anyone but Cornwallis himself.

DEFINING "AMERICAN"

"The World Turned Upside Down"

"The World Turned Upside Down," reputedly played during the surrender of the British at Yorktown, was a traditional English ballad from the seventeenth century. It was also the theme of a popular British print that circulated in the 1790s (**Figure 6.16**).

Figure 6.16 In many of the images in this popular print, entitled "The World Turned Upside Down or the Folly of Man," animals and humans have switched places. In one, children take care of their parents, while in another, the sun, moon, and stars appear below the earth.

Why do you think these images were popular in Great Britain in the decade following the Revolutionary War? What would these images imply to Americans?

Click and Explore

Visit the **Public Domain Review** (http://openstaxcollege.org/l/worldupside) to explore the images in an eighteenth-century British chapbook (a pamphlet for tracts or ballads) titled "The World Turned Upside Down." The chapbook is illustrated with woodcuts similar to those in the popular print mentioned above.

THE TREATY OF PARIS

The British defeat at Yorktown made the outcome of the war all but certain. In light of the American victory, the Parliament of Great Britain voted to end further military operations against the rebels and to begin peace negotiations. Support for the war effort had come to an end, and British military forces began to evacuate the former American colonies in 1782. When hostilities had ended, Washington resigned as commander in chief and returned to his Virginia home.

In April 1782, Benjamin Franklin, John Adams, and John Jay had begun informal peace negotiations in Paris. Officials from Great Britain and the United States finalized the treaty in 1783, signing the Treaty of Paris (**Figure 6.17**) in September of that year. The treaty recognized the independence of the United

States; placed the western, eastern, northern, and southern boundaries of the nation at the Mississippi River, the Atlantic Ocean, Canada, and Florida, respectively; and gave New Englanders fishing rights in the waters off Newfoundland. Under the terms of the treaty, individual states were encouraged to refrain from persecuting Loyalists and to return their confiscated property.

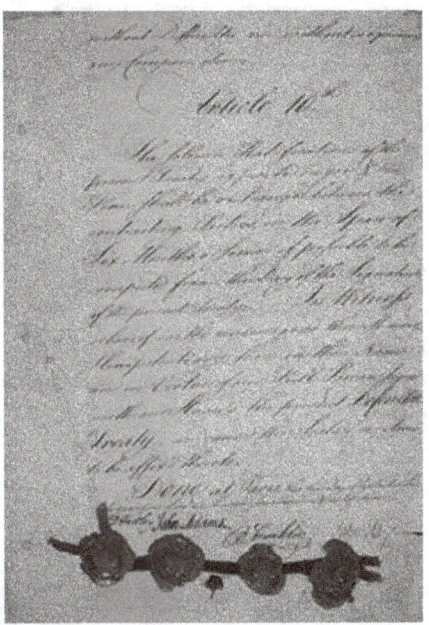

Figure 6.17 The last page of the Treaty of Paris, signed on September 3, 1783, contained the signatures and seals of representatives for both the British and the Americans. From right to left, the seals pictured belong to David Hartley, who represented Great Britain, and John Adams, Benjamin Franklin, and John Jay for the Americans.

6.4 Identity during the American Revolution

By the end of this section, you will be able to:
- Explain Loyalist and Patriot sentiments
- Identify different groups that participated in the Revolutionary War

The American Revolution in effect created multiple civil wars. Many of the resentments and antagonisms that fed these conflicts predated the Revolution, and the outbreak of war acted as the catalyst they needed to burst forth. In particular, the middle colonies of New York, New Jersey, and Pennsylvania had deeply divided populations. Loyalty to Great Britain came in many forms, from wealthy elites who enjoyed the prewar status quo to runaway slaves who desired the freedom that the British offered.

LOYALISTS

Historians disagree on what percentage of colonists were Loyalists; estimates range from 20 percent to over 30 percent. In general, however, of British America's population of 2.5 million, roughly one-third remained loyal to Great Britain, while another third committed themselves to the cause of independence. The remaining third remained apathetic, content to continue with their daily lives as best they could and preferring not to engage in the struggle.

Many Loyalists were royal officials and merchants with extensive business ties to Great Britain, who viewed themselves as the rightful and just defenders of the British constitution. Others simply resented local business and political rivals who supported the Revolution, viewing the rebels as hypocrites and schemers who selfishly used the break with the Empire to increase their fortunes. In New York's Hudson Valley, animosity among the tenants of estates owned by Revolutionary leaders turned them to the cause of King and Empire.

During the war, all the states passed **confiscation acts**, which gave the new revolutionary governments in the former colonies the right to seize Loyalist land and property. To ferret out Loyalists, revolutionary governments also passed laws requiring the male population to take oaths of allegiance to the new states. Those who refused lost their property and were often imprisoned or made to work for the new local revolutionary order.

William Franklin, Benjamin Franklin's only surviving son, remained loyal to Crown and Empire and served as royal governor of New Jersey, a post he secured with his father's help. During the war, revolutionaries imprisoned William in Connecticut; however, he remained steadfast in his allegiance to Great Britain and moved to England after the Revolution. He and his father never reconciled.

As many as nineteen thousand colonists served the British in the effort to put down the rebellion, and after the Revolution, as many as 100,000 colonists left, moving to England or north to Canada rather than staying in the new United States (**Figure 6.18**). Eight thousand whites and five thousand free blacks went to Britain. Over thirty thousand went to Canada, transforming that nation from predominately French to predominantly British. Another sizable group of Loyalists went to the British West Indies, taking their slaves with them.

Figure 6.18 *The Coming of the Loyalists*, a ca. 1880 work that artist Henry Sandham created at least a century after the Revolution, shows Anglo-American colonists arriving by ship in New Brunswick, Canada.

MY STORY

✣ *Hannah Ingraham on Removing to Nova Scotia*

Hannah Ingraham was eleven years old in 1783, when her Loyalist family removed from New York to Ste. Anne's Point in the colony of Nova Scotia. Later in life, she compiled her memories of that time.

> [Father] said we were to go to Nova Scotia, that a ship was ready to take us there, so we made all haste to get ready. . . . Then on Tuesday, suddenly the house was surrounded by rebels and father was taken prisoner and carried away. . . . When morning came, they said he was free to go.
>
> We had five wagon loads carried down the Hudson in a sloop and then we went on board the transport that was to bring us to Saint John. I was just eleven years old when we left our farm to come here. It was the last transport of the season and had on board all those who could not come sooner. The first transports had come in May so the people had all the summer before them to get settled. . . .
>
> We lived in a tent at St. Anne's until father got a house ready. . . . There was no floor laid, no windows, no chimney, no door, but we had a roof at least. A good fire was blazing and mother had a big loaf of bread and she boiled a kettle of water and put a good piece of butter in a pewter bowl. We toasted the bread and all sat around the bowl and ate our breakfast that morning and mother said: "Thank God we are no longer in dread of having shots fired through our house. This is the sweetest meal I ever tasted for many a day."

What do these excerpts tell you about life as a Loyalist in New York or as a transplant to Canada?

SLAVES AND INDIANS

While some slaves who fought for the Patriot cause received their freedom, revolutionary leaders—unlike the British—did not grant such slaves their freedom as a matter of course. Washington, the owner of more than two hundred slaves during the Revolution, refused to let slaves serve in the army, although he did allow free blacks. (In his will, Washington did free his slaves.) In the new United States, the Revolution largely reinforced a racial identity based on skin color. Whiteness, now a national identity, denoted freedom and stood as the key to power. Blackness, more than ever before, denoted servile status. Indeed, despite their class and ethnic differences, white revolutionaries stood mostly united in their hostility to both blacks and Indians.

MY STORY

◎ *Boyrereau Brinch and Boston King on the Revolutionary War*

In the Revolutionary War, some blacks, both free and enslaved, chose to fight for the Americans (**Figure 6.19**). Others chose to fight for the British, who offered them freedom for joining their cause. Read the excerpts below for the perspective of a black veteran from each side of the conflict.

Figure 6.19 Jean-Baptiste-Antoine de Verger created this 1781 watercolor, which depicts American soldiers at the Siege of Yorktown. Verger was an officer in Rochambeau's army, and his diary holds firsthand accounts of his experiences in the campaigns of 1780 and 1781. This image contains one of the earliest known representations of a black Continental soldier.

Boyrereau Brinch was captured in Africa at age sixteen and brought to America as a slave. He joined the Patriot forces and was honorably discharged and emancipated after the war. He told his story to Benjamin Prentiss, who published it as *The Blind African Slave* in 1810.

> Finally, I was in the battles at Cambridge, White Plains, Monmouth, Princeton, Newark, Frog's Point, Horseneck where I had a ball pass through my knapsack. All which battels [sic] the reader can obtain a more perfect account of in history, than I can give. At last we returned to West Point and were discharged [1783], as the war was over. Thus was I, a slave for five years fighting for liberty. After we were disbanded, I returned to my old master at Woodbury [Connecticut], with whom I lived one year, my services in the American war, having emancipated me from further slavery, and from being bartered or sold. . . . Here I enjoyed the pleasures of a freeman; my food was sweet, my labor pleasure: and one bright gleam of life seemed to shine upon me.

Boston King was a Charleston-born slave who escaped his master and joined the Loyalists. He made his way to Nova Scotia and later Sierra Leone, where he published his memoirs in 1792. The excerpt below describes his experience in New York after the war.

> When I arrived at New-York, my friends rejoiced to see me once more restored to liberty, and joined me in praising the Lord for his mercy and goodness. . . . [In 1783] the horrors and devastation of war happily terminated, and peace was restored between America and Great Britain, which diffused universal joy among all parties, except us, who had escaped from slavery and taken refuge in the English army; for a report prevailed at New-York, that all the slaves, in number 2000, were to be delivered up to their masters, altho' some of them had been three or four years among the English. This dreadful rumour filled us all with inexpressible anguish and terror, especially when we saw our old masters coming from Virginia, North-Carolina, and other parts, and seizing upon their slaves in the streets of New-York, or even dragging them out of their beds. Many of the slaves had very cruel masters, so that the thoughts of returning home with them embittered life to us. For some days we lost our appetite for food, and sleep departed from our eyes. The English had compassion upon us in the day of distress, and issued out a Proclamation, importing, That all slaves should be free, who had taken refuge in the British lines, and claimed the sanction and privileges of

the Proclamations respecting the security and protection of Negroes. In consequence of this, each of us received a certificate from the commanding officer at New-York, which dispelled all our fears, and filled us with joy and gratitude.

What do these two narratives have in common, and how are they different? How do the two men describe freedom?

For slaves willing to run away and join the British, the American Revolution offered a unique occasion to escape bondage. Of the half a million slaves in the American colonies during the Revolution, twenty thousand joined the British cause. At Yorktown, for instance, thousands of black troops fought with Lord Cornwallis. Slaves belonging to George Washington, Thomas Jefferson, Patrick Henry, and other revolutionaries seized the opportunity for freedom and fled to the British side. Between ten and twenty thousand slaves gained their freedom because of the Revolution; arguably, the Revolution created the largest slave uprising and the greatest emancipation until the Civil War. After the Revolution, some of these African Loyalists emigrated to Sierra Leone on the west coast of Africa. Others removed to Canada and England. It is also true that people of color made heroic contributions to the cause of American independence. However, while the British offered slaves freedom, most American revolutionaries clung to notions of black inferiority.

Powerful Indian peoples who had allied themselves with the British, including the Mohawk and the Creek, also remained loyal to the Empire. A Mohawk named Joseph Brant, whose given name was Thayendanegea (**Figure 6.20**), rose to prominence while fighting for the British during the Revolution. He joined forces with Colonel Barry St. Leger during the 1777 campaign, which ended with the surrender of General Burgoyne at Saratoga. After the war, Brant moved to the Six Nations reserve in Canada. From his home on the shores of Lake Ontario, he remained active in efforts to restrict white encroachment onto Indian lands. After their defeat, the British did not keep promises they'd made to help their Indian allies keep their territory; in fact, the Treaty of Paris granted the United States huge amounts of supposedly British-owned regions that were actually Indian lands.

(a) (b)

Figure 6.20 What similarities can you see in these two portraits of Joseph Brant, one by Gilbert Stuart in 1786 (a) and one by Charles Wilson Peale in 1797 (b)? What are the differences? Why do you think the artists made the specific choices they did?

PATRIOTS

The American revolutionaries (also called Patriots or Whigs) came from many different backgrounds and included merchants, shoemakers, farmers, and sailors. What is extraordinary is the way in which the struggle for independence brought a vast cross-section of society together, animated by a common cause.

During the war, the revolutionaries faced great difficulties, including massive supply problems; clothing, ammunition, tents, and equipment were all hard to come by. After an initial burst of enthusiasm in 1775 and 1776, the shortage of supplies became acute in 1777 through 1779, as Washington's difficult winter at Valley Forge demonstrates.

Funding the war effort also proved very difficult. Whereas the British could pay in gold and silver, the American forces relied on paper money, backed by loans obtained in Europe. This first American money was called **Continental currency**; unfortunately, it quickly fell in value. "Not worth a Continental" soon became a shorthand term for something of no value. The new revolutionary government printed a great amount of this paper money, resulting in runaway inflation. By 1781, inflation was such that 146 Continental dollars were worth only one dollar in gold. The problem grew worse as each former colony, now a revolutionary state, printed its own currency.

WOMEN

In colonial America, women shouldered enormous domestic and child-rearing responsibilities. The war for independence only increased their workload and, in some ways, solidified their roles. Rebel leaders required women to produce articles for war—everything from clothing to foodstuffs—while also keeping their homesteads going. This was not an easy task when their husbands and sons were away fighting. Women were also expected to provide food and lodging for armies and to nurse wounded soldiers.

The Revolution opened some new doors for women, however, as they took on public roles usually reserved for men. The Daughters of Liberty, an informal organization formed in the mid-1760s to oppose British revenue-raising measures, worked tirelessly to support the war effort. Esther DeBerdt Reed of Philadelphia, wife of Governor Joseph Reed, formed the Ladies Association of Philadelphia and led a fundraising drive to provide sorely needed supplies to the Continental Army. In "The Sentiments of an American Woman" (1780), she wrote to other women, "The time is arrived to display the same sentiments which animated us at the beginning of the Revolution, when we renounced the use of teas, however agreeable to our taste, rather than receive them from our persecutors; when we made it appear to them that we placed former necessaries in the rank of superfluities, when our liberty was interested; when our republican and laborious hands spun the flax, prepared the linen intended for the use of our soldiers; when exiles and fugitives we supported with courage all the evils which are the concomitants of war." Reed and other elite women in Philadelphia raised almost $300,000 in Continental money for the war.

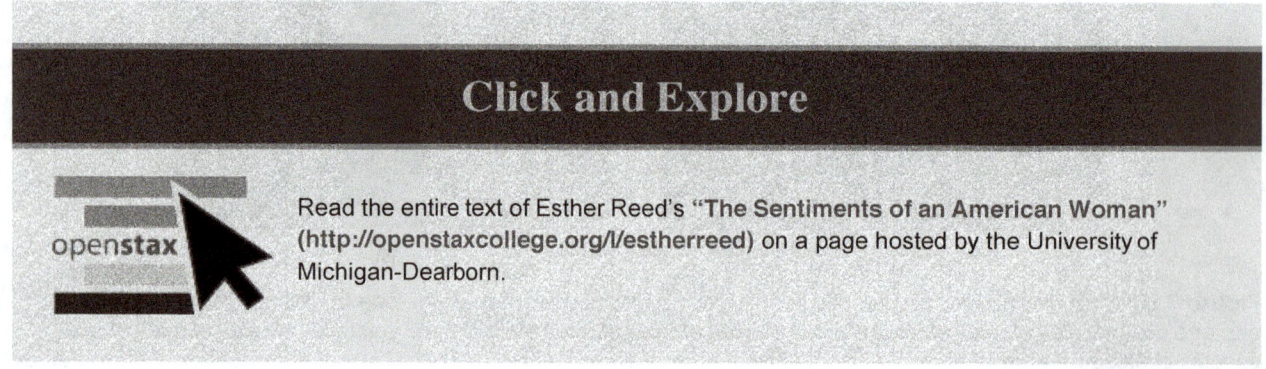

Click and Explore

Read the entire text of Esther Reed's "The Sentiments of an American Woman" (http://openstaxcollege.org/l/estherreed) on a page hosted by the University of Michigan-Dearborn.

Women who did not share Reed's elite status nevertheless played key economic roles by producing homespun cloth and food. During shortages, some women formed mobs and wrested supplies from those who hoarded them. Crowds of women beset merchants and demanded fair prices for goods; if a merchant refused, a riot would ensue. Still other women accompanied the army as "camp followers," serving as cooks, washerwomen, and nurses. A few also took part in combat and proved their equality with men through violence against the hated British.

CHAPTER 7

Creating Republican Governments, 1776–1790

Figure 7.1 John Trumbull, Washington's aide-de-camp, painted this wartime image of Washington on a promontory above the Hudson River. Just behind Washington, his slave William "Billy" Lee has his eyes firmly fixed on his master. In the far background, British warships fire on an American fort.

Chapter Outline

7.1 Common Sense: From Monarchy to an American Republic
7.2 How Much Revolutionary Change?
7.3 Debating Democracy
7.4 The Constitutional Convention and Federal Constitution

Introduction

After the Revolutionary War, the ideology that "all men are created equal" failed to match up with reality, as the revolutionary generation could not solve the contradictions of freedom and slavery in the new United States. Trumbull's 1780 painting of George Washington (**Figure 7.1**) hints at some of these contradictions. What attitude do you think Trumbull was trying to convey? Why did Trumbull include Washington's slave Billy Lee, and what does Lee represent in this painting?

During the 1770s and 1780s, Americans took bold steps to define American equality. Each state held constitutional conventions and crafted state constitutions that defined how government would operate and who could participate in political life. Many elite revolutionaries recoiled in horror from the idea of majority rule—the basic principle of democracy—fearing that it would effectively create a "mob rule" that would bring about the ruin of the hard-fought struggle for independence. Statesmen everywhere believed that a republic should replace the British monarchy: a government where the important affairs would be entrusted only to representative men of learning and refinement.

7.1 Common Sense: From Monarchy to an American Republic

By the end of this section, you will be able to:
- Compare and contrast monarchy and republican government
- Describe the tenets of republicanism

While monarchies dominated eighteenth-century Europe, American revolutionaries were determined to find an alternative to this method of government. Radical pamphleteer Thomas Paine, whose enormously popular essay *Common Sense* was first published in January 1776, advocated a republic: a state without a king. Six months later, Jefferson's Declaration of Independence affirmed the break with England but did not suggest what form of government should replace monarchy, the only system most English colonists had ever known. In the late eighteenth century, republics were few and far between. Genoa, Venice, and the Dutch Republic provided examples of states without monarchs, but many European Enlightenment thinkers questioned the stability of a republic. Nonetheless, after their break from Great Britain, Americans turned to republicanism for their new government.

REPUBLICANISM AS A POLITICAL PHILOSOPHY

Monarchy rests on the practice of dynastic succession, in which the monarch's child or other relative inherits the throne. Contested dynastic succession produced chronic conflict and warfare in Europe. In the eighteenth century, well-established monarchs ruled most of Europe and, according to tradition, were obligated to protect and guide their subjects. However, by the mid-1770s, many American colonists believed that George III, the king of Great Britain, had failed to do so. Patriots believed the British monarchy under George III had been corrupted and the king turned into a tyrant who cared nothing for the traditional liberties afforded to members of the British Empire. The disaffection from monarchy explains why a republic appeared a better alternative to the revolutionaries.

American revolutionaries looked to the past for inspiration for their break with the British monarchy and their adoption of a republican form of government. The Roman Republic provided guidance. Much like

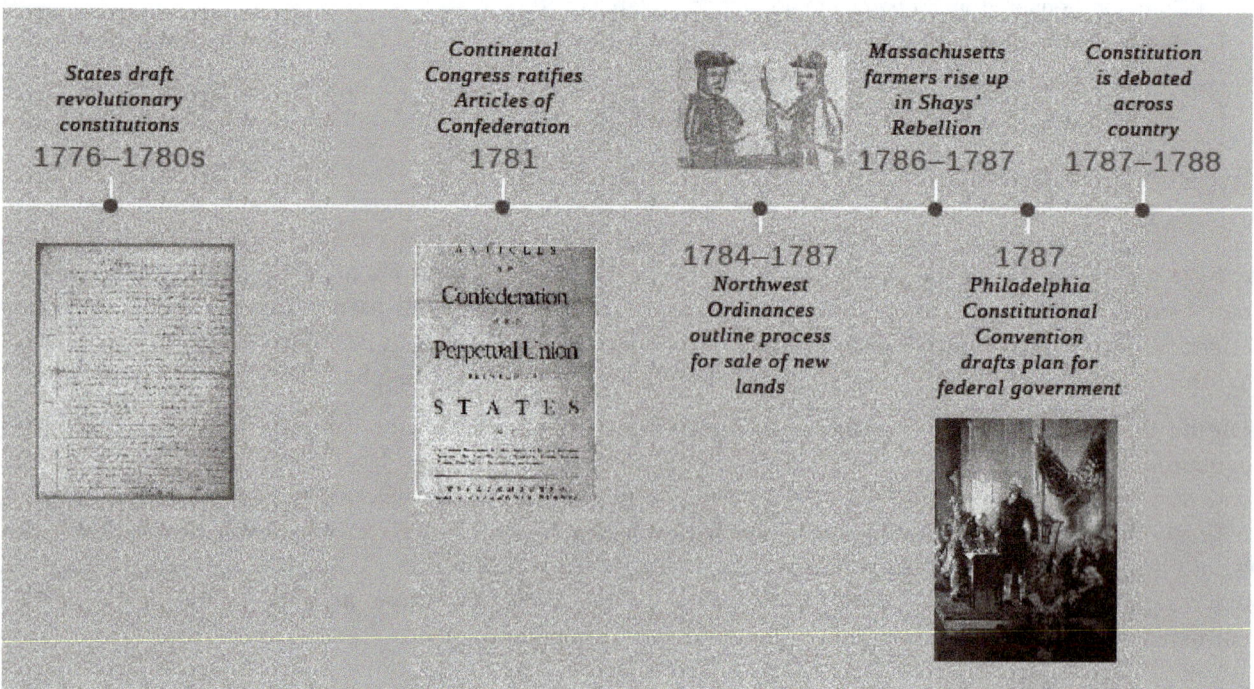

Figure 7.2

the Americans in their struggle against Britain, Romans had thrown off monarchy and created a republic in which Roman citizens would appoint or select the leaders who would represent them.

Click and Explore

Visit the Metropolitan Museum of Art (http://openstaxcollege.org/l/ceracchi) to see a Roman-style bust of George Washington, complete with toga. In 1791, Italian sculptor Giuseppe Ceracchi visited Philadelphia, hoping the government might commission a monument of his creation. He did not succeed, but the bust of Washington, one of the ones he produced to demonstrate his skill, illustrates the connection between the American and Roman republics that revolutionaries made.

While republicanism offered an alternative to monarchy, it was also an alternative to **democracy**, a system of government characterized by **majority rule**, where the majority of citizens have the power to make decisions binding upon the whole. To many revolutionaries, especially wealthy landowners, merchants, and planters, democracy did not offer a good replacement for monarchy. Indeed, **conservative Whigs** defined themselves in opposition to democracy, which they equated with anarchy. In the tenth in a series of essays later known as *The Federalist Papers*, Virginian James Madison wrote: "Democracies have ever been spectacles of turbulence and contention; have ever been found incompatible with personal security or the rights of property; and have in general been as short in their lives as they have been violent in their deaths." Many shared this perspective and worked hard to keep democratic tendencies in check. It is easy to understand why democracy seemed threatening: majority rule can easily overpower minority rights, and the wealthy few had reason to fear that a hostile and envious majority could seize and redistribute their wealth.

While many now assume the United States was founded as a democracy, history, as always, is more complicated. Conservative Whigs believed in government by a patrician class, a ruling group composed of a small number of privileged families. **Radical Whigs** favored broadening the popular participation in political life and pushed for democracy. The great debate after independence was secured centered on this question: Who should rule in the new American republic?

REPUBLICANISM AS A SOCIAL PHILOSOPHY

According to political theory, a republic requires its citizens to cultivate virtuous behavior; if the people are virtuous, the republic will survive. If the people become corrupt, the republic will fall. Whether republicanism succeeded or failed in the United States would depend on civic virtue and an educated citizenry. Revolutionary leaders agreed that the ownership of property provided one way to measure an individual's virtue, arguing that property holders had the greatest stake in society and therefore could be trusted to make decisions for it. By the same token, non-property holders, they believed, should have very little to do with government. In other words, unlike a democracy, in which the mass of non-property holders could exercise the political right to vote, a republic would limit political rights to property holders. In this way, republicanism exhibited a bias toward the elite, a preference that is understandable given the colonial legacy. During colonial times, wealthy planters and merchants in the American colonies had looked to the British ruling class, whose social order demanded deference from those of lower rank, as a model of behavior. Old habits died hard.

DEFINING "AMERICAN"

✪ Benjamin Franklin's Thirteen Virtues for Character Development

In the 1780s, Benjamin Franklin carefully defined thirteen virtues to help guide his countrymen in maintaining a virtuous republic. His choice of thirteen is telling since he wrote for the citizens of the thirteen new American republics. These virtues were:

1. Temperance. Eat not to dullness; drink not to elevation.
2. Silence. Speak not but what may benefit others or yourself; avoid trifling conversation.
3. Order. Let all your things have their places; let each part of your business have its time.
4. Resolution. Resolve to perform what you ought; perform without fail what you resolve.
5. Frugality. Make no expense but to do good to others or yourself; i.e., waste nothing.
6. Industry. Lose no time; be always employ'd in something useful; cut off all unnecessary actions.
7. Sincerity. Use no hurtful deceit; think innocently and justly, and, if you speak, speak accordingly.
8. Justice. Wrong none by doing injuries, or omitting the benefits that are your duty.
9. Moderation. Avoid extremes; forbear resenting injuries so much as you think they deserve.
10. Cleanliness. Tolerate no uncleanliness in body, cloaths, or habitation.
11. Tranquillity. Be not disturbed at trifles, or at accidents common or unavoidable.
12. Chastity. Rarely use venery but for health or offspring, never to dullness, weakness, or the injury of your own or another's peace or reputation.
13. Humility. Imitate Jesus and Socrates.

Franklin's thirteen virtues suggest that hard work and good behavior will bring success. What factors does Franklin ignore? How would he likely address a situation in which children inherit great wealth rather than working for it? How do Franklin's values help to define the notion of republican virtue?

Click and Explore

Check how well you are demonstrating all thirteen of Franklin's virtues (http://openstaxcollege.org/l/13virtues) on thirteenvirtues.com, where you can register to track your progress.

George Washington served as a role model par excellence for the new republic, embodying the exceptional talent and public virtue prized under the political and social philosophy of republicanism. He did not seek to become the new king of America; instead he retired as commander in chief of the Continental Army and returned to his Virginia estate at Mount Vernon to resume his life among the planter elite. Washington modeled his behavior on that of the Roman aristocrat Cincinnatus, a representative of the patrician or ruling class, who had also retired from public service in the Roman Republic and returned to his estate to pursue agricultural life.

The aristocratic side of republicanism—and the belief that the true custodians of public virtue were those who had served in the military—found expression in the Society of the Cincinnati, of which Washington was the first president general (**Figure 7.3**). Founded in 1783, the society admitted only officers of the Continental Army and the French forces, not militia members or minutemen. Following the rule of primogeniture, the eldest sons of members inherited their fathers' memberships. The society still exists today and retains the motto *Omnia relinquit servare rempublicam* ("He relinquished everything to save the Republic").

Figure 7.3 This membership certificate for the Society of the Cincinnati commemorates "the great Event which gave Independence to North America."

7.2 How Much Revolutionary Change?

By the end of this section, you will be able to:
- Describe the status of women in the new republic
- Describe the status of nonwhites in the new republic

Elite republican revolutionaries did not envision a completely new society; traditional ideas and categories of race and gender, order and decorum remained firmly entrenched among members of their privileged class. Many Americans rejected the elitist and aristocratic republican order, however, and advocated radical changes. Their efforts represented a groundswell of sentiment for greater equality, a part of the democratic impulse unleashed by the Revolution.

THE STATUS OF WOMEN

In eighteenth-century America, as in Great Britain, the legal status of married women was defined as **coverture**, meaning a married woman (or *feme covert*) had no legal or economic status independent of her husband. She could not conduct business or buy and sell property. Her husband controlled any property she brought to the marriage, although he could not sell it without her agreement. Married women's status as *femes covert* did not change as a result of the Revolution, and wives remained economically dependent on their husbands. The women of the newly independent nation did not call for the right to vote, but some, especially the wives of elite republican statesmen, began to agitate for equality under the law between husbands and wives, and for the same educational opportunities as men.

Some women hoped to overturn coverture. From her home in Braintree, Massachusetts, Abigail Adams (**Figure 7.4**) wrote to her husband, Whig leader John Adams, in 1776, "In the new code of laws which I suppose it will be necessary for you to make, I desire you would remember the ladies and be more generous and favorable to them than your ancestor. Do not put such unlimited power in the husbands. Remember, all men would be tyrants if they could." Abigail Adams ran the family homestead during the Revolution, but she did not have the ability to conduct business without her husband's consent. Elsewhere in the famous 1776 letter quoted above, she speaks of the difficulties of running the homestead when her husband is away. Her frustration grew when her husband responded in an April 1776 letter: "As to your extraordinary Code of Laws, I cannot but laugh. We have been told that our Struggle has loosened the bands of Government every where. That Children and Apprentices were disobedient—that schools and Colledges were grown turbulent—that Indians slighted their Guardians and Negroes grew insolent to their Masters. But your Letter was the first Intimation that another Tribe more numerous and powerfull than all the rest were grown discontented. . . . Depend on it, We know better than to repeal our Masculine systems."

Figure 7.4 Abigail Adams (a), shown here in a 1766 portrait by Benjamin Blythe, is best remembered for her eloquent letters to her husband, John Adams (b), who would later become the second president of the United States.

Another privileged member of the revolutionary generation, Mercy Otis Warren, also challenged gender assumptions and traditions during the revolutionary era (**Figure 7.5**). Born in Massachusetts, Warren actively opposed British reform measures before the outbreak of fighting in 1775 by publishing anti-British works. In 1812, she published a three-volume history of the Revolution, a project she had started in the late 1770s. By publishing her work, Warren stepped out of the female sphere and into the otherwise male-dominated sphere of public life.

Inspired by the Revolution, Judith Sargent Murray of Massachusetts advocated women's economic independence and equal educational opportunities for men and women (**Figure 7.5**). Murray, who came from a well-to-do family in Gloucester, questioned why boys were given access to education as a birthright while girls had very limited educational opportunities. She began to publish her ideas about educational equality beginning in the 1780s, arguing that God had made the minds of women and men equal.

(a) (b)

Figure 7.5 John Singleton Copley's 1772 portrait of Judith Sargent Murray (a) and 1763 portrait of Mercy Otis Warren (b) show two of America's earliest advocates for women's rights. Notice how their fine silk dresses telegraph their privileged social status.

Murray's more radical ideas championed woman's economic independence. She argued that a woman's education should be extensive enough to allow her to maintain herself—and her family—if there was no male breadwinner. Indeed, Murray was able to make money of her own from her publications. Her ideas were both radical and traditional, however: Murray also believed that women were much better at raising children and maintaining the morality and virtue of the family than men.

Adams, Murray, and Warren all came from privileged backgrounds. All three were fully literate, while many women in the American republic were not. Their literacy and station allowed them to push for new roles for women in the atmosphere of unique possibility created by the Revolution and its promise of change. Female authors who published their work provide evidence of how women in the era of the American Revolution challenged traditional gender roles.

Overall, the Revolution reconfigured women's roles by undermining the traditional expectations of wives and mothers, including subservience. In the home, the separate domestic sphere assigned to women, women were expected to practice republican virtues, especially frugality and simplicity. Republican motherhood meant that women, more than men, were responsible for raising good children, instilling in them all the virtue necessary to ensure the survival of the republic. The Revolution also opened new doors to educational opportunities for women. Men understood that the republic needed women to play a substantial role in upholding republicanism and ensuring the survival of the new nation. Benjamin Rush, a Whig educator and physician from Philadelphia, strongly advocated for the education of girls and young women as part of the larger effort to ensure that republican virtue and republican motherhood would endure.

THE MEANING OF RACE

By the time of the Revolution, slavery had been firmly in place in America for over one hundred years. In many ways, the Revolution served to reinforce the assumptions about race among white Americans. They viewed the new nation as a white republic; blacks were slaves, and Indians had no place. Racial hatred of blacks increased during the Revolution because many slaves fled their white masters for the freedom offered by the British. The same was true for Indians who allied themselves with the British; Jefferson wrote in the Declaration of Independence that separation from the Empire was necessary because George

III had incited "the merciless Indian savages" to destroy the white inhabitants on the frontier. Similarly, Thomas Paine argued in *Common Sense* that Great Britain was guilty of inciting "the Indians and Negroes to destroy us." For his part, Benjamin Franklin wrote in the 1780s that, in time, alcoholism would wipe out the Indians, leaving the land free for white settlers.

MY STORY

Phillis Wheatley: "On Being Brought from Africa to America"

Phillis Wheatley (Figure 7.6) was born in Africa in 1753 and sold as a slave to the Wheatley family of Boston; her African name is lost to posterity. Although most slaves in the eighteenth century had no opportunities to learn to read and write, Wheatley achieved full literacy and went on to become one of the best-known poets of the time, although many doubted her authorship of her poems because of her race.

Figure 7.6 This portrait of Phillis Wheatley from the frontispiece of *Poems on various subjects, religious and moral* shows the writer at work. Despite her status as a slave, her poems won great renown in America and in Europe.

Wheatley's poems reflected her deep Christian beliefs. In the poem below, how do her views on Christianity affect her views on slavery?

> Twas mercy brought me from my Pagan land,
> Taught my benighted soul to understand
> That there's a God, that there's a Saviour too:
> Once I redemption neither sought nor knew.
> Some view our sable race with scornful eye,
> "Their colour is a diabolic dye."
> Remember, Christians, Negroes, black as Cain,
> May be refin'd, and join th' angelic train.
> —Phillis Wheatley, "On Being Brought from Africa to America"

Slavery

Slavery offered the most glaring contradiction between the idea of equality stated in the Declaration of Independence ("all men are created equal") and the reality of race relations in the late eighteenth century.

Racism shaped white views of blacks. Although he penned the Declaration of Independence, Thomas Jefferson owned more than one hundred slaves, of whom he freed only a few either during his lifetime or in his will (Figure 7.7). He thought blacks were inferior to whites, dismissing Phillis Wheatley by arguing,

"Religion indeed has produced a Phillis Wheatley; but it could not produce a poet." White slaveholders took their female slaves as mistresses, as most historians agree that Jefferson did with one of his slaves, Sally Hemings. Together, they had several children.

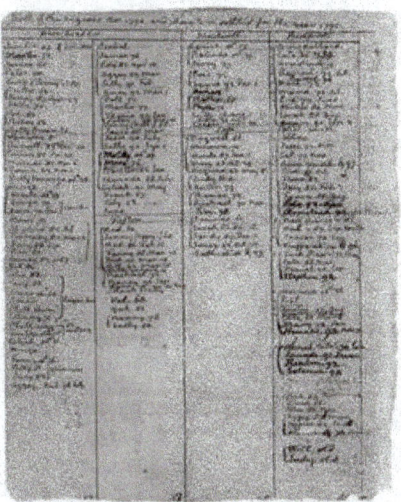

Figure 7.7 This page, taken from one of Thomas Jefferson's record books from 1795, lists his slaves.

Browse the Thomas Jefferson Papers (http://openstaxcollege.org/l/TJefferson) at the Massachusetts Historical Society to examine Jefferson's "farm books," in which he kept records of his land holdings, animal husbandry, and slaves, including specific references to Sally Hemings.

Jefferson understood the contradiction fully, and his writings reveal hard-edged racist assumptions. In his *Notes on the State of Virginia* in the 1780s, Jefferson urged the end of slavery in Virginia and the removal of blacks from that state. He wrote: "It will probably be asked, Why not retain and incorporate the blacks into the state, and thus save the expense of supplying, by importation of white settlers, the vacancies they will leave? Deep rooted prejudices entertained by the whites; ten thousand recollections, by the blacks, of the injuries they have sustained; new provocations; the real distinctions which nature has made; and many other circumstances, will divide us into parties, and produce convulsions which will probably never end but in the extermination of the one or the other race. —To these objections, which are political, may be added others, which are physical and moral." Jefferson envisioned an "empire of liberty" for white farmers and relied on the argument of sending blacks out of the United States, even if doing so would completely destroy the slaveholders' wealth in their human property.

Southern planters strongly objected to Jefferson's views on abolishing slavery and removing blacks from America. When Jefferson was a candidate for president in 1796, an anonymous "Southern Planter" wrote, "If this wild project succeeds, under the auspices of Thomas Jefferson, President of the United States, and three hundred thousand slaves are set free in Virginia, farewell to the safety, prosperity, the importance, perhaps the very existence of the Southern States" (**Figure 7.8**). Slaveholders and many other Americans protected and defended the institution.

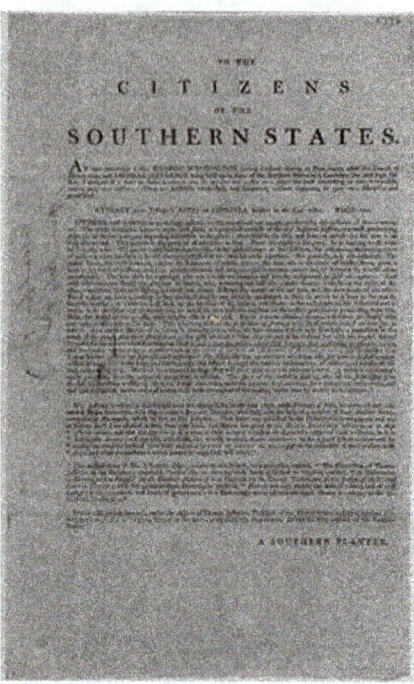

Figure 7.8 This 1796 broadside to "the Citizens of the Southern States" by "a Southern Planter" argued that Thomas Jefferson's advocacy of the emancipation of slaves in his *Notes on the State of Virginia* posed a threat to the safety, the prosperity, and even the existence of the southern states.

Freedom

While racial thinking permeated the new country, and slavery existed in all the new states, the ideals of the Revolution generated a movement toward the abolition of slavery. Private **manumissions**, by which slaveholders freed their slaves, provided one pathway from bondage. Slaveholders in Virginia freed some ten thousand slaves. In Massachusetts, the Wheatley family manumitted Phillis in 1773 when she was twenty-one. Other revolutionaries formed societies dedicated to abolishing slavery. One of the earliest efforts began in 1775 in Philadelphia, where Dr. Benjamin Rush and other Philadelphia Quakers formed what became the Pennsylvania Abolition Society. Similarly, wealthy New Yorkers formed the New York Manumission Society in 1785. This society worked to educate black children and devoted funds to protect free blacks from kidnapping.

Slavery persisted in the North, however, and the example of Massachusetts highlights the complexity of the situation. The 1780 Massachusetts constitution technically freed all slaves. Nonetheless, several hundred individuals remained enslaved in the state. In the 1780s, a series of court decisions undermined slavery in Massachusetts when several slaves, citing assault by their masters, successfully sought their freedom in court. These individuals refused to be treated as slaves in the wake of the American Revolution. Despite these legal victories, about eleven hundred slaves continued to be held in the New England states in 1800. The contradictions illustrate the difference between the letter and the spirit of the laws abolishing slavery in Massachusetts. In all, over thirty-six thousand slaves remained in the North, with the highest concentrations in New Jersey and New York. New York only gradually phased out slavery, with the last slaves emancipated in the late 1820s.

Indians

The 1783 Treaty of Paris, which ended the war for independence, did not address Indians at all. All lands held by the British east of the Mississippi and south of the Great Lakes (except Spanish Florida) now belonged to the new American republic (**Figure 7.9**). Though the treaty remained silent on the issue, much of the territory now included in the boundaries of the United States remained under the control of native peoples. Earlier in the eighteenth century, a "middle ground" had existed between powerful native groups in the West and British and French imperial zones, a place where the various groups interacted and accommodated each other. As had happened in the French and Indian War and Pontiac's Rebellion, the Revolutionary War turned the middle ground into a battle zone that no one group controlled.

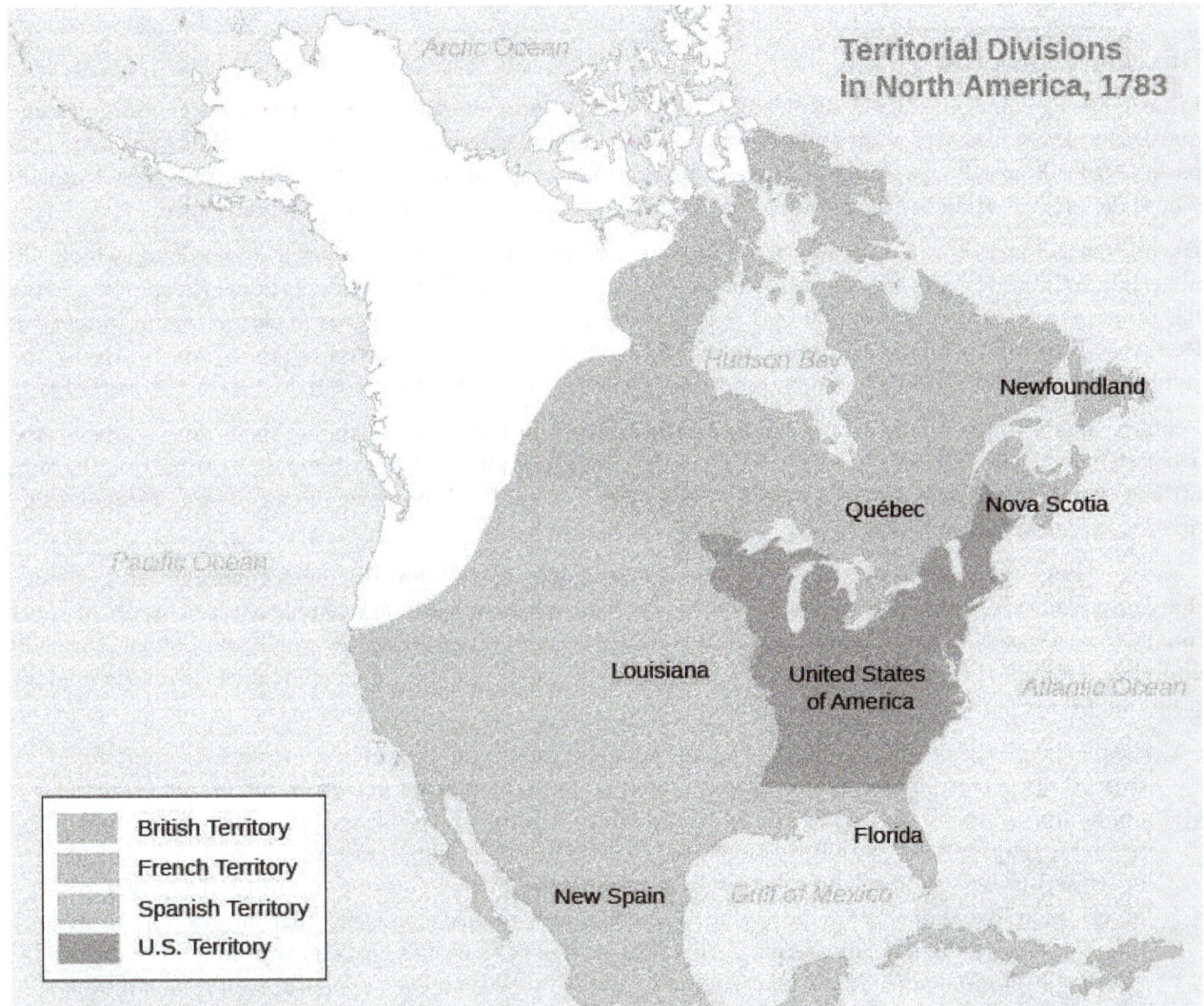

Figure 7.9 The 1783 Treaty of Paris divided North America into territories belonging to the United States and several European countries, but it failed to address Indian lands at all.

During the Revolution, a complex situation existed among Indians. Many villages remained neutral. Some native groups, such as the Delaware, split into factions, with some supporting the British while other Delaware maintained their neutrality. The Iroquois Confederacy, a longstanding alliance of tribes, also split up: the Mohawk, Cayuga, Onondaga, and Seneca fought on the British side, while the Oneida and Tuscarora supported the revolutionaries. Ohio River Valley tribes such as the Shawnee, Miami, and Mungo had been fighting for years against colonial expansion west; these groups supported the British. Some native peoples who had previously allied with the French hoped the conflict between the colonies and Great Britain might lead to French intervention and the return of French rule. Few Indians sided with the American revolutionaries, because almost all revolutionaries in the middle ground viewed them as an enemy to be destroyed. This racial hatred toward native peoples found expression in the American massacre of ninety-six Christian Delawares in 1782. Most of the dead were women and children.

After the war, the victorious Americans turned a deaf ear to Indian claims to what the revolutionaries saw as their hard-won land, and they moved aggressively to assert control over western New York and Pennsylvania. In response, Mohawk leader Joseph Brant helped to form the Western Confederacy, an alliance of native peoples who pledged to resist American intrusion into what was then called the Northwest. The Northwest Indian War (1785–1795) ended with the defeat of the Indians and their claims. Under the Treaty of Greenville (1795), the United States gained dominion over land in Ohio.

RELIGION AND THE STATE

Prior to the Revolution, several colonies had official, tax-supported churches. After the Revolution, some questioned the validity of state-authorized churches; the limitation of public office-holding to those of a particular faith; and the payment of taxes to support churches. In other states, especially in New England where the older Puritan heritage cast a long shadow, religion and state remained intertwined.

During the colonial era in Virginia, the established church had been the Church of England, which did not tolerate Catholics, Baptists, or followers or other religions. In 1786, as a revolutionary response against the privileged status of the Church of England, Virginia's lawmakers approved the Virginia Statute for Religious Freedom, which ended the Church of England's hold and allowed religious liberty. Under the statute, no one could be forced to attend or support a specific church or be prosecuted for his or her beliefs.

Pennsylvania's original constitution limited officeholders in the state legislature to those who professed a belief in both the Old and the New Testaments. This religious test prohibited Jews from holding that office, as the New Testament is not part of Jewish belief. In 1790, however, Pennsylvania removed this qualification from its constitution.

The New England states were slower to embrace freedom of religion. In the former Puritan colonies, the Congregational Church (established by seventeenth-century Puritans) remained the church of most inhabitants. Massachusetts, Connecticut, and New Hampshire all required the public support of Christian churches. Article III of the Massachusetts constitution blended the goal of republicanism with the goal of promoting Protestant Christianity. It reads:

> As the happiness of a people, and the good order and preservation of civil government, essentially depend upon piety, religion and morality; and as these cannot be generally diffused through a community, but by the institution of the public worship of GOD, and of public instructions in piety, religion and morality: Therefore, to promote their happiness and to secure the good order and preservation of their government, the people of this Commonwealth have a right to invest their legislature with power to authorize and require, and the legislature shall, from time to time, authorize and require, the several towns, parishes, precincts, and other bodies-politic, or religious societies, to make suitable provision, at their own expense, for the institution of the public worship of GOD, and for the support and maintenance of public protestant teachers of piety, religion and morality, in all cases where such provision shall not be made voluntarily. . . .
>
> And every denomination of Christians, demeaning themselves peaceably, and as good subjects of the Commonwealth, shall be equally under the protection of the law: And no subordination of any one sect or denomination to another shall ever be established by law.

> ### Click and Explore
>
>
>
> Read more about religion and state governments at the Religion and the Founding of the American Republic (http://openstaxcollege.org/l/farmbook1) exhibition page on the Library of Congress site. What was the meaning of the term "nursing fathers" of the church?

7.3 Debating Democracy

By the end of this section, you will be able to:
- Explain the development of state constitutions
- Describe the features of the Articles of Confederation
- Analyze the causes and consequences of Shays' Rebellion

The task of creating republican governments in each of the former colonies, now independent states, presented a new opportunity for American revolutionaries to define themselves anew after casting off British control. On the state and national levels, citizens of the new United States debated who would hold the keys to political power. The states proved to be a laboratory for how much democracy, or majority rule, would be tolerated.

THE STATE CONSTITUTIONS

In 1776, John Adams urged the thirteen independent colonies—soon to be states—to write their own state constitutions. Enlightenment political thought profoundly influenced Adams and other revolutionary leaders seeking to create viable republican governments. The ideas of the French philosopher Montesquieu, who had advocated the separation of powers in government, guided Adams's thinking. Responding to a request for advice on proper government from North Carolina, Adams wrote *Thoughts on Government*, which influenced many state legislatures. Adams did not advocate democracy; rather, he wrote, "there is no good government but what is republican." Fearing the potential for tyranny with only one group in power, he suggested a system of **checks and balances** in which three separate branches of government—executive, legislative, and judicial—would maintain a balance of power. He also proposed that each state remain sovereign, as its own republic. The state constitutions of the new United States illustrate different approaches to addressing the question of how much democracy would prevail in the thirteen republics. Some states embraced democratic practices, while others adopted far more aristocratic and republican ones.

Click and Explore

 Visit the **Avalon Project** (http://openstaxcollege.org/l/statecons) to read the constitutions of the seven states (Virginia, New Jersey, North Carolina, Maryland, Connecticut, Pennsylvania, and Delaware) that had written constitutions by the end of 1776.

The 1776 Pennsylvania constitution and the 1784 New Hampshire constitution both provide examples of democratic tendencies. In Pennsylvania, the requirement to own property in order to vote was eliminated, and if a man was twenty-one or older, had paid taxes, and had lived in the same location for one year, he could vote (**Figure 7.10**). This opened voting to most free white male citizens of Pennsylvania. The 1784 New Hampshire constitution allowed every small town and village to send representatives to the state government, making the lower house of the legislature a model of democratic government.

Figure 7.10 The 1776 Pennsylvania constitution, the first page of which is shown here, adhered to more democratic principles than some other states' constitutions did initially.

Conservative Whigs, who distrusted the idea of majority rule, recoiled from the abolition of property qualifications for voting and office holding in Pennsylvania. Conservative Whig John Adams reacted with horror to the 1776 Pennsylvania constitution, declaring that it was "so democratical that it must produce confusion and every evil work." In his mind and those of other conservative Whigs, this constitution simply put too much power in the hands of men who had no business exercising the right to vote. Pennsylvania's constitution also eliminated the executive branch (there was no governor) and the upper house. Instead, Pennsylvania had a one-house—a **unicameral**—legislature.

The Maryland and South Carolina constitutions provide examples of efforts to limit the power of a democratic majority. Maryland's, written in 1776, restricted office holding to the wealthy planter class. A man had to own at least £5,000 worth of personal property to be the governor of Maryland, and possess an estate worth £1,000 to be a state senator. This latter qualification excluded over 90 percent of the white males in Maryland from political office. The 1778 South Carolina constitution also sought to protect the interests of the wealthy. Governors and lieutenant governors of the state had to have "a settled plantation or freehold in their and each of their own right of the value of at least ten thousand pounds currency, clear of debt." This provision limited high office in the state to its wealthiest inhabitants. Similarly, South Carolina state senators had to own estates valued at £2,000.

John Adams wrote much of the 1780 Massachusetts constitution, which reflected his fear of too much democracy. It therefore created two legislative chambers, an upper and lower house, and a strong governor with broad veto powers. Like South Carolina, Massachusetts put in place office-holding requirements: To be governor under the new constitution, a candidate had to own an estate worth at least £1,000. To serve in the state senate, a man had to own an estate worth at least £300 and have at least £600 in total wealth. To vote, he had to be worth at least sixty pounds. To further keep democracy in check, judges were appointed, not elected. One final limit was the establishment of the state capitol in the commercial center of Boston, which made it difficult for farmers from the western part of the state to attend legislative sessions.

THE ARTICLES OF CONFEDERATION

Most revolutionaries pledged their greatest loyalty to their individual states. Recalling the experience of British reform efforts imposed in the 1760s and 1770s, they feared a strong national government and took some time to adopt the Articles of Confederation, the first national constitution. In June 1776, the Continental Congress prepared to announce independence and began to think about the creation of a new government to replace royal authority. Reaching agreement on the Articles of Confederation proved difficult as members of the Continental Congress argued over western land claims. Connecticut, for example, used its colonial charter to assert its claim to western lands in Pennsylvania and the Ohio Territory (**Figure 7.11**).

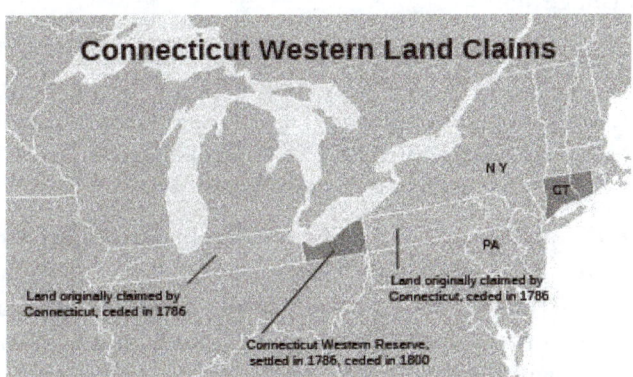

Figure 7.11 Connecticut, like many other states, used its state constitution to stake claims to uncharted western lands.

Members of the Continental Congress also debated what type of representation would be best and tried to figure out how to pay the expenses of the new government. In lieu of creating a new federal government, the Articles of Confederation created a "league of friendship" between the states. Congress readied the Articles in 1777 but did not officially approve them until 1781 (**Figure 7.12**). The delay of four years illustrates the difficulty of getting the thirteen states to agree on a plan of national government. Citizens viewed their respective states as sovereign republics and guarded their prerogatives against other states.

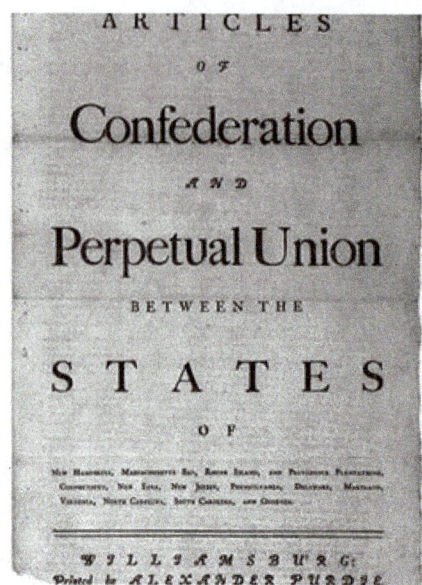

Figure 7.12 The first page of the 1777 Articles of Confederation, printed by Alexander Purdie, emphasized the "perpetual union" between the states.

The Articles of Confederation authorized a unicameral legislature, a continuation of the earlier Continental Congress. The people could not vote directly for members of the national Congress; rather, state legislatures decided who would represent the state. In practice, the national Congress was composed of state delegations. There was no president or executive office of any kind, and there was no national judiciary (or Supreme Court) for the United States.

Passage of any law under the Articles of Confederation proved difficult. It took the consensus of nine states for any measure to pass, and amending the Articles required the consent of all the states, also extremely difficult to achieve. Further, any acts put forward by the Congress were non-binding; states had the option to enforce them or not. This meant that while the Congress had power over Indian affairs and foreign policy, individual states could choose whether or not to comply.

The Congress did not have the power to tax citizens of the United States, a fact that would soon have serious consequences for the republic. During the Revolutionary War, the Continental Congress had sent requisitions for funds to the individual former colonies (now revolutionary states). These states already had an enormous financial burden because they had to pay for militias as well as supply them. In the end, the states failed to provide even half the funding requested by the Congress during the war, which led to a national debt in the tens of millions by 1784.

By the 1780s, some members of the Congress were greatly concerned about the financial health of the republic, and they argued that the national government needed greater power, especially the power to tax. This required amending the Articles of Confederation with the consent of all the states. Those who called for a stronger federal government were known as nationalists. The nationalist group that pushed for the power to tax included Washington's chief of staff, Alexander Hamilton; Virginia planter James Madison; Pennsylvania's wealthy merchant Robert Morris (who served under the Confederation government as superintendent of finance in the early 1780s); and Pennsylvania lawyer James Wilson. Two New Yorkers, Gouverneur Morris and James Duane, also joined the effort to address the debt and the weakness of the Confederation government.

These men proposed a 5 percent tax on imports coming into the United States, a measure that would have yielded enough revenue to clear the debt. However, their proposal failed to achieve unanimous support from the states when Rhode Island rejected it. Plans for a national bank also failed to win unanimous support. The lack of support illustrates the Americans' deep suspicion of a powerful national government, a suspicion that originated from the unilateral and heavy-handed reform efforts that the British Parliament imposed on the colonies in the 1760s and 1770s. Without revenue, the Congress could not pay back American creditors who had lent it money. However, it did manage to make interest payments to foreign creditors in France and the Dutch Republic, fearful that defaulting on those payments would destroy the republic's credit and leave it unable to secure loans.

One soldier in the Continental Army, Joseph Plumb Martin, recounted how he received no pay in paper money after 1777 and only one month's payment in specie, or hard currency, in 1781. Like thousands of other soldiers, Martin had fought valiantly against the British and helped secure independence, but had not been paid for his service. In the 1780s and beyond, men like Martin would soon express their profound dissatisfaction with their treatment. Their anger found expression in armed uprisings and political divisions.

Establishing workable foreign and commercial policies under the Articles of Confederation also proved difficult. Each state could decide for itself whether to comply with treaties between the Congress and foreign countries, and there were no means of enforcement. Both Great Britain and Spain understood the weakness of the Confederation Congress, and they refused to make commercial agreements with the United States because they doubted they would be enforced. Without stable commercial policies, American exporters found it difficult to do business, and British goods flooded U.S. markets in the 1780s, in a repetition of the economic imbalance that existed before the Revolutionary War.

The Confederation Congress under the Articles did achieve success through a series of directives called land ordinances, which established rules for the settlement of western lands in the public domain and the admission of new states to the republic. The ordinances were designed to prepare the land for sale to citizens and raise revenue to boost the failing economy of the republic. In the land ordinances, the Confederation Congress created the Mississippi and Southwest Territories and stipulated that slavery would be permitted there. The system of dividing the vast domains of the United States stands as a towering achievement of the era, a blueprint for American western expansion.

The Ordinance of 1784, written by Thomas Jefferson and the first of what were later called the Northwest Ordinances, directed that new states would be formed from a huge area of land below the Great Lakes, and these new states would have equal standing with the original states. The Ordinance of 1785 called for the division of this land into rectangular plots in order to prepare for the government sale of land. Surveyors would divide the land into townships of six square miles, and the townships would be subdivided into thirty-six plots of 640 acres each, which could be further subdivided. The price of an acre of land was set at a minimum of one dollar, and the land was to be sold at public auction under the direction of the Confederation.

The Ordinance of 1787 officially turned the land into an incorporated territory called the Northwest Territory and prohibited slavery north of the Ohio River (**Figure 7.13**). The map of the 1787 Northwest Territory shows how the public domain was to be divided by the national government for sale. Townships of thirty-six square miles were to be surveyed. Each had land set aside for schools and other civic purposes. Smaller parcels could then be made: a 640-acre section could be divided into quarter-sections of 160 acres, and then again into sixteen sections of 40 acres. The geometric grid pattern established by the ordinance is still evident today on the American landscape. Indeed, much of the western United States, when viewed from an airplane, is composed of an orderly grid system.

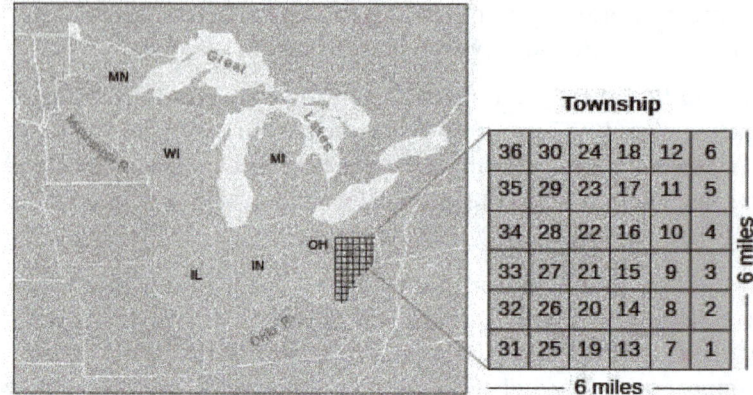

Figure 7.13 The Northwest Ordinance of 1787 created territories and an orderly method for the admission of new states.

Visit Window Seat (http://openstaxcollege.org/l/thescream) to explore aerial views of the grid system established by the Northwest Ordinance of 1787, which is still evident in much of the Midwest.

The land ordinances proved to be the great triumph of the Confederation Congress. The Congress would appoint a governor for the territories, and when the population in the territory reached five thousand free adult settlers, those citizens could create their own legislature and begin the process of moving toward statehood. When the population reached sixty thousand, the territory could become a new state.

SHAYS' REBELLION

Despite Congress's victory in creating an orderly process for organizing new states and territories, land sales failed to produce the revenue necessary to deal with the dire economic problems facing the new country in the 1780s. Each state had issued large amounts of paper money and, in the aftermath of the Revolution, widespread internal devaluation of that currency occurred as many lost confidence in the value of state paper money and the Continental dollar. A period of extreme inflation set in. Added to this dilemma was American citizens' lack of specie (gold and silver currency) to conduct routine business. Meanwhile, demobilized soldiers, many of whom had spent their formative years fighting rather than learning a peacetime trade, searched desperately for work.

The economic crisis came to a head in 1786 and 1787 in western Massachusetts, where farmers were in a difficult position: they faced high taxes and debts, which they found nearly impossible to pay with the worthless state and Continental paper money. For several years after the peace in 1783, these indebted citizens had petitioned the state legislature for redress. Many were veterans of the Revolutionary War who had returned to their farms and families after the fighting ended and now faced losing their homes.

Their petitions to the state legislature raised economic and political issues for citizens of the new state. How could people pay their debts and state taxes when paper money proved unstable? Why was the state government located in Boston, the center of the merchant elite? Why did the 1780 Massachusetts constitution cater to the interests of the wealthy? To the indebted farmers, the situation in the 1780s seemed hauntingly familiar; the revolutionaries had routed the British, but a new form of seemingly corrupt and self-serving government had replaced them.

In 1786, when the state legislature again refused to address the petitioners' requests, Massachusetts citizens took up arms and closed courthouses across the state to prevent foreclosure (seizure of land in lieu of overdue loan payments) on farms in debt. The farmers wanted their debts forgiven, and they demanded that the 1780 constitution be revised to address citizens beyond the wealthy elite who could serve in the legislature.

Many of the rebels were veterans of the war for independence, including Captain Daniel Shays from Pelham (**Figure 7.14**). Although Shays was only one of many former officers in the Continental Army who took part in the revolt, authorities in Boston singled him out as a ringleader, and the uprising became known as Shays' Rebellion. The Massachusetts legislature responded to the closing of the courthouses with a flurry of legislation, much of it designed to punish the rebels. The government offered the rebels clemency if they took an oath of allegiance. Otherwise, local officials were empowered to use deadly force against them without fear of prosecution. Rebels would lose their property, and if any militiamen refused to defend the state, they would be executed.

Figure 7.14 This woodcut, from Bickerstaff's Boston Almanack of 1787, depicts Daniel Shays and Job Shattuck. Shays and Shattuck were two of the leaders of the rebels who rose up against the Massachusetts government in 1786 to 1787. As Revolutionary War veterans, both men wear the uniform of officers of the Continental Army.

Despite these measures, the rebellion continued. To address the uprising, Governor James Bowdoin raised a private army of forty-four hundred men, funded by wealthy Boston merchants, without the approval of the legislature. The climax of Shays' Rebellion came in January 1787, when the rebels attempted to seize the federal armory in Springfield, Massachusetts. A force loyal to the state defeated them there, although the rebellion continued into February.

Shays' Rebellion resulted in eighteen deaths overall, but the uprising had lasting effects. To men of property, mostly conservative Whigs, Shays' Rebellion strongly suggested the republic was falling into anarchy and chaos. The other twelve states had faced similar economic and political difficulties, and continuing problems seemed to indicate that on a national level, a democratic impulse was driving the population. Shays' Rebellion convinced George Washington to come out of retirement and lead the convention called for by Alexander Hamilton to amend the Articles of Confederation in order to deal with insurgencies like the one in Massachusetts and provide greater stability in the United States.

7.4 The Constitutional Convention and Federal Constitution

By the end of this section, you will be able to:
- Identify the central issues of the 1787 Constitutional Convention and their solutions
- Describe the conflicts over the ratification of the federal constitution

The economic problems that plagued the thirteen states of the Confederation set the stage for the creation of a strong central government under a federal constitution. Although the original purpose of the convention was to amend the Articles of Confederation, some—though not all—delegates moved quickly to create a new framework for a more powerful national government. This proved extremely controversial. Those who attended the convention split over the issue of robust, centralized government and questions of how Americans would be represented in the federal government. Those who opposed the proposal for a stronger federal government argued that such a plan betrayed the Revolution by limiting the voice of the American people.

THE CONSTITUTIONAL CONVENTION

There had been earlier efforts to address the Confederation's perilous state. In early 1786, Virginia's James Madison advocated a meeting of states to address the widespread economic problems that plagued the new nation. Heeding Madison's call, the legislature in Virginia invited all thirteen states to meet in Annapolis, Maryland, to work on solutions to the issue of commerce between the states. Eight states responded to the invitation. But the resulting 1786 Annapolis Convention failed to provide any solutions because only five states sent delegates. These delegates did, however, agree to a plan put forward by Alexander Hamilton for a second convention to meet in May 1787 in Philadelphia. Shays' Rebellion gave greater urgency to the planned convention. In February 1787, in the wake of the uprising in western Massachusetts, the Confederation Congress authorized the Philadelphia convention. This time, all the states except Rhode Island sent delegates to Philadelphia to confront the problems of the day.

The stated purpose of the Philadelphia Convention in 1787 was to amend the Articles of Confederation. Very quickly, however, the attendees decided to create a new framework for a national government. That framework became the United States Constitution, and the Philadelphia convention became known as the Constitutional Convention of 1787. Fifty-five men met in Philadelphia in secret; historians know of the proceedings only because James Madison kept careful notes of what transpired. The delegates knew that what they were doing would be controversial; Rhode Island refused to send delegates, and New Hampshire's delegates arrived late. Two delegates from New York, Robert Yates and John Lansing, left the convention when it became clear that the Articles were being put aside and a new plan of national government was being drafted. They did not believe the delegates had the authority to create a strong national government.

Click and Explore

Read "Reasons for Dissent from the Proposed Constitution" (http://openstaxcollege.org/l/YatesLansing) in order to understand why Robert Yates and John Lansing, New York's delegates to the 1787 Philadelphia Convention, didn't believe the convention should draft a new plan of national government.

THE QUESTION OF REPRESENTATION

One issue that the delegates in Philadelphia addressed was the way in which representatives to the new national government would be chosen. Would individual citizens be able to elect representatives? Would representatives be chosen by state legislatures? How much representation was appropriate for each state?

James Madison put forward a proposition known as the Virginia Plan, which called for a strong national government that could overturn state laws (**Figure 7.15**). The plan featured a **bicameral** or two-house legislature, with an upper and a lower house. The people of the states would elect the members of the lower house, whose numbers would be determined by the population of the state. State legislatures would send delegates to the upper house. The number of representatives in the upper chamber would also be based on the state's population. This **proportional representation** gave the more populous states, like Virginia, more political power. The Virginia Plan also called for an executive branch and a judicial branch, both of which were absent under the Articles of Confederation. The lower and upper house together were to appoint members to the executive and judicial branches. Under this plan, Virginia, the most populous state, would dominate national political power and ensure its interests, including slavery, would be safe.

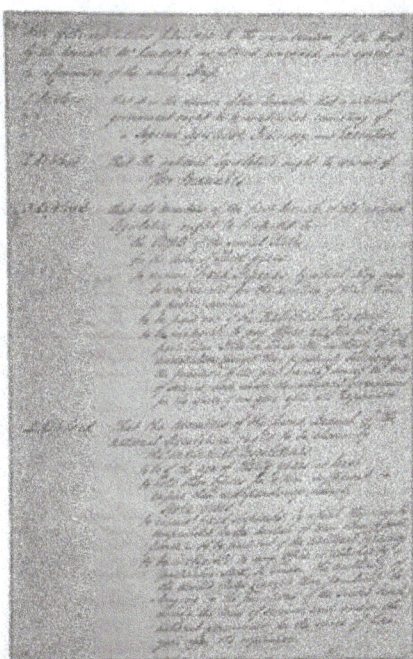

Figure 7.15 James Madison's Virginia Plan, shown here, proposed a strong national government with proportional state representation.

The Virginia Plan's call for proportional representation alarmed the representatives of the smaller states. William Paterson introduced a New Jersey Plan to counter Madison's scheme, proposing that all states have equal votes in a unicameral national legislature. He also addressed the economic problems of the day by calling for the Congress to have the power to regulate commerce, to raise revenue though taxes on imports and through postage, and to enforce Congressional requisitions from the states.

Roger Sherman from Connecticut offered a compromise to break the deadlock over the thorny question of representation. His **Connecticut Compromise**, also known as the Great Compromise, outlined a different bicameral legislature in which the upper house, the Senate, would have equal representation for all states; each state would be represented by two senators chosen by the state legislatures. Only the lower house, the House of Representatives, would have proportional representation.

THE QUESTION OF SLAVERY

The question of slavery stood as a major issue at the Constitutional Convention because slaveholders wanted slaves to be counted along with whites, termed "free inhabitants," when determining a state's total population. This, in turn, would augment the number of representatives accorded to those states in the lower house. Some northerners, however, such as New York's Gouverneur Morris, hated slavery and did not even want the term included in the new national plan of government. Slaveholders argued that slavery imposed great burdens upon them and that, because they carried this liability, they deserved special consideration; slaves needed to be counted for purposes of representation.

The issue of counting or not counting slaves for purposes of representation connected directly to the question of taxation. Beginning in 1775, the Second Continental Congress asked states to pay for war by collecting taxes and sending the tax money to the Congress. The amount each state had to deliver in tax revenue was determined by a state's total population, including both free and enslaved individuals. States routinely fell far short of delivering the money requested by Congress under the plan. In April 1783, the Confederation Congress amended the earlier system of requisition by having slaves count as three-fifths of the white population. In this way, slaveholders gained a significant tax break. The delegates in Philadelphia adopted this same three-fifths formula in the summer of 1787.

Under the **three-fifths compromise** in the 1787 Constitution, each slave would be counted as three-fifths of a white person. Article 1, Section 2 stipulated that "Representatives and direct Taxes shall be apportioned among the several states . . . according to their respective Number, which shall be determined by adding to the whole number of free Persons, including those bound for service for a Term of Years [white servants], and excluding Indians not taxed, three fifths of all other persons." Since representation in the House of Representatives was based on the population of a state, the three-fifths compromise gave extra political power to slave states, although not as much as if the total population, both free and slave, had been used. Significantly, no direct federal income tax was immediately imposed. (The Sixteenth Amendment, ratified in 1913, put in place a federal income tax.) Northerners agreed to the three-fifths compromise because the Northwest Ordinance of 1787, passed by the Confederation Congress, banned slavery in the future states of the northwest. Northern delegates felt this ban balanced political power between states with slaves and those without. The three-fifths compromise gave an advantage to slaveholders; they added three-fifths of their human property to their state's population, allowing them to send representatives based in part on the number of slaves they held.

THE QUESTION OF DEMOCRACY

Many of the delegates to the Constitutional Convention had serious reservations about democracy, which they believed promoted anarchy. To allay these fears, the Constitution blunted democratic tendencies that appeared to undermine the republic. Thus, to avoid giving the people too much direct power, the delegates made certain that senators were chosen by the state legislatures, not elected directly by the people (direct elections of senators came with the Seventeenth Amendment to the Constitution, ratified in 1913). As an additional safeguard, the delegates created the **Electoral College**, the mechanism for choosing the president. Under this plan, each state has a certain number of electors, which is its number of senators (two) plus its number of representatives in the House of Representatives. Critics, then as now, argue that this process prevents the direct election of the president.

THE FIGHT OVER RATIFICATION

The draft constitution was finished in September 1787. The delegates decided that in order for the new national government to be implemented, each state must first hold a special ratifying convention. When nine of the thirteen had approved the plan, the constitution would go into effect.

When the American public learned of the new constitution, opinions were deeply divided, but most people were opposed. To salvage their work in Philadelphia, the architects of the new national government began a campaign to sway public opinion in favor of their blueprint for a strong central government. In the fierce debate that erupted, the two sides articulated contrasting visions of the American republic and of democracy. Supporters of the 1787 Constitution, known as **Federalists**, made the case that a centralized republic provided the best solution for the future. Those who opposed it, known as **Anti-Federalists**, argued that the Constitution would consolidate all power in a national government, robbing the states of the power to make their own decisions. To them, the Constitution appeared to mimic the old corrupt and centralized British regime, under which a far-off government made the laws. Anti-Federalists argued that wealthy aristocrats would run the new national government, and that the elite would not represent ordinary citizens; the rich would monopolize power and use the new government to formulate policies that benefited their class—a development that would also undermine local state elites. They also argued that the Constitution did not contain a bill of rights.

New York's ratifying convention illustrates the divide between the Federalists and Anti-Federalists. When one Anti-Federalist delegate named Melancton Smith took issue with the scheme of representation as being too limited and not reflective of the people, Alexander Hamilton responded:

> It has been observed by an honorable gentleman [Smith], that a pure democracy, if it were practicable, would be the most perfect government. Experience has proven, that no position in politics is more false than this. The ancient democracies, in which the people themselves deliberated, never possessed one feature of good government. Their very character was tyranny; their figure deformity: When they assembled, the field of debate presented an ungovernable mob, not only incapable of deliberation, but prepared for every enormity. In these assemblies, the enemies of the people brought forward their plans of ambition systematically. They were opposed by their enemies of another party; and it became a matter of contingency, whether the people subjected themselves to be led blindly by one tyrant or by another.

The Federalists, particularly John Jay, Alexander Hamilton, and James Madison, put their case to the public in a famous series of essays known as *The Federalist Papers*. These were first published in New York and subsequently republished elsewhere in the United States.

DEFINING "AMERICAN"

James Madison on the Benefits of Republicanism

The tenth essay in *The Federalist Papers*, often called Federalist No. 10, is one of the most famous. Written by James Madison (Figure 7.16), it addresses the problems of political parties ("factions"). Madison argued that there were two approaches to solving the problem of political parties: a republican government and a democracy. He argued that a large republic provided the best defense against what he viewed as the tumult of direct democracy. Compromises would be reached in a large republic and citizens would be represented by representatives of their own choosing.

Figure 7.16 John Vanderlyn's 1816 portrait depicts James Madison, one of the leading Federalists who supported the 1787 Constitution.

> From this view of the subject, it may be concluded, that a pure Democracy, by which I mean a Society consisting of a small number of citizens, who assemble and administer the Government in person, can admit of no cure for the mischiefs of faction. A common passion or interest will, in almost every case, be felt by a majority of the whole; a communication and concert result from the form of Government itself; and there is nothing to check the inducements to sacrifice the weaker party, or an obnoxious individual. Hence it is, that such Democracies have ever been spectacles of turbulence and contention; have ever been found incompatible with personal security, or the rights of property; and have in general been as short in their lives, as they have been violent in their deaths. Theoretic politicians, who have patronized this species of Government, have erroneously supposed, that by reducing mankind to a perfect equality in their political rights, they would, at the same time, be perfectly equalized and assimilated in their possessions, their opinions, and their passions.
>
> A Republic, by which I mean a Government in which the scheme of representation takes place, opens a different prospect, and promises the cure for which we are seeking. Let us examine the points in which it varies from pure Democracy, and we shall comprehend both the nature of the cure, and the efficacy which it must derive from the Union.
>
> The two great points of difference, between a Democracy and a Republic, are, first, the delegation of the Government, in the latter, to a small number of citizens elected by the rest: Secondly, the greater number of citizens, and greater sphere of country, over which the latter may be extended.

Does Madison recommend republicanism or democracy as the best form of government? What arguments does he use to prove his point?

Click and Explore

Read the full text of **Federalist No. 10** (http://openstaxcollege.org/l/federalist10) on Wikisource. What do you think are Madison's most and least compelling arguments? How would different members of the new United States view his arguments?

Including all the state ratifying conventions around the country, a total of fewer than two thousand men voted on whether to adopt the new plan of government. In the end, the Constitution only narrowly won approval (**Figure 7.17**). In New York, the vote was thirty in favor to twenty-seven opposed. In Massachusetts, the vote to approve was 187 to 168, and some claim supporters of the Constitution resorted to bribes in order to ensure approval. Virginia ratified by a vote of eighty-nine to seventy-nine, and Rhode Island by thirty-four to thirty-two. The opposition to the Constitution reflected the fears that a new national government, much like the British monarchy, created too much centralized power and, as a result, deprived citizens in the various states of the ability to make their own decisions.

Figure 7.17 The first page of the 1787 United States Constitution, shown here, begins: "We the People of the United States, in Order to form a more perfect Union, establish Justice, insure domestic Tranquility, provide for the common defence, promote the general Welfare, and secure the Blessings of Liberty to ourselves and our Posterity, do ordain and establish this Constitution for the United States of America."

CHAPTER 8
Growing Pains: The New Republic, 1790–1820

Figure 8.1 "The happy Effects of the Grand Systom [sic] of shutting Ports against the English!!" appeared in 1808. Less than a year earlier, Thomas Jefferson had recommended (and Congress had passed) the Embargo Act of 1807, which barred American ships from leaving their ports.

Chapter Outline
8.1 Competing Visions: Federalists and Democratic-Republicans
8.2 The New American Republic
8.3 Partisan Politics
8.4 The United States Goes Back to War

Introduction

The partisan political cartoon above (**Figure 8.1**) lampoons Thomas Jefferson's 1807 Embargo Act, a move that had a devastating effect on American commerce. American farmers and merchants complain to President Jefferson, while the French emperor Napoleon Bonaparte whispers to him, "You shall be King hereafter." This image illustrates one of many political struggles in the years after the fight for ratification of the Constitution. In the nation's first few years, no organized political parties existed. This began to change as U.S. citizens argued bitterly about the proper size and scope of the new national government. As a result, the 1790s witnessed the rise of opposing political parties: the Federalists and the Democratic-Republicans. Federalists saw unchecked democracy as a dire threat to the republic, and they pointed to the excesses of the French Revolution as proof of what awaited. Democratic-Republicans opposed the Federalists' notion that only the wellborn and well educated were able to oversee the republic; they saw it as a pathway to oppression by an aristocracy.

8.1 Competing Visions: Federalists and Democratic-Republicans

By the end of this section, you will be able to:
- Describe the competing visions of the Federalists and the Democratic-Republicans
- Identify the protections granted to citizens under the Bill of Rights
- Explain Alexander Hamilton's financial programs as secretary of the treasury

In June 1788, New Hampshire became the ninth state to ratify the federal Constitution, and the new plan for a strong central government went into effect. Elections for the first U.S. Congress were held in 1788 and 1789, and members took their seats in March 1789. In a reflection of the trust placed in him as the personification of republican virtue, George Washington became the first president in April 1789. John Adams served as his vice president; the pairing of a representative from Virginia (Washington) with one from Massachusetts (Adams) symbolized national unity. Nonetheless, political divisions quickly became apparent. Washington and Adams represented the Federalist Party, which generated a backlash among those who resisted the new government's assertions of federal power.

FEDERALISTS IN POWER

Though the Revolution had overthrown British rule in the United States, supporters of the 1787 federal constitution, known as Federalists, adhered to a decidedly British notion of social hierarchy. The Federalists did not, at first, compose a political party. Instead, Federalists held certain shared assumptions. For them, political participation continued to be linked to property rights, which barred many citizens from voting or holding office. Federalists did not believe the Revolution had changed the traditional social roles between women and men, or between whites and other races. They did believe in clear distinctions in rank and intelligence. To these supporters of the Constitution, the idea that all were equal appeared ludicrous. Women, blacks, and native peoples, they argued, had to know their place as secondary to white male citizens. Attempts to impose equality, they feared, would destroy the republic. The United States was not created to be a democracy.

The architects of the Constitution committed themselves to leading the new republic, and they held a majority among the members of the new national government. Indeed, as expected, many assumed the new executive posts the first Congress created. Washington appointed Alexander Hamilton, a leading

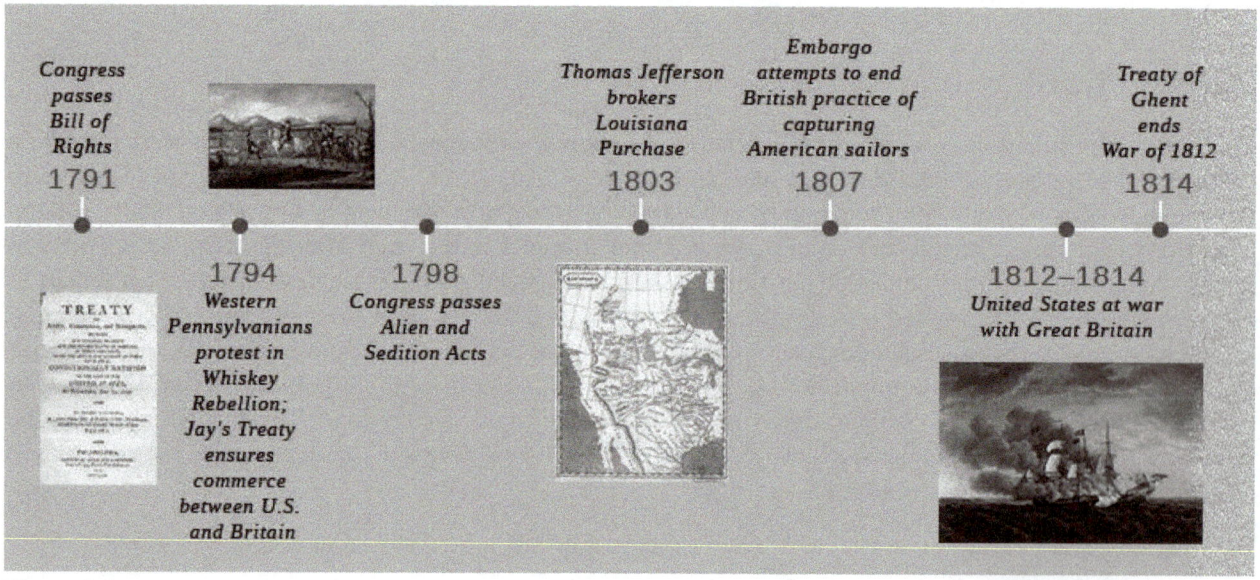

Figure 8.2

Federalist, as secretary of the treasury. For secretary of state, he chose Thomas Jefferson. For secretary of war, he appointed Henry Knox, who had served with him during the Revolutionary War. Edmond Randolph, a Virginia delegate to the Constitutional Convention, was named attorney general. In July 1789, Congress also passed the Judiciary Act, creating a Supreme Court of six justices headed by those who were committed to the new national government.

Congress passed its first major piece of legislation by placing a duty on imports under the 1789 Tariff Act. Intended to raise revenue to address the country's economic problems, the act was a victory for nationalists, who favored a robust, powerful federal government and had worked unsuccessfully for similar measures during the Confederation Congress in the 1780s. Congress also placed a fifty-cent-per-ton duty (based on materials transported, not the weight of a ship) on foreign ships coming into American ports, a move designed to give the commercial advantage to American ships and goods.

THE BILL OF RIGHTS

Many Americans opposed the 1787 Constitution because it seemed a dangerous concentration of centralized power that threatened the rights and liberties of ordinary U.S. citizens. These opponents, known collectively as Anti-Federalists, did not constitute a political party, but they united in demanding protection for individual rights, and several states made the passing of a bill of rights a condition of their acceptance of the Constitution. Rhode Island and North Carolina rejected the Constitution because it did not already have this specific bill of rights.

Federalists followed through on their promise to add such a bill in 1789, when Virginia Representative James Madison introduced and Congress approved the **Bill of Rights** (Table 8.1). Adopted in 1791, the bill consisted of the first ten amendments to the Constitution and outlined many of the personal rights state constitutions already guaranteed.

Table 8.1 Rights Protected by the First Ten Amendments

Amendment 1	Right to freedoms of religion and speech; right to assemble and to petition the government for redress of grievances
Amendment 2	Right to keep and bear arms to maintain a well-regulated militia
Amendment 3	Right not to house soldiers during time of war
Amendment 4	Right to be secure from unreasonable search and seizure
Amendment 5	Rights in criminal cases, including to due process and indictment by grand jury for capital crimes, as well as the right not to testify against oneself
Amendment 6	Right to a speedy trial by an impartial jury
Amendment 7	Right to a jury trial in civil cases
Amendment 8	Right not to face excessive bail or fines, or cruel and unusual punishment
Amendment 9	Rights retained by the people, even if they are not specifically enumerated by the Constitution
Amendment 10	States' rights to powers not specifically delegated to the federal government

The adoption of the Bill of Rights softened the Anti-Federalists' opposition to the Constitution and gave the new federal government greater legitimacy among those who otherwise distrusted the new centralized power created by men of property during the secret 1787 Philadelphia Constitutional Convention.

> **Click and Explore**
>
>  Visit the **National Archives** (http://openstaxcollege.org/l/BillRights) to consider the first ten amendments to the Constitution as an expression of the fears many citizens harbored about the powers of the new federal government. What were these fears? How did the Bill of Rights calm them?

ALEXANDER HAMILTON'S PROGRAM

Alexander Hamilton, Washington's secretary of the treasury, was an ardent nationalist who believed a strong federal government could solve many of the new country's financial ills. Born in the West Indies, Hamilton had worked on a St. Croix plantation as a teenager and was in charge of the accounts at a young age. He knew the Atlantic trade very well and used that knowledge in setting policy for the United States. In the early 1790s, he created the foundation for the U.S. financial system. He understood that a robust federal government would provide a solid financial foundation for the country.

The United States began mired in debt. In 1789, when Hamilton took up his post, the federal debt was over $53 million. The states had a combined debt of around $25 million, and the United States had been unable to pay its debts in the 1780s and was therefore considered a credit risk by European countries. Hamilton wrote three reports offering solutions to the economic crisis brought on by these problems. The first addressed public credit, the second addressed banking, and the third addressed raising revenue.

The Report on Public Credit

For the national government to be effective, Hamilton deemed it essential to have the support of those to whom it owed money: the wealthy, domestic creditor class as well as foreign creditors. In January 1790, he delivered his "Report on Public Credit" (**Figure 8.3**), addressing the pressing need of the new republic to become creditworthy. He recommended that the new federal government honor all its debts, including all paper money issued by the Confederation and the states during the war, at face value. Hamilton especially wanted wealthy American creditors who held large amounts of paper money to be invested, literally, in the future and welfare of the new national government. He also understood the importance of making the new United States financially stable for creditors abroad. To pay these debts, Hamilton proposed that the federal government sell bonds—federal interest-bearing notes—to the public. These bonds would have the backing of the government and yield interest payments. Creditors could exchange their old notes for the new government bonds. Hamilton wanted to give the paper money that states had issued during the war the same status as government bonds; these federal notes would begin to yield interest payments in 1792.

 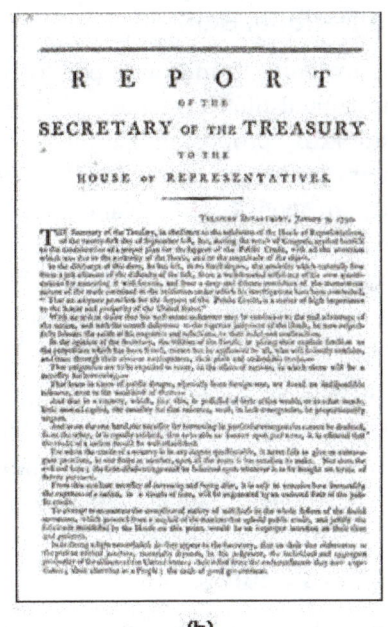

Figure 8.3 As the first secretary of the treasury, Alexander Hamilton (a), shown here in a 1792 portrait by John Trumbull, released the "Report on Public Credit" (b) in January 1790.

Hamilton designed his "Report on Public Credit" (later called "First Report on Public Credit") to ensure the survival of the new and shaky American republic. He knew the importance of making the United States financially reliable, secure, and strong, and his plan provided a blueprint to achieve that goal. He argued that his plan would satisfy creditors, citing the goal of "doing justice to the creditors of the nation." At the same time, the plan would work "to promote the increasing respectability of the American name; to answer the calls for justice; to restore landed property to its due value; to furnish new resources both to agriculture and commerce; to cement more closely the union of the states; to add to their security against foreign attack; to establish public order on the basis of upright and liberal policy."

Hamilton's program ignited a heated debate in Congress. A great many of both Confederation and state notes had found their way into the hands of speculators, who had bought them from hard-pressed veterans in the 1780s and paid a fraction of their face value in anticipation of redeeming them at full value at a later date. Because these speculators held so many notes, many in Congress objected that Hamilton's plan would benefit them at the expense of the original note-holders. One of those who opposed Hamilton's 1790 report was James Madison, who questioned the fairness of a plan that seemed to cheat poor soldiers.

Not surprisingly, states with a large debt, like South Carolina, supported Hamilton's plan, while states with less debt, like North Carolina, did not. To gain acceptance of his plan, Hamilton worked out a compromise with Virginians Madison and Jefferson, whereby in return for their support he would give up New York City as the nation's capital and agree on a more southern location, which they preferred. In July 1790, a site along the Potomac River was selected as the new "federal city," which became the District of Columbia.

Hamilton's plan to convert notes to bonds worked extremely well to restore European confidence in the U.S. economy. It also proved a windfall for creditors, especially those who had bought up state and Confederation notes at far less than face value. But it immediately generated controversy about the size and scope of the government. Some saw the plan as an unjust use of federal power, while Hamilton argued that Article 1, Section 8 of the Constitution granted the government "implied powers" that gave the green light to his program.

The Report on a National Bank

As secretary of the treasury, Hamilton hoped to stabilize the American economy further by establishing a national bank. The United States operated with a flurry of different notes from multiple state banks and no coherent regulation. By proposing that the new national bank buy up large volumes of state bank notes and demanding their conversion into gold, Hamilton especially wanted to discipline those state banks that issued paper money irresponsibly. To that end, he delivered his "Report on a National Bank" in December 1790, proposing a Bank of the United States, an institution modeled on the Bank of England. The bank would issue loans to American merchants and bills of credit (federal bank notes that would circulate as money) while serving as a repository of government revenue from the sale of land. Stockholders would own the bank, along with the federal government.

Like the recommendations in his "Report on Public Credit," Hamilton's bank proposal generated opposition. Jefferson, in particular, argued that the Constitution did not permit the creation of a national bank. In response, Hamilton again invoked the Constitution's implied powers. President Washington backed Hamilton's position and signed legislation creating the bank in 1791.

The Report on Manufactures

The third report Hamilton delivered to Congress, known as the "Report on Manufactures," addressed the need to raise revenue to pay the interest on the national debt. Using the power to tax as provided under the Constitution, Hamilton put forth a proposal to tax American-made whiskey. He also knew the importance of promoting domestic manufacturing so the new United States would no longer have to rely on imported manufactured goods. To break from the old colonial system, Hamilton therefore advocated tariffs on all foreign imports to stimulate the production of American-made goods. To promote domestic industry further, he proposed federal subsidies to American industries. Like all of Hamilton's programs, the idea of government involvement in the development of American industries was new.

With the support of Washington, the entire Hamiltonian economic program received the necessary support in Congress to be implemented. In the long run, Hamilton's financial program helped to rescue the United States from its state of near-bankruptcy in the late 1780s. His initiatives marked the beginning of an American capitalism, making the republic creditworthy, promoting commerce, and setting for the nation a solid financial foundation. His policies also facilitated the growth of the stock market, as U.S. citizens bought and sold the federal government's interest-bearing certificates.

THE DEMOCRATIC-REPUBLICAN PARTY AND THE FIRST PARTY SYSTEM

James Madison and Thomas Jefferson felt the federal government had overstepped its authority by adopting the treasury secretary's plan. Madison found Hamilton's scheme immoral and offensive. He argued that it turned the reins of government over to the class of speculators who profited at the expense of hardworking citizens.

Jefferson, who had returned to the United States in 1790 after serving as a diplomat in France, tried unsuccessfully to convince Washington to block the creation of a national bank. He also took issue with what he perceived as favoritism given to commercial classes in the principal American cities. He thought urban life widened the gap between the wealthy few and an underclass of landless poor workers who, because of their oppressed condition, could never be good republican property owners. Rural areas, in contrast, offered far more opportunities for property ownership and virtue. In 1783 Jefferson wrote, "Those who labor in the earth are the chosen people of God, if ever he had a chosen people." Jefferson believed that self-sufficient, property-owning republican citizens or yeoman farmers held the key to the success and longevity of the American republic. (As a creature of his times, he did not envision a similar role for either women or nonwhite men.) To him, Hamilton's program seemed to encourage economic inequalities and work against the ordinary American yeoman.

Opposition to Hamilton, who had significant power in the new federal government, including the ear of President Washington, began in earnest in the early 1790s. Jefferson turned to his friend Philip Freneau to help organize the effort through the publication of the *National Gazette* as a counter to the Federalist press, especially the *Gazette of the United States* (**Figure 8.4**). From 1791 until 1793, when it ceased publication, Freneau's partisan paper attacked Hamilton's program and Washington's administration. "Rules for Changing a Republic into a Monarchy," written by Freneau, is an example of the type of attack aimed at the national government, and especially at the elitism of the Federalist Party. Newspapers in the 1790s became enormously important in American culture as partisans like Freneau attempted to sway public opinion. These newspapers did not aim to be objective; instead, they served to broadcast the views of a particular party.

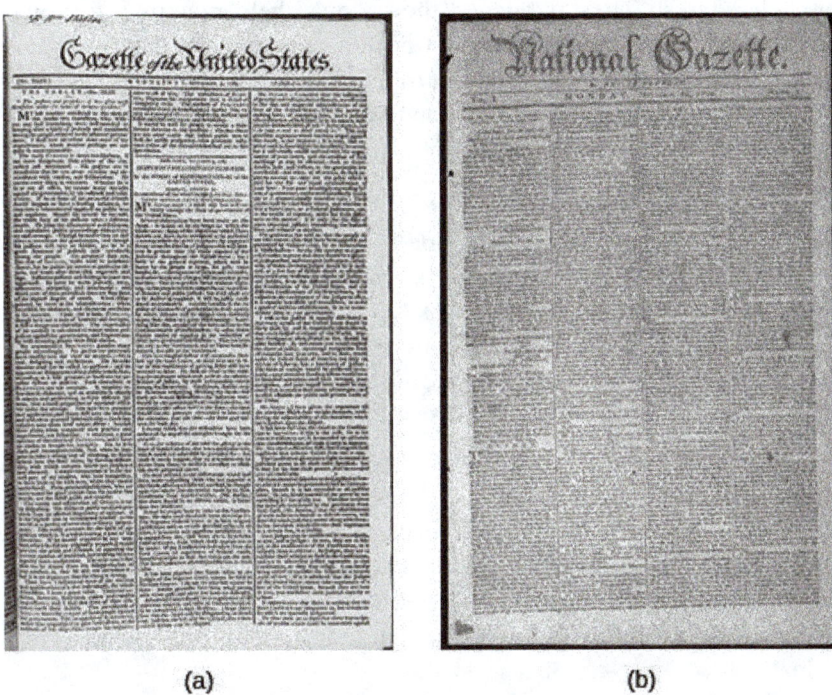

Figure 8.4 Here, the front page of the Federalist *Gazette of the United States* from September 9, 1789 (a), is shown beside that of the oppositional *National Gazette* from November 14, 1791 (b). The *Gazette of the United States* featured articles, sometimes written pseudonymously or anonymously, from leading Federalists like Alexander Hamilton and John Adams. The *National Gazette* was founded two years later to counter their political influence.

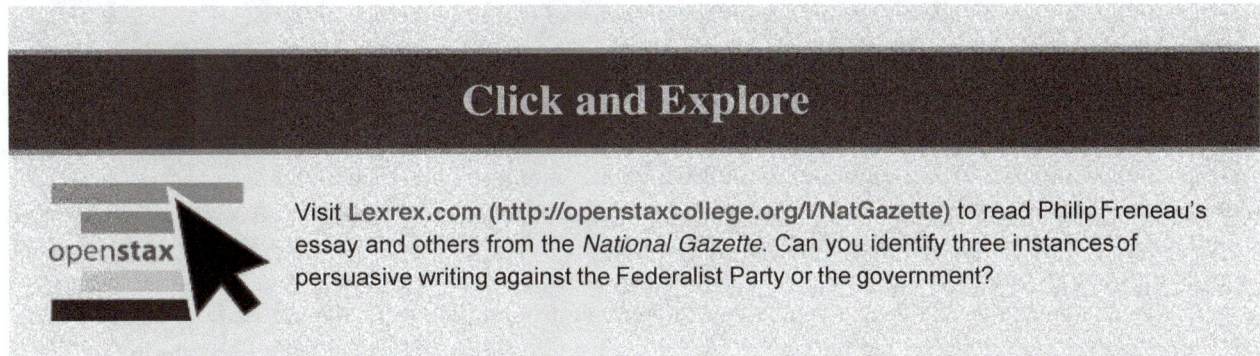

Visit Lexrex.com (http://openstaxcollege.org/l/NatGazette) to read Philip Freneau's essay and others from the *National Gazette*. Can you identify three instances of persuasive writing against the Federalist Party or the government?

Opposition to the Federalists led to the formation of Democratic-Republican societies, composed of men who felt the domestic policies of the Washington administration were designed to enrich the few while ignoring everyone else. **Democratic-Republicans** championed limited government. Their fear of centralized power originated in the experience of the 1760s and 1770s when the distant, overbearing, and seemingly corrupt British Parliament attempted to impose its will on the colonies. The 1787 federal constitution, written in secret by fifty-five wealthy men of property and standing, ignited fears of a similar menacing plot. To opponents, the Federalists promoted aristocracy and a monarchical government—a betrayal of what many believed to be the goal of the American Revolution.

While wealthy merchants and planters formed the core of the Federalist leadership, members of the Democratic-Republican societies in cities like Philadelphia and New York came from the ranks of artisans. These citizens saw themselves as acting in the spirit of 1776, this time not against the haughty British but by what they believed to have replaced them—a commercial class with no interest in the public good. Their political efforts against the Federalists were a battle to preserve republicanism, to promote the public good against private self-interest. They published their views, held meetings to voice their opposition, and sponsored festivals and parades. In their strident newspapers attacks, they also worked to undermine the traditional forms of deference and subordination to aristocrats, in this case the Federalist elites. Some members of northern Democratic-Republican clubs denounced slavery as well.

DEFINING CITIZENSHIP

While questions regarding the proper size and scope of the new national government created a divide among Americans and gave rise to political parties, a consensus existed among men on the issue of who qualified and who did not qualify as a citizen. The 1790 Naturalization Act defined citizenship in stark racial terms. To be a citizen of the American republic, an immigrant had to be a "free white person" of "good character." By excluding slaves, free blacks, Indians, and Asians from citizenship, the act laid the foundation for the United States as a republic of white men.

Full citizenship that included the right to vote was restricted as well. Many state constitutions directed that only male property owners or taxpayers could vote. For women, the right to vote remained out of reach except in the state of New Jersey. In 1776, the fervor of the Revolution led New Jersey revolutionaries to write a constitution extending the right to vote to unmarried women who owned property worth £50. Federalists and Democratic-Republicans competed for the votes of New Jersey women who met the requirements to cast ballots. This radical innovation continued until 1807, when New Jersey restricted voting to free white males.

8.2 The New American Republic

> By the end of this section, you will be able to:
> - Identify the major foreign and domestic uprisings of the early 1790s
> - Explain the effect of these uprisings on the political system of the United States

The colonies' alliance with France, secured after the victory at Saratoga in 1777, proved crucial in their victory against the British, and during the 1780s France and the new United States enjoyed a special relationship. Together they had defeated their common enemy, Great Britain. But despite this shared experience, American opinions regarding France diverged sharply in the 1790s when France underwent its own revolution. Democratic-Republicans seized on the French revolutionaries' struggle against monarchy as the welcome harbinger of a larger republican movement around the world. To the Federalists, however, the French Revolution represented pure anarchy, especially after the execution of the French king in 1793. Along with other foreign and domestic uprisings, the French Revolution helped harden the political divide in the United States in the early 1790s.

THE FRENCH REVOLUTION

The French Revolution, which began in 1789, further split American thinkers into different ideological camps, deepening the political divide between Federalists and their Democratic-Republican foes. At first, in 1789 and 1790, the revolution in France appeared to most in the United States as part of a new chapter in the rejection of corrupt monarchy, a trend inspired by the American Revolution. A constitutional monarchy replaced the absolute monarchy of Louis XVI in 1791, and in 1792, France was declared a republic. Republican liberty, the creed of the United States, seemed to be ushering in a new era in France. Indeed, the American Revolution served as an inspiration for French revolutionaries.

The events of 1793 and 1794 challenged the simple interpretation of the French Revolution as a happy chapter in the unfolding triumph of republican government over monarchy. The French king was executed in January 1793 (**Figure 8.5**), and the next two years became known as **the Terror**, a period of extreme violence against perceived enemies of the revolutionary government. Revolutionaries advocated direct representative democracy, dismantled Catholicism, replaced that religion with a new philosophy known as the Cult of the Supreme Being, renamed the months of the year, and relentlessly employed the guillotine against their enemies. Federalists viewed these excesses with growing alarm, fearing that the radicalism of the French Revolution might infect the minds of citizens at home. Democratic-Republicans interpreted the same events with greater optimism, seeing them as a necessary evil of eliminating the monarchy and aristocratic culture that supported the privileges of a hereditary class of rulers.

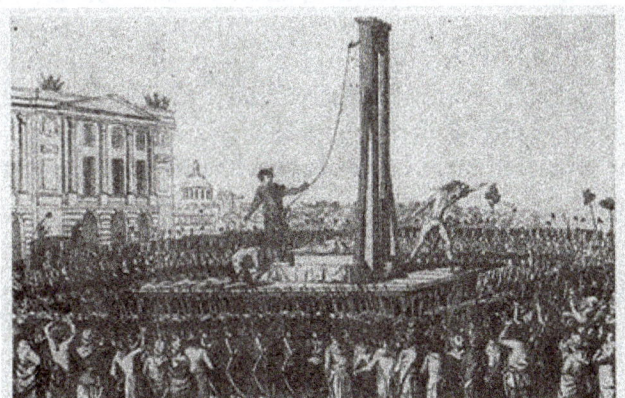

Figure 8.5 An image from a 1791 Hungarian journal depicts the beheading of Louis XVI during the French Revolution. The violence of the revolutionary French horrified many in the United States—especially Federalists, who saw it as an example of what could happen when the mob gained political control and instituted direct democracy.

The controversy in the United States intensified when France declared war on Great Britain and Holland in February 1793. France requested that the United States make a large repayment of the money it had borrowed from France to fund the Revolutionary War. However, Great Britain would judge any aid given to France as a hostile act. Washington declared the United States neutral in 1793, but Democratic-Republican groups denounced neutrality and declared their support of the French republicans. The Federalists used the violence of the French revolutionaries as a reason to attack Democratic-Republicanism in the United States, arguing that Jefferson and Madison would lead the country down a similarly disastrous path.

Click and Explore

Visit Liberty, Equality, Fraternity (http://openstaxcollege.org/l/revolution) for images, texts, and songs relating to the French Revolution. This momentous event's impact extended far beyond Europe, influencing politics in the United States and elsewhere in the Atlantic World.

THE CITIZEN GENÊT AFFAIR AND JAY'S TREATY

In 1793, the revolutionary French government sent Edmond-Charles Genêt to the United States to negotiate an alliance with the U.S. government. France empowered Genêt to issue **letters of marque**—documents authorizing ships and their crews to engage in piracy—to allow him to arm captured British ships in American ports with U.S. soldiers. Genêt arrived in Charleston, South Carolina, amid great Democratic-Republican fanfare. He immediately began commissioning American privateer ships and organizing volunteer American militias to attack Spanish holdings in the Americas, then traveled to Philadelphia, gathering support for the French cause along the way. President Washington and Hamilton denounced Genêt, knowing his actions threatened to pull the United States into a war with Great Britain. The **Citizen Genêt affair**, as it became known, spurred Great Britain to instruct its naval commanders in the West Indies to seize all ships trading with the French. The British captured hundreds of American ships and their cargoes, increasing the possibility of war between the two countries.

In this tense situation, Great Britain worked to prevent a wider conflict by ending its seizure of American ships and offered to pay for captured cargoes. Hamilton saw an opportunity and recommended to Washington that the United States negotiate. Supreme Court Justice John Jay was sent to Britain, instructed by Hamilton to secure compensation for captured American ships; ensure the British leave the Northwest outposts they still occupied despite the 1783 Treaty of Paris; and gain an agreement for American trade in the West Indies. Even though Jay personally disliked slavery, his mission also required him to seek compensation from the British for slaves who left with the British at the end of the Revolutionary War.

The resulting 1794 agreement, known as Jay's Treaty, fulfilled most of his original goals. The British would turn over the frontier posts in the Northwest, American ships would be allowed to trade freely in the West Indies, and the United States agreed to assemble a commission charged with settling colonial debts U.S. citizens owed British merchants. The treaty did not address the important issue of **impressment**, however—the British navy's practice of forcing or "impressing" American sailors to work and fight on British warships. Jay's Treaty led the Spanish, who worried that it signaled an alliance between the United States and Great Britain, to negotiate a treaty of their own—Pinckney's Treaty—that allowed American commerce to flow through the Spanish port of New Orleans. Pinckney's Treaty allowed American farmers, who were moving in greater numbers to the Ohio River Valley, to ship their products down the Ohio and Mississippi Rivers to New Orleans, where they could be transported to East Coast markets.

Jay's Treaty confirmed the fears of Democratic-Republicans, who saw it as a betrayal of republican France, cementing the idea that the Federalists favored aristocracy and monarchy. Partisan American newspapers tried to sway public opinion, while the skillful writing of Hamilton, who published a number of essays on the subject, explained the benefits of commerce with Great Britain.

THE FRENCH REVOLUTION'S CARIBBEAN LEGACY

Unlike the American Revolution, which ultimately strengthened the institution of slavery and the powers of American slaveholders, the French Revolution inspired slave rebellions in the Caribbean, including a 1791 slave uprising in the French colony of Saint-Domingue (modern-day Haiti). Thousands of slaves joined together to overthrow the brutal system of slavery. They took control of a large section of the island, burning sugar plantations and killing the white planters who had forced them to labor under the lash.

In 1794, French revolutionaries abolished slavery in the French empire, and both Spain and England attacked Saint-Domingue, hoping to add the colony to their own empires. Toussaint L'Ouverture, a former domestic slave, emerged as the leader in the fight against Spain and England to secure a Haiti free of slavery and further European colonialism. Because revolutionary France had abolished slavery, Toussaint aligned himself with France, hoping to keep Spain and England at bay (**Figure 8.6**).

Figure 8.6 An 1802 portrait shows Toussaint L'Ouverture, "*Chef des Noirs Insurgés de Saint Domingue*" ("Leader of the Black Insurgents of Saint Domingue"), mounted and armed in an elaborate uniform.

Events in Haiti further complicated the partisan wrangling in the United States. White refugee planters from Haiti and other French West Indian islands, along with slaves and free people of color, left the Caribbean for the United States and for Louisiana, which at the time was held by Spain. The presence of these French migrants raised fears, especially among Federalists, that they would bring the contagion of French radicalism to the United States. In addition, the idea that the French Revolution could inspire a successful slave uprising just off the American coastline filled southern whites and slaveholders with horror.

THE WHISKEY REBELLION

While the wars in France and the Caribbean divided American citizens, a major domestic test of the new national government came in 1794 over the issue of a tax on whiskey, an important part of Hamilton's financial program. In 1791, Congress had authorized a tax of 7.5 cents per gallon of whiskey and rum. Although most citizens paid without incident, trouble erupted in four western Pennsylvania counties in an uprising known as the Whiskey Rebellion.

Farmers in the western counties of Pennsylvania produced whiskey from their grain for economic reasons. Without adequate roads or other means to transport a bulky grain harvest, these farmers distilled their grains into gin and whiskey, which were more cost-effective to transport. Since these farmers depended on the sale of whiskey, some citizens in western Pennsylvania (and elsewhere) viewed the new tax as further proof that the new national government favored the commercial classes on the eastern seaboard at the expense of farmers in the West. On the other hand, supporters of the tax argued that it helped stabilize the economy and its cost could easily be passed on to the consumer, not the farmer-distiller. However, in the spring and summer months of 1794, angry citizens rebelled against the federal officials in charge of enforcing the federal excise law. Like the Sons of Liberty before the American Revolution, the whiskey rebels used violence and intimidation to protest policies they saw as unfair. They tarred and feathered federal officials, intercepted the federal mail, and intimidated wealthy citizens (**Figure 8.7**). The extent of their discontent found expression in their plan to form an independent western commonwealth, and they even began negotiations with British and Spanish representatives, hoping to secure their support for independence from the United States. The rebels also contacted their backcountry neighbors in Kentucky and South Carolina, circulating the idea of secession.

Figure 8.7 This painting, attributed to Frederick Kemmelmeyer ca. 1795, depicts the massive force George Washington led to put down the Whiskey Rebellion of the previous year. Federalists made clear they would not tolerate mob action.

With their emphasis on personal freedoms, the whiskey rebels aligned themselves with the Democratic-Republican Party. They saw the tax as part of a larger Federalist plot to destroy their republican liberty and, in its most extreme interpretation, turn the United States into a monarchy. The federal government lowered the tax, but when federal officials tried to subpoena those distillers who remained intractable, trouble escalated. Washington responded by creating a thirteen-thousand-man militia, drawn from several states, to put down the rebellion. This force made it known, both domestically and to the European powers that looked on in anticipation of the new republic's collapse, that the national government would do everything in its power to ensure the survival of the United States.

DEFINING "AMERICAN"

Alexander Hamilton: "Shall the majority govern or be governed?"

Alexander Hamilton frequently wrote persuasive essays under pseudonyms, like "Tully," as he does here. In this 1794 essay, Hamilton denounces the whiskey rebels and majority rule.

> It has been observed that the means most likely to be employed to turn the insurrection in the western country to the detriment of the government, would be artfully calculated among other things 'to divert your attention from the true question to be decided.'
>
> Let us see then what is this question. It is plainly this—shall the majority govern or be governed? shall the nation rule, or be ruled? shall the general will prevail, or the will of a faction? shall there be government, or no government? . . .
>
> The Constitution *you* have ordained for yourselves and your posterity contains this express clause, 'The Congress *shall have power* to lay and collect taxes, duties, imposts, and *Excises*, to pay the debts, and provide for the common defence and general welfare of the United States.' You have then, by a solemn and deliberate act, the most important and sacred that a nation can perform, pronounced and decreed, that your Representatives in Congress shall have power to lay Excises. You have done nothing since to reverse or impair that decree. . . .
>
> But the four western counties of Pennsylvania, undertake to rejudge and reverse your decrees, you have said, 'The Congress *shall have power* to lay *Excises*.' They say, 'The Congress *shall not have* this power.' . . .
>
> There is no road to *despotism* more sure or more to be dreaded than that which begins at *anarchy*."
>
> —Alexander Hamilton's "Tully No. II" for the *American Daily Advertiser*, Philadelphia, August 26, 1794

What are the major arguments put forward by Hamilton in this document? Who do you think his audience is?

WASHINGTON'S INDIAN POLICY

Relationships with Indians were a significant problem for Washington's administration, but one on which white citizens agreed: Indians stood in the way of white settlement and, as the 1790 Naturalization Act made clear, were not citizens. After the War of Independence, white settlers poured into lands west of the Appalachian Mountains. As a result, from 1785 to 1795, a state of war existed on the frontier between these settlers and the Indians who lived in the Ohio territory. In both 1790 and 1791, the Shawnee and Miami had defended their lands against the whites who arrived in greater and greater numbers from the East. In response, Washington appointed General Anthony Wayne to bring the Western Confederacy—a loose alliance of tribes—to heel. In 1794, at the Battle of Fallen Timbers, Wayne was victorious. With the 1795 Treaty of Greenville (**Figure 8.8**), the Western Confederacy gave up their claims to Ohio.

Figure 8.8 Notice the contrasts between the depictions of federal and native representatives in this painting of the signing of the Treaty of Greenville in 1795. What message or messages did the artist intend to convey?

8.3 Partisan Politics

By the end of this section, you will be able to:
- Identify key examples of partisan wrangling between the Federalists and Democratic-Republicans
- Describe how foreign relations affected American politics
- Assess the importance of the Louisiana Purchase

George Washington, who had been reelected in 1792 by an overwhelming majority, refused to run for a third term, thus setting a precedent for future presidents. In the presidential election of 1796, the two parties—Federalist and Democratic-Republican—competed for the first time. Partisan rancor over the French Revolution and the Whiskey Rebellion fueled the divide between them, and Federalist John Adams defeated his Democratic-Republican rival Thomas Jefferson by a narrow margin of only three electoral votes. In 1800, another close election swung the other way, and Jefferson began a long period of Democratic-Republican government.

THE PRESIDENCY OF JOHN ADAMS

The war between Great Britain and France in the 1790s shaped U.S. foreign policy. As a new and, in comparison to the European powers, extremely weak nation, the American republic had no control over European events, and no real leverage to obtain its goals of trading freely in the Atlantic. To Federalist president John Adams, relations with France posed the biggest problem. After the Terror, the French Directory ruled France from 1795 to 1799. During this time, Napoleon rose to power.

AMERICANA

The Art of Ralph Earl

Ralph Earl was an eighteenth-century American artist, born in Massachusetts, who remained loyal to the British during the Revolutionary War. He fled to England in 1778, but he returned to New England in the mid-1780s and began painting portraits of leading Federalists.

His portrait of Connecticut Federalist Oliver Ellsworth and his wife Abigail conveys the world as Federalists liked to view it: an orderly landscape administered by men of property and learning. His portrait of dry goods merchant Elijah Boardman shows Boardman as well-to-do and highly cultivated; his books include the works of Shakespeare and Milton (**Figure 8.9**).

(a)

(b)

Figure 8.9 Ralph Earl's portraits are known for placing their subjects in an orderly world, as seen here in the 1801 portrait of Oliver and Abigail Wolcott Ellsworth (a) and the 1789 portrait of Elijah Boardman (b).

What similarities do you see in the two portraits by Ralph Earl? What do the details of each portrait reveal about the sitters? About the artist and the 1790s?

Because France and Great Britain were at war, the French Directory issued decrees stating that any ship carrying British goods could be seized on the high seas. In practice, this meant the French would target American ships, especially those in the West Indies, where the United States conducted a brisk trade with the British. France declared its 1778 treaty with the United States null and void, and as a result, France and the United States waged an undeclared war—or what historians refer to as the Quasi-War—from 1796 to 1800. Between 1797 and 1799, the French seized 834 American ships, and Adams urged the buildup of the U.S. Navy, which consisted of only a single vessel at the time of his election in 1796 (**Figure 8.10**).

Figure 8.10 This 1799 print, entitled "Preparation for WAR to defend Commerce," shows the construction of a naval ship, part of the effort to ensure the United States had access to free trade in the Atlantic world.

In 1797, Adams sought a diplomatic solution to the conflict with France and dispatched envoys to negotiate terms. The French foreign minister, Charles-Maurice de Talleyrand, sent emissaries who told the American envoys that the United States must repay all outstanding debts owed to France, lend France 32 million guilders (Dutch currency), and pay a £50,000 bribe before any negotiations could take place. News of the attempt to extract a bribe, known as the **XYZ affair** because the French emissaries were referred to as X, Y, and Z in letters that President Adams released to Congress, outraged the American public and turned public opinion decidedly against France (**Figure 8.11**). In the court of public opinion, Federalists appeared to have been correct in their interpretation of France, while the pro-French Democratic-Republicans had been misled.

Figure 8.11 This anonymous 1798 cartoon, *Property Protected à la Françoise*, satirizes the XYZ affair. Five Frenchmen are shown plundering the treasures of a woman representing the United States. One man holds a sword labeled "French Argument" and a sack of gold and riches labeled "National Sack and Diplomatic Perquisites," while the others collect her valuables. A group of other Europeans look on and commiserate that France treated them the same way.

Click and Explore

Read the "transcript" of the above cartoon in the America in Caricature, 1765–1865 (http://openstaxcollege.org/l/cartoon) collection at Indiana University's Lilly Library.

The complicated situation in Haiti, which remained a French colony in the late 1790s, also came to the attention of President Adams. The president, with the support of Congress, had created a U.S. Navy that now included scores of vessels. Most of the American ships cruised the Caribbean, giving the United States the edge over France in the region. In Haiti, the rebellion leader Toussaint, who had to contend with various domestic rivals seeking to displace him, looked to end an U.S. embargo on France and its colonies, put in place in 1798, so that his forces would receive help to deal with the civil unrest. In early 1799, in order to capitalize upon trade in the lucrative West Indies and undermine France's hold on the island, Congress ended the ban on trade with Haiti—a move that acknowledged Toussaint's leadership, to the horror of American slaveholders. Toussaint was able to secure an independent black republic in Haiti by 1804.

THE ALIEN AND SEDITION ACTS

The surge of animosity against France during the Quasi-War led Congress to pass several measures that in time undermined Federalist power. These 1798 war measures, known as the Alien and Sedition Acts, aimed to increase national security against what most had come to regard as the French menace. The Alien Act and the Alien Enemies Act took particular aim at French immigrants fleeing the West Indies by giving the president the power to deport new arrivals who appeared to be a threat to national security. The act expired in 1800 with no immigrants having been deported. The Sedition Act imposed harsh penalties—up to five years' imprisonment and a massive fine of $5,000 in 1790 dollars—on those convicted of speaking or writing "in a scandalous or malicious" manner against the government of the United States. Twenty-five men, all Democratic-Republicans, were indicted under the act, and ten were convicted. One of these was Congressman Matthew Lyon (**Figure 8.12**), representative from Vermont, who had launched his own newspaper, *The Scourge Of Aristocracy and Repository of Important Political Truth*.

Figure 8.12 This 1798 cartoon, "Congressional Pugilists," shows partisan chaos in the U.S. House of Representatives as Matthew Lyon, a Democratic-Republican from Vermont, holds forth against his opponent, Federalist Roger Griswold.

The Alien and Sedition Acts raised constitutional questions about the freedom of the press provided under the First Amendment. Democratic-Republicans argued that the acts were evidence of the Federalists' intent to squash individual liberties and, by enlarging the powers of the national government, crush states' rights. Jefferson and Madison mobilized the response to the acts in the form of statements known as the Virginia and Kentucky Resolutions, which argued that the acts were illegal and unconstitutional. The resolutions introduced the idea of nullification, the right of states to nullify acts of Congress, and advanced the argument of states' rights. The resolutions failed to rally support in other states, however. Indeed, most other states rejected them, citing the necessity of a strong national government.

The Quasi-War with France came to an end in 1800, when President Adams was able to secure the Treaty of Mortefontaine. His willingness to open talks with France divided the Federalist Party, but the treaty reopened trade between the two countries and ended the French practice of taking American ships on the high seas.

THE REVOLUTION OF 1800 AND THE PRESIDENCY OF THOMAS JEFFERSON

The **Revolution of 1800** refers to the first transfer of power from one party to another in American history, when the presidency passed to Democratic-Republican Thomas Jefferson (**Figure 8.13**) in the 1800 election. The peaceful transition calmed contemporary fears about possible violent reactions to a new party's taking the reins of government. The passing of political power from one political party to another without bloodshed also set an important precedent.

Figure 8.13 Thomas Jefferson's victory in 1800 signaled the ascendency of the Democratic-Republicans and the decline of Federalist power.

The election did prove even more divisive than the 1796 election, however, as both the Federalist and Democratic-Republican Parties waged a mudslinging campaign unlike any seen before. Because the Federalists were badly divided, the Democratic-Republicans gained political ground. Alexander Hamilton, who disagreed with President Adams's approach to France, wrote a lengthy letter, meant for people within his party, attacking his fellow Federalist's character and judgment and ridiculing his handling of foreign affairs. Democratic-Republicans got hold of and happily reprinted the letter.

Jefferson viewed participatory democracy as a positive force for the republic, a direct departure from Federalist views. His version of participatory democracy only extended, however, to the white yeoman farmers in whom Jefferson placed great trust. While Federalist statesmen, like the architects of the 1787 federal constitution, feared a pure democracy, Jefferson was far more optimistic that the common American farmer could be trusted to make good decisions. He believed in majority rule, that is, that the majority of yeoman should have the power to make decisions binding upon the whole. Jefferson had cheered the French Revolution, even when the French republic instituted the Terror to ensure the monarchy would not return. By 1799, however, he had rejected the cause of France because of his opposition to Napoleon's seizure of power and creation of a dictatorship.

Over the course of his two terms as president—he was reelected in 1804—Jefferson reversed the policies of the Federalist Party by turning away from urban commercial development. Instead, he promoted agriculture through the sale of western public lands in small and affordable lots. Perhaps Jefferson's most lasting legacy is his vision of an "empire of liberty." He distrusted cities and instead envisioned a rural republic of land-owning white men, or yeoman republican farmers. He wanted the United States to be the breadbasket of the world, exporting its agricultural commodities without suffering the ills of urbanization and industrialization. Since American yeomen would own their own land, they could stand up against those who might try to buy their votes with promises of property. Jefferson championed the rights of states and insisted on limited federal government as well as limited taxes. This stood in stark contrast to the Federalists' insistence on a strong, active federal government. Jefferson also believed in fiscal austerity. He pushed for—and Congress approved—the end of all internal taxes, such as those on whiskey and rum. The most significant trimming of the federal budget came at the expense of the military; Jefferson did not believe in maintaining a costly military, and he slashed the size of the navy Adams had worked to build up. Nonetheless, Jefferson responded to the capture of American ships and sailors by pirates off the coast of North Africa by leading the United States into war against the Muslim Barbary States in 1801, the first conflict fought by Americans overseas.

The slow decline of the Federalists, which began under Jefferson, led to a period of one-party rule in national politics. Historians call the years between 1815 and 1828 the "Era of Good Feelings" and highlight the "Virginia dynasty" of the time, since the two presidents who followed Jefferson—James Madison and James Monroe—both hailed from his home state. Like him, they owned slaves and represented the Democratic-Republican Party. Though Federalists continued to enjoy popularity, especially in the Northeast, their days of prominence in setting foreign and domestic policy had ended.

PARTISAN ACRIMONY

The earliest years of the nineteenth century were hardly free of problems between the two political parties. Early in Jefferson's term, controversy swirled over President Adams's judicial appointments of many Federalists during his final days in office. When Jefferson took the oath of office, he refused to have the commissions for these Federalist justices delivered to the appointed officials.

One of Adams's appointees, William Marbury, had been selected to be a justice of the peace in the District of Columbia, and when his commission did not arrive, he petitioned the Supreme Court for an explanation from Jefferson's secretary of state, James Madison. In deciding the case, **Marbury v. Madison**, in 1803, Chief Justice John Marshall agreed that Marbury had the right to a legal remedy, establishing that individuals had rights even the president of the United States could not abridge. However, Marshall also found that Congress's Judicial Act of 1789, which would have given the Supreme Court the power to grant Marbury remedy, was unconstitutional because the Constitution did not allow for cases like Marbury's to come directly before the Supreme Court. Thus, Marshall established the principle of judicial review, which strengthened the court by asserting its power to review (and possibly nullify) the actions of Congress and the president. Jefferson was not pleased, but neither did Marbury get his commission.

The animosity between the political parties exploded into open violence in 1804, when Aaron Burr, Jefferson's first vice president, and Alexander Hamilton engaged in a duel. When Democratic-Republican Burr lost his bid for the office of governor of New York, he was quick to blame Hamilton, who had long hated him and had done everything in his power to discredit him. On July 11, the two antagonists met in Weehawken, New Jersey, to exchange bullets in a duel in which Burr shot and mortally wounded Hamilton.

THE LOUISIANA PURCHASE

Jefferson, who wanted to expand the United States to bring about his "empire of liberty," realized his greatest triumph in 1803 when the United States bought the Louisiana territory from France. For $15 million—a bargain price, considering the amount of land involved—the United States doubled in size. Perhaps the greatest real estate deal in American history, the **Louisiana Purchase** greatly enhanced the Jeffersonian vision of the United States as an agrarian republic in which yeomen farmers worked the land. Jefferson also wanted to bolster trade in the West, seeing the port of New Orleans and the Mississippi River (then the western boundary of the United States) as crucial to American agricultural commerce. In his mind, farmers would send their produce down the Mississippi River to New Orleans, where it would be sold to European traders.

The purchase of Louisiana came about largely because of circumstances beyond Jefferson's control, though he certainly recognized the implications of the transaction. Until 1801, Spain had controlled New Orleans and had given the United States the right to traffic goods in the port without paying customs duties. That year, however, the Spanish had ceded Louisiana (and New Orleans) to France. In 1802, the United States lost its right to deposit goods free in the port, causing outrage among many, some of whom called for war with France.

Jefferson instructed Robert Livingston, the American envoy to France, to secure access to New Orleans, sending James Monroe to France to add additional pressure. The timing proved advantageous. Because black slaves in the French colony of Haiti had successfully overthrown the brutal plantation regime, Napoleon could no longer hope to restore the empire lost with France's defeat in the French and Indian

War (1754–1763). His vision of Louisiana and the Mississippi Valley as the source for food for Haiti, the most profitable sugar island in the world, had failed. The emperor therefore agreed to the sale in early 1803.

Explore the collected maps and documents relating to the Louisiana Purchase and its history at the **Library of Congress** (http://openstaxcollege.org/l/LaPurchase) site.

The true extent of the United States' new territory remained unknown (**Figure 8.14**). Would it provide the long-sought quick access to Asian markets? Geographical knowledge was limited; indeed, no one knew precisely what lay to the west or how long it took to travel from the Mississippi to the Pacific. Jefferson selected two fellow Virginians, Meriwether Lewis and William Clark, to lead an expedition to the new western lands. Their purpose was to discover the commercial possibilities of the new land and, most importantly, potential trade routes. From 1804 to 1806, Lewis and Clark traversed the West.

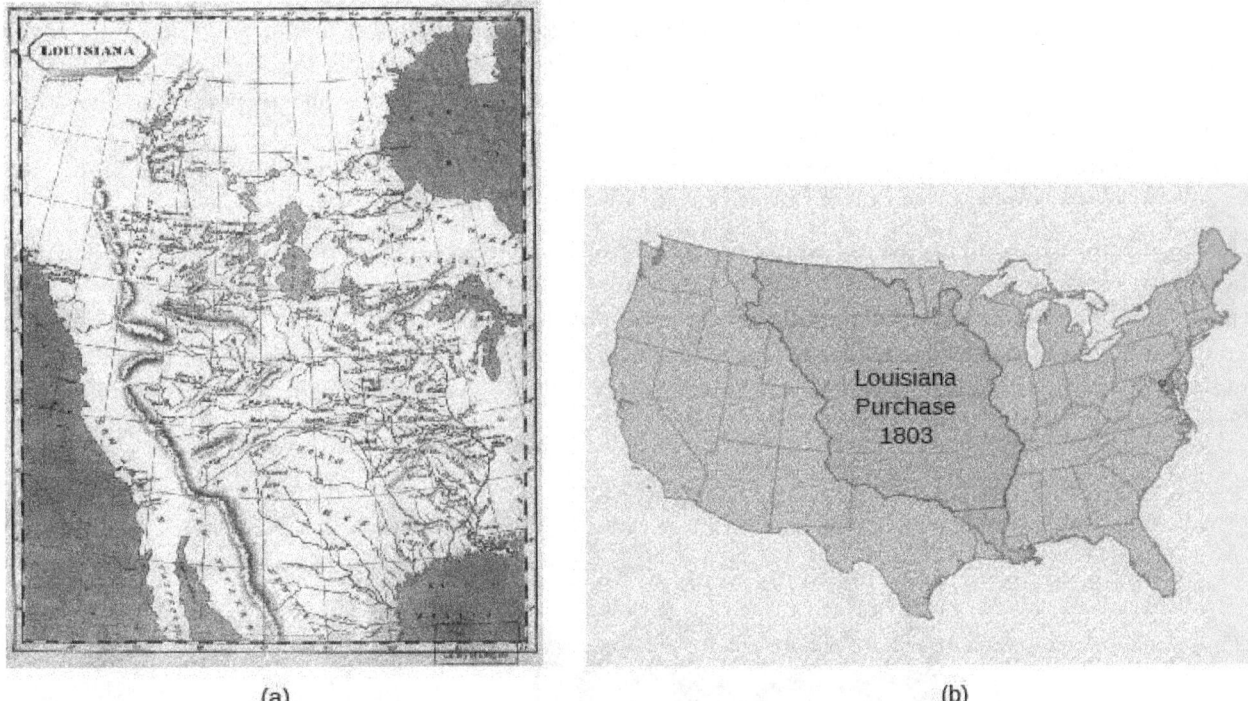

Figure 8.14 This 1804 map (a) shows the territory added to the United States in the Louisiana Purchase of 1803. Compare this depiction to the contemporary map (b). How does the 1804 version differ from what you know of the geography of the United States?

The Louisiana Purchase helped Jefferson win reelection in 1804 by a landslide. Of 176 electoral votes cast, all but 14 were in his favor. The great expansion of the United States did have its critics, however, especially northerners who feared the addition of more slave states and a corresponding lack of representation of their interests in the North. And under a strict interpretation of the Constitution, it remained unclear whether the president had the power to add territory in this fashion. But the vast majority of citizens cheered the increase in the size of the republic. For slaveholders, new western lands would be a boon; for slaves, the Louisiana Purchase threatened to entrench their suffering further.

8.4 The United States Goes Back to War

By the end of this section, you will be able to:
- Describe the causes and consequences of the War of 1812
- Identify the important events of the War of 1812 and explain their significance

The origins of the War of 1812, often called the Second War of American Independence, are found in the unresolved issues between the United States and Great Britain. One major cause was the British practice of impressment, whereby American sailors were taken at sea and forced to fight on British warships; this issue was left unresolved by Jay's Treaty in 1794. In addition, the British in Canada supported Indians in their fight against further U.S. expansion in the Great Lakes region. Though Jefferson wanted to avoid what he called "entangling alliances," staying neutral proved impossible.

THE EMBARGO OF 1807

France and England, engaged in the Napoleonic Wars, which raged between 1803 and 1815, both declared open season on American ships, which they seized on the high seas. England was the major offender, since the Royal Navy, following a time-honored practice, "impressed" American sailors by forcing them into its service. The issue came to a head in 1807 when the HMS *Leopard*, a British warship, fired on a U.S. naval ship, the *Chesapeake*, off the coast of Norfolk, Virginia. The British then boarded the ship and took four sailors. Jefferson chose what he thought was the best of his limited options and responded to the crisis through the economic means of a sweeping ban on trade, the Embargo Act of 1807. This law prohibited American ships from leaving their ports until Britain and France stopped seizing them on the high seas. As a result of the embargo, American commerce came to a near-total halt.

The logic behind the embargo was that cutting off all trade would so severely hurt Britain and France that the seizures at sea would end. However, while the embargo did have some effect on the British economy, it was American commerce that actually felt the brunt of the impact (**Figure 8.15**). The embargo hurt American farmers, who could no longer sell their goods overseas, and seaport cities experienced a huge increase in unemployment and an uptick in bankruptcies. All told, American business activity declined by 75 percent from 1808 to 1809.

Figure 8.15 In this political cartoon from 1807, a snapping turtle (holding a shipping license) grabs a smuggler in the act of sneaking a barrel of sugar to a British ship. The smuggler cries, "Oh, this cursed Ograbme!" ("Ograbme" is "embargo" spelled backwards.)

This content is available for free at http://cnx.org/content/col11740/latest/

Enforcement of the embargo proved very difficult, especially in the states bordering British Canada. Smuggling was widespread; Smugglers' Notch in Vermont, for example, earned its name from illegal trade with British Canada. Jefferson attributed the problems with the embargo to lax enforcement.

At the very end of his second term, Jefferson signed the Non-Intercourse Act of 1808, lifting the unpopular embargoes on trade except with Britain and France. In the election of 1808, American voters elected another Democratic-Republican, James Madison. Madison inherited Jefferson's foreign policy issues involving Britain and France. Most people in the United States, especially those in the West, saw Great Britain as the major problem.

TECUMSEH AND THE WESTERN CONFEDERACY

Another underlying cause of the War of 1812 was British support for native resistance to U.S. western expansion. For many years, white settlers in the American western territories had besieged the Indians living there. Under Jefferson, two Indian policies existed: forcing Indians to adopt American ways of agricultural life, or aggressively driving Indians into debt in order to force them to sell their lands.

In 1809, Tecumseh, a Shawnee war chief, rejuvenated the Western Confederacy. His brother, Tenskwatawa, was a prophet among the Shawnee who urged a revival of native ways and rejection of Anglo-American culture, including alcohol. In 1811, William Henry Harrison, the governor of the Indiana Territory, attempted to eliminate the native presence by attacking Prophetstown, a Shawnee settlement named in honor of Tenskwatawa. In the ensuing Battle of Tippecanoe, U.S. forces led by Harrison destroyed the settlement (**Figure 8.16**). They also found ample evidence that the British had supplied the Western Confederacy with weapons, despite the stipulations of earlier treaties.

Figure 8.16 Portrait (a), painted by Charles Bird King in 1820, is a depiction of Shawnee prophet Tenskwatawa. Portrait (b) is Rembrandt Peele's 1813 depiction of William Henry Harrison. What are the significant similarities and differences between the portraits? What was each artist trying to convey?

THE WAR OF 1812

The seizure of American ships and sailors, combined with the British support of Indian resistance, led to strident calls for war against Great Britain. The loudest came from the "war hawks," led by Henry Clay from Kentucky and John C. Calhoun from South Carolina, who would not tolerate British insults to American honor. Opposition to the war came from Federalists, especially those in the Northeast, who knew war would disrupt the maritime trade on which they depended. In a narrow vote, Congress authorized the president to declare war against Britain in June 1812.

The war went very badly for the United States at first. In August 1812, the United States lost Detroit to the British and their Indian allies, including a force of one thousand men led by Tecumseh. By the end of the year, the British controlled half the Northwest. The following year, however, U.S. forces scored several victories. Captain Oliver Hazard Perry and his naval force defeated the British on Lake Erie. At the Battle of the Thames in Ontario, the United States defeated the British and their native allies, and Tecumseh was counted among the dead. Indian resistance began to ebb, opening the Indiana and Michigan territories for white settlement.

These victories could not turn the tide of the war, however. With the British gaining the upper hand during the Napoleonic Wars and Napoleon's French army on the run, Great Britain now could divert skilled combat troops from Europe to fight in the United States. In July 1814, forty-five hundred hardened British soldiers sailed up the Chesapeake Bay and burned Washington, DC, to the ground, forcing President Madison and his wife to run for their lives (**Figure 8.17**). According to one report, they left behind a dinner the British officers ate. That summer, the British shelled Baltimore, hoping for another victory. However, they failed to dislodge the U.S. forces, whose survival of the bombardment inspired Francis Scott Key to write "The Star-Spangled Banner."

Figure 8.17 George Munger painted *The President's House* shortly after the War of 1812, ca. 1814–1815. The painting shows the result of the British burning of Washington, DC.

AMERICANA

Francis Scott Key's "In Defense of Fort McHenry"

After the British bombed Baltimore's Fort McHenry in 1814 but failed to overcome the U.S. forces there, Francis Scott Key was inspired by the sight of the American flag, which remained hanging proudly in the aftermath. He wrote the poem "In Defense of Fort McHenry," which was later set to the tune of a British song called "The Anacreontic Song" and eventually became the U.S. national anthem, "The Star-Spangled Banner."

> Oh, say, can you see, by the dawn's early light,
> What so proudly we hailed at the twilight's last gleaming?
> Whose broad stripes and bright stars, thru the perilous fight,
> O'er the ramparts we watched, were so gallantly streaming?
> And the rockets' red glare, the bombs bursting in air,
> Gave proof through the night that our flag was still there.
> O say, does that star-spangled banner yet wave
> O'er the land of the free and the home of the brave?
>
> On the shore dimly seen through the mists of the deep,
> Where the foe's haughty host in dread silence reposes,
> What is that which the breeze, o'er the towering steep,
> As it fitfully blows, half conceals, half discloses?
> Now it catches the gleam of the morning's first beam,
> In full glory reflected, now shines on the stream:
> Tis the star-spangled banner: O, long may it wave
> O'er the land of the free and the home of the brave!
>
> And where is that band who so vauntingly swore
> That the havoc of war and the battle's confusion
> A home and a country should leave us no more?
> Their blood has washed out their foul footsteps' pollution.
> No refuge could save the hireling and slave
> From the terror of flight or the gloom of the grave:
> And the star-spangled banner in triumph doth wave
> O'er the land of the free and the home of the brave.
>
> O, thus be it ever when freemen shall stand,
> Between their loved home and the war's desolation!
> Blest with victory and peace, may the heav'n-rescued land
> Praise the Power that hath made and preserved us a nation!
> Then conquer we must, when our cause it is just,
> And this be our motto: "In God is our trust"
> And the star-spangled banner in triumph shall wave
> O'er the land of the free and the home of the brave!
> —Francis Scott Key, "In Defense of Fort McHenry," 1814

What images does Key use to describe the American spirit? Most people are familiar with only the first verse of the song; what do you think the last three verses add?

Click and Explore

Visit the **Smithsonian Institute** (http://openstaxcollege.org/l/flag) to explore an interactive feature on the flag that inspired "The Star-Spangled Banner," where clickable "hot spots" on the flag reveal elements of its history.

With the end of the war in Europe, Britain was eager to end the conflict in the Americas as well. In 1814, British and U.S. diplomats met in Flanders, in northern Belgium, to negotiate the Treaty of Ghent, signed in December. The boundaries between the United States and British Canada remained as they were before the war, an outcome welcome to those in the United States who feared a rupture in the country's otherwise steady expansion into the West.

The War of 1812 was very unpopular in New England because it inflicted further economic harm on a region dependent on maritime commerce. This unpopularity caused a resurgence of the Federalist Party in New England. Many Federalists deeply resented the power of the slaveholding Virginians (Jefferson and then Madison), who appeared indifferent to their region. The depth of the Federalists' discontent is illustrated by the proceedings of the December 1814 Hartford Convention, a meeting of twenty-six Federalists in Connecticut, where some attendees issued calls for New England to secede from the United States. These arguments for disunion during wartime, combined with the convention's condemnation of the government, made Federalists appear unpatriotic. The convention forever discredited the Federalist Party and led to its downfall.

EPILOGUE: THE BATTLE OF NEW ORLEANS

Due to slow communication, the last battle in the War of 1812 happened after the Treaty of Ghent had been signed ending the war. Andrew Jackson had distinguished himself in the war by defeating the Creek Indians in March 1814 before invading Florida in May of that year. After taking Pensacola, he moved his force of Tennessee fighters to New Orleans to defend the strategic port against British attack.

On January 8, 1815 (despite the official end of the war), a force of battle-tested British veterans of the Napoleonic Wars attempted to take the port. Jackson's forces devastated the British, killing over two thousand. New Orleans and the vast Mississippi River Valley had been successfully defended, ensuring the future of American settlement and commerce. The Battle of New Orleans immediately catapulted Jackson to national prominence as a war hero, and in the 1820s, he emerged as the head of the new Democratic Party.

CHAPTER 9
Jacksonian Democracy, 1820–1840

Figure 9.1 In *President's Levee, or all Creation going to the White House, Washington* (1841), by Robert Cruikshank, the artist depicts Andrew Jackson's inauguration in 1829, with crowds surging into the White House to join the celebrations. Rowdy revelers destroyed many White House furnishings in their merriment. A new political era of democracy had begun, one characterized by the rule of the majority.

Chapter Outline

9.1 A New Political Style: From John Quincy Adams to Andrew Jackson
9.2 The Rise of American Democracy
9.3 The Nullification Crisis and the Bank War
9.4 Indian Removal
9.5 The Tyranny and Triumph of the Majority

Introduction

The most extraordinary political development in the years before the Civil War was the rise of American democracy. Whereas the founders envisioned the United States as a republic, not a democracy, and had placed safeguards such as the Electoral College in the 1787 Constitution to prevent simple majority rule, the early 1820s saw many Americans embracing majority rule and rejecting old forms of deference that were based on elite ideas of virtue, learning, and family lineage.

A new breed of politicians learned to harness the magic of the many by appealing to the resentments, fears, and passions of ordinary citizens to win elections. The charismatic Andrew Jackson gained a reputation as a fighter and defender of American expansion, emerging as the quintessential figure leading the rise of American democracy. In the image above (**Figure 9.1**), crowds flock to the White House to celebrate his inauguration as president. While earlier inaugurations had been reserved for Washington's political elite, Jackson's was an event for the people, so much so that the pushing throngs caused thousands of dollars of damage to White House property. Characteristics of modern American democracy, including the turbulent nature of majority rule, first appeared during the Age of Jackson.

9.1 A New Political Style: From John Quincy Adams to Andrew Jackson

By the end of this section, you will be able to:
- Explain and illustrate the new style of American politics in the 1820s
- Describe the policies of John Quincy Adams's presidency and explain the political divisions that resulted

In the 1820s, American political culture gave way to the democratic urges of the citizenry. Political leaders and parties rose to popularity by championing the will of the people, pushing the country toward a future in which a wider swath of citizens gained a political voice. However, this expansion of political power was limited to white men; women, free blacks, and Indians remained—or grew increasingly—disenfranchised by the American political system.

THE DECLINE OF FEDERALISM

The first party system in the United States shaped the political contest between the Federalists and the Democratic-Republicans. The Federalists, led by Washington, Hamilton, and Adams, dominated American politics in the 1790s. After the election of Thomas Jefferson—the Revolution of 1800—the Democratic-Republicans gained ascendance. The gradual decline of the Federalist Party is evident in its losses in the presidential contests that occurred between 1800 and 1820. After 1816, in which Democratic-Republican James Monroe defeated his Federalist rival Rufus King, the Federalists never ran another presidential candidate.

Before the 1820s, a **code of deference** had underwritten the republic's political order. Deference was the practice of showing respect for individuals who had distinguished themselves through military accomplishments, educational attainment, business success, or family pedigree. Such individuals were members of what many Americans in the early republic agreed was a natural aristocracy. Deference shown

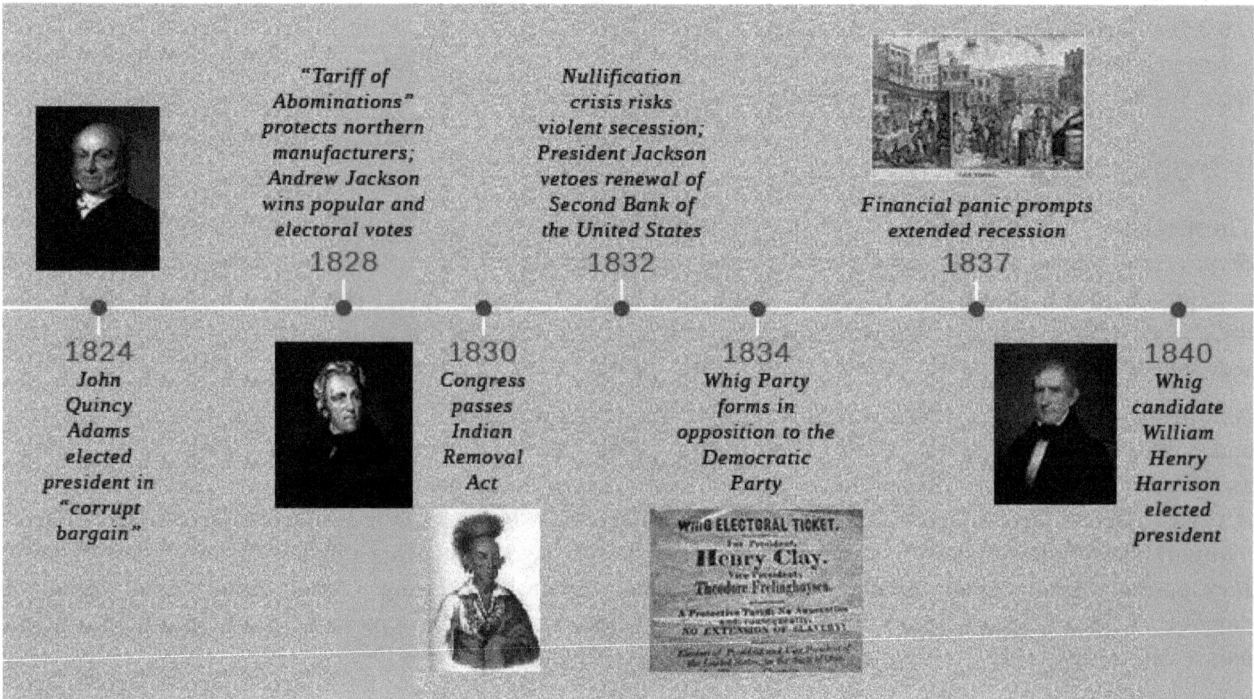

Figure 9.2

to them dovetailed with republicanism and its emphasis on virtue, the ideal of placing the common good above narrow self-interest. Republican statesmen in the 1780s and 1790s expected and routinely received deferential treatment from others, and ordinary Americans deferred to their "social betters" as a matter of course.

For the generation who lived through the American Revolution, for instance, George Washington epitomized republican virtue, entitling him to great deference from his countrymen. His judgment and decisions were considered beyond reproach. An Anglican minister named Mason Locke Weems wrote the classic tale of Washington's unimpeachable virtue in his 1800 book, *The Life of Washington*. Generations of nineteenth-century American children read its fictional story of a youthful Washington chopping down one of his father's cherry trees and, when confronted by his father, confessing: "I cannot tell a lie" (**Figure 9.3**). The story spoke to Washington's unflinching honesty and integrity, encouraging readers to remember the deference owed to such towering national figures.

Figure 9.3 "*Father, I Can Not Tell a Lie: I Cut the Tree*" (1867) by John McRae, after a painting by George Gorgas White, illustrates Mason Locke Weems's tale of Washington's honesty and integrity as revealed in the incident of the cherry tree. Although it was fiction, this story about Washington taught generations of children about the importance of virtue.

Washington and those who celebrated his role as president established a standard for elite, virtuous leadership that cast a long shadow over subsequent presidential administrations. The presidents who followed Washington shared the first president's pedigree. With the exception of John Adams, who was from Massachusetts, all the early presidents—Thomas Jefferson, James Madison, and James Monroe—were members of Virginia's elite slaveholder aristocracy.

DEMOCRATIC REFORMS

In the early 1820s, deference to pedigree began to wane in American society. A new type of deference—to the will of the majority and not to a ruling class—took hold. The spirit of democratic reform became most evident in the widespread belief that all white men, regardless of whether they owned property, had the right to participate in elections.

Before the 1820s, many state constitutions had imposed property qualifications for voting as a means to keep democratic tendencies in check. However, as Federalist ideals fell out of favor, ordinary men from the middle and lower classes increasingly questioned the idea that property ownership was an indication of virtue. They argued for **universal manhood suffrage**, or voting rights for all white male adults.

New states adopted constitutions that did not contain property qualifications for voting, a move designed to stimulate migration across their borders. Vermont and Kentucky, admitted to the Union in 1791 and 1792 respectively, granted the right to vote to all white men regardless of whether they owned property or paid taxes. Ohio's state constitution placed a minor taxpaying requirement on voters but otherwise allowed for expansive white male suffrage. Alabama, admitted to the Union in 1819, eliminated property qualifications for voting in its state constitution. Two other new states, Indiana (1816) and Illinois (1818), also extended the right to vote to white men regardless of property. Initially, the new state of Mississippi (1817) restricted voting to white male property holders, but in 1832 it eliminated this provision.

In Connecticut, Federalist power largely collapsed in 1818 when the state held a constitutional convention. The new constitution granted the right to vote to all white men who paid taxes or served in the militia. Similarly, New York amended its state constitution in 1821–1822 and removed the property qualifications for voting.

Expanded voting rights did not extend to women, Indians, or free blacks in the North. Indeed, race replaced property qualifications as the criterion for voting rights. American democracy had a decidedly racist orientation; a white majority limited the rights of black minorities. New Jersey explicitly restricted the right to vote to white men only. Connecticut passed a law in 1814 taking the right to vote away from free black men and restricting suffrage to white men only. By the 1820s, 80 percent of the white male population could vote in New York State elections. No other state had expanded suffrage so dramatically. At the same time, however, New York effectively disenfranchised free black men in 1822 (black men had had the right to vote under the 1777 constitution) by requiring that "men of color" must possess property over the value of $250.

PARTY POLITICS AND THE ELECTION OF 1824

In addition to expanding white men's right to vote, democratic currents also led to a new style of political party organization, most evident in New York State in the years after the War of 1812. Under the leadership of Martin Van Buren, New York's "Bucktail" Republican faction (so named because members wore a deer's tail on their hats, a symbol of membership in the Tammany Society) gained political power by cultivating loyalty to the will of the majority, not to an elite family or renowned figure. The Bucktails emphasized a pragmatic approach. For example, at first they opposed the Erie Canal project, but when the popularity of the massive transportation venture became clear, they supported it.

One of the Bucktails' greatest achievements in New York came in the form of revisions to the state constitution in the 1820s. Under the original constitution, a Council of Appointments selected local officials such as sheriffs and county clerks. The Bucktails replaced this process with a system of direct elections, which meant thousands of jobs immediately became available to candidates who had the support of the majority. In practice, Van Buren's party could nominate and support their own candidates based on their loyalty to the party. In this way, Van Buren helped create a political machine of disciplined party members who prized loyalty above all else, a harbinger of future patronage politics in the United States. This system of rewarding party loyalists is known as the **spoils system** (from the expression, "To the victor belong the spoils"). Van Buren's political machine helped radically transform New York politics.

Party politics also transformed the national political landscape, and the election of 1824 proved a turning point in American politics. With tens of thousands of new voters, the older system of having members of Congress form congressional caucuses to determine who would run no longer worked. The new voters had regional interests and voted on them. For the first time, the popular vote mattered in a presidential election. Electors were chosen by popular vote in eighteen states, while the six remaining states used the older system in which state legislatures chose electors.

With the caucus system defunct, the presidential election of 1824 featured five candidates, all of whom ran as Democratic-Republicans (the Federalists having ceased to be a national political force). The crowded field included John Quincy Adams, the son of the second president, John Adams. Candidate Adams had broken with the Federalists in the early 1800s and served on various diplomatic missions, including the mission to secure peace with Great Britain in 1814. He represented New England. A second candidate, John C. Calhoun from South Carolina, had served as secretary of war and represented the slaveholding South. He dropped out of the presidential race to run for vice president. A third candidate, Henry Clay, the Speaker of the House of Representatives, hailed from Kentucky and represented the western states. He favored an active federal government committed to internal improvements, such as roads and canals, to bolster national economic development and settlement of the West. William H. Crawford, a slaveholder from Georgia, suffered a stroke in 1823 that left him largely incapacitated, but he ran nonetheless and had the backing of the New York machine headed by Van Buren. Andrew Jackson, the famed "hero of New Orleans," rounded out the field. Jackson had very little formal education, but he was popular for his military victories in the War of 1812 and in wars against the Creek and the Seminole. He had been elected to the Senate in 1823, and his popularity soared as pro-Jackson newspapers sang the praises of the courage and daring of the Tennessee slaveholder (**Figure 9.4**).

Figure 9.4 The two most popular presidential candidates in the election of 1824 were Andrew Jackson (a), who won the popular vote but failed to secure the requisite number of votes in the Electoral College, and John Quincy Adams (b), who emerged victorious after a contentious vote in the U.S. House of Representatives.

Results from the eighteen states where the popular vote determined the electoral vote gave Jackson the election, with 152,901 votes to Adams's 114,023, Clay's 47,217, and Crawford's 46,979. The Electoral College, however, was another matter. Of the 261 electoral votes, Jackson needed 131 or better to win but secured only 99. Adams won 84, Crawford 41, and Clay 37. Because Jackson did not receive a majority vote from the Electoral College, the election was decided following the terms of the Twelfth Amendment, which stipulated that when a candidate did not receive a majority of electoral votes, the election went to the House of Representatives, where each state would provide one vote. House Speaker Clay did not want to see his rival, Jackson, become president and therefore worked within the House to secure the presidency for Adams, convincing many to cast their vote for the New Englander. Clay's efforts paid off; despite not having won the popular vote, John Quincy Adams was certified by the House as the next president. Once in office, he elevated Henry Clay to the post of secretary of state.

Jackson and his supporters cried foul. To them, the election of Adams reeked of anti-democratic corruption. So too did the appointment of Clay as secretary of state. John C. Calhoun labeled the whole affair a **"corrupt bargain"** (**Figure 9.5**). Everywhere, Jackson supporters vowed revenge against the anti-majoritarian result of 1824.

Figure 9.5 John C. Calhoun (a) believed that the assistance Henry Clay (b) gave to John Quincy Adams in the U.S. House of Representatives' vote to decide the presidential election of 1824 indicated that a "corrupt bargain" had been made.

THE PRESIDENCY OF JOHN QUINCY ADAMS

Secretary of State Clay championed what was known as the **American System** of high tariffs, a national bank, and federally sponsored internal improvements of canals and roads. Once in office, President Adams embraced Clay's American System and proposed a national university and naval academy to train future leaders of the republic. The president's opponents smelled elitism in these proposals and pounced on what they viewed as the administration's catering to a small privileged class at the expense of ordinary citizens.

Clay also envisioned a broad range of internal transportation improvements. Using the proceeds from land sales in the West, Adams endorsed the creation of roads and canals to facilitate commerce and the advance of settlement in the West. Many in Congress vigorously opposed federal funding of internal improvements, citing among other reasons that the Constitution did not give the federal government the power to fund these projects. However, in the end, Adams succeeded in extending the Cumberland Road into Ohio (a federal highway project). He also broke ground for the Chesapeake and Ohio Canal on July 4, 1828.

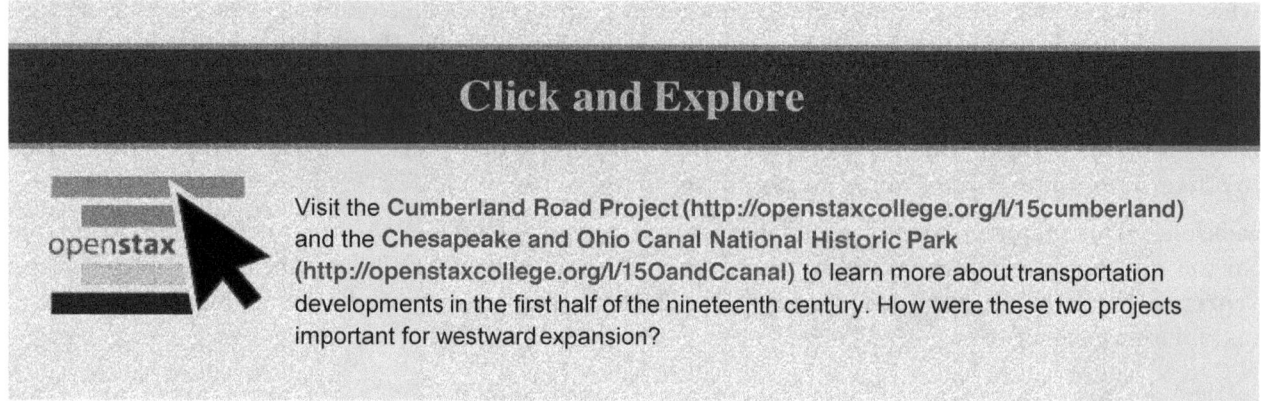

Visit the **Cumberland Road Project** (http://openstaxcollege.org/l/15cumberland) and the **Chesapeake and Ohio Canal National Historic Park** (http://openstaxcollege.org/l/15OandCcanal) to learn more about transportation developments in the first half of the nineteenth century. How were these two projects important for westward expansion?

Tariffs, which both Clay and Adams promoted, were not a novel idea; since the birth of the republic they had been seen as a way to advance domestic manufacturing by making imports more expensive. Congress had approved a tariff in 1789, for instance, and Alexander Hamilton had proposed a protective tariff in

1790. Congress also passed tariffs in 1816 and 1824. Clay spearheaded the drive for the federal government to impose high tariffs to help bolster domestic manufacturing. If imported goods were more expensive than domestic goods, then people would buy American-made goods.

President Adams wished to promote manufacturing, especially in his home region of New England. To that end, in 1828 he proposed a high tariff on imported goods, amounting to 50 percent of their value. The tariff raised questions about how power should be distributed, causing a fiery debate between those who supported states' rights and those who supported the expanded power of the federal government (**Figure 9.6**). Those who championed states' rights denounced the 1828 measure as the **Tariff of Abominations**, clear evidence that the federal government favored one region, in this case the North, over another, the South. They made their case by pointing out that the North had an expanding manufacturing base while the South did not. Therefore, the South imported far more manufactured goods than the North, causing the tariff to fall most heavily on the southern states.

Figure 9.6 *The Monkey System or 'Every one for himself at the expense of his neighbor!!!!!!!!!'* (1831) critiqued Henry Clay's proposed tariff and system of internal improvements. In this political cartoon by Edward Williams Clay, four caged monkeys labeled "Home," "Consumption," "Internal," and "Improv" (improvements)—different parts of the nation's economy—steal each other's food while Henry Clay, in the foreground, extols the virtues of his "grand original American System." (credit: Project Gutenberg Archives)

The 1828 tariff generated additional fears among southerners. In particular, it suggested to them that the federal government would unilaterally take steps that hurt the South. This line of reasoning led some southerners to fear that the very foundation of the South—slavery—could come under attack from a hostile northern majority in Congress. The spokesman for this southern view was President Adams's vice president, John C. Calhoun.

> ## DEFINING "AMERICAN"
>
> ### ✪ John C. Calhoun on the Tariff of 1828
>
> Vice President John C. Calhoun, angry about the passage of the Tariff of 1828, anonymously wrote a report titled "South Carolina Exposition and Protest" (later known as "Calhoun's Exposition") for the South Carolina legislature. As a native of South Carolina, Calhoun articulated the fear among many southerners that the federal government could exercise undue power over the states.
>
>> If it be conceded, as it must be by every one who is the least conversant with our institutions, that the sovereign powers delegated are divided between the General and State Governments, and that the latter hold their portion by the same tenure as the former, it would seem impossible to deny to the States the right of deciding on the infractions of their powers, and the proper remedy to be applied for their correction. The right of judging, in such cases, is an essential attribute of sovereignty, of which the States cannot be divested without losing their sovereignty itself, and being reduced to a subordinate corporate condition. In fact, to divide power, and to give to one of the parties the exclusive right of judging of the portion allotted to each, is, in reality, not to divide it at all; and to reserve such exclusive right to the General Government (it matters not by what department) to be exercised, is to convert it, in fact, into a great consolidated government, with unlimited powers, and to divest the States, in reality, of all their rights, It is impossible to understand the force of terms, and to deny so plain a conclusion.
>> —John C. Calhoun, "South Carolina Exposition and Protest," 1828
>
> What is Calhoun's main point of protest? What does he say about the sovereignty of the states?

9.2 The Rise of American Democracy

> By the end of this section, you will be able to:
> - Describe the key points of the election of 1828
> - Explain the scandals of Andrew Jackson's first term in office

A turning point in American political history occurred in 1828, which witnessed the election of Andrew Jackson over the incumbent John Quincy Adams. While democratic practices had been in ascendance since 1800, the year also saw the further unfolding of a democratic spirit in the United States. Supporters of Jackson called themselves Democrats or the Democracy, giving birth to the Democratic Party. Political authority appeared to rest with the majority as never before.

THE CAMPAIGN AND ELECTION OF 1828

During the 1800s, democratic reforms made steady progress with the abolition of property qualifications for voting and the birth of new forms of political party organization. The 1828 campaign pushed new democratic practices even further and highlighted the difference between the Jacksonian expanded electorate and the older, exclusive Adams style. A slogan of the day, "Adams who can write/Jackson who can fight," captured the contrast between Adams the aristocrat and Jackson the frontiersman.

The 1828 campaign differed significantly from earlier presidential contests because of the party organization that promoted Andrew Jackson. Jackson and his supporters reminded voters of the "corrupt bargain" of 1824. They framed it as the work of a small group of political elites deciding who would lead the nation, acting in a self-serving manner and ignoring the will of the majority (**Figure 9.7**). From Nashville, Tennessee, the Jackson campaign organized supporters around the nation through editorials in partisan newspapers and other publications. Pro-Jackson newspapers heralded the "hero of New Orleans" while denouncing Adams. Though he did not wage an election campaign filled with public appearances,

Jackson did give one major campaign speech in New Orleans on January 8, the anniversary of the defeat of the British in 1815. He also engaged in rounds of discussion with politicians who came to his home, the Hermitage, in Nashville.

Figure 9.7 The bitter rivalry between Andrew Jackson and Henry Clay was exacerbated by the "corrupt bargain" of 1824, which Jackson made much of during his successful presidential campaign in 1828. This drawing, published in the 1830s during the debates over the future of the Second Bank of the United States, shows Clay sewing up Jackson's mouth while the "cure for calumny [slander]" protrudes from his pocket.

At the local level, Jackson's supporters worked to bring in as many new voters as possible. Rallies, parades, and other rituals further broadcast the message that Jackson stood for the common man against the corrupt elite backing Adams and Clay. Democratic organizations called Hickory Clubs, a tribute to Jackson's nickname, Old Hickory, also worked tirelessly to ensure his election.

In November 1828, Jackson won an overwhelming victory over Adams, capturing 56 percent of the popular vote and 68 percent of the electoral vote. As in 1800, when Jefferson had won over the Federalist incumbent John Adams, the presidency passed to a new political party, the Democrats. The election was the climax of several decades of expanding democracy in the United States and the end of the older politics of deference.

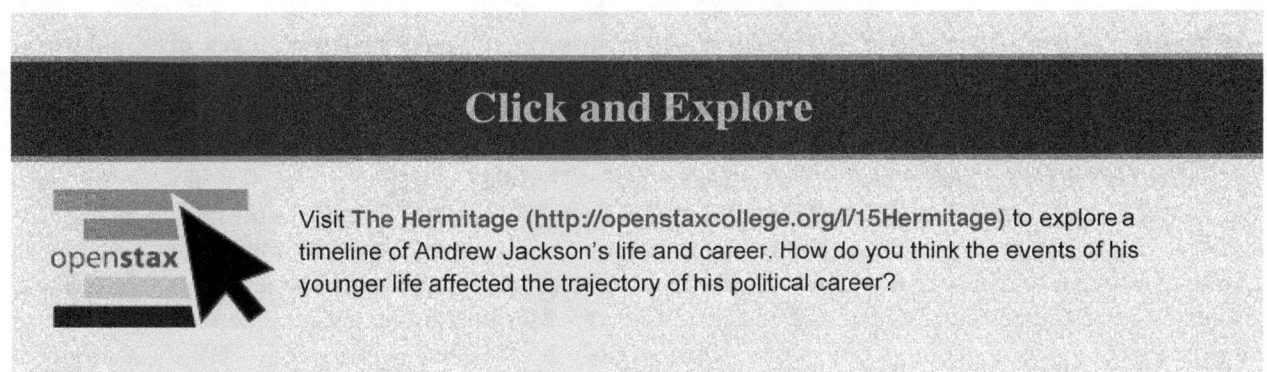

Visit The Hermitage (http://openstaxcollege.org/l/15Hermitage) to explore a timeline of Andrew Jackson's life and career. How do you think the events of his younger life affected the trajectory of his political career?

SCANDAL IN THE PRESIDENCY

Amid revelations of widespread fraud, including the disclosure that some $300,000 was missing from the Treasury Department, Jackson removed almost 50 percent of appointed civil officers, which allowed him to handpick their replacements. This replacement of appointed federal officials is called **rotation in office**.

Lucrative posts, such as postmaster and deputy postmaster, went to party loyalists, especially in places where Jackson's support had been weakest, such as New England. Some Democratic newspaper editors who had supported Jackson during the campaign also gained public jobs.

Jackson's opponents were angered and took to calling the practice the spoils system, after the policies of Van Buren's Bucktail Republican Party. The rewarding of party loyalists with government jobs resulted in spectacular instances of corruption. Perhaps the most notorious occurred in New York City, where a Jackson appointee made off with over $1 million. Such examples seemed proof positive that the Democrats were disregarding merit, education, and respectability in decisions about the governing of the nation.

In addition to dealing with rancor over rotation in office, the Jackson administration became embroiled in a personal scandal known as the Petticoat affair. This incident exacerbated the division between the president's team and the insider class in the nation's capital, who found the new arrivals from Tennessee lacking in decorum and propriety. At the center of the storm was Margaret ("Peggy") O'Neal, a well-known socialite in Washington, DC (**Figure 9.8**). O'Neal cut a striking figure and had connections to the republic's most powerful men. She married John Timberlake, a naval officer, and they had three children. Rumors abounded, however, about her involvement with John Eaton, a U.S. senator from Tennessee who had come to Washington in 1818.

Figure 9.8 Peggy O'Neal was so well known that advertisers used her image to sell products to the public. In this anonymous nineteenth-century cigar-box lid, her portrait is flanked by vignettes showing her scandalous past. On the left, President Andrew Jackson presents her with flowers. On the right, two men fight a duel for her.

Timberlake committed suicide in 1828, setting off a flurry of rumors that he had been distraught over his wife's reputed infidelities. Eaton and Mrs. Timberlake married soon after, with the full approval of President Jackson. The so-called Petticoat affair divided Washington society. Many Washington socialites snubbed the new Mrs. Eaton as a woman of low moral character. Among those who would have nothing to do with her was Vice President John C. Calhoun's wife, Floride. Calhoun fell out of favor with President Jackson, who defended Peggy Eaton and derided those who would not socialize with her, declaring she was "as chaste as a virgin." (Jackson had personal reasons for defending Eaton: he drew a parallel between Eaton's treatment and that of his late wife, Rachel, who had been subjected to attacks on her reputation related to her first marriage, which had ended in divorce.) Martin Van Buren, who defended the Eatons and organized social gatherings with them, became close to Jackson, who came to rely on a group of informal advisers that included Van Buren and was dubbed the **Kitchen Cabinet**. This select group of presidential supporters highlights the importance of party loyalty to Jackson and the Democratic Party.

9.3 The Nullification Crisis and the Bank War

By the end of this section, you will be able to:
- Explain the factors that contributed to the Nullification Crisis
- Discuss the origins and creation of the Whig Party

The crisis over the Tariff of 1828 continued into the 1830s and highlighted one of the currents of democracy in the Age of Jackson: namely, that many southerners believed a democratic majority could be harmful to their interests. These southerners saw themselves as an embattled minority and claimed the right of states to nullify federal laws that appeared to threaten state sovereignty. Another undercurrent was the resentment and anger of the majority against symbols of elite privilege, especially powerful financial institutions like the Second Bank of the United States.

THE NULLIFICATION CRISIS

The Tariff of 1828 had driven Vice President Calhoun to pen his "South Carolina Exposition and Protest," in which he argued that if a national majority acted against the interest of a regional minority, then individual states could void—or nullify—federal law. By the early 1830s, the battle over the tariff took on new urgency as the price of cotton continued to fall. In 1818, cotton had been thirty-one cents per pound. By 1831, it had sunk to eight cents per pound. While production of cotton had soared during this time and this increase contributed to the decline in prices, many southerners blamed their economic problems squarely on the tariff for raising the prices they had to pay for imported goods while their own income shrank.

Resentment of the tariff was linked directly to the issue of slavery, because the tariff demonstrated the use of federal power. Some southerners feared the federal government would next take additional action against the South, including the abolition of slavery. The theory of **nullification**, or the voiding of unwelcome federal laws, provided wealthy slaveholders, who were a minority in the United States, with an argument for resisting the national government if it acted contrary to their interests. James Hamilton, who served as governor of South Carolina in the early 1830s, denounced the "despotic majority that oppresses us." Nullification also raised the specter of secession; aggrieved states at the mercy of an aggressive majority would be forced to leave the Union.

On the issue of nullification, South Carolina stood alone. Other southern states backed away from what they saw as the extremism behind the idea. President Jackson did not make the repeal of the 1828 tariff a priority and denied the nullifiers' arguments. He and others, including former President Madison, argued that Article 1, Section 8 of the Constitution gave Congress the power to "lay and collect taxes, duties, imposts, and excises." Jackson pledged to protect the Union against those who would try to tear it apart over the tariff issue. "The union shall be preserved," he declared in 1830.

To deal with the crisis, Jackson advocated a reduction in tariff rates. The Tariff of 1832, passed in the summer, lowered the rates on imported goods, a move designed to calm southerners. It did not have the desired effect, however, and Calhoun's nullifiers still claimed their right to override federal law. In November, South Carolina passed the Ordinance of Nullification, declaring the 1828 and 1832 tariffs null and void in the Palmetto State. Jackson responded, however, by declaring in the December 1832 Nullification Proclamation that a state did not have the power to void a federal law.

With the states and the federal government at an impasse, civil war seemed a real possibility. The next governor of South Carolina, Robert Hayne, called for a force of ten thousand volunteers (**Figure 9.9**) to defend the state against any federal action. At the same time, South Carolinians who opposed the nullifiers told Jackson that eight thousand men stood ready to defend the Union. Congress passed the Force Bill of 1833, which gave the federal government the right to use federal troops to ensure compliance with federal law. The crisis—or at least the prospect of armed conflict in South Carolina—was defused by the Compromise Tariff of 1833, which reduced tariff rates considerably. Nullifiers in South Carolina accepted it, but in a move that demonstrated their inflexibility, they nullified the Force Bill.

Figure 9.9 The governor of South Carolina, Robert Hayne, elected in 1832, was a strong proponent of states' rights and the theory of nullification.

The Nullification Crisis illustrated the growing tensions in American democracy: an aggrieved minority of elite, wealthy slaveholders taking a stand against the will of a democratic majority; an emerging sectional divide between South and North over slavery; and a clash between those who believed in free trade and those who believed in protective tariffs to encourage the nation's economic growth. These tensions would color the next three decades of politics in the United States.

THE BANK WAR

Congress established the Bank of the United States in 1791 as a key pillar of Alexander Hamilton's financial program, but its twenty-year charter expired in 1811. Congress, swayed by the majority's hostility to the bank as an institution catering to the wealthy elite, did not renew the charter at that time. In its place, Congress approved a new national bank—the Second Bank of the United States—in 1816. It too had a twenty-year charter, set to expire in 1836.

The Second Bank of the United States was created to stabilize the banking system. More than two hundred banks existed in the United States in 1816, and almost all of them issued paper money. In other words, citizens faced a bewildering welter of paper money with no standard value. In fact, the problem of paper money had contributed significantly to the Panic of 1819.

In the 1820s, the national bank moved into a magnificent new building in Philadelphia. However, despite Congress's approval of the Second Bank of the United States, a great many people continued to view it as tool of the wealthy, an anti-democratic force. President Jackson was among them; he had faced economic crises of his own during his days speculating in land, an experience that had made him uneasy about paper money. To Jackson, hard currency—that is, gold or silver—was the far better alternative. The president also personally disliked the bank's director, Nicholas Biddle.

A large part of the allure of mass democracy for politicians was the opportunity to capture the anger and resentment of ordinary Americans against what they saw as the privileges of a few. One of the leading opponents of the bank was Thomas Hart Benton, a senator from Missouri, who declared that the bank served "to make the rich richer, and the poor poorer." The self-important statements of Biddle, who claimed to have more power that President Jackson, helped fuel sentiments like Benton's.

In the reelection campaign of 1832, Jackson's opponents in Congress, including Henry Clay, hoped to use their support of the bank to their advantage. In January 1832, they pushed for legislation that would re-charter it, even though its charter was not scheduled to expire until 1836. When the bill for re-chartering passed and came to President Jackson, he used his executive authority to veto the measure.

The defeat of the Second Bank of the United States demonstrates Jackson's ability to focus on the specific issues that aroused the democratic majority. Jackson understood people's anger and distrust toward the bank, which stood as an emblem of special privilege and big government. He skillfully used that perception to his advantage, presenting the bank issue as a struggle of ordinary people against a rapacious elite class who cared nothing for the public and pursued only their own selfish ends. As Jackson portrayed it, his was a battle for small government and ordinary Americans. His stand against what bank opponents called the "**monster bank**" proved very popular, and the Democratic press lionized him for it (**Figure 9.10**). In the election of 1832, Jackson received nearly 53 percent of the popular vote against his opponent Henry Clay.

Figure 9.10 In *General Jackson Slaying the Many Headed Monster* (1836), the artist, Henry R. Robinson, depicts President Jackson using a cane marked "Veto" to battle a many-headed snake representing state banks, which supported the national bank. Battling alongside Martin Van Buren and Jack Downing, Jackson addresses the largest head, that of Nicholas Biddle, the director of the national bank: "Biddle thou Monster Avaunt [go away]!! . . ."

Jackson's veto was only one part of the war on the "monster bank." In 1833, the president removed the deposits from the national bank and placed them in state banks. Biddle, the bank's director, retaliated by restricting loans to the state banks, resulting in a reduction of the money supply. The financial turmoil only increased when Jackson issued an executive order known as the Specie Circular, which required that western land sales be conducted using gold or silver only. Unfortunately, this policy proved a disaster when the Bank of England, the source of much of the hard currency borrowed by American businesses, dramatically cut back on loans to the United States. Without the flow of hard currency from England, American depositors drained the gold and silver from their own domestic banks, making hard currency scarce. Adding to the economic distress of the late 1830s, cotton prices plummeted, contributing to a financial crisis called the Panic of 1837. This economic panic would prove politically useful for Jackson's opponents in the coming years and Van Buren, elected president in 1836, would pay the price for Jackson's hard-currency preferences.

WHIGS

Jackson's veto of the bank and his Specie Circular helped galvanize opposition forces into a new political party, the **Whigs**, a faction that began to form in 1834. The name was significant; opponents of Jackson saw him as exercising tyrannical power, so they chose the name Whig after the eighteenth-century political party that resisted the monarchical power of King George III. One political cartoon dubbed the president "King Andrew the First" and displayed Jackson standing on the Constitution, which has been ripped to shreds (**Figure 9.11**).

Figure 9.11 This anonymous 1833 political caricature (a) represents President Andrew Jackson as a despotic ruler, holding a scepter in one hand and a veto in the other. Contrast the image of "King Andrew" with a political cartoon from 1831 (b) of Jackson overseeing a scene of uncontrollable chaos as he falls from a hickory chair "coming to pieces at last."

Whigs championed an active federal government committed to internal improvements, including a national bank. They made their first national appearance in the presidential election of 1836, a contest that pitted Jackson's handpicked successor, Martin Van Buren, against a field of several Whig candidates. Indeed, the large field of Whig candidates indicated the new party's lack of organization compared to the Democrats. This helped Van Buren, who carried the day in the Electoral College. As the effects of the Panic of 1837 continued to be felt for years afterward, the Whig press pinned the blame for the economic crisis on Van Buren and the Democrats.

Explore a **Library of Congress** (http://openstaxcollege.org/l/15PolPrints) collection of 1830s political cartoons from the pages of *Harper's Weekly* to learn more about how Andrew Jackson was viewed by the public in that era.

This content is available for free at http://cnx.org/content/col11740/latest/

9.4 Indian Removal

By the end of this section, you will be able to:
- Explain the legal wrangling that surrounded the Indian Removal Act
- Describe how depictions of Indians in popular culture helped lead to Indian removal

Pro-Jackson newspapers touted the president as a champion of opening land for white settlement and moving native inhabitants beyond the boundaries of "American civilization." In this effort, Jackson reflected majority opinion: most Americans believed Indians had no place in the white republic. Jackson's animosity toward Indians ran deep. He had fought against the Creek in 1813 and against the Seminole in 1817, and his reputation and popularity rested in large measure on his firm commitment to remove Indians from states in the South. The 1830 Indian Removal Act and subsequent displacement of the Creek, Choctaw, Chickasaw, Seminole, and Cherokee tribes of the Southeast fulfilled the vision of a white nation and became one of the identifying characteristics of the Age of Jackson.

INDIANS IN POPULAR CULTURE

Popular culture in the first half of the nineteenth century reflected the aversion to Indians that was pervasive during the Age of Jackson. Jackson skillfully played upon this racial hatred to engage the United States in a policy of ethnic cleansing, eradicating the Indian presence from the land to make way for white civilization.

In an age of mass democracy, powerful anti-Indian sentiments found expression in mass culture, shaping popular perceptions. James Fenimore Cooper's very popular historical novel, *The Last of the Mohicans*, published in 1826 as part of his Leatherstocking series, told the tale of Nathaniel "Natty" Bumppo (aka Hawkeye), who lived among Indians but had been born to white parents. Cooper provides a romantic version of the French and Indian War in which Natty helps the British against the French and the feral, bloodthirsty Huron. Natty endures even as his Indian friends die, including the noble Uncas, the last Mohican, in a narrative that dovetailed with most people's approval of Indian removal.

Indians also made frequent appearances in art. George Catlin produced many paintings of native peoples, which he offered as true representations despite routinely emphasizing their supposed savage nature. *The Cutting Scene, Mandan O-kee-pa Ceremony* (**Figure 9.12**) is one example. Scholars have long questioned the accuracy of this portrayal of a rite of passage among the Mandan people. Accuracy aside, the painting captured the imaginations of white viewers, reinforcing their disgust at the savagery of Indians.

Figure 9.12 *The Cutting Scene, Mandan O-kee-pa Ceremony*, an 1832 painting by George Catlin, depicts a rite-of-passage ceremony that Catlin said he witnessed. It featured wooden splints inserted into the chest and back muscles of young men. Such paintings increased Indians' reputation as savages.

AMERICANA

✪ *The Paintings of George Catlin*

George Catlin seized upon the public fascination with the supposedly exotic and savage Indian, seeing an opportunity to make money by painting them in a way that conformed to popular white stereotypes (**Figure 9.13**). In the late 1830s, he toured major cities with his Indian Gallery, a collection of paintings of native peoples. Though he hoped his exhibition would be profitable, it did not bring him financial security.

(a)   (b)

Figure 9.13 In *Attacking the Grizzly Bear* (a), painted in 1844, Catlin focused on the Indians' own vanishing culture, while in *Wi-jún-jon, Pigeon's Egg Head (The Light) Going To and Returning From Washington* (b), painted in 1837–1839, he contrasted their ways with those of whites by showing an Assiniboine chief transformed by a visit to Washington, DC.

Catlin routinely painted Indians in a supposedly aboriginal state. In *Attacking the Grizzly Bear*, the hunters do not have rifles and instead rely on spears. Such a portrayal stretches credibility as native peoples had long been exposed to and adopted European weapons. Indeed, the painting's depiction of Indians riding horses, which were introduced by the Spanish, makes clear that, as much as Catlin and white viewers wanted to believe in the primitive and savage native, the reality was otherwise.

In *Wi-jún-jon, Pigeon's Egg Head (The Light) Going To and Returning From Washington*, the viewer is shown a before and after portrait of Wi-jún-jon, who tried to emulate white dress and manners after going to Washington, DC. What differences do you see between these two representations of Wi-jún-jon? Do you think his attempt to imitate whites was successful? Why or why not? What do you think Catlin was trying to convey with this depiction of Wi-jún-jon's assimilation?

THE INDIAN REMOVAL ACT

In his first message to Congress, Jackson had proclaimed that Indian groups living independently within states, as sovereign entities, presented a major problem for state sovereignty. This message referred directly to the situation in Georgia, Mississippi, and Alabama, where the Creek, Choctaw, Chickasaw, Seminole, and Cherokee peoples stood as obstacles to white settlement. These groups were known as the **Five Civilized Tribes**, because they had largely adopted Anglo-American culture, speaking English and practicing Christianity. Some held slaves like their white counterparts.

Whites especially resented the Cherokee in Georgia, coveting the tribe's rich agricultural lands in the northern part of the state. The impulse to remove the Cherokee only increased when gold was discovered on their lands. Ironically, while whites insisted the Cherokee and other native peoples could never be good citizens because of their savage ways, the Cherokee had arguably gone farther than any other indigenous group in adopting white culture. The *Cherokee Phoenix*, the newspaper of the Cherokee, began publication in 1828 (**Figure 9.14**) in English and the Cherokee language. Although the Cherokee followed the lead of their white neighbors by farming and owning property, as well as embracing Christianity and owning their own slaves, this proved of little consequence in an era when whites perceived all Indians as incapable of becoming full citizens of the republic.

Figure 9.14 This image depicts the front page of the *Cherokee Phoenix* newspaper from May 21, 1828. The paper was published in both English and the Cherokee language.

Jackson's anti-Indian stance struck a chord with a majority of white citizens, many of whom shared a hatred of nonwhites that spurred Congress to pass the 1830 Indian Removal Act. The act called for the removal of the Five Civilized Tribes from their home in the southeastern United States to land in the West, in present-day Oklahoma. Jackson declared in December 1830, "It gives me pleasure to announce to Congress that the benevolent policy of the Government, steadily pursued for nearly thirty years, in relation to the removal of the Indians beyond the white settlements is approaching to a happy consummation. Two important tribes have accepted the provision made for their removal at the last session of Congress, and it is believed that their example will induce the remaining tribes also to seek the same obvious advantages."

The Cherokee decided to fight the federal law, however, and took their case to the Supreme Court. Their legal fight had the support of anti-Jackson members of Congress, including Henry Clay and Daniel Webster, and they retained the legal services of former attorney general William Wirt. In *Cherokee Nation v. Georgia*, Wirt argued that the Cherokee constituted an independent foreign nation, and that an injunction (a stop) should be placed on Georgia laws aimed at eradicating them. In 1831, the Supreme Court found the Cherokee did not meet the criteria for being a foreign nation.

Another case involving the Cherokee also found its way to the highest court in the land. This legal struggle—*Worcester v. Georgia*—asserted the rights of non-natives to live on Indian lands. Samuel Worcester was a Christian missionary and federal postmaster of New Echota, the capital of the Cherokee nation. A Congregationalist, he had gone to live among the Cherokee in Georgia to further the spread of Christianity, and he strongly opposed Indian removal.

By living among the Cherokee, Worcester had violated a Georgia law forbidding whites, unless they were agents of the federal government, to live in Indian territory. Worcester was arrested, but because his federal job as postmaster gave him the right to live there, he was released. Jackson supporters then succeeded in taking away Worcester's job, and he was re-arrested. This time, a court sentenced him and nine others for violating the Georgia state law banning whites from living on Indian land. Worcester was sentenced to four years of hard labor. When the case of *Worcester v. Georgia* came before the Supreme Court in 1832, Chief Justice John Marshall ruled in favor of Worcester, finding that the Cherokee constituted "distinct political communities" with sovereign rights to their own territory.

DEFINING "AMERICAN"

Chief Justice John Marshall's Ruling in Worcester v. Georgia

In 1832, Chief Justice of the Supreme Court John Marshall ruled in favor of Samuel Worcester in *Worcester v. Georgia*. In doing so, he established the principle of tribal sovereignty. Although this judgment contradicted *Cherokee Nation v. Georgia*, it failed to halt the Indian Removal Act. In his opinion, Marshall wrote the following:

> From the commencement of our government Congress has passed acts to regulate trade and intercourse with the Indians; which treat them as nations, respect their rights, and manifest a firm purpose to afford that protection which treaties stipulate. All these acts, and especially that of 1802, which is still in force, manifestly consider the several Indian nations as distinct political communities, having territorial boundaries, within which their authority is exclusive, and having a right to all the lands within those boundaries, which is not only acknowledged, but guaranteed by the United States. . . .
>
> The Cherokee Nation, then, is a distinct community, occupying its own territory, with boundaries accurately described, in which the laws of Georgia can have no force, and which the citizens of Georgia have no right to enter but with the assent of the Cherokees themselves or in conformity with treaties and with the acts of Congress. The whole intercourse between the United States and this nation is, by our Constitution and laws, vested in the government of the United States.
>
> The act of the State of Georgia under which the plaintiff in error was prosecuted is consequently void, and the judgment a nullity. . . . The Acts of Georgia are repugnant to the Constitution, laws, and treaties of the United States.

How does this opinion differ from the outcome of *Cherokee Nation v. Georgia* just one year earlier? Why do you think the two outcomes were different?

The Supreme Court did not have the power to enforce its ruling in *Worcester v. Georgia*, however, and it became clear that the Cherokee would be compelled to move. Those who understood that the only option was removal traveled west, but the majority stayed on their land. In order to remove them, the president relied on the U.S. military. In a series of forced marches, some fifteen thousand Cherokee were finally relocated to Oklahoma. This forced migration, known as the **Trail of Tears**, caused the deaths of as many as four thousand Cherokee (**Figure 9.15**). The Creek, Choctaw, Chickasaw, and Seminole peoples were also compelled to go. The removal of the Five Civilized Tribes provides an example of the power of majority opinion in a democracy.

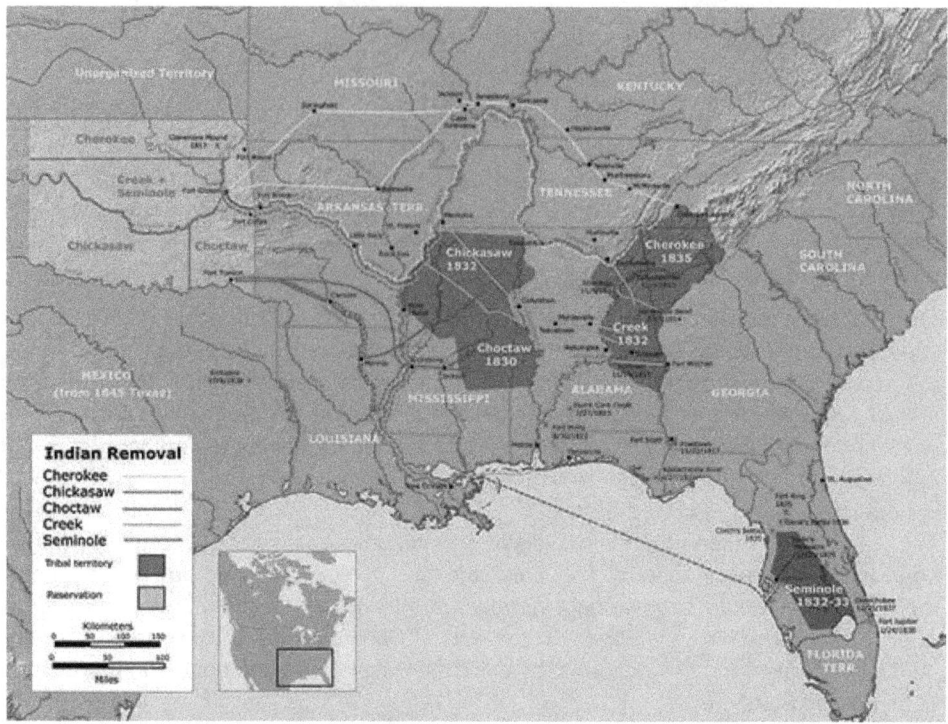

Figure 9.15 After the passage of the Indian Removal Act, the U.S. military forced the Cherokee, Creek, Choctaw, Chickasaw, and Seminole to relocate from the Southeast to an area in the western territory (now Oklahoma), marching them along the routes shown here.

 Explore the interactive **Trail of Tears map** (http://openstaxcollege.org/l/15NativeAm) at PBS.org to see the routes the Five Civilized Tribes traveled when they were expelled from their lands. Then listen to a collection of **Cherokee oral histories** (http://openstaxcollege.org/l/15NativeAm2) including verses of a Cherokee-language song about the Trail of Tears. What do you think is the importance of oral history in documenting the Cherokee experience?

BLACK HAWK'S WAR

The policy of removal led some Indians to actively resist. In 1832, the Fox and the Sauk, led by Sauk chief Black Hawk (Makataimeshekiakiah), moved back across the Mississippi River to reclaim their ancestral home in northern Illinois. A brief war in 1832, Black Hawk's War, ensued. White settlers panicked at the return of the native peoples, and militias and federal troops quickly mobilized. At the Battle of Bad Axe (also known as the Bad Axe Massacre), they killed over two hundred men, women, and children. Some seventy white settlers and soldiers also lost their lives in the conflict (**Figure 9.16**). The war, which lasted only a matter of weeks, illustrates how much whites on the frontier hated and feared Indians during the Age of Jackson.

Figure 9.16 Charles Bird King's 1837 portrait *Sauk Chief Makataimeshekiakiah, or Black Hawk* (a), depicts the Sauk chief who led the Fox and Sauk peoples in an ill-fated effort to return to their native lands in northern Illinois. This engraving depicting the Battle of Bad Axe (b) shows U.S. soldiers on a steamer firing on Indians aboard a raft. (credit b: modification of work by Library of Congress)

9.5 The Tyranny and Triumph of the Majority

By the end of this section, you will be able to:
- Explain Alexis de Tocqueville's analysis of American democracy
- Describe the election of 1840 and its outcome

To some observers, the rise of democracy in the United States raised troubling questions about the new power of the majority to silence minority opinion. As the will of the majority became the rule of the day, everyone outside of mainstream, white American opinion, especially Indians and blacks, were vulnerable to the wrath of the majority. Some worried that the rights of those who opposed the will of the majority would never be safe. Mass democracy also shaped political campaigns as never before. The 1840 presidential election marked a significant turning point in the evolving style of American democratic politics.

ALEXIS DE TOCQUEVILLE

Perhaps the most insightful commentator on American democracy was the young French aristocrat Alexis de Tocqueville, whom the French government sent to the United States to report on American prison reforms (**Figure 9.17**). Tocqueville marveled at the spirit of democracy that pervaded American life. Given his place in French society, however, much of what he saw of American democracy caused him concern.

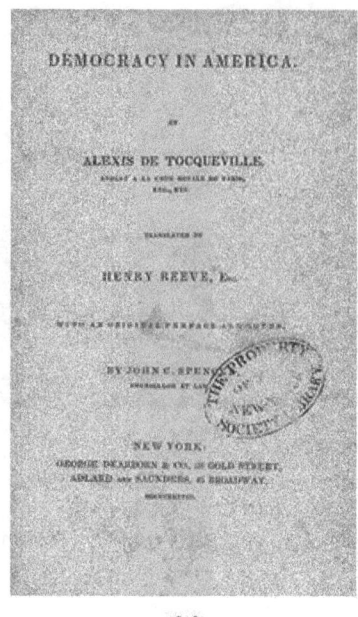 

Figure 9.17 Alexis de Tocqueville is best known for his insightful commentary on American democracy found in *De la démocratie en Amérique*. The first volume of Tocqueville's two-volume work was immediately popular throughout Europe. The first English translation, by Henry Reeve and titled *Democracy in America* (a), was published in New York in 1838. Théodore Chassériau painted this portrait of Alexis de Tocqueville in 1850 (b).

Tocqueville's experience led him to believe that democracy was an unstoppable force that would one day overthrow monarchy around the world. He wrote and published his findings in 1835 and 1840 in a two-part work entitled *Democracy in America*. In analyzing the democratic revolution in the United States, he wrote that the major benefit of democracy came in the form of equality before the law. A great deal of the social revolution of democracy, however, carried negative consequences. Indeed, Tocqueville described a new type of tyranny, the **tyranny of the majority**, which overpowers the will of minorities and individuals and was, in his view, unleashed by democracy in the United States.

In this excerpt from *Democracy in America*, Alexis de Tocqueville warns of the dangers of democracy when the majority will can turn to tyranny:

> When an individual or a party is wronged in the United States, to whom can he apply for redress? If to public opinion, public opinion constitutes the majority; if to the legislature, it represents the majority, and implicitly obeys its injunctions; if to the executive power, it is appointed by the majority, and remains a passive tool in its hands; the public troops consist of the majority under arms; the jury is the majority invested with the right of hearing judicial cases; and in certain States even the judges are elected by the majority. However iniquitous or absurd the evil of which you complain may be, you must submit to it as well as you can.
> The authority of a king is purely physical, and it controls the actions of the subject without subduing his private will; but the majority possesses a power which is physical and moral at the same time; it acts upon the will as well as upon the actions of men, and it represses not only all contest, but all controversy. I know no country in which there is so little true independence of mind and freedom of discussion as in America.

Click and Explore

Take the Alexis de Tocqueville Tour (http://openstaxcollege.org/l/15Tocqueville) to experience nineteenth-century America as Tocqueville did, by reading his journal entries about the states and territories he visited with fellow countryman Gustave de Beaumont. What regional differences can you draw from his descriptions?

THE 1840 ELECTION

The presidential election contest of 1840 marked the culmination of the democratic revolution that swept the United States. By this time, the **second party system** had taken hold, a system whereby the older Federalist and Democratic-Republican Parties had been replaced by the new Democratic and Whig Parties. Both Whigs and Democrats jockeyed for election victories and commanded the steady loyalty of political partisans. Large-scale presidential campaign rallies and emotional propaganda became the order of the day. Voter turnout increased dramatically under the second party system. Roughly 25 percent of eligible voters had cast ballots in 1828. In 1840, voter participation surged to nearly 80 percent.

The differences between the parties were largely about economic policies. Whigs advocated accelerated economic growth, often endorsing federal government projects to achieve that goal. Democrats did not view the federal government as an engine promoting economic growth and advocated a smaller role for the national government. The membership of the parties also differed: Whigs tended to be wealthier; they were prominent planters in the South and wealthy urban northerners—in other words, the beneficiaries of the market revolution. Democrats presented themselves as defenders of the common people against the elite.

In the 1840 presidential campaign, taking their cue from the Democrats who had lionized Jackson's military accomplishments, the Whigs promoted William Henry Harrison as a war hero based on his 1811 military service against the Shawnee chief Tecumseh at the Battle of Tippecanoe. John Tyler of Virginia ran as the vice presidential candidate, leading the Whigs to trumpet, "Tippecanoe and Tyler too!" as a campaign slogan.

The campaign thrust Harrison into the national spotlight. Democrats tried to discredit him by declaring, "Give him a barrel of hard [alcoholic] cider and settle a pension of two thousand a year on him, and take my word for it, he will sit the remainder of his days in his log cabin." The Whigs turned the slur to their advantage by presenting Harrison as a man of the people who had been born in a log cabin (in fact, he came from a privileged background in Virginia), and the contest became known as the **log cabin campaign** (**Figure 9.18**). At Whig political rallies, the faithful were treated to whiskey made by the E. C. Booz Company, leading to the introduction of the word "booze" into the American lexicon. Tippecanoe Clubs, where booze flowed freely, helped in the marketing of the Whig candidate.

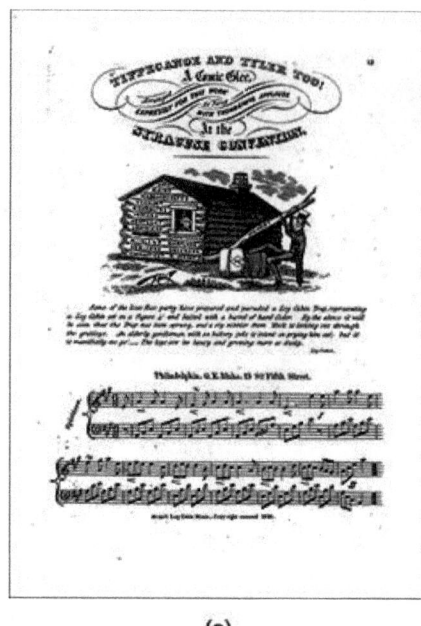 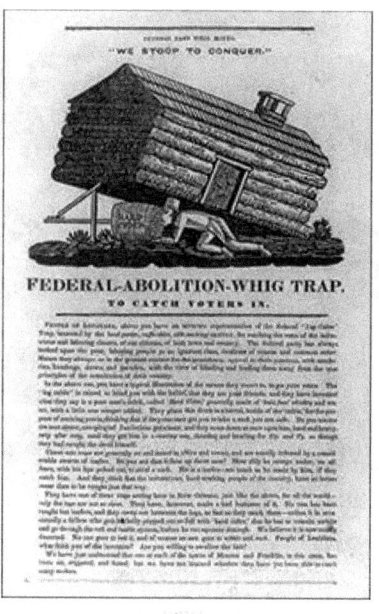

Figure 9.18 The Whig campaign song "Tippecanoe and Tyler Too!" (a) and the anti-Whig flyers (b) that were circulated in response to the "log cabin campaign" illustrate the partisan fervor of the 1840 election.

The Whigs' efforts, combined with their strategy of blaming Democrats for the lingering economic collapse that began with the hard-currency Panic of 1837, succeeded in carrying the day. A mass campaign with political rallies and party mobilization had molded a candidate to fit an ideal palatable to a majority of American voters, and in 1840 Harrison won what many consider the first modern election.

APPENDIX A

The Declaration of Independence

When in the Course of human events, it becomes necessary for one people to dissolve the political bands which have connected them with another, and to assume among the powers of the earth, the separate and equal station to which the Laws of Nature and of Nature's God entitle them, a decent respect to the opinions of mankind requires that they should declare the causes which impel them to the separation.

We hold these truths to be self-evident, that all men are created equal, that they are endowed by their Creator with certain unalienable Rights, that among these are Life, Liberty and the pursuit of Happiness. —That to secure these rights, Governments are instituted among Men, deriving their just powers from the consent of the governed, —That whenever any Form of Government becomes destructive of these ends, it is the Right of the People to alter or to abolish it, and to institute new Government, laying its foundation on such principles and organizing its powers in such form, as to them shall seem most likely to effect their Safety and Happiness. Prudence, indeed, will dictate that Governments long established should not be changed for light and transient causes; and accordingly all experience hath shewn, that mankind are more disposed to suffer, while evils are sufferable, than to right themselves by abolishing the forms to which they are accustomed. But when a long train of abuses and usurpations, pursuing invariably the same Object evinces a design to reduce them under absolute Despotism, it is their right, it is their duty, to throw off such Government, and to provide new Guards for their future security. —Such has been the patient sufferance of these Colonies; and such is now the necessity which constrains them to alter their former Systems of Government. The history of the present King of Great Britain is a history of repeated injuries and usurpations, all having in direct object the establishment of an absolute Tyranny over these States. To prove this, let Facts be submitted to a candid world.

He has refused his Assent to Laws, the most wholesome and necessary for the public good.

He has forbidden his Governors to pass Laws of immediate and pressing importance, unless suspended in their operation till his Assent should be obtained; and when so suspended, he has utterly neglected to attend to them.

He has refused to pass other Laws for the accommodation of large districts of people, unless those people would relinquish the right of Representation in the Legislature, a right inestimable to them and formidable to tyrants only.

He has called together legislative bodies at places unusual, uncomfortable, and distant from the depository of their public Records, for the sole purpose of fatiguing them into compliance with his measures.

He has dissolved Representative Houses repeatedly, for opposing with manly firmness his invasions on the rights of the people.

He has refused for a long time, after such dissolutions, to cause others to be elected; whereby the Legislative powers, incapable of Annihilation, have returned to the People at large for their exercise; the State remaining in the mean time exposed to all the dangers of invasion from without, and convulsions within.

He has endeavoured to prevent the population of these States; for that purpose obstructing the Laws for Naturalization of Foreigners; refusing to pass others to encourage their migrations hither, and raising the conditions of new Appropriations of Lands.

He has obstructed the Administration of Justice, by refusing his Assent to Laws for establishing Judiciary powers.

He has made Judges dependent on his Will alone, for the tenure of their offices, and the amount and payment of their salaries.

He has erected a multitude of New Offices, and sent hither swarms of Officers to harrass our people, and eat out their substance.

He has kept among us, in times of peace, Standing Armies without the Consent of our legislatures.

He has affected to render the Military independent of and superior to the Civil power.

He has combined with others to subject us to a jurisdiction foreign to our constitution, and unacknowledged by our laws; giving his Assent to their Acts of pretended Legislation:

For Quartering large bodies of armed troops among us:

For protecting them, by a mock Trial, from punishment for any Murders which they should commit on the Inhabitants of these States:

For cutting off our Trade with all parts of the world:

For imposing Taxes on us without our Consent:

For depriving us in many cases, of the benefits of Trial by Jury:

For transporting us beyond Seas to be tried for pretended offences:

For abolishing the free System of English Laws in a neighbouring Province, establishing therein an Arbitrary government, and enlarging its Boundaries so as to render it at once an example and fit instrument for introducing the same absolute rule into these Colonies:

For taking away our Charters, abolishing our most valuable Laws, and altering fundamentally the Forms of our Governments:

For suspending our own Legislatures, and declaring themselves invested with power to legislate for us in all cases whatsoever.

He has abdicated Government here, by declaring us out of his Protection and waging War against us.

He has plundered our seas, ravaged our Coasts, burnt our towns, and destroyed the lives of our people.

He is at this time transporting large Armies of foreign Mercenaries to compleat the works of death, desolation and tyranny, already begun with circumstances of Cruelty & perfidy scarcely paralleled in the most barbarous ages, and totally unworthy the Head of a civilized nation.

He has constrained our fellow Citizens taken Captive on the high Seas to bear Arms against their Country, to become the executioners of their friends and Brethren, or to fall themselves by their Hands.

He has excited domestic insurrections amongst us, and has endeavoured to bring on the inhabitants of our frontiers, the merciless Indian Savages, whose known rule of warfare, is an undistinguished destruction of all ages, sexes and conditions.

In every stage of these Oppressions We have Petitioned for Redress in the most humble terms: Our repeated Petitions have been answered only by repeated injury. A Prince whose character is thus marked by every act which may define a Tyrant, is unfit to be the ruler of a free people.

Nor have We been wanting in attentions to our Brittish brethren. We have warned them from time to time of attempts by their legislature to extend an unwarrantable jurisdiction over us. We have reminded them of the circumstances of our emigration and settlement here. We have appealed to their native justice and magnanimity, and we have conjured them by the ties of our common kindred to disavow these usurpations, which, would inevitably interrupt our connections and correspondence. They too have been deaf to the voice of justice and of consanguinity. We must, therefore, acquiesce in the necessity, which denounces our Separation, and hold them, as we hold the rest of mankind, Enemies in War, in Peace Friends.

We, therefore, the Representatives of the united States of America, in General Congress, Assembled, appealing to the Supreme Judge of the world for the rectitude of our intentions, do, in the Name, and by Authority of the good People of these Colonies, solemnly publish and declare, That these United Colonies are, and of Right ought to be Free and Independent States; that they are Absolved from all Allegiance to the British Crown, and that all political connection between them and the State of Great Britain, is and ought to be totally dissolved; and that as Free and Independent States, they have full Power to levy War, conclude Peace, contract Alliances, establish Commerce, and to do all other Acts and Things which Independent States may of right do. And for the support of this Declaration, with a firm reliance on the protection of divine Providence, we mutually pledge to each other our Lives, our Fortunes and our sacred Honor.

The 56 signatures on the Declaration appear in the positions indicated:

Column 1
Georgia:
Button Gwinnett
Lyman Hall
George Walton
Column 2
North Carolina:
William Hooper
Joseph Hewes
John Penn
South Carolina:
Edward Rutledge
Thomas Heyward, Jr.
Thomas Lynch, Jr.
Arthur Middleton
Column 3
Massachusetts:
John Hancock
Maryland:
Samuel Chase
William Paca
Thomas Stone
Charles Carroll of Carrollton
Virginia:
George Wythe
Richard Henry Lee
Thomas Jefferson
Benjamin Harrison
Thomas Nelson, Jr.
Francis Lightfoot Lee
Carter Braxton
Column 4
Pennsylvania:
Robert Morris
Benjamin Rush
Benjamin Franklin
John Morton
George Clymer
James Smith
George Taylor
James Wilson
George Ross
Delaware:
Caesar Rodney

George Read
Thomas McKean
Column 5
New York:
William Floyd
Philip Livingston
Francis Lewis
Lewis Morris
New Jersey:
Richard Stockton
John Witherspoon
Francis Hopkinson
John Hart
Abraham Clark
Column 6
New Hampshire:
Josiah Bartlett
William Whipple
Massachusetts:
Samuel Adams
John Adams
Robert Treat Paine
Elbridge Gerry
Rhode Island:
Stephen Hopkins
William Ellery
Connecticut:
Roger Sherman
Samuel Huntington
William Williams
Oliver Wolcott
New Hampshire:
Matthew Thornton

APPENDIX B
The Constitution of the United States

We the People of the United States, in Order to form a more perfect Union, establish Justice, insure domestic Tranquility, provide for the common defence, promote the general Welfare, and secure the Blessings of Liberty to ourselves and our Posterity, do ordain and establish this Constitution for the United States of America.

Article. I.

Section. 1.

All legislative Powers herein granted shall be vested in a Congress of the United States, which shall consist of a Senate and House of Representatives.

Section. 2.

The House of Representatives shall be composed of Members chosen every second Year by the People of the several States, and the Electors in each State shall have the Qualifications requisite for Electors of the most numerous Branch of the State Legislature.

No Person shall be a Representative who shall not have attained to the Age of twenty five Years, and been seven Years a Citizen of the United States, and who shall not, when elected, be an Inhabitant of that State in which he shall be chosen.

Representatives and direct Taxes shall be apportioned among the several States which may be included within this Union, according to their respective Numbers, which shall be determined by adding to the whole Number of free Persons, including those bound to Service for a Term of Years, and excluding Indians not taxed, three fifths of all other Persons. The actual Enumeration shall be made within three Years after the first Meeting of the Congress of the United States, and within every subsequent Term of ten Years, in such Manner as they shall by Law direct. The Number of Representatives shall not exceed one for every thirty Thousand, but each State shall have at Least one Representative; and until such enumeration shall be made, the State of New Hampshire shall be entitled to chuse three, Massachusetts eight, Rhode-Island and Providence Plantations one, Connecticut five, New-York six, New Jersey four, Pennsylvania eight, Delaware one, Maryland six, Virginia ten, North Carolina five, South Carolina five, and Georgia three.

When vacancies happen in the Representation from any State, the Executive Authority thereof shall issue Writs of Election to fill such Vacancies.

The House of Representatives shall chuse their Speaker and other Officers; and shall have the sole Power of Impeachment.

Section. 3.

The Senate of the United States shall be composed of two Senators from each State, chosen by the Legislature thereof, for six Years; and each Senator shall have one Vote.

Immediately after they shall be assembled in Consequence of the first Election, they shall be divided as equally as may be into three Classes. The Seats of the Senators of the first Class shall be vacated at the Expiration of the second Year, of the second Class at the Expiration of the fourth Year, and of the third Class at the Expiration of the sixth Year, so that one third may be chosen every second Year; and if Vacancies happen by Resignation, or otherwise, during the Recess of the Legislature of any State, the Executive thereof may make temporary Appointments until the next Meeting of the Legislature, which shall then fill such Vacancies.

No Person shall be a Senator who shall not have attained to the Age of thirty Years, and been nine Years a Citizen of the United States, and who shall not, when elected, be an Inhabitant of that State for which he shall be chosen.

The Vice President of the United States shall be President of the Senate, but shall have no Vote, unless they be equally divided.

The Senate shall chuse their other Officers, and also a President pro tempore, in the Absence of the Vice President, or when he shall exercise the Office of President of the United States.

The Senate shall have the sole Power to try all Impeachments. When sitting for that Purpose, they shall be on Oath or Affirmation. When the President of the United States is tried, the Chief Justice shall preside: And no Person shall be convicted without the Concurrence of two thirds of the Members present.

Judgment in Cases of Impeachment shall not extend further than to removal from Office, and disqualification to hold and enjoy any Office of honor, Trust or Profit under the United States: but the Party convicted shall nevertheless be liable and subject to Indictment, Trial, Judgment and Punishment, according to Law.

Section. 4.

The Times, Places and Manner of holding Elections for Senators and Representatives, shall be prescribed in each State by the Legislature thereof; but the Congress may at any time by Law make or alter such Regulations, except as to the Places of chusing Senators.

The Congress shall assemble at least once in every Year, and such Meeting shall be on the first Monday in December, unless they shall by Law appoint a different Day.

Section. 5.

Each House shall be the Judge of the Elections, Returns and Qualifications of its own Members, and a Majority of each shall constitute a Quorum to do Business; but a smaller Number may adjourn from day to day, and may be authorized to compel the Attendance of absent Members, in such Manner, and under such Penalties as each House may provide.

Each House may determine the Rules of its Proceedings, punish its Members for disorderly Behaviour, and, with the Concurrence of two thirds, expel a Member.

Each House shall keep a Journal of its Proceedings, and from time to time publish the same, excepting such Parts as may in their Judgment require Secrecy; and the Yeas and Nays of the Members of either House on any question shall, at the Desire of one fifth of those Present, be entered on the Journal.

Neither House, during the Session of Congress, shall, without the Consent of the other, adjourn for more than three days, nor to any other Place than that in which the two Houses shall be sitting.

Section. 6.

The Senators and Representatives shall receive a Compensation for their Services, to be ascertained by Law, and paid out of the Treasury of the United States. They shall in all Cases, except Treason, Felony and Breach of the Peace, be privileged from Arrest during their Attendance at the Session of their respective Houses, and in going to and returning from the same; and for any Speech or Debate in either House, they shall not be questioned in any other Place.

No Senator or Representative shall, during the Time for which he was elected, be appointed to any civil Office under the Authority of the United States, which shall have been created, or the Emoluments whereof shall have been encreased during such time; and no Person holding any Office under the United States, shall be a Member of either House during his Continuance in Office.

Section. 7.

All Bills for raising Revenue shall originate in the House of Representatives; but the Senate may propose or concur with Amendments as on other Bills.

Every Bill which shall have passed the House of Representatives and the Senate, shall, before it become a Law, be presented to the President of the United States; If he approve he shall sign it, but if not he shall return it, with his Objections to that House in which it shall have originated, who shall enter the Objections at large on their Journal, and proceed to reconsider it. If after such Reconsideration two thirds of that House shall agree to pass the Bill, it shall be sent, together with the Objections, to the other House, by which it shall likewise be reconsidered, and if approved by two thirds of that House, it shall become a Law. But in all such Cases the Votes of both Houses shall be determined by yeas and Nays, and the Names of the Persons voting for and against the Bill shall be entered on the Journal of each House respectively. If any Bill shall not be returned by the President within ten Days (Sundays excepted) after it shall have been presented to him, the Same shall be a Law, in like Manner as if he had signed it, unless the Congress by their Adjournment prevent its Return, in which Case it shall not be a Law.

Every Order, Resolution, or Vote to which the Concurrence of the Senate and House of Representatives may be necessary (except on a question of Adjournment) shall be presented to the President of the United States; and before the Same shall take Effect, shall be approved by him, or being disapproved by him, shall be repassed by two thirds of the Senate and House of Representatives, according to the Rules and Limitations prescribed in the Case of a Bill.

Section. 8.

The Congress shall have Power To lay and collect Taxes, Duties, Imposts and Excises, to pay the Debts and provide for the common Defence and general Welfare of the United States; but all Duties, Imposts and Excises shall be uniform throughout the United States;

To borrow Money on the credit of the United States;

To regulate Commerce with foreign Nations, and among the several States, and with the Indian Tribes;

To establish an uniform Rule of Naturalization, and uniform Laws on the subject of Bankruptcies throughout the United States;

To coin Money, regulate the Value thereof, and of foreign Coin, and fix the Standard of Weights and Measures;

To provide for the Punishment of counterfeiting the Securities and current Coin of the United States;

To establish Post Offices and post Roads;

To promote the Progress of Science and useful Arts, by securing for limited Times to Authors and Inventors the exclusive Right to their respective Writings and Discoveries;

To constitute Tribunals inferior to the supreme Court;

To define and punish Piracies and Felonies committed on the high Seas, and Offences against the Law of Nations;

To declare War, grant Letters of Marque and Reprisal, and make Rules concerning Captures on Land and Water;

To raise and support Armies, but no Appropriation of Money to that Use shall be for a longer Term than two Years;

To provide and maintain a Navy;

To make Rules for the Government and Regulation of the land and naval Forces;

To provide for calling forth the Militia to execute the Laws of the Union, suppress Insurrections and repel Invasions;

To provide for organizing, arming, and disciplining, the Militia, and for governing such Part of them as may be employed in the Service of the United States, reserving to the States respectively, the Appointment of the Officers, and the Authority of training the Militia according to the discipline prescribed by Congress;

To exercise exclusive Legislation in all Cases whatsoever, over such District (not exceeding ten Miles square) as may, by Cession of particular States, and the Acceptance of Congress, become the Seat of the Government of the United States, and to exercise like Authority over all Places purchased by the Consent of the Legislature of the State in which the Same shall be, for the Erection of Forts, Magazines, Arsenals, dock-Yards, and other needful Buildings;—And

To make all Laws which shall be necessary and proper for carrying into Execution the foregoing Powers, and all other Powers vested by this Constitution in the Government of the United States, or in any Department or Officer thereof.

Section. 9.

The Migration or Importation of such Persons as any of the States now existing shall think proper to admit, shall not be prohibited by the Congress prior to the Year one thousand eight hundred and eight, but a Tax or duty may be imposed on such Importation, not exceeding ten dollars for each Person.

The Privilege of the Writ of Habeas Corpus shall not be suspended, unless when in Cases of Rebellion or Invasion the public Safety may require it.

No Bill of Attainder or ex post facto Law shall be passed.

No Capitation, or other direct, Tax shall be laid, unless in Proportion to the Census or enumeration herein before directed to be taken.

No Tax or Duty shall be laid on Articles exported from any State.

No Preference shall be given by any Regulation of Commerce or Revenue to the Ports of one State over those of another: nor shall Vessels bound to, or from, one State, be obliged to enter, clear, or pay Duties in another.

No Money shall be drawn from the Treasury, but in Consequence of Appropriations made by Law; and a regular Statement and Account of the Receipts and Expenditures of all public Money shall be published from time to time.

No Title of Nobility shall be granted by the United States: And no Person holding any Office of Profit or Trust under them, shall, without the Consent of the Congress, accept of any present, Emolument, Office, or Title, of any kind whatever, from any King, Prince, or foreign State.

Section. 10.

No State shall enter into any Treaty, Alliance, or Confederation; grant Letters of Marque and Reprisal; coin Money; emit Bills of Credit; make any Thing but gold and silver Coin a Tender in Payment of Debts; pass any Bill of Attainder, ex post facto Law, or Law impairing the Obligation of Contracts, or grant any Title of Nobility.

No State shall, without the Consent of the Congress, lay any Imposts or Duties on Imports or Exports, except what may be absolutely necessary for executing it's inspection Laws: and the net Produce of all Duties and Imposts, laid by any State on Imports or Exports, shall be for the Use of the Treasury of the United States; and all such Laws shall be subject to the Revision and Controul of the Congress.

No State shall, without the Consent of Congress, lay any Duty of Tonnage, keep Troops, or Ships of War in time of Peace, enter into any Agreement or Compact with another State, or with a foreign Power, or engage in War, unless actually invaded, or in such imminent Danger as will not admit of delay.

Article. II.

Section. 1.

The executive Power shall be vested in a President of the United States of America. He shall hold his Office during the Term of four Years, and, together with the Vice President, chosen for the same Term, be elected, as follows

Each State shall appoint, in such Manner as the Legislature thereof may direct, a Number of Electors, equal to the whole Number of Senators and Representatives to which the State may be entitled in the Congress: but no Senator or Representative, or Person holding an Office of Trust or Profit under the United States, shall be appointed an Elector.

The Electors shall meet in their respective States, and vote by Ballot for two Persons, of whom one at least shall not be an Inhabitant of the same State with themselves. And they shall make a List of all the Persons voted for, and of the Number of Votes for each; which List they shall sign and certify, and transmit sealed to the Seat of the Government of the United States, directed to the President of the Senate. The President of the Senate shall, in the Presence of the Senate and House of Representatives, open all the Certificates, and the Votes shall then be counted. The Person having the greatest Number of Votes shall be the President, if such Number be a Majority of the whole Number of Electors appointed; and if there be more than one who have such Majority, and have an equal Number of Votes, then the House of Representatives shall immediately chuse by Ballot one of them for President; and if no Person have a Majority, then from the five highest on the List the said House shall in like Manner chuse the President. But in chusing the President, the Votes shall be taken by States, the Representation from each State having one Vote; A quorum for this Purpose shall consist of a Member or Members from two thirds of the States, and a Majority of all the States shall be necessary to a Choice. In every Case, after the Choice of the President, the Person having the greatest Number of Votes of the Electors shall be the Vice President. But if there should remain two or more who have equal Votes, the Senate shall chuse from them by Ballot the Vice President.

The Congress may determine the Time of chusing the Electors, and the Day on which they shall give their Votes; which Day shall be the same throughout the United States.

No Person except a natural born Citizen, or a Citizen of the United States, at the time of the Adoption of this Constitution, shall be eligible to the Office of President; neither shall any Person be eligible to that Office who shall not have attained to the Age of thirty five Years, and been fourteen Years a Resident within the United States.

In Case of the Removal of the President from Office, or of his Death, Resignation, or Inability to discharge the Powers and Duties of the said Office, the Same shall devolve on the Vice President, and the Congress may by Law provide for the Case of Removal, Death, Resignation or Inability, both of the President and Vice President, declaring what Officer shall then act as President, and such Officer shall act accordingly, until the Disability be removed, or a President shall be elected.

The President shall, at stated Times, receive for his Services, a Compensation, which shall neither be encreased nor diminished during the Period for which he shall have been elected, and he shall not receive within that Period any other Emolument from the United States, or any of them.

Before he enter on the Execution of his Office, he shall take the following Oath or Affirmation:—"I do solemnly swear (or affirm) that I will faithfully execute the Office of President of the United States, and will to the best of my Ability, preserve, protect and defend the Constitution of the United States."

Section. 2.

The President shall be Commander in Chief of the Army and Navy of the United States, and of the Militia of the several States, when called into the actual Service of the United States; he may require the Opinion, in writing, of the principal Officer in each of the executive Departments, upon any Subject relating to the Duties of their respective Offices, and he shall have Power to grant Reprieves and Pardons for Offences against the United States, except in Cases of Impeachment.

He shall have Power, by and with the Advice and Consent of the Senate, to make Treaties, provided two thirds of the Senators present concur; and he shall nominate, and by and with the Advice and Consent of the Senate, shall appoint Ambassadors, other public Ministers and Consuls, Judges of the supreme Court, and all other Officers of the United States, whose Appointments are not herein otherwise provided for, and which shall be established by Law: but the Congress may by Law vest the Appointment of such inferior Officers, as they think proper, in the President alone, in the Courts of Law, or in the Heads of Departments.

The President shall have Power to fill up all Vacancies that may happen during the Recess of the Senate, by granting Commissions which shall expire at the End of their next Session.

Section. 3.

He shall from time to time give to the Congress Information of the State of the Union, and recommend to their Consideration such Measures as he shall judge necessary and expedient; he may, on extraordinary Occasions, convene both Houses, or either of them, and in Case of Disagreement between them, with Respect to the Time of Adjournment, he may adjourn them to such Time as he shall think proper; he shall receive Ambassadors and other public Ministers; he shall take Care that the Laws be faithfully executed, and shall Commission all the Officers of the United States.

Section. 4.

The President, Vice President and all civil Officers of the United States, shall be removed from Office on Impeachment for, and Conviction of, Treason, Bribery, or other high Crimes and Misdemeanors.

Article III.

Section. 1.

The judicial Power of the United States, shall be vested in one supreme Court, and in such inferior Courts as the Congress may from time to time ordain and establish. The Judges, both of the supreme and inferior Courts, shall hold their Offices during good Behaviour, and shall, at stated Times, receive for their Services, a Compensation, which shall not be diminished during their Continuance in Office.

Section. 2.

The judicial Power shall extend to all Cases, in Law and Equity, arising under this Constitution, the Laws of the United States, and Treaties made, or which shall be made, under their Authority;—to all Cases affecting Ambassadors, other public Ministers and Consuls;—to all Cases of admiralty and maritime Jurisdiction;—to Controversies to which the United States shall be a Party;—to Controversies between two or more States;— between a State and Citizens of another State,—between Citizens of different States,—between Citizens of the same State claiming Lands under Grants of different States, and between a State, or the Citizens thereof, and foreign States, Citizens or Subjects.

In all Cases affecting Ambassadors, other public Ministers and Consuls, and those in which a State shall be Party, the supreme Court shall have original Jurisdiction. In all the other Cases before mentioned, the supreme Court shall have appellate Jurisdiction, both as to Law and Fact, with such Exceptions, and under such Regulations as the Congress shall make.

The Trial of all Crimes, except in Cases of Impeachment, shall be by Jury; and such Trial shall be held in the State where the said Crimes shall have been committed; but when not committed within any State, the Trial shall be at such Place or Places as the Congress may by Law have directed.

Section. 3.

Treason against the United States, shall consist only in levying War against them, or in adhering to their Enemies, giving them Aid and Comfort. No Person shall be convicted of Treason unless on the Testimony of two Witnesses to the same overt Act, or on Confession in open Court.

The Congress shall have Power to declare the Punishment of Treason, but no Attainder of Treason shall work Corruption of Blood, or Forfeiture except during the Life of the Person attainted.

Article. IV.

Section. 1.

Full Faith and Credit shall be given in each State to the public Acts, Records, and judicial Proceedings of every other State. And the Congress may by general Laws prescribe the Manner in which such Acts, Records and Proceedings shall be proved, and the Effect thereof.

Section. 2.

The Citizens of each State shall be entitled to all Privileges and Immunities of Citizens in the several States.

A Person charged in any State with Treason, Felony, or other Crime, who shall flee from Justice, and be found in another State, shall on Demand of the executive Authority of the State from which he fled, be delivered up, to be removed to the State having Jurisdiction of the Crime.

No Person held to Service or Labour in one State, under the Laws thereof, escaping into another, shall, in Consequence of any Law or Regulation therein, be discharged from such Service or Labour, but shall be delivered up on Claim of the Party to whom such Service or Labour may be due.

Section. 3.

New States may be admitted by the Congress into this Union; but no new State shall be formed or erected within the Jurisdiction of any other State; nor any State be formed by the Junction of two or more States, or Parts of States, without the Consent of the Legislatures of the States concerned as well as of the Congress.

The Congress shall have Power to dispose of and make all needful Rules and Regulations respecting the Territory or other Property belonging to the United States; and nothing in this Constitution shall be so construed as to Prejudice any Claims of the United States, or of any particular State.

Section. 4.

The United States shall guarantee to every State in this Union a Republican Form of Government, and shall protect each of them against Invasion; and on Application of the Legislature, or of the Executive (when the Legislature cannot be convened), against domestic Violence.

Article. V.

The Congress, whenever two thirds of both Houses shall deem it necessary, shall propose Amendments to this Constitution, or, on the Application of the Legislatures of two thirds of the several States, shall call a Convention for proposing Amendments, which, in either Case, shall be valid to all Intents and Purposes, as Part of this Constitution, when ratified by the Legislatures of three fourths of the several States, or by Conventions in three fourths thereof, as the one or the other Mode of Ratification may be proposed by the Congress; Provided that no Amendment which may be made prior to the Year One thousand eight hundred and eight shall in any Manner affect the first and fourth Clauses in the Ninth Section of the first Article; and that no State, without its Consent, shall be deprived of its equal Suffrage in the Senate.

Article. VI.

All Debts contracted and Engagements entered into, before the Adoption of this Constitution, shall be as valid against the United States under this Constitution, as under the Confederation.

This Constitution, and the Laws of the United States which shall be made in Pursuance thereof; and all Treaties made, or which shall be made, under the Authority of the United States, shall be the supreme Law of the Land; and the Judges in every State shall be bound thereby, any Thing in the Constitution or Laws of any State to the Contrary notwithstanding.

The Senators and Representatives before mentioned, and the Members of the several State Legislatures, and all executive and judicial Officers, both of the United States and of the several States, shall be bound by Oath or Affirmation, to support this Constitution; but no religious Test shall ever be required as a Qualification to any Office or public Trust under the United States.

Article. VII.

The Ratification of the Conventions of nine States, shall be sufficient for the Establishment of this Constitution between the States so ratifying the Same.

Done in Convention by the Unanimous Consent of the States present the Seventeenth Day of September in the Year of our Lord one thousand seven hundred and Eighty seven and of the Independance of the United States of America the Twelfth In witness whereof We have hereunto subscribed our Names,

G. Washington
Presidt and deputy from Virginia

Delaware
Geo: Read
Gunning Bedford jun
John Dickinson
Richard Bassett
Jaco: Broom

Maryland
James McHenry
Dan of St Thos. Jenifer
Danl. Carroll

Virginia
John Blair
James Madison Jr.

North Carolina
Wm. Blount
Richd. Dobbs Spaight
Hu Williamson

South Carolina
J. Rutledge
Charles Cotesworth Pinckney
Charles Pinckney
Pierce Butler

Georgia
William Few
Abr Baldwin

New Hampshire
John Langdon
Nicholas Gilman

Massachusetts
Nathaniel Gorham
Rufus King

Connecticut
Wm. Saml. Johnson
Roger Sherman

New York
Alexander Hamilton

New Jersey
Wil: Livingston
David Brearley
Wm. Paterson
Jona: Dayton

Pensylvania
B Franklin
Thomas Mifflin
Robt. Morris
Geo. Clymer
Thos. FitzSimons
Jared Ingersoll
James Wilson
Gouv Morris

Constitutional Amendments

The U.S. Bill of Rights (Amendments 1–10)

The Preamble to The Bill of Rights

Congress of the United States begun and held at the City of New-York, on Wednesday the fourth of March, one thousand seven hundred and eighty nine.

The Conventions of a number of the States, having at the time of their adopting the Constitution, expressed a desire, in order to prevent misconstruction or abuse of its powers, that further declaratory and restrictive clauses should be added: And as extending the ground of public confidence in the Government, will best ensure the beneficent ends of its institution.

Resolved by the Senate and House of Representatives of the United States of America, in Congress assembled, two thirds of both Houses concurring, that the following Articles be proposed to the Legislatures of the several States, as amendments to the Constitution of the United States, all, or any of which Articles, when ratified by three fourths of the said Legislatures, to be valid to all intents and purposes, as part of the said Constitution; viz.

Articles in addition to, and Amendment of the Constitution of the United States of America, proposed by Congress, and ratified by the Legislatures of the several States, pursuant to the fifth Article of the original Constitution.

Note: The following text is a transcription of the first ten amendments to the Constitution in their original form. These amendments were ratified December 15, 1791, and form what is known as the "Bill of Rights."

Amendment I

Congress shall make no law respecting an establishment of religion, or prohibiting the free exercise thereof; or abridging the freedom of speech, or of the press; or the right of the people peaceably to assemble, and to petition the Government for a redress of grievances.

Amendment II

A well regulated Militia, being necessary to the security of a free State, the right of the people to keep and bear Arms, shall not be infringed.

Amendment III

No Soldier shall, in time of peace be quartered in any house, without the consent of the Owner, nor in time of war, but in a manner to be prescribed by law.

Amendment IV

The right of the people to be secure in their persons, houses, papers, and effects, against unreasonable searches and seizures, shall not be violated, and no Warrants shall issue, but upon probable cause, supported by Oath or affirmation, and particularly describing the place to be searched, and the persons or things to be seized.

Amendment V

No person shall be held to answer for a capital, or otherwise infamous crime, unless on a presentment or indictment of a Grand Jury, except in cases arising in the land or naval forces, or in the Militia, when in actual service in time of War or public danger; nor shall any person be subject for the same offence to be twice put in jeopardy of life or limb; nor shall be compelled in any criminal case to be a witness against himself, nor be deprived of life, liberty, or property, without due process of law; nor shall private property be taken for public use, without just compensation.

Amendment VI

In all criminal prosecutions, the accused shall enjoy the right to a speedy and public trial, by an impartial jury of the State and district wherein the crime shall have been committed, which district shall have been previously ascertained by law, and to be informed of the nature and cause of the accusation; to be confronted with the witnesses against him; to have compulsory process for obtaining witnesses in his favor, and to have the Assistance of Counsel for his defence.

Amendment VII

In Suits at common law, where the value in controversy shall exceed twenty dollars, the right of trial by jury shall be preserved, and no fact tried by a jury, shall be otherwise re-examined in any Court of the United States, than according to the rules of the common law.

Amendment VIII

Excessive bail shall not be required, nor excessive fines imposed, nor cruel and unusual punishments inflicted.

Amendment IX

The enumeration in the Constitution, of certain rights, shall not be construed to deny or disparage others retained by the people.

Amendment X

The powers not delegated to the United States by the Constitution, nor prohibited by it to the States, are reserved to the States respectively, or to the people.

Amendment XI

The Judicial power of the United States shall not be construed to extend to any suit in law or equity, commenced or prosecuted against one of the United States by Citizens of another State, or by Citizens or Subjects of any Foreign State.

Amendment XII

The Electors shall meet in their respective states and vote by ballot for President and Vice-President, one of whom, at least, shall not be an inhabitant of the same state with themselves; they shall name in their ballots the person voted for as President, and in distinct ballots the person voted for as Vice-President, and they shall make distinct lists of all persons voted for as President, and of all persons voted for as Vice-President, and of the number of votes for each, which lists they shall sign and certify, and transmit sealed to the seat of the government of the United States, directed to the President of the Senate; — the President of the Senate shall, in the presence of the Senate and House of Representatives, open all the certificates and the votes shall then be counted; — The person having the greatest number of votes for President, shall be the President, if such number be a majority of the whole number of Electors appointed; and if no person have such majority, then from the persons having the highest numbers not exceeding three on the list of those voted for as President, the House of Representatives shall choose immediately, by ballot, the President. But in choosing the President, the votes shall be taken by states, the representation from each state having one vote; a quorum for this purpose shall consist of a member or members from two-thirds of the states, and a majority of all the states shall be necessary to a choice. [And if the House of Representatives shall not choose a President whenever the right of choice shall devolve upon them, before the fourth day of March next following, then the Vice-President shall act as President, as in case of the death or other constitutional disability of the President. —]* The person having the greatest number of votes as Vice-President, shall be the Vice-President, if such number be a majority of the whole number of Electors appointed, and if no person have a majority, then from the two highest numbers on the list, the Senate shall choose the Vice-President; a quorum for the purpose shall consist of two-thirds of the whole number of Senators, and a majority of the whole number shall be necessary to a choice. But no person constitutionally ineligible to the office of President shall be eligible to that of Vice-President of the United States.

Superseded by Section 3 of the 20th amendment.

Amendment XIII

Section 1.

Neither slavery nor involuntary servitude, except as a punishment for crime whereof the party shall have been duly convicted, shall exist within the United States, or any place subject to their jurisdiction.

Section 2.

Congress shall have power to enforce this article by appropriate legislation.

Amendment XIV

Section 1.

All persons born or naturalized in the United States, and subject to the jurisdiction thereof, are citizens of the United States and of the State wherein they reside. No State shall make or enforce any law which shall abridge the privileges or immunities of citizens of the United States; nor shall any State deprive any person of life, liberty, or property, without due process of law; nor deny to any person within its jurisdiction the equal protection of the laws.

Section 2.

Representatives shall be apportioned among the several States according to their respective numbers, counting the whole number of persons in each State, excluding Indians not taxed. But when the right to vote at any election for the choice of electors for President and Vice-President of the United States, Representatives in Congress, the Executive and Judicial officers of a State, or the members of the Legislature thereof, is denied to any of the male inhabitants of such State, being twenty-one years of age,* and citizens of the United States, or in any way abridged, except for participation in rebellion, or other crime, the basis of representation therein shall be reduced in the proportion which the number of such male citizens shall bear to the whole number of male citizens twenty-one years of age in such State.

Section 3.

No person shall be a Senator or Representative in Congress, or elector of President and Vice-President, or hold any office, civil or military, under the United States, or under any State, who, having previously taken an oath, as a member of Congress, or as an officer of the United States, or as a member of any State legislature, or as an executive or judicial officer of any State, to support the Constitution of the United States, shall have engaged in insurrection or rebellion against the same, or given aid or comfort to the enemies thereof. But Congress may by a vote of two-thirds of each House, remove such disability.

Section 4.

The validity of the public debt of the United States, authorized by law, including debts incurred for payment of pensions and bounties for services in suppressing insurrection or rebellion, shall not be questioned. But neither the United States nor any State shall assume or pay any debt or obligation incurred in aid of insurrection or rebellion against the United States, or any claim for the loss or emancipation of any slave; but all such debts, obligations and claims shall be held illegal and void.

Section 5.

The Congress shall have the power to enforce, by appropriate legislation, the provisions of this article.

Changed by Section 1 of the 26th amendment.

Amendment XV

Section 1.

The right of citizens of the United States to vote shall not be denied or abridged by the United States or by any State on account of race, color, or previous condition of servitude—

Section 2.

The Congress shall have the power to enforce this article by appropriate legislation.

Amendment XVI

The Congress shall have power to lay and collect taxes on incomes, from whatever source derived, without apportionment among the several States, and without regard to any census or enumeration.

Amendment XVII

The Senate of the United States shall be composed of two Senators from each State, elected by the people thereof, for six years; and each Senator shall have one vote. The electors in each State shall have the qualifications requisite for electors of the most numerous branch of the State legislatures.

When vacancies happen in the representation of any State in the Senate, the executive authority of such State shall issue writs of election to fill such vacancies: *Provided*, That the legislature of any State may empower the executive thereof to make temporary appointments until the people fill the vacancies by election as the legislature may direct.

This amendment shall not be so construed as to affect the election or term of any Senator chosen before it becomes valid as part of the Constitution.

Amendment XVIII

Section 1.

After one year from the ratification of this article the manufacture, sale, or transportation of intoxicating liquors within, the importation thereof into, or the exportation thereof from the United States and all territory subject to the jurisdiction thereof for beverage purposes is hereby prohibited.

Section 2.

The Congress and the several States shall have concurrent power to enforce this article by appropriate legislation.

Section 3.

This article shall be inoperative unless it shall have been ratified as an amendment to the Constitution by the legislatures of the several States, as provided in the Constitution, within seven years from the date of the submission hereof to the States by the Congress.

Amendment XIX

The right of citizens of the United States to vote shall not be denied or abridged by the United States or by any State on account of sex.

Congress shall have power to enforce this article by appropriate legislation.

Amendment XX

Section 1.

The terms of the President and the Vice President shall end at noon on the 20th day of January, and the terms of Senators and Representatives at noon on the 3d day of January, of the years in which such terms would have ended if this article had not been ratified; and the terms of their successors shall then begin.

Section 2.

The Congress shall assemble at least once in every year, and such meeting shall begin at noon on the 3d day of January, unless they shall by law appoint a different day.

Section 3.

If, at the time fixed for the beginning of the term of the President, the President elect shall have died, the Vice President elect shall become President. If a President shall not have been chosen before the time fixed for the beginning of his term, or if the President elect shall have failed to qualify, then the Vice President elect shall act as President until a President shall have qualified; and the Congress may by law provide for the case wherein neither a President elect nor a Vice President elect shall have qualified, declaring who shall then act as President, or the manner in which one who is to act shall be selected, and such person shall act accordingly until a President or Vice President shall have qualified.

Section 4.

The Congress may by law provide for the case of the death of any of the persons from whom the House of Representatives may choose a President whenever the right of choice shall have devolved upon them, and for the case of the death of any of the persons from whom the Senate may choose a Vice President whenever the right of choice shall have devolved upon them.

Section 5.

Sections 1 and 2 shall take effect on the 15th day of October following the ratification of this article.

Section 6.

This article shall be inoperative unless it shall have been ratified as an amendment to the Constitution by the legislatures of three-fourths of the several States within seven years from the date of its submission.

Amendment XXI

Section 1.

The eighteenth article of amendment to the Constitution of the United States is hereby repealed.

Section 2.

The transportation or importation into any State, Territory, or possession of the United States for delivery or use therein of intoxicating liquors, in violation of the laws thereof, is hereby prohibited.

Section 3.

This article shall be inoperative unless it shall have been ratified as an amendment to the Constitution by conventions in the several States, as provided in the Constitution, within seven years from the date of the submission hereof to the States by the Congress.

Amendment XXII

Section 1.

No person shall be elected to the office of the President more than twice, and no person who has held the office of President, or acted as President, for more than two years of a term to which some other person was elected President shall be elected to the office of the President more than once. But this Article shall not apply to any person holding the office of President when this Article was proposed by the Congress, and shall not prevent any person who may be holding the office of President, or acting as President, during the term within which this Article becomes operative from holding the office of President or acting as President during the remainder of such term.

Section 2.

This article shall be inoperative unless it shall have been ratified as an amendment to the Constitution by the legislatures of three-fourths of the several States within seven years from the date of its submission to the States by the Congress.

Amendment XXIII

Section 1.

The District constituting the seat of Government of the United States shall appoint in such manner as the Congress may direct:

A number of electors of President and Vice President equal to the whole number of Senators and Representatives in Congress to which the District would be entitled if it were a State, but in no event more than the least populous State; they shall be in addition to those appointed by the States, but they shall be considered, for the purposes of the election of President and Vice President, to be electors appointed by a State; and they shall meet in the District and perform such duties as provided by the twelfth article of amendment.

Section 2.

The Congress shall have power to enforce this article by appropriate legislation.

Amendment XXIV

Section 1.

The right of citizens of the United States to vote in any primary or other election for President or Vice President, for electors for President or Vice President, or for Senator or Representative in Congress, shall not be denied or abridged by the United States or any State by reason of failure to pay any poll tax or other tax.

Section 2.

The Congress shall have power to enforce this article by appropriate legislation.

Amendment XXV

Section 1.

In case of the removal of the President from office or of his death or resignation, the Vice President shall become President.

Section 2.

Whenever there is a vacancy in the office of the Vice President, the President shall nominate a Vice President who shall take office upon confirmation by a majority vote of both Houses of Congress.

Section 3.

Whenever the President transmits to the President pro tempore of the Senate and the Speaker of the House of Representatives his written declaration that he is unable to discharge the powers and duties of his office, and until he transmits to them a written declaration to the contrary, such powers and duties shall be discharged by the Vice President as Acting President.

Section 4.

Whenever the Vice President and a majority of either the principal officers of the executive departments or of such other body as Congress may by law provide, transmit to the President pro tempore of the Senate and the Speaker of the House of Representatives their written declaration that the President is unable to discharge the powers and duties of his office, the Vice President shall immediately assume the powers and duties of the office as Acting President.

Thereafter, when the President transmits to the President pro tempore of the Senate and the Speaker of the House of Representatives his written declaration that no inability exists, he shall resume the powers and duties of his office unless the Vice President and a majority of either the principal officers of the executive department or of such other body as Congress may by law provide, transmit within four days to the President pro tempore of the Senate and the Speaker of the House of Representatives their written declaration that the President is unable to discharge the powers and duties of his office. Thereupon Congress shall decide the issue, assembling within forty-eight hours for that purpose if not in session. If the Congress, within twenty-one days after receipt of the latter written declaration, or, if Congress is not in session, within twenty-one days after Congress is required to assemble, determines by two-thirds vote of both Houses that the President is unable to discharge the powers and duties of his office, the Vice President shall continue to discharge the same as Acting President; otherwise, the President shall resume the powers and duties of his office.

Amendment XXVI

Section 1.

The right of citizens of the United States, who are eighteen years of age or older, to vote shall not be denied or abridged by the United States or by any State on account of age.

Section 2.

The Congress shall have power to enforce this article by appropriate legislation.

Amendment XXVII

No law, varying the compensation for the services of the Senators and Representatives, shall take effect, until an election of Representatives shall have intervened.

CPSIA information can be obtained
at www.ICGtesting.com
Printed in the USA
LVHW05s0750110818
586440LV00004B/6/P